A PIONEER WOMAN DOCTOR'S LIFE

Bethenia Owens-Adair, M.D.

Contents

PUBLISHER'S NOTES

Bethenia Angelina Owens Hill Adair's complicated and extraordinary life is nearly peerless for her time. One would have expected her to have fallen into a life of poverty rather than rise to the heights she achieved through incredible determination and fortitude. As she relates below, she was born in 1840 to Thomas and Sarah Owens in Missouri. The 1850 federal census, however, gives her age as 12, so she may have been born in 1838. According to records and to her own account, she was only 14 when she married LeGrand Henderson Hill, who was abusive to her and her child. Despite great opposition to divorce by society, friends, and family, she left Hill and never went back.

At eighteen years old, divorced and barely able to read and write, Bethenia had bigger plans for her life than anyone could have expected. Gaining legal access to her maiden name, she never relinquished it, using, much ahead of her time, a hyphenated name when she remarried.

The University of Pennsylvania opened the first American medical school in 1765 and it was 1847—more than 80 years later—before Elizabeth Blackwell became the first woman admitted to an American medical school. Even by 1905, only four percent of medical school graduates were women in the U.S. and there was little change in those numbers until the mid-1960s. Bethenia's decision to study medicine was only slightly less mad than if she'd decided to become a soldier; her choice of life was to be met with obstacles at every single step.

With indomitable courage, she never shrank from a challenge. One can only imagine the great comfort and relief it was to Dr. Adair's female patients to be attended by someone of their own sex, who would better listen to and understand their complaints. She was an early advocate of physical exercise for women, even making the shocking recommendation that they ride horses astride instead of side-saddle. Her involvement in the temperance movement came more from her experience as a doctor seeing families destroyed by alcoholism than from any moralistic motivation.

1

Dr. Adair's life was a remarkable testament to persistence and determination. She died on September 11, 1926 in Clatsop, Oregon.

SALUTATORY

In giving this book to the public, I have a two-fold purpose—

First: A desire to assist in the preservation of the early history of Oregon;

Second: Through the story of my life, and the few selections from my earliest and later writings—preserved in newspaper clippings,—I have endeavored to show how the pioneer women labored and struggled to gain an entrance into the various avenues of industry, and to make it respectable to earn her honest bread by the side of her brother, man.

In this day and age of progress and plenty, women are found in all the pursuits of life, from the cradle to the grave, and it is hard now, and will be more so, for women a century hence, to believe what their privileges have cost their early mothers in tears, anguish, and contumely, as they ascended, step by step, that slippery and dangerous highway, clinging courageously to the rope and tackle of progress, taking in the slack here and there, never flinching, and never turning back. Several chapters have been contributed by a life-long friend.

"Every book is a quotation, and every house is a quotation out of all forests, and mines, and stone-quarries; and every man is a quotation from all his ancestors."—Emerson.

I was born February 7th, 1840, in Van Huron county, Missouri, being the second daughter of Thomas and Sarah Damron Owens.

My father and mother crossed the plains with the first emigrant wagons of 1843, and settled on Clatsop plains, Clatsop county, Oregon, at the mouth of the Columbia, the wonderful "River of the West," in sound of the ceaseless roar of that mightiest of oceans, the grand old Pacific. Though then very small and delicate in stature, and of a highly nervous and sensitive nature, I possessed a strong and vigorous constitution, and a most wonderful endurance and recuperative power. These qualities were inherited, not only from my parents, but from my grandparents, as well. My grandfather Owens was a man of exceptional financial ability. He had a large plantation in Kentucky, mid owned many slaves, and many stores throughout the state. He was a grandson of Sir Thomas Owens, of Wales, of historic fame.

My grandmother Owens was of German descent; a rather small, but executive woman, who took charge of, and ably administered the affairs of the plantation, during my grandfather's absence, which was most of the time. She was precisely the kind of woman President Roosevelt most admires;—a woman of energy, industry, and capability in managing her home affairs, and the mother of twelve children, all of whom grew to maturity, married, and went on giving vigorous sons and daughters to this young and growing republic.

My grandfather Damron was a man of equal worth. He was a noted Indian fighter, and was employed by the Government, during its wars with the Shawnees and Delawares, as a scout and spy. He performed many deeds of remarkable bravery and daring, one of which was the rescue of a mother and five children from the Indians, who had captured them, at the imminent risk of his own life; in recognition of this act of signal bravery the Government presented him with a handsome silver-mounted rifle, worth three hundred dollars.

My grandmother Damron was my grandfather's second wife. She was of Irish descent, and noted for her great personal beauty.

My father, a tall, athletic Kentuckian, served as sheriff of Pike county for many years, beginning as a deputy at the age of sixteen. It was often said of him: "Thomas Owens is not afraid of man or devil."

My mother was of slight build, but perfect form, with bright blue eyes, and soft brown hair. She weighed but ninety-six pounds when she was married, at the age of sixteen.

My earliest recollection reaches back to the first step taken by my brother, Josiah Parrish Owens, I being five years old, and he between seven and eight months. It was in the smooth, cleanly swept back yard, on a soft, warm July afternoon. Mother sat just outside the door, sewing. My sister Diana, who was past seven, and old for her years, and who never seemed to care much for play, (unlike most children,) sat near mother, busy with her patch-work. My brother Flem (about three) and I were playing with the baby. In his infantile glee he crept away from us, raised himself on his feet, and looked smiling at mother, who held out her arms, when he toddled to her, taking at least a dozen steps, before she caught him. From this time on, he never seemed to desire to creep. It was a red-letter day to us, as our baby, named for Rev. J. L. Parrish, of missionary fame, was the pride of our home. My brother Flem, two years my junior, was my constant companion. He grew rapidly, and soon overtook me in size, as I was small, and grew slowly, but I was tough and active, and usually led in all our pursuits of work or play. Not until I was past twelve, did he ever succeed in throwing me. One day he came in the kitchen, where I was washing the dinner dishes and, with a broad smile on his face (he was such a good-natured boy!) said: "Pap told me to go to the barn for two bundles of oats for the horses; now the first one that is thrown down must go for the oats."

Instantly the dish-cloth was dropped, and we clinched.

I had noticed for some time that he was gaining on me, but I could not refuse to take a "dare," and he had not yet thrown me.

6

Round, and round the room we went, bending and swaying, like two young saplings, till, seeing his chance, he put out his foot and tripped me. I fell on a chair which happened to be in the way, and my mouth came in contact with one of its posts, which broke off a piece of one of my front teeth. Poor brother picked up the fragment of tooth, burst out crying, and ran off to the barn for the oats.

He had just learned this new accomplishment in wrestling, which he had kept secret from me, to his life-long regret, for in those times and parts dentistry was almost an unknown art. It was at least eighteen years after that before I found a dentist who could repair the injury. Dr. Hatch, of Portland, did the work, and I was more than pleased to have that unsightly gap filled in with shining gold. The rarity of such an artistic piece of work in the mouth added to its attractiveness. The first attempt, by the way, was a failure, the filling soon becoming loose; but the second was a success, and was still perfect when the tooth was extracted thirty-five years later. This tooth I keep, as a souvenir in remembrance of that particular tussle with my dear, good brother;—not the last, however, by any means, for we were, as I said, constant companions, and I was a veritable "tom-boy," and gloried in the fact. It was father's custom to pat me on the head, and call me his "boy."

The regret of my life up to the age of thirty-five, was that I had not been born a boy, for I realized very early in life that a girl was hampered and hemmed in on all sides simply by the accident of sex.

Brother and I were always trying our muscular strength, and before I was thirteen, I bet him I could carry four sacks of flour, or two hundred pounds. I stood between a table and a box, on which we had put two sacks of flour each. Then brother placed a sack of flour on each of my shoulders, and held them steady, while I managed to get the other two sacks (one on the table and the other on the box on each side of me) under each arm, and then I walked triumphantly off, carrying all four sacks! In that memorable year of 1847, after the shocking Whitman massacre, my father was preparing to go, with other Clatsop volunteers, to fight the Indians. When all was ready for his departure, as he stood in the midst of his

7

weeping wife and children, a Mr. McDonald, who was then working for father, stepped forward and said:

"Mr. Owens, I am a single man, and have no one to care for me, but I am poor. Give me your outfit, and money for my expenses, and I will go in your place."

Yielding to the entreaties of his family, my father finally assented, and Mr. McDonald went, but he never returned. He was killed, I think, by an accident. We have always remembered him gratefully, believing that he may have saved our father's life to us; and at least, he freely gave his own.

I was the family nurse; and it was seldom that I had not a child in my arms, and more clinging to me. Where there is a baby every two years, there is always no end of nursing to be done; especially when the mother's time is occupied, as it was then, every moment, from early morning till late at night, with much outdoor as well as indoor work. She seldom found time to devote to the baby, except to give it the breast.

When the weather was fine we fairly lived out of doors, baby and all, I hauling the baby in its rude little sled, or cart, which bumped along, and from which baby was often thrown out, but seldom seriously hurt, and never killed; with a two-year-old on one hip, and a four-year-old hanging to my skirts, in order to keep up; but more often on brother Flem's back; so we went, playing here, and working there, during all the pleasant weather. When it rained, we had access to the barn, where we could swing, play "hide and seek," and slide down the hay-mow, from the top to the bottom. Many a time I have carried the children to the top, from where, with the baby in my arms, and the two next younger clinging to me, I would slide to the bottom, to their great delight.

I was fond of hunting hen's nests, which I seldom failed to find. One afternoon, I crawled under the barn, as I knew there were eggs there. The ground was hard and smooth, and so near the barn-floor that moving-room was at a premium. About the center of the space, I found a nest full of eggs, and squeezed under till I could reach and gather them into my apron. Then, as I could not turn around, I began to slide out backward. When passing a sleeper, a knot in it caught between the waistband of my dress and the first button above. Try as best I might, I could not get loose. Brother was waiting for me outside, and when he found I could not possibly extricate myself, he ran to mother for help. Father was away from home. Mother saw that the only way to release me was to break the button-hole above my belt. Lying wedged in there on my face, I could not reach the button, or break either the button-hole, or strong belt. The barn was full of hay, which it would take several men at least a day,—perhaps more—to remove so as to get down to the middle of the barn floor; and to tunnel under to me would require about as much time and labor. So she told me to push and work myself backward and sidewise. I obeyed, and after long and persistent effort, I succeeded in tearing the button-hole out, thus enabling me to back once more into freedom and fresh air. After I got clear of the sleeper, I reached back and unbuttoned all my buttons, to make sure I did not get hung up again. My eggs were near by, and I brought them out with me.

That was not the last time I crawled under that barn for eggs, but I had learned a lesson never to be forgotten, for I never again went into a tight place like that without preparing beforehand to leave all my clothes behind, if necessary,—that is, if I should again be hung up on a knot or a Peg.

When I was about twelve years old, a teacher by the name of Beaufort came to teach a three months' school in our neighborhood. School-books were extremely scarce, and sometimes whole families were taught out of one book. All the children over four years old attended the school, for children did not remain babies long when other babies came along so fast and crowded them out of the cradle. Boys and girls of fourteen and fifteen were expected to do a full day's work on the farm or in the house, and even the younger ones were all taught to be helpful and useful, and to do their full share in taking care of themselves.

The new teacher was a fine, handsome young man, who held himself aloof from the young people of his age, and kept his person so clean, neat and trim that the country young men disliked him.

Mr. Beaufort boarded at our house, and we children walked the two miles to school with him, daily. He was greatly liked by the children, to whom he was most kind, playing with them, and often taking two or three of the little tots, or as many as could hang on, and, thus handicapped, he would run races with the older children, to the hilarious joy of the little youngsters, who thought they had won the race.

I simply worshiped my handsome teacher, who taught me how to run, to jump, to lasso, to spring up on the horse's back, and so many other things that I appreciated. On one occasion there was a picnic at our house, it being the largest and best on Clatsop plains;—and while there, the young men began to joke and guy the young teacher about his white hands. He took it good-naturedly, and finally said:

"I will bet you $200 in cash, my watch and chain, and all I have, against $100, and whatever you can put up, that I can dig, measure and stack more potatoes than any other man on Clatsop."

This stirred their blood, and touched their pride, and his challenge was accepted. He was to dig, measure and stack in three piles, sixty bushels of potatoes in ten hours, he to select his ground on which to dig. My father said to Legrand Hill, who was then working for him, and whom I married two years later: "Now, my boy, take my advice: don't fool away your summer's work. I have been watching that young man, for three months. He is as strong as a bear, and active as a cat."

But, like the other young men (and some of the older ones) he needed no advice. He bet his watch, and two hundred bundles, or sheaves, of oats on the issue.

Mr. Beaufort selected his ground in Mr. Jewett's potato patch, on the farm now belonging to Mr. Josiah West, near the main county road. The day before the contest, he had staked out his ground, and smoothed off the spots on which to pile his potatoes.

The day dawned bright and beautiful, and found everybody there, including men, women, children and Indians. All brought good things to eat for luncheon, and came to spend the day, and see the fun.

Time-keepers being selected, and the hour being near at hand, the teacher removed his coat, vest, and long, handsome blue silk Spanish scarf, and hung them on the fence. Suspenders were unknown in those days. He then loosened his leather belt, and taking off his boots, he encased his feet in a pair of handsome beaded moccasins; then, drawing a pair of soft buckskin gloves over his smooth white hands, he picked up the new hoe, from the handle of which he had sawed off about half, and stepped to the middle of the plot, as the time-keeper called the hour. He took off his hat, and made a graceful bow to the assembled company. Then, stepping across a hill and standing with a foot on each side of it, he, with two or three strokes of the hoe, laid bare the potatoes, and with both hands scooped them up into his half bushel measure.

It did not require more than two or three hills to more than fill the measure. Then, with a few elastic leaps, he emptied them on one of the places he had prepared for them. For two or three hours he kept the tellers busy counting; and then he took it more leisurely, laughing and joking as he worked, and he finished his task long before night. All the beholders were fully convinced, after the first hour's work, that the stakes were his. That was a "red letter" day for that handsome and accomplished young teacher. He had "raked in" watches, rings, scarf-pins and about all the spare money the young men, and some old ones in that settlement possessed.

After he had finished his sixty bushels, he turned several handsprings, and, reaching the fence, he put his hands on the top rail, and sprang over, with one bound.

That was a revelation in potato-digging to the Clatsopites, who all dug with a long-handled hoe, while the Indians used a short stick, or their hands, for the purpose, at the same time sitting or crawling on their hands and knees. That was the last, and one of the best lessons that my honored teacher taught on Clatsop. He left in a few days and we never heard of him again, but his memory is always fresh in my mind. He was, in my young, crude, and it might be called barren life, a green, flower-strewn oasis, with a fountain of cool water in its midst.

I was then but twelve years old; small, but perfect in form, health, and vigor. Brother Flem towered far above me, and sister Diana, "The Beauty of Clatsop," was taller than our mother.

My love for my handsome, kind and intelligent teacher knew no bounds. Diana said I was always "tagging him around;" and mother chided me for being so rude, saying, "You ought to know that he must get tired of you and the children sometimes."

However I found many opportunities of being in his society, and I improved them all; especially as mother was so over-worked she was only too glad to be relieved of the care of the baby, and the two other smaller children. Taking my brood, I would seek out, my friend, who invariably met me with a welcoming smile, for he had learned to love the two tiny girls, and the big, fat baby, who warmly returned his affection.

He would catch up one of the older little ones, toss her above his head in such a way that she would rest across his shoulders, with her little arm around his head. Then he would take the baby and hug it close, and, picking up the other little midget, under his other arm, we would be off for a race. And how we all enjoyed it! The children would scream with delight, and my own happiness, though less demonstrative, was no less deep. We often went to the fields where father was plowing, cultivating or haying. Many a time did he lift me lightly to the back of the near horse, hand me the baby, and seating one of the others behind me, with one on his shoulder, walk beside the horse with his hand reached out to hold us from falling. Father liked him, too, and was always pleased to have him around.

It was a sad, sad day when he left us. First, he bade father and mother good-bye; and then the children. He snatched up the baby from the floor, tossed her up, and kissed her. I was trying to keep back my tears. He smiled down on me with his handsome blue eyes, and said to mother: "I guess I'll take this one with me."

Mother answered, "All right; she is such a tom-boy I can never make a girl of her, anyway."

He took my little hand in his, and I went with him through the gate, and some distance down the road. Then he said: "Now, little one, you must go back. You are a nice little girl, and some day you will make a fine woman; but you must remember and study your book hard, and when you get to be a woman everybody will love you;—and don't forget your first teacher, *will* you?" He had gathered me up, and smiling, kissed me, and then set me down with my face toward home. I ran back, and seeing the children on the fence-, all looking, I ran off around the back of the house, and hid, and cried a long time. Of course they all laughed at me, and often times afterward, when I was especially rebellious and wayward, which was not infrequently, I would be confronted with, "I wish the teacher had taken you with him," to which I never failed to answer promptly and fervently, "*I* wish he had, too!"

About this time, a Mr. and Mrs. McCrary moved on the adjoining farm, owned by a Mr. McDaniel, a bachelor.

Their little house was not more than a quarter of a mile from ours, just over, and beyond a pretty, grassy ridge. I did not like the man, but I fell in love with his tall, splendid wife. She was quite a little older than my mother, but very different from her. She was tall, and very fair, with pleasant gray eyes;—not pretty in form or features, but she was one of the most admirable and beautiful characters I have met with in all my life. To me she looked beautiful, and I loved her ardently. No child could have loved a mother more than I loved this pure, noble woman. It is said that "love begets love," and it surely did, in this case, for she returned my love with a true mother-love. She was not blessed with children of her own. The affection between us remained unbroken throughout her long subsequent life, of nearly fifty years; and now I can realize, looking back, that the lovely example of her beautiful life has had much to do with molding my own, and I doubt not, the characters of many of those around her. Their worldly goods were few when they settled near us, but she made the most of what little she had,—only two small rooms scantily furnished,—but every thing in them was kept immaculate, and she, with her kind words, sweet smiles, and winning ways, her hair combed smoothly back from his high, prominent forehead, an ample white kerchief crossed and pinned smoothly over her bosom, and her long, checked apron ironed without one wrinkle, fastened trimly about her waist, was a fitting, and charming mistress of her spotless little home.

My mother was a neat and tasteful woman, but she said

"Mrs. McCrary always looked as if she had come out of a band-box."

It was my habit to visit my friend once a day;—often several times. Whatever might be my task, I would try to finish it as quickly as possible, that I might slip off, and fly to Mrs. McCrary's. It did seem like flying, for my feet scarcely touched the ground, as I ran. I received many scoldings, for running off thus, without permission, and was repeatedly told that grown people did not want to be bothered with children, but, unless I was positively forbidden, I still went.

Mrs. McCrary seemed always so glad to see me, and had so many pretty and pleasant things to say to me, that it was no wonder I was drawn so strongly to her. She did not visit much, and never gossiped. She was a reader, but books and papers were very scarce in those days. She always treated me as if I were a little lady of some consequence.

For instance, she would say:

"Why, your visits are just like bright, sparkling, refreshing sunbeams to me."

If a button was gone from my dress, or apron, a pin went into its place, and she would say:

"Now, that looks so much nicer!"

Again she would frequently say:

"I am just going to comb out those long, pretty braids of yours;" and she would take down my hair, which came half way to the floor, and brush and comb it, and then take down the little mirror from the wall, and hold it before me, turning it from side to side, so that I could see how long and nice it was, waving over my shoulder, saying: "We'll leave it so awhile, it makes you look so like a fairy."

Sometimes she would tell me a fairy story, at the same time showing me how to knit, crochet or sew. All this time talking, and drawing me out, correcting my mistakes with such delicacy that even my super-sensitive nature was not wounded. She infused such a charm into everything she did and said that I was not only interested, but most anxious to learn. She impressed upon my mind in the most positive language just how the thing should be done, showing me by example, at the same time, always having me assist her when possible; invariably excusing my blunders, and praising my progress.

Was she making biscuits, she would have me stand by, while she showed me every step of the process. First she would take down the clean board, and say: "Now you take so many cups of sifted flour, so many cups of milk, so much butter, so much salt, so much soda for so many persons. When you knead the biscuits, be sure you do not put the flour too near the edge of the board, or it will get on the floor; and stand a little farther back from the table, or you will get your apron mussed."

"Do you know, I have seen women who could wear one apron all the week and then it would not be as soiled as that of some women would be in one day. That shows the difference between a neat and slovenly person."

"Some people always have a place for everything, and keep things where they belong, while others keep their things hap-hazard, and never know where to find them,—and so make themselves a great deal more work, and have a much harder time to get along. You will never be that kind of a person, for your mother is a good housekeeper, and you will grow up to be an orderly housekeeper, too."

Was it any wonder that I loved that wise, good woman? I was as wax in her hands, and could I have been under her influence until I had reached maturity, instead of but one year, I could, and would have escaped many of the sorrows and hardships of my life.

Mr. McCrary soon took up a claim on Young's river, a part of which is now known as "Greenwood Cemetery," but it was then quite remote, and could be reached only by boat.

After the lapse of many years, on my return to Clatsop, I heard that Mrs. McCrary, now a widow, was spending the winter in Astoria, and I embraced the first opportunity to visit her. Oh, what a joyful meeting was ours! And with what interest and emotion did we recall and rehearse the past!

She was the same grand woman. Hardships and griefs—of which she had suffered many—seemed to have made her more lovely and saintly. She said to me: "Well, I am getting old, but you are young, and fresh, with the bloom and beauty of womanhood upon you, and

16

yet I can see much to remind me of the little bare-footed girl who brought me so much pleasure the year I lived near your father's;" and she laughed happily.

Again we parted; and year after year came and went. I became a physician, married a second time, and went to live on our Sunnymead farm in Clatsop county. One dark night a messenger came with a lantern, saying that Mrs. McCrary was suffering dreadfully from an abscess, and wanted me. Would I go? Yes, by every fond recollection;—by every tie of gratitude and affection— most assuredly I would go! And a walk of one mile over a rough tide-land road brought us to the Lewis and Clarke river, which we had to cross in a boat, to where a horse was awaiting us. Then three miles farther, and we were at our destination. I first administered an opiate; then lanced the ulcers, and applied a hot poultice and a hot-water bag, and she was soon comfortable and free from pain: Then she said:

"Oh, how good God is, to send you to me in my trouble; and I do not regret my sickness, since it brought you here. I want you to get right in bed with me. I am ashamed to be so selfish as not to let you sleep in another room, after this long, hard trip, but if you had given me a bushel of opiates I could not sleep, I am so hungry for a good, long talk."

"Do not for a moment think," I replied, "that you are depriving me of anything, for I am quite as anxious as you are for such a talk"; and we did talk, from 2 a m till breakfast the next morning, living over much of our past lives from my early childhood.

A year or so later, she came to Clatsop to visit her friends, the Carnahans, who now own my father's old donation land claim.

While there, she had a severe attack of pneumonia, and, for a time, I despaired of her life; but she calmly said:

"I know my time has come. I am ready and anxious to go; for I have lived beyond my usefulness. You are doing all you can, and I do not blame you, but I feel that I ought to go now."

But her time was not yet come, and, after many weeks, she made a good recovery, and went to Portland, Oregon, to live with her adopted son, Capt. Kane Olney, whom she took, in infancy, and raised him to manhood.

I saw her frequently afterward, when I was in Portland, and in 1899, before removing to North Yakima, Wash. [about two hours east of Seattle, across the Cascade Mountains], I called to say good-bye to her. I found her reading the Oregonian. On seeing me, she rose to her feet at once, and met me with her old, gracious, heart-warming smile.

"I see you are reading the Oregonian," I said.

"Yes," she said, "I spend much of my time in reading. If I only could remember what I read! My memory, you see, is only half-way across the floor. That is just about the length of it now."

"Never mind your present memory," I reassured her, "your past will not desert you, and the good you have done in this world will linger long after you and I have been laid to rest."

This pleasant, cheerful way in which she alluded to her loss of memory illustrates the wonderful charm and beauty with which she invested life; so that all its rough, unsightly, and annoying features were sure, under her sunny way of meeting and presenting them, to become less disagreeable, and often even perfectly charming. That was the last time I ever saw that grand, noble woman,—one of God's masterpieces. Her walk in life was lowly, but sunshine and flowers followed her and illumined her pathway, and it could be truly said of her that no one ever came in contact with her without being made better.

An amusing little occurrence took place when I was just past thirteen. Father had working for him at the time a diminutive, stuttering Englishman.

This man had been trying to make love to me for some time, and, notwithstanding my scornful rejection of his attentions, and positively rude treatment of him, he persisted in them.

One morning I was washing. For heating water, and boiling the clothes, we used a huge pot, which hung on a crane, in the big, open fire-place, in a room used for washing, and as a general store-room. Under the open stairway were several partly filled barrels of cranberries, and other articles. That little imp, knowing I was there, and watching his opportunity, slipped up behind me, as I was stirring down the clothes with a long broom-handle, and, catching me around the waist, hugged, and tried to kiss me, and then he jumped back and laughed triumphantly, endeavoring to escape by the open door; but, like a tiger, I leaped between him and the door, giving him such a whack with the broom handle that he staggered, and rushed under the stairs, and plunged his head into the cranberry barrel, thus presenting a fair field for the strokes which, in my fury, I laid on thick and fast, with all the strength I possessed. He screamed, and mother, hearing the disturbance, ran down stairs, and had to actually pull me off by main strength. When he got his head out of the barrel, he sputtered and stammered, and could not utter a single coherent word. In towering contempt, I exclaimed: "You little skunk, if you ever dare come near me again, I'll kill you!"

About this time another occurrence happened that made a lasting impression on my mind.

One bright morning a young farmer about 27 years old came rushing excitedly up with his coat on his arm, to mother, who was in the back yard, saying:

"Where is Tom Owens?"

Mother asked: "What do you want of him? He is not here."

"I want him!" he vociferated, "And I intend to whip him within an inch of his life."

He was a large fellow, as tall as father, and much heavier.

Mother said: "Now, Luke, go home, and get over your mad fit; Owens has never done you any harm. But I tell you if you do get him roused, he will beat you half to death, and I don't want to see you get hurt." But he had no notion of getting hurt.

Just then we saw father coming up the road on horseback. Luke saw him, too, and started for him, mother calling, and begging him to come back, but he rushed on. The children were terribly frightened, and began to cry. Mother said: "Stop your crying. Your father is not going to be hurt." She, however, walked out with us to where we could see and hear everything. Father stopped his horse, and Luke, throwing down his coat, began gesticulating, swearing, and daring father to get down and fight him, but father sat calmly on his horse and said:

"Now, Luke, you are only a boy; you don't know what you are doing; go home, and let me alone. I don't want to hurt you."

At this, Luke sprang at him, calling him a coward, and attempting to pull him off his horse, but before he could catch his foot, father was off his horse on the opposite side, and giving the bridle a pull, turned the horse from him; and the first thing he did, when Luke came lunging at him, was to knock him down with a single blow. Then he held him down, and choked him till he cried "Enough!" when father released him, saying: "Go to the house and wash and clean yourself up; my wife will give you water and towels." Luke lost no time in obeying, and mother brought water and towels, and assisted him. His nose was bleeding profusely, and he was covered with blood, but he was not half so badly hurt as he was scared.

Mother said, "Well, Luke, I am very sorry you did not take my advice. I knew you would get hurt."

He was very penitent, and much humiliated, and when father came up, bringing his coat, and assisted him in putting it on, they shook hands, and were friends ever after.

It afterward transpired that some of the neighbors, knowing him to be a bragging bully, and thinking he needed a taking down, had put him up to coming, by telling him that Mr. Owens had said he had stolen something.

In 1853, finding that his 640 acres on Clatsop could no longer supply feed for his rapidly increasing herds, father decided to remove to Southern Oregon, where he could have an abundance of range for them.

He at once set about building a large flat-boat, or scow, in which to move his family, household goods, and what stock he could not, or did not wish to sell.

In the fall, after the crops were harvested, and everything disposed of that we did not want to move, father shipped his cattle and horses to St. Helens, and sent them on by the trail, to the valley. He then returned, and moved the family and our teams to Portland, then a very small town on the Willamette river.

After disposing of the boat, we loaded up the two wagons, and were ready to start for the valley. It had been raining, and I well remember what a terrific time we had getting through the dense timber west and south of Portland, father leading, driving one team, and mother following, with the second. Mr. John Hobson, my brother-in-law, had, meantime, gotten the horses and cattle through the timber, and, leaving the other men to herd them, on good pasturage, came back and met us in the woods, for which we were very thankful. We came up with the herd near the Burton place, in North Yamhill, the next day, and bidding Mr. Hobson and one of the other two men good-bye, we proceeded on to Roseburg, arriving there without mishap.

Brother Flem and I, with the assistance of one man, who was not half equal to either one of us for the purpose, drove the herd.

Father said we were worth more than any two men he could hire. There was an abundance of grass; the weather was fine, and this part of the journey was really a picnic for us all.

Upon leaving home, I had insisted upon taking my big cat, Tab, against the judgment of my parents. After a good deal of argument, and many tears on my part, I carried my point, and Tab went with us. After getting well on our way, I let him out when we made camp, putting him in the covered wagon, and fastening down the cover when we were ready to start again.

One morning the horses had strayed off, and father sent me after them. When I returned with them, everything was packed, ready to leave, and I forgot Tab. We had gone perhaps a mile, when I thought of him, and rushing back to mother's wagon, I asked if she had put him in. No, she had not thought of him, or seen him.

Without another word, I put whip to my horse, and galloped back to camp, but no Tab was to be found. I rode up and down the pretty little stream calling for Tab, but saw no signs of him, and with sad heart, and wet eyes, I rode ahead, and overtook the wagons. When we stopped at noon, mother sent me to the wagon for something, and as I unfastened and lifted the cover, what did I see but my big, beautiful, beloved Tab, ready to greet me with an affectionate "Meouw!"

From that time on, he always crawled into the wagon of his own accord, when the horses were being hitched on preparatory to starting. He enjoyed the trip as well as any of us. On reaching Roseburg, we found our old friend and neighbor Mr. Perry had a house all ready for us, and we moved right in. Father took up a claim just across the Umpqua river, from the then little village of Roseburg. This gave him a wide scope of range for all his stock.

He at once bought lumber for a good house, and began hauling it on the building-spot, in order to be ready to build early in the spring. Then, during the winter, he built a ferry-boat for his own accommodation, and that of the public. As the river could not be forded during a part of the year, and was really dangerous, the ferry was quite a source of revenue to us. During the winter, Mr. Hill came to visit us. His parents and their family had come to Oregon the year before, and settled in the Rogue River valley, near the Siskiyou mountains.

It was now arranged that we should be married the next spring, when father's house was far enough completed to move in. During the winter and early spring, I put in all my spare time in preparing for my approaching marriage. I had four quilts already pieced, ready for the lining; mother had given me the lining for them all, and the cotton for two. I carded wool for the other two, and we quilted and finished them all. She also gave me muslin for four sheets, two pairs of pillow-cases, two tablecloths, and four towels. I cut and made two calico dresses for myself, and assisted mother in the making of my wedding dress, which was a pretty, sky-blue figured lawn. I had

22

everything done, and neatly folded away long before the wedding day arrived. Mr. Hill came early in April, and assisted us in moving into the new house.

On May 4th, 1854, with only our old friends, the Perrys, and the minister present, beside our own family, we were married. I was still small for my age. My husband was five feet eleven inches in height, and I could stand under his outstretched arm. I grew very slowly, and did not reach my full stature until I was 25 years old, which is now 5 feet 4 inches.

Just prior to our marriage, Mr. Hill had bought a farm of 320 acres on credit, four miles from my father's home, for $600, to be paid for in two years.

The improvements on it consisted of a small cabin, 12x14 in dimensions, made of round logs, with the bark on them, each notched deeply enough at its end to dovetail into its neighbors above and below it. The cracks still remaining after this rude fitting were filled with mixed mud and grass, but this cabin had never yet been "chinked." It was covered with "shakes" (thick, hand-made shingles three feet long), which were kept in place by poles, tied down at each end. The door was so low that a man had to stoop to go in and out, and it was fastened with the proverbial latch and string. The cabin had neither floor nor chimney, and the wide cracks admitted both draughts and vermin. Later I gathered grass and fern, mixed them with mud, and filled these cracks, thus shutting out the snakes and lizards, which abounded in that region, and which had made me frequent and alarming visits. The window consisted of two panes of glass set in an opening made by sawing out a section of one of the logs for that purpose.

About twelve acres of land were fenced, and had been seeded to oats and wheat for one or two years. A rough, open shed sufficed to shelter six or eight head of stock, and surrounding it was a corral for milking cows, and a calf-pen adjoining it.

Our furniture consisted of a pioneer bed, made by boring three holes in the logs of the wall in one corner, in which to drive the rails. Thus the bedstead required but one leg. The table was a mere rough shelf, fastened to the wall, and supported by two legs. Three smaller shelves answered for a cupboard, and were amply sufficient for my slender supply of dishes, which comprised mostly tin ware, which, in those days, was kept scrupulously bright and shining. My sugar bowl, cream jug, steel knives and forks (two-tined) and one set of German silver teaspoons, I had bought with my own little savings before my marriage.

My cooking utensils were a pot, tea-kettle and bake-oven (all of iron), a frying-pan and coffee-pot, a churn, six milk pans, a wash tub and board, a large twenty or thirty-gallon iron pot for washing purposes, etc., and a water bucket and tin dipper. All these things, including a full supply of groceries, I got on my father's account, as he had told me to go to the store and purchase what I wanted. This I did in the afternoon of my wedding day, the ceremony having taken place at 10 a. m. He also gave me a fine riding mare, Queen (my saddle I had already earned long before), one fresh cow and a heifer calf, which I selected; also one cow which would be fresh in the early fall, and a wagon and harness. In addition, mother gave me a good feather bed, and pillows, a good straw bed, a pair of blankets and two extra quilts. My husband's possessions were a horse and saddle, a gun, and less than twenty dollars in money; but I considered this a most excellent start in life. I knew what my father and mother had done, and I then believed that my husband was the equal of any man living.

The late Hon. John Hobson, Collector of Customs at Astoria, once said to me:

"Your father could make money faster than any man I ever saw. He came here in 1843. with fifty cents in his pocket, and I do not think there was one hundred dollars in the whole county (Clatsop), and in less than ten years he was worth over twenty thousand dollars."

Consequently, I had high hopes and great expectations for the future. My husband was a strong, healthy man; I had been trained to work, and bred to thrift and economy, and everything looked bright and beautiful to me. My soul overflowed with love and hope, and I could sing the dear old home-songs from morning to night. My happy, buoyant nature enabled me to enjoy anything,—even cooking out of doors, over a smoky fire, without even a covering over my head; for at first we had neither fireplace nor stove.

It was sweet, smiling spring,—the season that I loved best. The hills were bedecked with the loveliest wild flowers, for the variety and abundance of which the Umpqua valley is especially noted.

And yet, from a child I was practical and methodical. I had everything packed, and ready to move to my new home as soon as we were married, and I insisted on going there the next morning, knowing that the garden ought to be in. Within a few days it was planted.

We depended on wild game for meat, and as my husband was a good marksman, he kept us well supplied. I always went with him, and we never came home empty-handed. He often killed two grouse from one tree by shooting the under bird first. The upper one seldom flew, and the hunter could bag it at the next shot. This seems to be a characteristic of the grouse. It is not startled by the sound of the gun's discharge, but if the upper bird is killed, its fall alarms those under, who immediately take to flight. I have myself seen hunters who know this fact kill three grouse in one tree by shooting the lower ones first.

Mr. Hill was always ready to go hunting, no matter what work was pressing to be done.

One evening he proposed a deer-hunt, so next morning we were off early. He decided to go to the top of the highest hill, as the wind coming from that direction would bear away our scent; so we rode our horses as far up as we could, and then staked them on good grass, and proceeded on foot to a point where he said we were sure to find deer. When near the summit, we crept with great caution, and peeped over. Sure enough! There, basking in the heat of the day, in the shade of the noble oak trees on that gentle, grassy slope, was a band of the soft-eyed beauties.

All save one were lying down; while the king of the herd stood quietly by, leisurely chewing his cud, with his head toward us, all unconscious that his last hour had come.

We were behind a large tree, and my husband rested his rifle on one of its limbs, and took deliberate aim. At the click of the trigger, the royal buck sprang into the air, and fell dead. The herd was thrown into consternation; and, as the wind blew from them to us, they bounded toward us. In an instant the gun was re-loaded, aimed, and a graceful doe succumbed. I now entreated that he shoot no more, and as it was then past noon, and we were a long way from home, he assented. We first went down to the big buck, and soon dismembered him, and cut off his head. After spending much time, and hard labor in tugging and pulling, we at last got him to the top of the hill, after which it was an easy task to carry the small deer up. Then we started down the long hill, he with the large animal, and I with the small one. In time we reached the horses, on which we lashed the carcasses. Then we led the horses to the foot of the hill, where we loaded both deer on one horse, and rode home ourselves on the other, getting home at dark. The early morning of the next day was spent in skinning and salting the meat. Then, taking the two large hams, we lost no time in riding over to father's for dinner, eager to tell of and talk over our hunting exploit. We well knew how much father and mother would enjoy the juicy steaks from those toothsome hams. Good coffee, hot buttermilk biscuits, or corn bread and fried venison, with cream gravy, and potatoes, was the favorite breakfast (or any other meal) of the southern man, and a hunter's delight. My mother was a cook worthy the name. Breakfast foods were then unknown, and as little needed, as such a thing as a dyspeptic was never heard of, and the word, even, was scarcely comprehended.

In the beginning of our married life, my father had advised my husband to begin at once to fell trees, and hew them, and put up a good house before winter set in. There was an abundance of suitable timber on our land, near by, but he was never in any hurry to get down to work. In one way and another he managed to idle away the summer, going to camp-meetings, reading novels, and hunting.

In September, when the mornings and evenings grew cold, we bought an old, second-hand stove, for $2.50, which we put up in one corner of the cabin. This was an inexpressible comfort to me. Soon after this, we had a heavy rain, lasting all one day and night. The following morning our house was flooded, and in one corner the water was bubbling up like a spring. This came from a gopher's hole. I have seen water spouting out of hillsides for days after a hard rain, due to gopher channels.

Our cabin stood on a hillside, an d the water was seeping and streaming down on us from the hill above. In order to protect ourselves from it, we were forced to dig a ditch on the upper side of the house, the bottom of which was below the foundation log; and thus the water was successfully carried away. It was late in the fall before the logs for the new, 16x20 foot house were even ready to be hauled out. My father had provided two doors, two windows, shingles, nails, and rough lumber for the floor. (No ready planed lumber was to be had in those days. All planing was done by hand.) He had these all on the ground long before Mr. Hill had finished the logs; but at last they were done,—cut the proper length, hewed flat on two sides, the bark removed, and deposited on the building-spot. They were notched to suit, as they were laid together, in building.

When all was ready, father came, with men to raise the house, and mother with him, bringing pies and cakes, and to help me with the dinner. Quilting parties, house-raisings, and hog-killings were always social events in pioneer life.

My father and the other men under his direction soon had the house up, with the openings for one door and windows sawed out; and all departed happy with the sun yet high in the heavens. Father said, before starting: "Now, Legrand, go right at it and put the roof on, for you can look out for a hard rain soon." Next morning I slipped out of bed at 4 o'clock, and milked the cow, and when breakfast was almost ready, I skipped in, and tickled my husband's feet to waken him, and put him in a good humor (for he was not pleased with father's advice).

At breakfast I said: "Now we have an early start, and we will just show father how soon we will have that roof on, and floor down." I was so excited over the prospect of having a fine new house, with a floor, and windows, that I felt equal to almost any task. In two days the rafters were up, and the roof was going on. Oh, how proud I was! Our new house looked so big and tall beside the little old hut, and it was so nice to be able to look up and see no cracks large enough to let a snake through: for, as the back of the old house was against the hill, it was but three or four feet there from the ground to the roof,

28

upon which the snakes often crawled to sun themselves. One of them actually did fall through into the house one day.

By the time the roof was on, Mr. Hill began to get tired, and suggested a hunt, but I begged and coaxed for at least one-half of the floor, so that we could move in, till he reluctantly went ahead. When sufficient floor was down to give room for our one-legged bed it was moved in, and I soon had it neatly made up. I then drove nails on which to hang our clothing, and other things that could be hung up, and then ornamented the floor by spreading one of my new, braided rugs in front of the bed, only wishing for room to put down the other to add to the charms of this growing paradise. No young wife of unlimited wealth ever could have looked with more pride and pleasure on her rich velvet, or Turkish rug than I did on that to me precious rug, made by my own hands from old and new scraps given me by my mother.

When a little over half the floor was done, Mr. Hill stopped to put in the door, which was not completed when he severely mashed the thumb of his left hand, which meant the loss of the nail, and a lay-off for some time.

Oh, dear! This was terrible. November was nearly gone; the cooking must be done on the old stove in the hut, and we must sit there, with the rain leaking all around us! The stove could not be moved into the new house till an opening was made for the pipe, and we had not sufficient pipe to reach out of it, had there been one. I was planning to get more pipe with the butter, and few eggs I could collect in the next few weeks. Our groceries had all come from the proceeds of my good cow, excepting what mother had given me. She always had a sack of good things ready for me whenever I visited her. Winter was upon us, and we were in a dilemma.

I was not yet 15, but, girl as I was, I could but realize that this condition was due not only to poor management, but to want of industry and perseverance. I did not then know, however, that a man with a perfect right hand and a quick and willing wife to help him, could have gone right ahead and finished the work. My husband now suggested that we go to father's for a "visit." I did not like this, for I realized that father did not approve of his shiftlessness, but I had to consent, for he had begun to exhibit temper when I objected to any of his plans or suggestions.

We got up the horses and saddled them, and, taking a change of clothing, and our cow and calf, and putting everything else into the new house, and nailing up the openings for the door and windows,— all of which was work no less hard than going on with the flooring, door and windows would have been,—we took ourselves and cow over to father's, where we were always welcome, and found plenty of good things to eat.

There we stayed for two weeks, when father got us pipe for the stove, and a box of groceries. He and mother also went home with us, and helped to put up the stove, and hang the door. After a time the remainder of the floor was laid, and the windows put in. Now the butter from the two cows supplied us with groceries. We had no neighbors nearer than father and mother.

Mr. Hill had been receiving letters frequently during the winter from his father, and married sisters, all living in Jackson county, Oregon, and doing well, and well pleased with that section. His father had bought a fine farm, and twenty or thirty cows, lived on the main road, not far from the Siskiyou mountains, and received large prices at his own door for every pound of butter and cheese he produced.

There was a rush for the California mines. They urged us to sell, and come out there in the spring. Spring was now at hand, and in April we were to pay three hundred dollars on our farm. We had not a dollar with which to meet the obligation. Nothing had been added to or taken from the place, excepting the house, and the hay for the stock, wheat for the chickens, and what the garden had yielded. The house, alone, had been permanently added, and that would not have been built but for my father's assistance. Mr. Hill was handy with tools, and could have had work at good wages, as a carpenter, at any time.

The former owner was anxious to get the place back, and he offered us $60 to return it to him. This was more than we had expected, and with high hopes, we decided to go as soon as we could in the spring.

I sold my chickens at the store for a pair of shoes, calico for two dresses, and a few other little things. I now again had bright hopes for the future, and felt quite rich in our worldly possessions of two horses, two cows, and one yearling heifer.

We traded the younger calf and the remains of the crop for another horse, as I should have to ride my horse Queen, and drive the cows. The following is a description of our trip through that memorable canyon, which we passed on our way to Jackson county, written several years ago for publication:

Transportation Facilities in Oregon and Northern California, as told by Dr. Owens-Adair.

To THE EDITOR: In the days of the early fifties, all freight, including the U. S. mail, was carried by pack trains. The mule was to Oregon what the camel is to the great desert. The roads were never good, at the best, and in winter the mud was so deep that the laden animals often became mired beyond the power to extricate themselves, and had to be literally "snaked" out, as the packers call it. Even in summer, the worst places were extremely difficult and dangerous to' pass. The packers were men of resource, ever ready for, and equal to an emergency. They had need to be, for those were times that tried and cultivated to their utmost every human power of endurance. Besides this, many of the pioneers were the flower of the East. More courageous, more forceful and enterprising, as well as more adventurous than their fellows, they pushed on to find a broader field for their exploitation, through obstacles that weaker men feared to attack; and found their reward in the free, whole-souled life of the frontier, and in the development of a sturdy character not to be obtained in the narrower, more conventional surroundings.. The first time I ever saw a pack-train was in the early spring of 1854. My father, Thomas Owens, and his family, were then living just north of the bridge crossing the famous Deer Creek, near by the Roseburg mill—the first flouring mill in Southern Oregon. Deer Creek runs through a beautiful valley, nestled between swelling hills and gentle slopes, and dotted picturesquely with fine oak, ash,

31

pine, manzanita, laurel, and other trees. The stream itself was thickly fringed with a generous and graceful growth of myrtle, crab-apple, vine-maple and willow; with luxuriant vines of a wild white grape climbing their trunks. These grapes were similar to those in cultivation, excepting in size, and were equally palatable and wholesome. Berries in great variety abounded, in their season, including strawberries, huckleberries, service-berries, the blue elderberry, blackberries and the wild Oregon grape, which is chiefly admired for its fragrant golden bloom, and its shining, holly-like foliage. Groves of wild plums also furnished conserves to the pioneer housewife. This valley was then the feeding and breeding-grounds of thousands of deer, from which it received its name. They were attracted by the abundance of grass and excellent water, and especially by the salt springs, or "licks," which abounded in the neighborhood. It was an ideal pioneer home, and on this fresh spring morning it spread, an enchanting picture, before our door, as we heard the jangling bells of the long mule pack train, plodding down the gentle slope toward the then primitive village of Roseburg. The roads were drying fast, but the mud was still deep and stiff in the low, level stretch near the creek. A freighted mule-train was a notable spectacle, and, as I said before, it was my first sight of one, as we had moved there but recently from Clatsop plains. We all hastened to the door to get a good view of it. On they came, the mules crowding each other down the hill with increasing activity, as if their legs as well as their spirits, were becoming "limbered" up by the warm sunshine, and soon reached the brink of that deceptive mud-hole, for, like thin ice, the dry crust gave way, and the foremost animals were "stuck" fast before their drivers could turn them to either side. Mules are commonly considered to be stupid creatures. However, these showed a great deal of sense. They realized their situation, and seemed to have perfect confidence in their rescuers, and stood perfectly still, without an effort to extricate themselves. In a twinkling three athletic fellows were at hand, uncoiling their long, strong, braided rawhide ropes, or liariats, which they always carry coiled at their pommels. One rode in beside the mired mules, and in some, to me, inexplicable manner, instantaneously fastened his lariat to the pack-saddle of the foremost beast, to which he secured the ends of the other ropes of his two companions. Then the quick, sharp word, "pull away!" was given; the two other horsemen repeated the command, and their trained animals pulled so gallantly that the helpless mule, with his pack, was landed safely on solid ground in a "jiffy," where he was soon on his feet again, shaking off the mud, and vigorously switching his thin little tail, as he started off to join the procession ahead. And so the work went on, till all were over the quagmire, and out of our sight. That formidable mudhole has long since been converted into a paved street in the now beautiful and flourishing little city of Roseburg.

I was married in 1854, and a year from that time, in the spring of 1855, my husband and I started to move farther south, to the foothills of the Siskiyou mountains, beyond Jacksonville. We had packed our possessions, which were few, in a wagon, to which was attached a span of horses. I was to ride my thoroughbred mare, Queen. We waited several days, however, in order to go with a drove of cattle, as their drivers were to have a wagon and team in which to haul their outfit, and we could thus assist each other. When the drove of some 150 head of cattle arrived, we all set off, on May 1st, and on the next afternoon, reached the then famous camping-ground at the entrance of the canyon, which is now a town called Canyonville, twenty-five miles south of Roseburg. It was ten miles through this dreadful can-yon, and it was called the worst ten miles of road between Portland, Oregon, and Yreka, California; but there was then no better way. There were several miles of it that had to be traveled through the bed of the creek, over and between immense boulders, and the creek itself had to be crossed ninety-six times! Besides all this, the road ran up and down hills, and on the edges of precipices into whose frightful depths few could look without dizziness. Many accidents occurred on this road. Pack animals and teams had gone over, never to be recovered. No one thought of attempting to start through this perilous pass excepting in the early morning, so we prepared to camp for the night. Late in the afternoon, to our great delight, a big train of seventy or eighty pack mules and their drivers came up. We greeted them with welcoming cheers, and they responded with equal good-fellowship. A council was held, and it was decided that the mule-train should go first, followed by the cattle, so that they might stir up and tread down the mud, and make it possible for the wagons which followed to get through. I was then only a little past fifteen; but a girl of fifteen was then considered a grown woman. Though small, I was in perfect health, and as active as a squirrel. I was at home in the saddle, and felt perfect confidence in myself and my beautiful Queen; so I looked forward to the next day's trip as a real picnic, which it certainly was, though of a very different kind from what I had imagined. The captain of the pack-train had offered to take me with them, as he said no untrained horse with a rider could ever get safely through that canyon without help, of which I was speedily convinced. I never saw my gallant cavalier, the captain of that big mule-train, again after parting the next day, but his memory is still fresh in my mind. I can see him now, as he stood by my beautiful Queen,—tall, handsome and graceful, critically examining every part of her-trappings, after which he smiled down on me, and walked away to his supply mule, coming back with a long, broad cinch, which he threw across my saddle, and quickly tightened over all, thus making everything doubly secure. Then, placing his right hand upon the back of my saddle, he bent forward, and extended his left for my foot, and with one light spring, I was seated in the saddle. Had this honest, cautious and capable frontiersman been the captain of the ill-fated *Gen. Slocum*,* or its inspector, 1020 helpless victims would not have been sacrificed to fire and flood, and heartless greed for gold. There were many brave and noble men in those days, clad in buckskin, battling with the wilds of the wilderness. Those were times "that tried men's souls," but those heroes "came, saw and conquered."

*The *General Slocum* was a passenger steamboat that sank in the East River of New York in 1904. It was the worst disaster in terms of loss of life in New York City until the September 11, 2001 terrorist attack. Over 1,000 people lost their lives in the boat accident.

After seating me, the captain mounted his own horse. All was now ready, and the train entered the canyon. The first half mile was delightful. It was a perfect spring morning. The sun was just rising over the hills, and all nature smiled a joyous response to his warm greeting. The happy birds twittered in the branches, and sweetly sang their morning anthems. The air was filled with the fragrance of the wealth of wild flowers that glorified the hillsides and sheltered valleys with their rich and varied tints,—for in no spot in the whole wide world have I seen so wonderful a variety, or such beauty of form and color, as in the native flora of this favored Umpqua Valley. It produces three different varieties of the sweetest scented honeysuckles, and at least three distinct and beautiful lilies, yellow, straw-colored, purple and white. Violets, gorgeous rhododendrons and azaleas—but it is impossible to enumerate all the treasures of that garden of our flower-garlanded Oregon. The noble trees, the rolling hills, the verdant valleys, the gorgeous wild flowers, with their intoxicating fragrance, the genial, golden sunshine, and the blue sky over-arching all, made a picture little short of perfection—a dream of beauty never to be forgotten. I was so filled with the romantic enthusiasm and exaltation of spirits inspired by such charming surroundings, that my young heart's buoyant emotions burst forth in snatches of song. My sympathetic Queen partook of my feelings, and felt the influence of the exhilarating atmosphere, and was off like a flash. I was but a feather on her back, and she was always ready to go when I gave her the rein. The captain had to put spurs to his horse to keep by my side. All too soon we caught up with the train, and entered the dense woods and deep mud, where romance retired, and stern reality stared us in the face. Much or the road resembled a corduroy road of logs, laid parallel, and perhaps two feet apart; though instead of logs, it was formed of ridges of stiff mud, with deep furrows between each, worn by the feet of hundreds of pack-animals stepping into the same tracks as they passed, the ruts becoming deeper, and the ridges higher, as time went on. The summer months dried the roads in this condition, making it next to impossible for a wagon to get through. The mule leaders, each wearing a bell of different tone from all the others, followed in single file. They knew the danger, and seldom "bunched up." There was usually a driver to each ten or twelve mules, and these drivers were here and there, always on the lookout, and ready for an emergency, or an accident, which often occurred.

The position of captain of a large mule freight-train, like that of the captain of a great ocean liner, was behind his command, that he might the better overlook and control its movements. We could hear the bells far ahead, and, as the captain and drivers knew the sound of each, if trouble occurred they instantly knew in what part of the train it was,. even though it were out of their sight, in a curve of the road ahead. Every now and then there would come a call to "halt," when two or more drivers would go on and assist in helping some fallen animal.

Our troubles soon began. The mud was so stiff and deep that in some places it was well-nigh impossible for the heavily laden animals to get through, and they frequently became "stuck," and had to be pulled out.

Entirely unaccustomed to such a road, my Queen became first nervous, and then frantic. She would try to step upon the hard ridges, and then slip, and plunge, and flounder, throwing mud all over herself and me.

But the strong, firm hand was on her bit, and the kind, masterful voice, speaking gentle, soothing words in her ear. Only through such treatment by the captain, and the presence of his own trained animal, could she ever have gotten through without injuring herself or her rider. I think she must have fallen twenty times on that trip, but the faithful captain held her gently, yet firmly, and in the most soothing tones, would appeal to her, as to a high-born lady, and his own sweetheart;—"Easy, easy, now, my lady "Come, now, my pretty birdie"; "Gently now, my pretty girl";—meantime patting and caressing her. She soon understood, and, in time, learned to trust him, and to submit willingly to his guidance—and often, after he had safely guided her around some frightful mud-hole, or almost impassable barrier, and turned, with a reassuring caress, to mount his own faithful horse, who always kept closely behind, Queen would put out her nose for another pat, which she would be sure to get. Then he would exclaim: "Oh, you're a beauty! Almost as lovely as a woman." When he was compelled to leave us by the roadside, to go forward to assist in extricating some unfortunate, he would say to me: "Now let me assist you off. It will rest you. I am afraid you will get very tired." Queen was restless in his absence, and anxiously watched for his coming. Intelligent animals always realize their surroundings, and soon learn, in danger, to depend on the superior human intelligence.

The woods reverberated with whoops, yells, and curses. The cattle "bunched up," crowded each other, and some rolled down the hill to their death. The wagons mired so deeply that they had to be pried up, and the teams doubled to pull them out. And so the long day wore on, until about 4 p m., after twelve hours of desperately hard work, the rear end of the mule train emerged from the canyon upon a beautiful green slope, bedecked with wild flowers. The first part of the pack-train had already been relieved of their burdens, and were quietly grazing with intense enjoyment upon the luscious grass. The sight, to me, was perfectly enchanting, as I jumped off my poor, tired Queen. We were both covered from head to feet with mud. Our good, gallant friend speedily relieved her of her trappings, and the next minute she was down, rolling on the clean grass, and rubbing the mud from her handsome coat. The hungry cattle now appeared, and instantly made for the grass. Water they had had all day in plenty, but no food. Some of the men who got out first volunteered to go back and help bring out the, wagons, which sorely needed their aid. With their strong ropes, hitched on in front of the horses, they kept them on their feet, and helped them through, and both man and beast rejoiced at the end of their severe exertions.

I assisted the packers, and we soon had a good supper for all, to which we sat down with appetites suited to the occasion, amid general congratulations on our good day's work. The next day we regretfully bade adieu to our good friends the packers, only wishing we could have kept up with them.

And this was frontier life! Hard, strenuous, often dangerous, but full of free, fresh out-of-door enjoyment, and rich in those noblest qualities of the race,—courage, resolution, patience, industry, honesty, hope, patriotism, chivalry, cheerfulness, helpful kindness and hearty good will.

The remainder of our trip after getting through the canyon, was uneventful, but pleasant. We remained several months with his father and mother, both assisting with the milking, and he on the farm and I in the house and dairy.

At this time there was much gold excitement in and around Yreka, and Mr. Hill decided to go there, and thinking we could not take the cows, he sold them. And now we had some money. Then he suggested that before we went off so far, we ride back and visit my folks. "It would only take a few weeks, and cost very little." By this time I was homesick, and, of course, glad to go, and so we went. I could see that father did not approve of Mr. Hill's having sold my cows. He said to him:

"Now take my advice, and settle down; and remember that a 'rolling stone gathers no moss.' It does not take long for a few head of cattle to grow into money."

Our visit over, we mounted our horses, and said goodbye again. Along the road, at convenient intervals, stood roadside inns, for the accommodation of travelers. One of the best of these was kept by two brothers, bachelors, one of whom stuttered badly. He was the cook and housekeeper. My husband knew them well, and always made it a point to stop there, coming and going.

Just after we had alighted, and Mr. Hill was leading our horses away, a man rode up, and inquired how far it was to the next stopping-place. Our landlord, anxious to reply promptly, began stuttering and sputtering, twisting his face into the most frightful contortions, and working himself all over, in the effort to reply. The stranger sat on his horse, gazing at him in amazement. At last the landlord blurted out:

"D—d—n it! go on! You'll get there b-before I can tell you!" and made for the house.

I told the man it was about four miles, and he rode on, convulsed with laughter. This expression was repeated as a by-word on similar occasions by all the country round for many years, and may be current there now, for aught I know.

From here we proceeded on to the mountain-house, then owned and kept by a Mr. Russell, the husband of Mr. Hill's youngest sister, who was one of the most lovely women I ever knew. She and I were about the same age, and we became very much attached to each other, and, I am happy to say, we have continued up to this time warm friends, with never a word to jar our pleasant relations. She, long since widowed, lives in Ashland, Oregon, surrounded by her admirable family, and honored and loved by all who know her. I can say, with pride, that I have retained the respect and confidence of all Mr. Hill's family, who are, and have been among the most respected and esteemed pioneers of Jackson county, Oregon.

We found the dwellers at the Mountain House in a state of great excitement. The day before, two men had been attacked and killed on the mountain, and the mail, and all travelers must wait till a sufficient number of men could be gathered together to make traveling safe, or till the soldiers could come to guard the U. S. mail and the teams.

At the end of three days a large company was collected;—at least half a dozen wagons with families, a long pack-train, and a good many horsemen, and miners with their pack animals. Men and women were not easily frightened in those days. With twenty men, well-armed, we felt no fear. We started over that mountain more like a party going to a picnic, than people going into deadly danger. The men, however, kept a sharp lookout for "the red devils," but saw none, and we reached Yreka safely, and in good time.

Mr. Hill had an aunt, his father's sister, a Mrs. Kelly, living there. She had had but one son, who had been recently killed in the war with the Rogue River Indians, and her great sorrow for his loss was still fresh. As soon as she heard we were in town, she came at once to see us, and said to my husband:

"Now, Legrand, you must get right to work; there's plenty to do here, at good wages. But you must not leave this little wife of yours alone, for there are too many rough, drinking men in the place; but she will be safe with me. I can help you both in many ways. So you pack up everything and move right over to my house." I was delighted, and she proved to be one of the dearest and best of mothers to me.

She was a woman of executive ability, and a real moneymaker; but, like most women of such ability, she had a husband who wheedled it out of her about as fast as she made it.

She kept from one to two cows and a flock of chickens, from which she sold milk and eggs, made pies and cakes for sale, and took in sewing. She received $3 for making a white shirt, and was paid for everything else in proportion. She was a most excellent seamstress, and she found in me a more than willing student, as I was anxious both to learn and to make money also. And so we worked together, she giving me all, and usually more than I earned.

Her husband was selfish and unsympathetic, and often scolded her for grieving for her dead boy, who was the son of her first husband. Then the poor mother would turn to me for sympathy, which she unfailingly received. She soon transferred her affection to me, and took great pride in making my clothes fit me perfectly, and in dressing me becomingly. Often she would say: "Now, I am going to see that you have plenty of nice clothes, and I shall not let you give it to Legrand to fool away." (He had lived with her for eight or ten years in his boyhood, and she thoroughly understood him, and felt that she had a right to advise him and instruct him as to what he ought to do. Had he followed her advice, he would have succeeded, instead of making a failure.)

"Legrand," she would say, "I want you to buy a lot, while you have the money to pay for it. First thing you know, the money will all be gone, and you'll have nothing to show for it. Then, get in, and build a house. It is high time you were getting settled."

In March a small, one-roomed, battened house, with a "lean-to" for a kitchen, and a lot, were for sale at $450,—only a block from Aunt Kelly's. , That was then a great bargain, and we bought it, paying $300 down, all the money left from the sale of my two cows, heifer and the wagon and horses. My Queen was out on pasture, and continued to be a "bone of contention," as she was only an expense. But I stoutly refused to have her sold, and Aunt Kelly stood by me, declaring he should not sell her, as she would herself pay for her pasturage before it should be done.

We moved into our new house in March, with the $150 mortgage hanging over us. On April 17th, 1856, our baby was born, and then Aunt Kelly begged me to give him to her, addressing me thus:

"Now, Bethenia, you just give him to me. I will take him, and educate him, and make him my heir. I will give him all I have, and that is more than his father will ever do for him. I know very well that Legrand will just fool around all his life, and never accomplish anything."

She seemed to think my consent to her having the child was all that was necessary. But my baby was too precious to give to anyone.

I continued to work with Aunt Kelly, who was always over-crowded with work, and as we were so near by each other, I could do much of it at my own home; so that, in time, I was able to get many little conveniences and comforts for the house, beside a good share of our groceries. Mr. Hill neither drank or used tobacco, but, as his aunt said, he simply idled away his time, doing a day's work here and there, but never continuing at anything. Then, too, he had a passion for trading and speculating, always himself coming out a loser; and thus the time dragged on, until September, 1857, when who should drive up, one glad day, but my father and mother. Father had heard how things were going with us, and had come, prepared to take us back with them in case we were willing to go, but he was to discreet to let this be known till later. He and mother wanted to see the country; the children were large enough to look out for things at home; and they especially desired to see my baby.

It did not take them long to understand that we were barely living "from hand to mouth," as it were, with most of the work coming on me, so father said:

"How would you like to go back to Roseburg? It is a growing town. I have several acres in it, and if you think you would like to make the change, I will give you an acre of land, and the material for a good

41

house, which you can put up this fall. The boys can help you, and there will always be plenty of work at carpentering in town."

To say that we were delighted with this proposal expresses it but faintly. We sold our house and lot in Yreka, realizing less than $100 out of the transaction, as the $150 mortgage and interest had to come out of the sum received for the property, but father said "A bird in the hand is worth two in the bush." We were soon packed, and ready to start again on our migrations. There was but one regret on my part, that was leaving dear old Aunt Kelly, who had been so good to me, and had taught me so many useful things. With many tears and sobs, I bade her good-bye. My tears were always near the surface in my young days, and overflowed easily. Mother frequently said, "Your tears lie very shallow; you are always either at the top or bottom." There was no middle ground for me, and my likes and dislikes were positive in the extreme.

The weather was fine, and we all enjoyed the trip, only one accident occurring, and that came near ending in a terrible tragedy.

Mr. Hill was driving the team. Mother sat on the back seat, holding in her arms my youngest sister (now Mrs. Alvah Pike, of Portland, Oregon). I sat on the front seat beside my husband, with my baby in my arms. My father was walking behind, leading my mare, Queen. As we were descending the Siskiyou mountains into Oregon, we came to a deep gulch, spanned by a high, narrow bridge, at least forty feet above the stream below, which ran among immense boulders. The road beyond was steep, narrow, and rocky, and turned sharply to the left. The moment we were across the bridge, Mr. Hill started up the horses briskly, applying the whip, to which they were totally unaccustomed in climbing a hill. In springing suddenly and strongly forward, one wheel of the wagon came violently in contact with a large rock, and, in his hasty attempt to bring them around, he pulled the lines too hard, and they began to back toward the bridge. I saw the danger, and, instantly, with one bound, I was on the ground, with my babe in my arms. Turning, I heard father's commanding voice shouting "Whoa!" and saw him running toward us. The next instant he had seized the spokes of the wheel, and thrown his full strength into one supreme effort to check

42

the wagon, which he succeeded in doing, just as the wheel was at the very edge of the bridge! Meanwhile, I had placed my baby on the ground and seized a solid chunk of wood that fortunately lay near, and wedged it under and behind the wheel. Thus an awful tragedy was averted. Not till the danger was past did I realize that I was hurt. I now found that I had sustained a severe sprain of the instep of my right foot, from which I have suffered very much at times, ever since. Mother removed my shoe, and wrapped my foot in a thick cloth, saturated with water from the creek under the memorable bridge that came so near being our death, after which we continued our journey, father now driving, which he continued thereafter to do on all bad places.

On reaching home, father told me I could go over and select my acre of land, and our building-spot, which I gladly did. He told Mr. Hill he could have the team, and he and the boys could haul the lumber for our house, so that he could get to work on it at once.

They hauled the lumber, but, in the meantime, Mr. Hill had been talking with a man about burning brick. This man had some land a mile from father's and a team, and he offered to go into equal partnership with Mr. Hill in the business of brickmaking there, each, beside his own work, furnishing one man to help, and I was to do the cooking for them all, for the use of the team.

Father endeavored, in every way, to dissuade him from going into this undertaking, telling him that it would be impossible, so late in the season, to prepare a yard, and burn a kiln of brick before winter; and that the soil had never been tested, and there was no certainty that it was suitable for the purpose, etc., but the more he talked the more determined Mr. Hill was to put all the little money we had into the venture, and so he moved me and my young child into a tent in a low, damp valley, near the river, and their work and mine was begun. But it was never half completed, for when they had only a few hundred of brick molded, it began to rain continuously, and put a stop to their work, and in addition to this ill-fortune, I was stricken down with typhoid fever. Father and mother came with the wagon, and moved us back to their home. It was now late in November; winter was upon us, and still our house was not touched. When I became convalescent, father urged Mr. Hill to begin the house. He replied that he wanted a deed to the acre of land before beginning the house.

Father then told him that he and mother had talked it over, and had decided to deed the property to me and the boy; that he had given us one good start, and now, after three and a half years, we had nothing left but one horse, and that he thought it best to secure a home for me and the child in my own name.

This enraged Mr. Hill, who said he would not build on the lot unless the deed was made to him, as he was the head of his family. Father advised him to think it over, and not to act rashly.

He sulked for a time, and then bargained for a lot in town, after which he hired a team, and hauled the lumber off from the acre to the lot, and began to build the house. All this time we were living off father, who said nothing; but furnished the shingles, and told Mr. Hill to get nails, and anything he needed, at the store, on his account, which he did. In time, the roof was on, and the kitchen partly finished, and we moved in. The kitchen was so open that the skunks, which were very numerous in that region at that time, came under the floor nights, and up into the kitchen, where they rattled around among the pots and pans, even jumping on the table, and devouring the food, if I did not keep everything securely covered, while I often lay and listened to their nocturnal antics, not daring to get up to drive them out, as the dire consequences of disturbing them suddenly were well known, and dreaded.

My health was poor. I had not been strong since the baby came, and I could not seem to recover from the effects of the fever. The baby was ill and fretful, much of the time, and things were going anything but smoothly. A short time before the climax, I went home and told my parents that I did not think I could stand it much longer. Mother was indignant, and told me to come home, and let him go; that "any man that could not make a living with the good starts and help he has had, never will make one; and with his temper, he is liable to kill you at any time."

Father broke down, and shed tears, saying:

"Oh, Bethenia, there has never been a divorce in my family, and I hope there never will be. I want you to go back, and try again, and do your best. After that, if you *cannot possibly* get along, come home." I went back, greatly relieved, for I knew that if I had to leave, I would be protected.

Our trouble usually started over the baby, who was unusually cross. He was such a sickly, tiny mite, with an abnormal, voracious appetite, but his father thought him old enough to be trained and disciplined, and would spank him unmercifully because he cried. This I could not endure, and war would be precipitated at once. A few days before our separation, his father fed him six hard-boiled eggs at supper, in spite of all I could do or say. I slept little that night, expecting that the child would be in convulsions before morning. And thus one thing led to another until the climax was reached.

Early one morning in March, after a tempestuous scene of this sort, Mr. Hill threw the baby on the bed, and rushed down in town. As soon as he was out of sight, I put on my hat and shawl, and, gathering a few necessaries together for the baby, I flew over to father's.

I found my brother ferrying a man across the river, and I went back with him. By this time, I was almost in a state of collapse, as I had ran all the way,—about three fourths of a mile. Brother, seeing that something was wrong, and always ready to smooth out the wrinkles, took the baby with a smile, saying: "Give me that little 'piggywig"; and shall I take you under my other arm? It seems to me you're getting smaller every year. Now, just hang on to me, and I'll get you up the hill, all right. Mother will have breakfast ready, and I guess a good square meal is what you need."

The next day father saw Mr. Hill, and found he had been trying to sell the house and lot. Father told him that he would come with me to get my clothes, and a few things I needed, and that he (Mr. Hill) could have the rest. That he (father) would take care of me from that time on, and that when he (Mr. Hill) sold the house and lot, I would sign the deed, as the lot was not paid for, and the unfinished house would, according to law, go with it.

45

However, before Mr. Hill found a purchaser, he had repented, and come several times to get me to go back to him. I said: "Legrand, I have told you many times that if we ever did separate, I would never go back, and I never will."

DETERMINATION

And now, at eighteen years of age, I found myself, broken in spirit and health, again in my father's house, from which, only four short years before, I had gone with such a happy heart, and such bright hopes for the future.

It seemed to me now that I should never be happy or strong again. I was, indeed, surrounded with difficulties seemingly insurmountable,—a husband for whom I had lost all love and respect, a divorce, the stigma of which would cling to me all my future life, and a sickly babe of two years in my arms, all rose darkly before me.

At this time, I could scarcely read or write, and four years of trials, and hardships and privations sufficient to crush a mature woman, had wrought a painful change in the fresh, blooming child who had so buoyantly taken the duties and burdens of wifehood and motherhood on her young shoulders. I realized my position fully, and resolved to meet it bravely, and do my very best.

Surrounded with an atmosphere of affection and cheerfulness, with an abundance of nourishing food, my health rapidly returned, and with it came an increasing desire for education, that I might fit myself for the duties of a mother, and for the life yet before me.

At this time, there was as: good a school as the country then afforded in Roseburg, distant not more than half a mile.

My little George, too, felt the beneficial change, fully as much as I did, for my mother's idea of raising children could not be improved upon—simply to give them sufficient wholesome food, keep them clean and happy, and let them live out of door as much as possible.

George was such a tiny creature, and so active in his movements that my young brothers and sisters felt him no burden, and always had him with them out of doors; so after pondering the matter for some time, I said one day: "Mother, do you think I might manage to go to school?" "Why, yes," she answered; "go right along. George is no trouble. The children will take care of him."

I joyfully accepted this opportunity, and from that day on, I was up early and out to the barn, assisting with the milking, and doing all the work possible in the house, until 8:30, when I went to school with the children, my younger brothers and sisters. Saturdays, with the aid of the children, I did the washing and ironing of the family, and kept up with my studies.

At the end of my first four months' term I had finished the third reader, and made good progress with my other studies of spelling, writing, geography and arithmetic.

In September, Mr. and Mrs. Hobson (Mrs. Hobson was my eldest sister, Diana) came to visit us; and on their return home, Diana begged me to go home with them, and I went.

With a light wagon, and a span of good horses, the trip over the same road and beautiful country through which I had passed five years before, was delightful.

Soon after we reached my sister's home on Clatsop, only two miles from my father's old farm, we went on a visit to our good and worthy neighbor, Mrs. Morrison, who said to me:

"Bethenia, why did you leave your husband?"

"Because he whipped my baby unmercifully, and struck and choked me,—and I was never born to be struck by mortal man!'"

"But did he commit adultery?"

"No."

"Then, my dear child, take my advice, and go back, and beg him on your knees to receive you,—for the scriptures forbid the separation of man and wife for any other cause than adultery." I replied: "I think there are other things quite as bad as that." She shook her head, with deep gravity, saying: "My child, you must not set up your opinion against the Holy Bible."

Several years later, when I was again on Clatsop, Mrs. Morrison gave a quilting party, to which the whole neighborhood was invited. The weather was propitious, and everybody was expected to come early. The night before the party, a daughter of Mrs. Morrison, herself the mother of a large family, and expecting another soon, fled from her home and brutal husband, to her father's house for protection. Her arms and face were bruised and swollen, and the livid marks of his cruel fingers were on her throat!

This was a terrible shock to the dear old lady's ideas of Bible interpretation, and when she saw me the next day, like the honest, sincere Christian that she was, she walked promptly up to me, and said, with much emotion:

"Bethenia, a few years ago I chastised you because you left your husband for brutal abuse. God has justly punished me, and now, before all these women, I want to ask your forgiveness. When I saw my own child bruised and mutilated, I realized that there are things as bad as adultery."

I threw my arms around that dear old neck, and we mingled our tears together.

Long years after, when her time had come to bid this earth adieu, and I was called to attend her professionally, at her bedside I met her three daughters, now past the meridian of life, with kind faces and beautiful gray hair, all lovingly anxious to make their beloved mother's last hours as peaceful as possible. It has never been my lot to witness a deathbed where more Christian devotion and resignation were manifested. A few years later, when Captain Morrison, her husband, received his last call, and followed his saintly wife, I was again summoned to render my professional services. And still later, when the secretary of the Pioneer Association asked me to write biographical sketches of all the Clatsop pioneer women coming to Oregon prior to 1849, to be preserved in the archives of the society, I did not forget to record the heroic deeds and self-sacrificing life of this grand woman, likening her, as her majestic carriage and exalted character well deserve, to Joan of Arc.

Before going to Clatsop, in the fall of 1859, with my sister, I applied for a divorce, and the custody of my child, and petitioned for the restoration of my maiden name of Owens.

49

In the spring of 1859, my brother Flem met me in Salem with a team, and together we returned to Roseburg in time for the session of court before which my case was to appear.

The suit was strongly contested on account of the child, which Mr. Hill's widowed mother was anxious to have, thinking her son would be thus induced to make his home with her, so that she might remain in her own home, all her other children now having homes of their own.

My father employed Hon. Stephen F. Chadwick [later the fifth governor of Oregon] on my behalf, and he won my suit, including the custody of my child, and the permission to resume my maiden name.

A circumstance which seems stranger than fiction occurred more than thirty years later, when I was visiting Ex-Governor and Mrs. Chadwick, at their home in Salem by special invitation, during the session of the Legislature.

They had visited us at our home in Sunnymead the summer before.

The Governor met me at the train, and seemed about in his usual health. We all attended the session of the Legislature that afternoon. At dinner the Governor had been conversing animatedly in his usual happy strain.

"Jane," he said to his wife, "we'll give the doctor a feast next Thursday evening. You know we are to have our church social then."

His daughter Mary who had just risen to change his plate, remarked: "We may not find so much to eat."

"Oh, yes, we shall," he rejoined; "I know how to get the best, and we will have it."

At that moment, as his daughter moved toward the sideboard, he gave a little characteristic cough, and she said: "Shall I get you a glass of water, papa?"

"No, I thank you," was his reply.

Turning toward the table the next instant with the dessert in her hand, she gave a piercing scream.

I was sitting between him and his wife.

Startled and alarmed, I looked up instantly, and saw the Governor sitting bolt upright, his head thrown back, and his face livid. I sprang to his side, laid him prone on the floor, and loosened his clothes, but to no avail. That noble heart was still;—the Governor was dead!

Never, never before did I so deeply, keenly feel how true it is that in the midst of life and joy come sorrow and death.

In the unexcelled language of Mrs. Hemans—

"Leaves have their time to fall,
And flowers to wither at the north wind's breath,
And stars to set,—but all
Thou hast *all* seasons for thine own, oh Death.
Thou art where friend meets friend,
Beneath the shadow of the elm to rest;—
Thou art where foe meets foe, and trumpets rend
The skies, and swords beat down the princely crest."

After the decree of the court was rendered giving me custody of my child, and my father's name, which I have never since discarded, and never will, I felt like a free woman.

The world began to look bright once more, as with renewed vigor and reviving hope, I sought work in all honorable directions, even accepting washing, which was one of the most profitable occupations among the few considered "proper" for women in those days.(I am here reminded of a characteristic, courageous, and, at the time, iconoclastic, declaration by Mrs. Duniway in the New Northwest, at the time of the bitter uprising against Chinese labor, and the summary expulsion of all Chinese from many localities on the Pacific Coast, to-wit: "White men will not wash. White women have no business to wash, and we *must* have Chinamen for that purpose!")

My father objected to my doing washing for a living, and said:

"Why can't you be contented to stay at home with us; I am able to support you and your child?"

But no. No amount of argument would shake my determination to earn my own livelihood, and that of my child, so father bought me a sewing-machine, the first that ever came into that town, and so, with sewing and nursing, a year passed very profitably.

My sister, Mrs. Hobson, now urged me to return to her on Clatsop, as she greatly needed my help. I went, but soon became restless, because of my intense thirst for learning. An education I must have, at whatever cost. Late in the fall of 1860, sister and I went over to Oysterville, Wash., to visit my old and much-beloved girl-friend, Mts. S. S. Munson. The few days which my sister had arranged to stay, passed all too quickly, so Captain and Mrs. Munson assured Mrs. Hobson that they would see that I reached home safely if I might stay till we "got our visit out."

I told Mrs. Munson of my great anxiety for an education, and she immediately said:

"Why not, then, stay with me, and go to school? We have a good school here, and I should like so much to have you with me, especially farther on."

To this generous offer I replied that I would gladly accept it if I could only find some way of earning my necessary expenses while attending school. Mrs. Munson replied: "There are my brother and his hired man; I can get you their washing, which will bring you in from $1.00 to $1.50 per week, which will be all you will need."

To this I gratefully assented; and I did their washing evenings. Work to me then, was scarcely more than play, and, as "change in work brings rest," I assisted in the other domestic work with pleasure, especially as Mrs. Munson was a methodical and excellent housekeeper, and I loved and enjoyed order and neatness in the home above all things.

Thus passed one of the pleasantest, and most profitable winters of my life, while, "whetted by what it fed on," my desire for knowledge grew daily stronger.

My sister, Mrs. Hobson, now urged me to come back to her, and I said to her:

"I am determined to get at least a common school education. I now know that I can support and educate myself and my boy, and I am resolved to do it; furthermore, I do not intend to do it over the washtub, either. Nor will I any longer work for my board and clothes, alone. You need me, and I am willing to stay with you the next six months, if you will arrange for me to go to school in Astoria next winter."

She agreed to this. Sometime later, I said to her: "Diana, don't you think I could teach a little summer school here on the plains? I can rise at four, and help with the milking, and get all the other work done by 8 a m., and I can do the washing mornings and evenings, and on Saturdays."

She said: "You can try," so the following day I asked Mr. Hobson if he would not get up a little school for me. He replied:

"Take the horse and go around among the neighbors and work it up yourself."

I lost no time in carrying out his suggestion, and succeeded in getting the promise of sixteen pupils, for which I was to receive $2 each for three months.

This was my first attempt to instruct others. I taught my school in the old Presbyterian church,—the first Presbyterian church-building ever erected in Oregon. Of my sixteen pupils, there were three who were more advanced than myself, but I took their books home with me nights, and, with the help of my brother-in-law, I managed to prepare the lessons beforehand, and they never suspected my incompetency.

From this school I received my first little fortune of $25; and I added to this by picking wild blackberries at odd times, which found a ready sale at fifty cents a gallon.

Fall found me settled at the old Boelling hotel in Astoria, with my nephew, Frank Hobson, and my little son George. Our board was paid, I taking care of our small room, and our clothes, with the privilege of doing our washing and ironing on Saturdays. And now I encountered one of my sharpest trials, for, on entering school, and being examined in mental arithmetic, I was placed in the primary class!

Mr. Deardorff, the principal, kindly offered to assist me in that study after school, and, later, permitted me to enter both classes. Words can never express my humiliation at having to recite with children of from eight to fourteen years of age. This, however, was of brief duration, for in a few weeks I had advanced to the next class above, and was soon allowed to enter the third (and highest) class in mental arithmetic.

At the end of the term of nine months, I had passed into most of the advanced classes;—not that I was an apt scholar, for m)' knowledge has always been acquired by the hardest labor,—but by sheer determination, industry and perseverance. At 4 a m my lamp was always burning, and I was poring over *my* books,—never allowing myself more than eight hours for sleep.

Nothing was permitted to come between me and this, the greatest opportunity of my life.

The following summer was spent on Clatsop with my sister, milking, making butter, and assisting in all the laborious, and never-ending work of a well-managed farm.

This was now 1862, during the civil war, and the State had called upon the counties to contribute to the Sanitary Commission, organized for the aid and comfort of our soldiers in the field. Public interest and sympathy in the cause was intense, and all were ready to do their part.

It was suggested, among other things, that Clatsop, being a dairy region, should furnish a mammoth cheese;—but who was able to make it, and where could a hoop of sufficient size be found?

It so happened that Mr. Hobson had a man working for him who had made cheese, and understood the process. He and I, therefore, volunteered to attempt the manufacture of the caseous monster, the milk to be furnished by the county. Milk was then abundant, and

Mr. Hobson suggested that a small hogshead might answer for a hoop, by sawing off both ends, and using the middle, the iron bands around which could be filed off after the cheese was made. This was done.

Several of the huge pots then so much in use for washing and soap-boiling, were provided, and also a number of large tubs for setting the curd; and, with an improvised press, we were ready for the milk, which came in in lavish abundance, for this was everybody's cheese.

When finished, the cheese was pronounced a complete success, and it certainly was, in size.

Previous to the State Fair, where it was to be exhibited before its final' disposal, it was taken to Astoria, where it was sold at auction, sold and re-sold until the sum of $145 was realized in Clatsop county from our big cheese, for the good cause.

After this, I was chosen to convey it, in the name of Clatsop county, to the State Fair at Salem, the capital, where, notwithstanding my assertion that I did not deserve it all, the full credit for it was given to me, and circulars were sent out setting forth in staring head-lines:

MRS. OWENS' BIG CHEESE FROM CLATSOPCOUNTY!!

IT HAS ALREADY BROUGHT $145 IN ASTORIA!!!

It will be on exhibition at the State Fair in Salem, after which it will be re-sold, and it and its proceeds sent to the soldiers in the field!!

This program was carried out, and I afterward heard that the total proceeds from our big cheese were between four and five hundred dollars.

As to whether the cheese itself ever reached the "boys in blue," and whether or not they found it palatable, and digestible, I was not informed.

Autumn having again arrived, I rented three rooms in what was then known as the "Old Gray House," in Astoria, a large, square, cupola-crowned wooden building, erected by the late W. H. Gray, author of a history of Oregon, and occupied by himself and family for a number of years as a residence. It stood on the beach, its front resting on the ground, and its back supported by piles, five or six feet in height, over the waters of the Columbia river; so that at high tide the house was almost entirely over the water, which at the highest tides flowed over the bank, and spread far out on the flats, toward the hills, requiring, at such times, a boat to reach the main town. This, however, was of rare occurrence.

My rooms were in the second story, and several rooms on the same floor were occupied by a Mr. and Mrs. Lowell, excellent and cultivated young people, of exceptional personal attractiveness. Their apartments were situated immediately across the hall from mine, and there were many empty rooms in the spacious old building, then otherwise unoccupied.

Many had been the happy social gatherings in its hospitable parlors below when occupied by Mr. Gray, his estimable wife, and their musically gifted, intelligent and social sons and daughters, and its vacant halls seem yet to ring with the sound of merry laughter, and pleasant voices of the past.

Here, in three small rooms, I set up housekeeping, with barely the necessary furniture, and a scanty larder, which was supplied by my savings from blackberry-picking, and other odd jobs of sewing, crocheting, etc. I was ready and eager for school, but my daily expenses (for two, as my child was always with me,) must be met, and this is how it was done: I engaged to do the washing for two large families, and the washing and ironing for another, for which last I received two dollars weekly, and which I did at my rooms, evenings and Saturdays.

Sunday night found me and little George at Capt. C.'s. At 4 a m. Monday I was in the kitchen at my task. George went with their children to school at 8:30, and at 10 a m., my washing done, I followed them.

Monday night, and Tuesday morning, this program was repeated at Dr. T.'s.

For all this work, I received five dollars each week, including the kindest treatment from all my employers. This enabled me to meet all my expenses, especially as, living on the beach, George and I were able to pick up most of our wood from the drift.

Thus I was as happy in my independence, I dare say, as is John D. Rockefeller, with all his "tainted" wealth, and far more hopeful for the long future yet before me.

There was, at this time, in Astoria, a kind and estimable gentleman, of middle age,—Capt. A. C. Farnsworth, by name, a Columbia River bar pilot. Being a special friend of Mr. and Mrs. Hobson, he was familiar with my struggles for an education, from the first.

One rainy evening, he called at my rooms. George had been snugly tucked into bed, and I was ironing at the table, with my book in front of me, for in this way I always studied while I worked, my hands, like those of the musician, being trained to do their mechanical part, with little assistance from my brains, which were employed mainly elsewhere.

Removing his heavy overcoat, and seating himself by the table, Captain Farnsworth said:

"Have you no time to talk?"

"Oh, yes," I responded; "I can talk and work, too." "Well," he continued, "I want you to put away that work. I have come to talk with you, and I want you to listen well to what I have to say."

I closed the book, removed the ironing cloth, and basket, and sat down, not knowing what was coming, but feeling very apprehensive. He saw this, and smiling reassuringly, said:

"Don't you ever get tired?"

"Oh, yes, but I get rested easily, and quickly."

"How long do you expect to go on in this way?"

"I don't know," I answered.

"I do not like to see you working in this way," he continued; "and I have come to see you as a friend; and I want to be a true friend. I am alone in the world. The nearest relative I have is a nephew. I have more money than I need, and I think I cannot do better with it than help you." Trembling, and with moist eyes, I exclaimed: "No, no! I cannot take money from you!"

"Now do not be foolish," he hastened to say; "but listen to me. I know you are thinking it will compromise you; besides, you are a great deal too independent for your own good. I am a good deal older than you are, and know vastly more of the world than you do, and I want you to thoroughly understand that if you accept the offer I make you, you are never to feel under the slightest obligation to me. My offer is this: You are to select, and attend any school in the United States, for as long a time as you choose, and I will furnish the money for all the expenses of yourself and boy, and no one shall ever know from me where the money came from. If you say so, I will promise never even to write to you."

Could there have been a more generous, unselfish offer? I was now in tears, but my self-will, independence, and inexperience decided me to refuse it. I preferred to rely on my own exertions, rather than to incur such an obligation from even so good a friend.

The acceptance of that offer would doubtless have changed my whole life, but who can tell if for better or for worse?

Captain Farnsworth was thoroughly disgusted with my obstinacy, and, though he continued a friend, he showed less interest in me from that time.

I am free to acknowledge that many were the times during my after years of struggles and hardships, in my supreme effort to get ahead, in which I bitterly repented my hasty decision, feeling that it was the mistake of my life. The acceptance of that offer would have far earlier opened the doors of science, and saved me many long years of bitter experience, and irretrievably lost opportunities.

Others, also, beside my generous friend, the Captain, had been observant of my efforts. At that time Col. James Taylor and Mir. David Ingalls were the school directors of that district, and, as the wife of the principal was prevented by illness from continuing as assistant in the school, they generously selected me to fill her place at a salary of $25 per month, for the remaining three months of the term. This was, indeed, a wave of prosperity! And, as one good thing sometimes brings another, I was offered a room and board, for the care of nine rooms in a private boarding-house, which I promptly accepted. I asked, and received, permission, while teaching in the primary department of the school, to recite in two of the advanced classes. I also joined a reading and singing class which met an evening of each week.

When I took my place as teacher there, a young lady from Oysterville, who was far ahead of me when I attended that school with her two years before, now recited to me, a circumstance that went far toward removing the sting of humiliation I had felt on being placed in the primary arithmetic class, as before related. Before the expiration of this term, I had received an offer to teach a three months' school in Bruceport, on Shoalwater Bay, at $25 per month and board. "And to board around."

Judge Cyrus Olney [6th Associate Justice of the Oregon Supreme Court, 1853-1858] was then county school superintendent, and it was with fear and trembling that I applied to him for examination and a certificate. But he said to me:

"I know you are competent to teach that school. I have had my eye on you for over a year, and I know you will do your duty. I will send you a certificate." And he did.

This was a great encouragement to me, and increased my determination to do my best.

I accepted the school, and with mv boy, I was away the very next day after my Astoria term closed, to Bruceport, where I began teaching at once. After I had taught here two weeks, a subscription was raised among the few families, and more numerous oystermen, for another three months' school, (making a six months' term, in all).

Before this was completed, I received and accepted an offer of the Oysterville school (the same school I first attended), where I "boarded around," as was then the prevailing custom. This enabled me to spend more time with my friends the Munsons, my friendship with whom has never grown less; and when, over forty years later, Captain Munson received his last call from his Great Commander, mine was the sadly pleasant task of covering his casket with beautiful flowers from my garden,—flowers not more fragrant than the memory of his constant kindness and genial, generous spirit will ever be to me. TI The Oysterville school then had the undesirable reputation of 'being ungovernable, and it was my reputation for good government that secured me the situation, a reputation which was not lessened by an incident that transpired soon after I took charge of the school.

Among my pupils was a well-grown boy of eighteen. He was a well-disposed youth, but silly and injudicious men had guyed him about having to mind a "school marm," and for a "joke," had put him up to breaking the rules, which I had written out, and hung up on the walls of the school room.

I had heard of this, and expected trouble. This boy whispered, and I rebuked him, explaining the necessity for the rule forbidding whispering in school, in the presence of the children. He soon repeated the offense, however, and I took no outward note of it, though aware that several of the pupils knew I had seen him.

On dismissing the school, I said to him, pleasantly:

"Remain after school, a moment, please; I want to speak to you."

He kept his seat, and as the last child passed out, I locked the door, removing the key, which I always carried.

Going back to him, I said, kindly:

"I know you are not a bad boy, but you are almost a man, and you should, and I intend you shall, set a good example before the younger members of this school. I will excuse you this time, with the understanding that if you repeat this offense, I will have to punish you before the whole school by giving you ten blows on the open hand with the ferrule, and if you attempt to resent this punishment, I will call in the directors; who will stand by and see it administered, for you must understand clearly that I am mistress of this school. You may go, now, and I hope I shall have no more trouble with you." I had none, thereafter.

The curiosity of some of the children prompted them to listen outside, and through the thin boarded walls they heard all that was said, and of course repeated it so that it was generally known.

On receiving the offer of the Oysterville school, my reply was: "I will engage to teach for you, if the directors will pledge their support to the government of the school."

This they readily did. There were three pupils in that school who made all the trouble;—an Irish girl, and two boys, and the girl was the ring-leader.

It was not long before one of these boys stuck a pin -into the girl sitting in front of him. I reprimanded him, but he only grinned impertinently. I told him to bring his lunch on the following day, and stay in during the noon hour. He failed to make his appearance the next morning, but in the afternoon, his older brother came, dragging him to school. I opened the door, and drew him in. He wore heavy shoes, and in his rage, he kicked me viciously. This was a trifle more than my temper could bear, and I seized him by the shoulder, and fairly churned the bench with him, which subdued the young gentleman (who had not expected to encounter such muscle in a lady) in short order.

At the close of the school, I gave him his choice between remaining in during the noon hour for one week, or receiving five blows on each palm with the ferrule at once. He chose the whipping, and I administered it.

The Irish girl was living with one of the directors, who afterward told me that she came running home that evening, exclaiming:

"Well! I tell you, it's no use fooling with that teacher. She don't scare worth a cent!"

This girl of twelve proved to be one of my best pupils, both in behavior and aptitude.

Before the close of this school I received a call from Clatsop to teach a four months' school there, at $40 a month, and board myself. It was again spring; that loveliest season of the year, when Nature clothes the brown old earth with richest green, and pours out upon it her boundless treasure of beautiful and fragrant blossoms;— "The time of the singing of birds," when my heart was always lightest.

With my boy, I moved into the old parsonage at Skipanon, which had long been unoccupied, and had been used for storing hay.

It stood in the midst of a green, grassy plot, now made sweet and beautiful by the thousands of wild violets and buttercups sprinkled over it.

This I could have free of cost, and so, with a few boards and nails, and a little help from the kind neighbors, two rooms of the old house were made habitable, for the spring and summer months. I was as "happy as a lark." I was an expert, as experts went, in those days, on the sewing machine, and with the crochet-needle. Crocheted nets were then much in vogue, and my crochet-needle was kept busy in making them. My work was always ready to take up, and thus every else unoccupied moment was filled in, and thus I made all our expenses for living, and more.

I had, in this way, so far, managed to save up all my school money, and at the end of this term of four months, at $10 per month, I would have $400. My ambition now was to have a home of my own, and, with this brilliant prospect in view, I bought a half lot in Astoria, and contracted with a carpenter to build me a small, three-roomed cottage, with a cosy little porch.

To this, my last school, I can look back with pleasure and satisfaction. The neighboring farmers and their families were kindness itself to me. They never forgot the teacher, and her little boy, but continually brought us good things to eat, and invitations to visit them over Sunday.

I was invariably up by five o'clock, looking over all the lessons for the day. Then came breakfast, and at 8:30 we were off for the pleasant mile walk to the school-house. Thus the four months sped pleasantly away, and when my school closed, my little home in Astoria was ready for me. It stood on the hack end of that beautiful and sightly lot on which I. W. Case, the banker, later built his handsome residence. I was as proud as a queen of my pretty little home, which was the first f had ever really owned; and the fact that f had earned it all myself made it doubly prized.

I had won the respect of all, and now work came to me from all directions. As I could "turn my hand" to almost anything, and was anxious to accumulate, I was never idle.

During all these years, Mr. Hill had been writing, and urging me to re-marry him, which I kindly, but steadily refused to do.

One winter night my machine was buzzing busily, while I sang as I sewed. There was a knock, I opened the door, and there stood the father of my child! He had come unannounced, thinking that his sudden appearance might overcome my opposition.

But alas for him! He found not the young, ignorant, inexperienced child-mother whom he had neglected and misused, but a full-grown, self-reliant, self-supporting woman, who could look upon him only with pity.

He soon realized that there was now a gulf between us which he could never hope to cross.

During all the years since we had parted, he had never even offered to contribute one dollar to his child's support, nor had I ever received a dollar from any source which I had not fully earned. He said:

"Can I come and take my boy down in town with me tomorrow? I will not ask you to awaken him tonight." I answered: "You may, if you will promise me that you will not try to run off with him, as you have so often threatened to do." He said:

"I will promise that."

However, not daring to trust his word, I hastened, early next morning, to the sheriff, and told him my trouble, and he smiled reassuringly, as he said: "Now don't you worry, my dear little woman, he will never get out of this town with your child."

In the fall I rented my little home, and went to visit my people in Roseburg. My brother and two of my sisters had married, and they all urged me to spend the winter among them.

During my stage trip to Roseburg, as we were descending a hill, one very cold night, some part of the stage, which was only a common farm wagon (a "dead-ax wagon" they called it then) gave way. The driver got out, and seeing that the break could not be temporarily repaired, fit for immediate use, he said to me:

"We are four miles from the next station, and it is as cold as blazes! Now you and the boy just lie still, and try to keep warm till I can get back with a horse for you to ride. I'll try to get here in two hours, if I possibly can; but it is dark, and the road is rough, so don't be scared if you hear the wolves howl; for they will not touch you. I will leave two of the horses here, in order to get back as soon as possible."

George and I were lying in the bed of the wagon, back of the driver's seat, on an armful of straw, under a blanket and a buffalo-robe. We had been comfortable up to this time, as I had started with a hot brick, but it was growing colder, and now we began to become chilled. I removed George's shoes, and put his cold feet against my body, and held him close to me.

The wolves began to howl; the wind, laden with fine snow, whistled and whirled about us. The wolves kept up their dreary howling; while the horses stamped, and champed their bits, for they, too, were cold, and liked not the proximity of the wolves no better than did we; but I was glad of their companionship, feeling that it was some protection. It was all of two and a half hours before the driver and another man came to our relief, bringing a horse for me. They wrapped George snugly in a blanket, and we started, the driver leading the other horses.

It was full daylight when we reached the station, where we were thawed out, and made comfortable. By noon we were again on our way and arrived at Roseburg in good time, where we received a warm welcome.

Mr. Abraham, my new brother-in-law, was a merchant, and, among them all, I was persuaded to go into the business of dressmaking and millinery. Consequently, when spring opened, I established myself in a house just across the street from Mr. Abraham's store, he buying me a nice little stock of goods. Here for two years I plodded along, working early and late, and getting ahead pecuniarily much faster than I had ever yet done. I had saved my earnings, with which I had bought my home there, and had a good start, and a growing business, with plenty to eat, drink and wear.

My front yard, 12x20, was a gorgeous glory of color, and my beautiful flowers were the admiration of all the passersby, while my back yard supplied an abundance of vegetables.

My boy was in school, and with the respect of the community, added, why was I not happy? I was. Work brought its own pleasure, and sweet rewards. Five a m never found me in bed, though often did I awake at two a m in my chair, with my work still in my hand. But the young are soon rested, and as a change of work gives rest and health, I was blest with both. I had a time and place for everything, and I have found adherence to this rule throughout my life to be one of the greatest aids to success in any pursuit.

It was also then, as it still is, my habit to plan today for tomorrow. And now I am going over my past life, step by step, gleaning here and there what I hope may be of service to those who come after me, knowing full well how undesirable and seemingly impossible such a life will seem to the youth of today, yet believing its lessons ought to be of use to them in this age of teeming wealth, and lavish expenditure, surrounded and protected as they are from all the hardships of frontier life, with the fountains of knowledge flowing free for them to drink, "without money, and without price."

No more is it necessary for the student to pore over the old, time-worn book, by the light of a pitch stick, or a tow-string in a broken mug of refuse kitchen grease;—and yet those times and methods produced from and for this nation a Franklin, a Jefferson, a Greeley, a Clay, a Webster, and a Lincoln, and a host of others of less transcendent fame, but who possessed the sterling qualities of intelligent, incorruptible citizenship, and who rendered an incalculable aggregate of invaluable service to their country, and whom, if the youth of this generation equal they will do well.

The very conquering of the apparently insurmountable obstacles to their progress by these illustrious citizens of our great Republic but added strength and luster to their character and proved their worth, as does the emery the steel.

The results of the methods of the past are before us, and command our highest admiration. Time will tell whether those of the present will prove a blessing or a curse to our beloved land.

As I have already said, I had had two years of uninterrupted success in my millinery and dressmaking business in Roseburg. The town had steadily grown, and now a new milliner made her advent. She moved in next door to me, and came right in, and looked me over, stock and all, also getting all the information I could give her. She told me incidentally that she had been a milliner for years: that she had learned the trade, and understood it thoroughly, and had come there to begin business, and intended to remain.

I was soon made to feel her power. She laughed at and ridiculed my pretensions, saying that mine was only a "picked-up" business, and that I did not know the first principles of the trade.

"*She* knew how to bleach and whiten all kinds of leghorn and white straws; she could renew and make over all shapes and kinds of* hats; she could also make hat-blocks, on which to press and shape hats, and make new frames," all of which was Greek to me, practically speaking. She came late in the fall, and her husband went, with his team, throughout the country, gathering up all the old hats, and advertising his wife's superior work as a milliner.

All this was not only humiliating to me personally, but was a severe blow to my business. I was at my wits' end to know what to do, and how to do it. One beautiful day I sat thinking the matter over while eating my dinner at the table in front of a window which overlooked my new neighbor's kitchen door. I had seen her husband drive past the evening before, and unload several open boxes filled with old hats, and that day they were getting ready for cleaning, bleaching, and pressing.

They set a table out in the sun, and placed upon it two new plaster of paris hat-blocks. Then the work began, not twenty feet from me. My house was above them, so that they could not see me, but I could not only see them, but could hear every word they said.

For more than an hour I sat there, and in that brief time I learned the art of cleaning, stiffening, fitting, bleaching, and pressing hats.

Oh, what a' revelation it was to me! My heart was beating fast, and I felt that I had never learned so much in any one hour of my life before. I saw how easily it was all done, and how much profit there was in it.

The new hats that year were very, very small ("pancakes"), and some of those old-fashioned hats would make three of them. Certainly two new ones could he made from each of most of the old ones. Of course, the remnants would be considered useless by the owners, and were turned to profit by the expert milliner.

I now knew that if I could get the blocks I could do the work, so I stepped down to the new milliner's shop, and asked her how much she would charge to make me two blocks.

She said: "Thirty dollars."

I said: "I will think it over. I did not expect them to be so high."

"You don't expect me to *give* away my business, do you?" she asked. Then, smiling, she added, "Can you press hats?"

I passed out, and as the door closed, I heard them laughing at my expense. This roused me almost to desperation, and I said to myself, "The day will come when I will show you that I cannot only press hats, but do several other things; and first of all, I will find out how to make hatblocks."

I now remembered a book I possessed, entitled, "Inquire Within." From this I learned how to mix plaster of paris for molds, and this gave me a foundation on which to experiment. I had the buckram frame, like those two new blocks of Mrs., and I knew they must have made and shaped their blocks by the use of those frames, so I bought 50 cents' worth of plaster of paris at the drug-store, and set to work. My first attempt was a failure, but it proved to me that I was on the right road. I was in such a state of anxiety and excitement that I slept little that night.

As soon as the stores were open in the morning, I purchased a dollar's worth of plaster of paris. During that anxious, wakeful night, I had gone over the ground thoroughly in my mind, and was confident of success; and succeed I did.

Words failed to express my triumphant joy that in less than twenty-four hours, I had obtained, and now held, the key to that mysterious knowledge whose wonderful results had charmed away my customers.

I began at once to put my freshly acquired knowledge into practice, resolving not to let a soul know how it was obtained.

That same evening a lady called, bringing an old white leghorn hat.

"I want one of those little 'pancake' hats made from this," she said. 'It has to be bleached and pressed, you know. Can you make it over?"

"Certainly, I can," I answered.

"Oh, I am so glad! Mrs.—said I would just have to take it to the new milliner, but I said I wasn't going to throw off on you: I'd come here first, anyway. Now we'll pick out the trimming. Oh, you haven't any of that beautiful lace bugle fringe, have you? I *must* have that for the rim, it is so stylish, now. Mrs.—has it; would you mind getting it there?"

"Oh, no, not at all," I said.

So, when the hat was cleaned, bleached, stiffened and pressed, and trimmed, all but the bugle lace, I wrapped it carefully, and with the package in my hand, I walked into the store of my rival with the pride of a full-grown peacock.

Laying my parcel on the counter, and lifting a freshly pressed straw braid hat of the same style as mine from the block which she kept there as an advertisement, I asked:

"How much of that bugle fringe does it take to go around this hat?"

"Three-quarters of a yard; price, $1.00 a yard," was her reply.

I laid down seventy-five cents, and said I would take three-quarters of a yard. As she was measuring it off, I said:

"Please put a pin in there, till I see if it will be enough," unwrapping my hat, and measuring around it with the lace, as I finished speaking. Finding it sufficient, I clipped it off with my belt scissors and dropped it into my hat before she could object, had she desired.

"Whose hat is that?" she asked.

"It is one I have just made over for one of my customers," I replied.

"Who pressed it?"

"I did."

"Who made the block?"

"I made it myself," I answered, and passed out. I heard no laughing behind me this time. Surely this was gratification enough for one day. She now knew that I was in possession of her secrets, but how I had learned them she never knew.

As has been said, I set about putting my newly acquired knowledge into practical use. Going about among the stores, I bought up all their old, out-of-date, unsalable milliner)', for almost nothing, and began at once to prepare it for future use, knowing that the fall styles in straws would be in demand in the spring, and that, in this way, with a small stock from San Francisco, I could make a good showing; which I did. But, though my goods were in every way equal to those of my rival, the customers passed me by, and bought of her. She managed to checkmate me at every turn.

Thus the summer and autumn wore away, and left me stranded, but not conquered. My time had not all been lost, however, and I knew that I had gained much that would be of service to me in the future.

I had surmounted other formidable difficulties, and I would yet wring a victory out of this defeat. For one thing, I had learned more of average human nature during that year than I had in all my previous life, and I saw that I must convince that community that I was not a pretender, but was, in reality, mistress of my business; and that could not be accomplished alone by the skillful making over of old hats and bonnets.

Therefore, in November, 1867, leaving my boy in charge of a minister and his wife, who occupied my little home; and borrowing $250, I left for San Francisco.

I had previously announced in both the Roseburg papers that I should spend the winter in the best millinery establishment in San Francisco, with the purpose of perfecting myself in the business, and would return in the spring, bringing with me all the latest and most attractive millinery. This I carried out to the letter.

Bearing letters of recommendation from two of the principal merchants of Roseburg who dealt with Madame Fouts, I was kindly received by her, and given every advantage. For three months I sat beside her head-trimmer, where I could see and hear everything. Those three months in San Francisco were worth more to me than ten years of such opportunities as I had hitherto had. Madame took me to the wholesale houses, and showed me how to purchase goods, and especially how to select odd lots of nice, but out of date materials, and how to convert these into new and attractive styles. I saw her daily selling hats which had not cost her over fifty cents, for from four to six dollars. Meantime, I worked only on my own goods, and when spring came, I had a lovely stock secured with very little expense. I wrote home ordering a show-window put into the front of my little store,—almost the first show-window in that town. I also had printed announcements struck off, and sent on ahead to all of my patrons, and to be posted, stating the day I had fixed for my grand opening.

I reached home a week or ten days beforehand, and had everything in complete and elegant readiness at the appointed time.

I now felt equal to the situation, and was mistress of my art, a fact which I used to the best possible advantage. The profits from the sales of that year amounted to $1,500, and the business continued to increase as long as I conducted it.

In 1870, I placed my son in the University of California, at Berkeley. I had always had a fondness for nursing, and had developed such a special capacity in that direction by assisting my neighbors in illness, that I was more and more besieged by the entreaties of my friends and doctors, which were hard to refuse, to come to their aid in sickness, oftentimes to the detriment of business, and now that money came easily, a desire began to grow within me for a medical education. One evening I was sent for by a friend with a very sick child. The old physician in my presence attempted to use an instrument for the relief of the little sufferer, and, in his long, bungling, and unsuccessful attempt he severely lacerated the tender flesh of the poor little girl. At last, he laid down the instrument ,to wipe his glasses. I picked it up, saying, "Let me try, Doctor.' and passed it instantly, with perfect ease, bringing immediate relief to the tortured child. The mother, who was standing by in agony at the sight of her child's mutilation, threw her arms around my neck, and sobbed out her thanks. Not so the doctor! He did not appreciate or approve of my interference, and he showed his displeasure at the time most emphatically. This apparently unimportant incident really decided my future, course.

A few days later, I called on my friend, Dr. Hamilton, and confiding to him my plans and ambitions, I asked for the loan of medical books. He gave me Gray's Anatomy. I came out of his private office into the drug-store, where I saw Hon. S. F. Chadwick, who had heard the conversation, and who came promptly forward and shook my hand warmly, saying: "Go ahead. It is in you; let it come out. You will win."

The Hon. Jesse Applegate, my dear and revered friend, who had fondled me as a babe, was the one other person who ever gave me a single word of encouragement to study medicine.

Realizing that I should meet opposition, especially from my own family, I kept my own counsel.

I now began in good earnest to arrange my business affairs so that I could leave for the East in one year from that time, meantime studying diligently to familiarize myself with the science of anatomy, the groundwork of my chosen profession. Later, I took Mrs. Duniway, of Portland, editor and proprietor of *The New Northwest,* into my confidence, and arranged with her to take my boy into her family, and give him work on her paper.

I also wrote to my old friend, Mrs. W. L. Adams, of Portland, and asked her to take a motherly interest in my boy. She responded promptly, saying:

"My husband, Dr. Adams, is in Philadelphia, partly for study, and partly for his health. Why not go there? He could be of great help to you, and it would be a relief to me to know that you were near in case of sickness. You can trust me to look after the welfare of your boy."

This letter was a genuine comfort to me, and I decided to accept her advice. In due time, I announced that in two weeks I would leave for Philadelphia, to enter a medical school. As I have said, I expected disapproval from my friends and relatives, but I was not prepared for the storm of opposition that followed. My family felt that they were disgraced, and even my own child was influenced and encouraged to think that I was doing him an irreparable injury, by my course. People sneered and laughed derisively. Most of my friends seemed to consider it their Christian duty to advise against, and endeavor to prevent me taking this "fatal" step. That crucial fortnight was a period in my life never to be forgotten. I was literally kept on the rack. But as all things must have an end, the day of my departure was at last at hand. My son had gone to Portland, and my family had given me up in despair. My business, all in good shape, was entrusted to a younger sister, who had been with me for the past year or more.

On that last afternoon, two friends, Mesdames Sheridan and Champaign, called to say good-bye. Mrs. C. Said:

"Well, this beats all! I always did think you were a smart woman, but you must have lost your senses, and gone stark crazy to leave such a business as you have, and run off on such a 'wild goose chase' as this."

I smiled and said: "You will change your mind when I come back a physician, and charge you more than I ever have for your hats and bonnets."

Her answer came, quick and sharp: "Not much! You are a good milliner, but I'll never have a woman doctor about me!"

Choking back the tears with a desperate effort, I calmly answered:

"Time will tell. People have been known to change their minds."

As a matter of fact, both these ladies did, in after years, call upon me for professional services many times, and we laughed together on recalling that conversation in Roseburg.

Eleven o'clock p m arrived at last, and I found myself seated in the California overland stage, beginning my long journey across the continent. It was a dark and stormy night, and I was the only inside passenger. There was no one to divert my thoughts from myself, or prevent the full realization of the dreary and desolate sense that I was starting out into an untried world alone, with only my own unaided resources to carry me through. The full moment of what I had undertaken now rose before me, and all I had left behind tugged at my heart-strings. My crushed and over-wrought soul cried out for sympathy, and forced me to give vent to my pent-up feelings in a flood of tears, while the stage floundered on through mud and slush, and the rain came down in torrents, as if sympathizing Nature were weeping a fitting accompaniment to my lonely, sorrowful mood.

And now I had ample opportunity to reason and reflect. I remembered that every great trouble of my life had proved a blessing in disguise, and had brought me renewed strength and courage.

"For so tenderly our sorrows hold the germs of future joys,

That even a disappointment brings us more than it destroys."

74

I had taken the decisive step, and I would never turn back. Those cheering words of my faithful attorney, Hon. S. F. Chadwick, who had so ably defended my divorce case, came back to me then as a sweet solace to my wounded spirit: "Go ahead. It is in you; let it come out. You will win!"

How many, many times have those inspiring words cheered me on through the dark hours of life.

They have helped me through countless difficulties, and knotty problems, which have since confronted me. Let us never forget or neglect to speak an encouraging word when we can. It costs us so little, and is worth so much to the recipient.

I strongly resolved that if there was anything in me, it should come out, and that, come what might, I would succeed.

We are told that when the decision is made, the battle is half won.

My decision was now irrevocably made, and I was comforted.

Stage travel was no hardship to me, for, like the sailor on his ship, I felt at home in the stage. For several years I had gone to San Francisco spring and fall by land, when the nearest railroad connection was at Marysville, Cal. At that time Colonel Hooker, to whom Hon. Jesse Applegate [Oregon pioneer and active in the early government] refers in his letter, was superintendent of the stage line. During the last three years I had given much thought to woman suffrage and temperance, and had written a number of articles for the Roseburg papers, and for *The New Northwest,* on these subjects, a few of which can be found in this volume by referring to the index. I had given much time and labor to temperance work, and had served in the highest office of the I. O. G. T. [International Organization of Good Templars]

On reaching Philadelphia, I matriculated in the Eclectic School of Medicine, and employed a private tutor. I also attended the lectures and clinics in the great Blockly Hospital twice a week, as did all the medical students of the city. In due time, I received my degree, and returned to Roseburg to wind up my business, which I had left in charge of my sister. A few days after my return, an old man without friends died, and the six physicians who had all attended him at various times, decided to hold an autopsy. At their meeting, Dr. Palmer, who had not forgotten my former "impudence" in using his instrument, made a motion to invite the new "Philadelphia" doctor to be present. This was carried, and a messenger was dispatched to me with a written invitation. I knew this meant no honor for me, but I said: "Give the doctors my compliments, and say that I will be there in a few minutes." The messenger left, and I followed close behind him. I waited outside until he went in and closed the door. I heard him say, in excited tones: "She said to give you her compliments, and that she'd be here in a minute." Then came a roar of laughter, after which I quietly opened the door and walked in, went forward, and shook hands with Dr. Hoover, who advanced to meet me, saying:

"Do you know that the autopsy is on the genital organs?" "No," I answered; "but one part of the human body should be as sacred to the physician as another."

Dr. Palmer here stepped back, saying: "I object to a woman's being present at a male autopsy, and if she is allowed to remain, I shall retire!" "I came here by written invitation," I said; "and I will leave it to a vote whether I go or stay; but first, I would like to ask Dr. Palmer what is the difference between the attendance of a woman at a male autopsy, and the attendance of a man at a female autopsy?"

Dr. Hoover said: "Well, I voted for you to come, and I will stick to it." Another said: "I voted yes, and I'll not go back on it."

Two more said the same, making a majority of the six. Dr. Hamilton then said: "I did not vote, but I have no objection," thus leaving Dr. Palmer only, who said: "Then I will retire," which he did amid the cheers and laughter of forty or fifty men and boys in and outside the old shed, where the corpse lay on a board, supported by two sawbucks, and covered with a worn gray blanket. They were there to see and hear all that was to be seen and done.

One of the doctors opened an old medicine case, and offered it to me.

"You do not want me to do the work, do you?" I asked, in surprise.

"Oh, yes, yes, go ahead," he said. I took the case and complied. The news of what was going on had spread to every house in town, and the excitement was at fever-heat.

When I had at last finished the dissection, the audience (not the doctors) gave me three cheers. As I passed out and down on my way home, the street was lined on both sides with men, women and children, all anxious to get a look at "the woman who dared," to see what sort of a strange, anomalous being she was. The women were shocked and scandalized! The men were disgusted, but amused, thinking it "such a good joke on the doctors."

When I moved to North Yakima, Wash., in 1899, a Mrs. Thomas Redfield called on me, and we were soon fast friends. At our first meeting she said:

"Of course, you don't remember me, but I remember well the first time I ever saw you."

"Where was it?" f asked.

"Well," laughed she, "it was when I was a young girl, and we lived in Roseburg. I was on the street with the rest of the crowd to see you, when you came out of that old shed where the doctors were holding the autopsy on that old man."

"And what did you think of me then?"

"Oh, of course, I thought you were a terrible woman! It was simply dreadful the way those people did go on at that time. Isn't it wonderful what a change has taken place since then?"

"Yes," I answered. "I suppose they felt like applying a coat of tar and feathers to me then; and it is a wonder they did not."

"Yes; I think they did."

And now, as I look back, I believe that all that saved me was the fact that my brothers, Flem and Josiah, lived there, and, although they disapproved of my actions quite as much as the rest of the community did, yet "blood is thicker than water," and they would have died in their tracks before they would have seen me subjected to indignities, or driven out of town. And as everybody knew they would shoot at the drop of a hat, good care was taken to lay no violent hands on me.

I did not stop to think, at the time, neither did I pause to consider what the consequences might be; I was prompted by my natural disposition to resent an insult, which I knew was intended.

As soon as possible after that autopsy, I closed up my business, and, taking my sister, and the remnant of my store goods, I removed to Portland, Oregon.

I frankly admit that I breathed more freely after I had bidden adieu to my family and few remaining friends, and was on board the train. I well knew that it was a relief, even to my own folks, to have me go, for it did seem as if I were only a "thorn in the flesh" to them then.

TO BECOME A DOCTOR?

I first occupied the ground-floor of a two-story brick building on the east side of First street, between Taylor and Yamhill. There were no brick buildings in Portland south of there at that time. I had two rooms fitted up for electrical and medicated baths. This was a new process of treatment, and it, in connection with my other practice, proved both attractive and remunerative. I obtained the knowledge in a New York institution, which had been open but a short time.

There was but one man, a German, in Portland who seemed to have any knowledge of electrical batteries, and he found much trouble in keeping my batteries in running order.

I was now well settled, and, notwithstanding occasional rebuffs here and there, and frequent slights from my brother M. D.'s, I went steadily on, gaining a step here, and a point there, and constantly advancing, with money coming in faster and faster.

My son George was now nineteen, and I entered him in the Medical Department of the Willamette University. It was certainly one of the proudest days of my life when he was graduated from it, two years later. From the beginning, I had set my heart on making a physician of him, and at last my life's ambition was crowned with success.

One morning, on returning from my round of professional visits, I found a woman lying on a couch in my office, with her husband and two neighbors beside her. She was suffering from double pneumonia, and when I first saw her I did not think she could live till night. They had brought her fifteen miles in an open wagon to Vancouver, and from there to Portland by boat. She had been sick for a year or two, and they had brought her for the baths, not knowing that her sudden change for the worse was due to pneumonia. They were very poor. Before she died, she begged me to take one of her three little girls, which I promised to do; and a few days later, her husband brought me the eldest, but smallest, of the three sisters. She was a puny, sickly looking little creature, and as she stood beside her father, who was also undersized, in her old, faded calico dress, up to her knees, her stockings tied up with strings, her shoes out at the toes, and holding a bundle done up in an old red cotton handkerchief, with a scared look on her pinched little face, the pair made a forlorn picture that stamped itself indelibly on my memory.

Taking the child by the hand, I said: "So this is my little girl? Come with me. This is your home, now." To her father: "When do you return home?"

"In a few hours," was his reply; "I want to get home, as the other children are alone on the farm."

"Then come in again before you go; I want to send some little presents to Mattie's brothers and sisters." Then I led Mattie to my back office, and gave her into the hands of the woman who assisted in the baths, telling her to give her a good bath. I found waiting to say good-bye, a Homeopathic doctor, who said, as Mattie passed through the door: "What on earth are you going to do with that child?"

"Oh, she is mine, now. Her mother gave her to me on her death-bed."

"Well, if I took a child, I would find a better looking one than that," she exclaimed.

"Oh, well," I rejoined, "you know 'beauty is only skin deep,' and 'fine feathers make fine birds/ so come and go with me to select some feathers for my bird."

On returning home, I found Mattie clean, and with her hair neatly combed, and she was soon dressed throughout in nice, new clothing, with a blue ribbon tied in her sun-burned hair. Her father soon returned, and I sent back with him all he had brought, excepting Mattie herself, together with a supply of cakes, nuts, and candy for Mattie's brother and sisters at home.

Two years later, this same Doctor called one evening, and said: "What did you ever do with that little girl you took when I was here last.

Mattie was sitting at the desk, busy with her lessons, for she had now been two years in the public schools.

"Come here. Mattie," I said, and she came and stood at my side.

The Doctor looked her over. "You don't tell me that this is the 'ornery' little thing you brought in here two years ago?" Mattie's face crimsoned, and her lip quivered. I put my arm around her waist, and drew her to me.

"Indeed," I said. "This is my own good Mattie Bell. She is sweet sixteen, now, and she is above my ears, and she will soon be above my head."

Time passed on. I was successful and prosperous, but not yet satisfied.

Again I was beginning to pine for more knowledge.

My sister asked for a course in Mills College, which I gave her. My son had his profession. "I have done my duty to those depending on me," I thought, "and now I will treat myself to a full medical course in the old school, and a trip to Europe. I shall then be equipped for business on an advanced scale."

I set about putting these plans into practice by establishing my son in the drug business in Goldendale, Wash. Then, after closing out everything, including some Roseburg property, I found myself in the possession of the sum of $8,000,—sufficient for all my needs.

Again my family and friends objected. They said: "You will soon be rich; why spend all you have for nothing?"

Strange to say, my old and honored friend, Jesse Applegate, now added his protest, also, and came from his home to Portland to plead with me he said: "You have a good foundation; close application will increase your knowledge and power. You can make of yourself what you will. You can do this, and at the same time increase, instead of spending your wealth, and remember, my friend, that wealth is power."

But I was deaf to all entreaties;—a better education I must and would have, and the best way to secure it was to go to the fountain-

81

head. This was my argument and belief. I had not forgotten my first San Francisco millinery trip, when F had to borrow the money for my expenses. The money for my present trip was *not* borrowed, and it had come to me through that decision and venture.

My mind was made up, and, like the gambler who has won once, I would risk all at one throw again; and so, on September 1st, 1878, on a bright, sunny day, I left Portland, again *en route* for Philadelphia; not this time with a storm without and within, but surrounded with sunshine, and followed by the good wishes of many friends.

It was my intention, if possible, to gain admission to the then renowned Jefferson Medical College.

Armed with letters from U. S. Senators, Governors, Professors, and Doctors, on reaching Philadelphia I at once called upon, and was entertained by Dr. Hannah Longshore, one of the first graduates of the Woman's Medical School of Philadelphia, and sister of Professor Longshore, founder of and professor in the Eclectic Medical School of Philadelphia for men and women.

I told her plainly just what I desired.

"I have no faith that you can get into Jefferson College," she said, "but I want to see you try it. I believe the time will come when the doors of every medical school in our land will be forced to open for women, as do the Eclectic and Homeopathic schools now. But the old schools, as you know, do not recognize them. If there is any man today who can open the doors of Jefferson College to women, it is Professor Gross."

"This is Saturday," I said, "and I will go at once to see him."

He received me with a gracious smile, requesting me to be seated, as I handed him the envelope containing my credentials.

While he was looking over the letters with a pleased expression on his fine face, I could scarcely realize that I was in the presence of the then greatest surgeon in the United States.

His slender, delicate hands were not suggestive of bloodletting.

I was lost in contemplation of this grand man, when he broke my reverie by saying, with the gentlest voice and manner:

"And now, my little lady, what can I do for you?"

"I have come to this grand old city in search of knowledge," I answered. "I hunger and thirst after it. I want to drink at the fountain-head. Can you not lead me into Jefferson College,—you, her greatest professor?"

He gazed at me with moist and sympathetic eyes for an instant. Then, in the gentlest, softest tones, he said:

"My dear little woman, how gladly I would open the doors of Jefferson to you; but that privilege is denied to me. The deciding power lies in the hands of the board of regents, and they are a whole age behind the times. They would simply be shocked, scandalized, and enraged at the mere mention of admitting a woman into Jefferson College. Why not go to the Woman's College? It is just as good. The examinations required to be passed are identically the same."

"I know that, Professor Gross," I responded; "but a Woman's College out West stands below par, and I must have a degree that is second to none." "Then the University of Michigan is the school for you," he said. "It is a long-term school, and a mixed school, and it is second to none in America."

"Thanks, Professor, a thousand thanks!" I gratefully exclaimed; "I will follow your advice, and go there at once."

"Why not remain another day, and breakfast with me?" he asked; "I should be pleased to extend the courtesy, and to know you better."

But, on consulting the University Announcements, we found that I had not a day to spare, and I therefore bade my new-found friend farewell, and with his blessing, started at once for Ann Arbor.

Arriving there, I was soon settled, and in my seat for the opening lecture, on the next day but one. During the ensuing nine months, I averaged sixteen hours a day in attending lectures, in hard study, and in all the exercises required in the course, after which I put in ten hours a day (excepting Sundays) in study during the vacation. Most of this time was given to Professor Ford's Question-Book. It was a book of questions without answers, on anatomy. Anatomy has always been the bug-bear of medical students.

I procured a blank book, and commencing at the beginning, I numbered each question, then looked up each answer, and wrote it out in full in my blank book. This book covered the anatomy, from beginning to end, and it was completed, with the exception of a few answers which I could not find.

At the opening of the next term, I took my book to Professor Ford for the correct answers to these, that I might fill in the blanks. Professor Ford took the book, and examined it carefully, and then said:

"You have done that which no other student in this University has ever done before, and more than I have expected one to do; and you have done it while the others have been enjoying a vacation. I shall not forget this. It will be of the highest value to you in the saving of time, and the fixing of these all-important facts in your memory."

It was my custom to rise at four a m., take a cold bath, followed by vigorous exercise; then study till breakfast, at seven. (I allowed myself half an hour for each meal.)

After supper came "Quizzes," and then study till nine p m., when I retired, to sleep soundly.

Between lectures, clinics, laboratory work, Quizzes, examinations, two good sermons on Sunday, and a church social now and then, the time was fully and pleasantly occupied. The constant change brought rest, and acted as a safety valve to our over-heated brains.

At the close of the second year, in June, 1880, I received my degree. During all that time, I had not suffered from a day's sickness, and had been present at every class lecture save one, my absence from it being due to my having been so deeply absorbed in my studies that I failed to hear the bell. This lapse almost broke my heart, which had been set on being able to say, at the end of the course, that I had not missed a single lecture.

Commencement was an important event at this, as in all Universities. It has been my habit, since the beginning of my correspondence, over forty-five years ago, to preserve all letters of interest or importance, and also to keep in a blank book a copy of my answers to many such. Hence I have a great mass of material from which to select in compiling this volume, and from which could be drawn matter to fill many larger books than the present. The following is an extract from a letter thus preserved:

Ann Arbor.

The past week has been one of unusual excitement in this great University of learning, comprising 3,000 students, but now all that has passed, and such a quiet and stillness prevails that it reminds me of the grave.

The commencement exercises were splendid, in the extreme. Would that my pen bad power to adequately paint the scene. The spacious, and perfectly-kept University grounds were resplendent in a full and glorious summer dress of green illuminated gorgeously with the crimson blue and gold of masses of flowers of every hue, whose intoxicating fragrance was gathered, co-mingled, and wafted by the soft breezes to the charmed nostrils of the enchanted, happy and hopeful throngs of manhood and womanhood who were so rarely privileged as to be present. Add to all this, thousands of waving banners and flags, the fluttering of countless colored badges, the sweet and thrilling strains of music furnished by three brass bands, and the gaily attired students, marching and counter-marching, preparatory to forming into line for the final grand march into University Hall, and you have a picture beyond words to fittingly present, and one so deeply and brightly stamped on my memory that it can never be effaced.

Each department entered, and was seated according to the time it became a part of the institution.

The immense hall was packed with humanity, and every available space was filled with flowers.

First, the band discoursed rare music.

President Angell then delivered his farewell address; after which came the presentation of the diplomas.

In the evening followed the faculties' grand reception, the most brilliant feature of all. The superb old hall was hung with rare and costly paintings, entwined with the Stars and Stripes. The sweetest strains of music blended with the fragrance of hot-house blossoms, charmed every finer sense, and gave a seeming foretaste of Heaven.

Wealth and beauty, in all their splendor, were there. Gorgeous trains and soft laces swept the polished floor. Tinted cheeks, and lips, sparkling eyes, and rounded arms and shoulders of rosy ivory, glowed with animation, while, with shaking of hands, joyous greetings, and enthusiastic congratulations, all "went merry as a marriage bell." Alumni meetings followed, and the festivities were closed by the President's reception to the graduates.

After graduating, having arranged for three years' absence from home, I went with one of my classmates to Chicago. Taking rooms, we devoted ourselves to hospital and clinical work.

While there, my son, Dr. Hill, joined me, and the first of October found us back at the University, where Dr. Hill entered for a post course, while I remained as a resident physician, which entitled me to all lectures. I attended all the advanced lectures in my department, theory and practice in the Homeopathic School, and English literature and history in the Literary Department.

At the end of six months, with my son and two lady physicians, I sailed for Europe. We visited Glasgow, Hamburg, Berlin, Potsdam, Munich, Dresden, Paris, London, and other cities.

While in Munich, we were one day being conducted through the great buildings where masterpieces of castings and mouldings were on exhibition, when the guide opened a door and ushered us into a large, circular room known as "The American Department."

The central figure was a heroic statue of Washington, on his great white charger, carrying the flag of his country. Around him were grouped the signers of the Declaration of Independence, and there, also, was the statuary representing our martyred Lincoln, striking off the fetters from the limbs of the black man. That sight, so beautiful, so real, so moving, was enough to stir the blood of the coldest American! For weeks,—it seemed months,—we had not seen "Old Glory," and now here it burst on our view, floating over the images of all we held nearest and dearest on earth! It was too much for my impulsive nature. Forgetting time and place, and oblivious to all around me, I rushed forward, fell on my knees at the feet of the Father of his Country, find gave vent to my pent-up feelings of joy, in exclamations of "Oh, my country, my country! My flag, my flag!" I was brought suddenly to my senses by the warning voice of Dr. Hill:

"Mother, mother! These people cannot understand a word of English! They will think you are crazy, and there is no telling what trouble you will get us into!"

I sprang to my feet, and looked behind me, expecting to see the *gens d'armes* coming to take charge of me, but, instead, I saw a picture that I never can forget. The door was filled with broadly smiling faces, showing more plainly than words could do that they thoroughly understood the situation, and heartily sympathized with the loyal *"Americaine"*

As our party passed out, they further showed their appreciation and approval by profuse smiles and bows; thus showing that the love of one's native land is "the touch of Nature that makes the whole world kin."

Arrived outside, Dr. Hill said: "Well, I never did see anything like it! Mother is always getting into scrapes; but somehow she always comes out on top."

Dr. Hill now became homesick, and declared he would rather see his Western sweetheart than all the cities in the world, so I gave him his return ticket, and $500 in money, and he lost no time in going back to Goldendale and getting married.

The two Doctors and I continued our journey through Austria, Prussia, France, Scotland, and England. In all the large cities, we visited the hospitals, and saw many of the world's greatest surgeons operate. My letters with state seals always secured us open doors, and invitations to enter. On reaching London, I found a letter from

87

my dear friend, now Mrs. Lillie Glenn O'Neil, urging me to come to her in July. This request from my dear Lillie (who always called me mother), the only and petted child of my old and honored friend, Dr. J. G. Glenn, now deceased, I could not refuse, and so bidding my two classmates adieu, I started for Portland, Oregon.

When I landed at New York, the Customs Collector demanded $70 duty on my instruments, which I had purchased in Paris. I said: "These instruments are for my own use. I am a physician. Here is a letter from the President of the University of Michigan, and letters from U. S. Senators, Governors, etc. I know you have no right to collect duty on my instruments, and if you take my goods, I will employ an attorney."

"You stay right here," he said, "till I come back, and you'll find you will have to pay the duty." After two hours, he returned, and said: "Take your things, and go on."

I speedily obeyed, glad to get out of his clutches. In a few hours my ticket to San Francisco was secured and I was *en route* thither.

In those days the steamer's passenger list was telegraphed ahead from San Francisco. On reaching the Portland wharf, I found a messenger with a carriage waiting to take me to the bedside of a patient. This was surely an auspicious beginning, and I felt more than elated, for I was delighted to get home, and anxious to be at work. My purse was greatly depleted, only $200 remaining of the $8,000 with which I had left home, three years before.

Within twenty-four hours I had secured nice rooms over the drug-store of my old and good friend, Dr. O. P. S. Plummer, and I lost no time in getting them fitted up, and ready for patients, who came, and continued to come, in increasing numbers.

A week or two after I was settled, Col. McC—. Called, and said:

"I am glad to welcome you back, and I thought I would take a few of your electrical medical baths. I have not really had an attack of rheumatism since that terrible time I had before, but I thought I had better take a few as a preventive."

I laughed, saying: "I have no baths, and never expect to have again."

"Really; you have not lost faith in them, have you?"

"Oh, no, I fully realize their worth; but you see, Colonel, I am now a full-fledged University physician of the old school, and I cannot afford to attach to myself the odium of the epithet, 'Bath Doctor.' One dollar and a half was considered a large price for those baths, by some of my customers, but no one expects to get a prescription for less than $2.00. Oh, no, I expect to carry my stock in trade in my head from this time on."

My friends, and my enemies, as well,—if they of the old slights and disapproval could be so called,—came to pay their respects, and many to receive my professional services; and from no place did I receive so much consideration and patronage as from Roseburg, my former home.

I often jokingly remarked: "I wonder, as I look back now, that I was not tarred and feathered after that autopsy affair: I can assure you it was no laughing matter then to break through the customs, prejudices and established rules of a new country, which is always a risky undertaking, especially if it is done by a woman, whose position is so sharply defined. Only a few years before that date, the students of Jefferson Medical College publicly "rotten-egged" the woman students, as they were leaving Blockly Hospital.

Soon after I was established, a doctor called whom I had known for many years, saying:

"I cannot succeed in Portland, and am going to make a change, and sell my belongings at auction. Come and look over what I have, and take what you want. I have many things you need that I do not wish to take,—and come to the sale."

"Why, Doctor," I said, "I have just come home, and have spent all my money." "No matter. You can have anything or all I have for sale, without a dollar. You will have money soon enough." "But I do not know that."

"I do. I only wish I was sure of making half as much. Before six months you will be taking in $600 a month."

I was astounded, for I knew he was in earnest; and yet his prophecy did come true. I had for so many years been clinging to the slippery ladder, struggling and fighting for my very existence, making headway surely, but so slowly, that I could not realize how much was now within my reach. But I knew it soon. Hundreds of incidents might be recorded to indicate my success during the next three years, and the unbounded satisfaction and happiness it brought me. One morning a woman, pale and trembling, came into my office, and said:

"I have been sick for many years, and the doctors say I cannot be cured. I have heard so much about you, that I have come to see if you cannot give me relief. We have paid out nearly all we have to doctors, and I know that if you cannot help me, you will say so."

Whom should this invalid be but my old Roseburg rival in the millinery business? I gave her a warm and cordial reception, saying: "I earnestly hope I may be able to help you."

After making a thorough examination of her case, which was one of ulceration of the bladder, I said: "I can help you. I will treat you for a few weeks, and will then teach you how to treat yourself, and if you will follow my advice and directions, I have faith that your health will be restored." With tears of hope and gratitude, she said: "No one can or will be more faithful and obedient than I will be. When shall I come again?"

"You are not able to come to the office now."

"But it is so far out to my son's where I am staying, and we are so poor." "That makes no difference; and don't you worry about my bill. I will take you home in my carriage, and will go to your son's every day and treat you until you are able to return home."

"Oh, you are heaping coals of fire on my head by all this kindness!" she exclaimed. "But I do want to tell you now that I always did have the greatest respect for you."

"Now, I do not look at it in that way," said I. "If you had not gone out to Roseburg, and goaded me on, by showing me how little I really knew about millinery, I might have been out there yet, making poor hats and bonnets. But you proved the truth of what a friend once said to me: 'If I wished to increase your height two and a half inches, I would attempt to press you down, and you would grow upward from sheer resentment.' So now, you see, my dear friend, that you have all along been my good angel in disguise. I owe you a great debt of gratitude, and I intend to repay it, with interest."

And I did, for her health was restored, and, from that hour, arose a friendship between us which lasted till her death. Only three years ago we exchanged photographs.

During 1878, before leaving for the East, I provided a home in Forest Grove for Mattie, where she could continue her studies. On my return she hastened to Portland to see her foster mother. She was now twenty, and full-grown.

"Well. Mattie," I said, "I thought you might be married by this time. Haven't you found a sweetheart?" I playfully asked her.

"No, I haven't; and I don't want one. I want to come and live with you."

"And what do you want to do? Would you like to be a doctor?"

"I will do anything you want me to do, and think I can do."

"Then go back and get your things. I will be settled and ready for you in a few days; and then I will make a doctor of you."

She was soon with me, my dear, good Mattie Belle. Had I had a hundred children, I am sure none could have been more faithful, or loved me better. She was always a sunbeam, not only in my heart, but in my home, as well. She graduated in medicine, but never left me till death claimed her, in 1893.

Thus passed three of the happiest and most prosperous years of my life. Health, hosts of friends, and unbroken prosperity; what more could I ask, or desire?

When asked, as I often was, why I did not marry, I always responded: "I am married. I am married to my profession,"—and I was honest in that belief.

But the time came which is said to come to all, when I was ready and willing to add another name to mine, and it came about in this way: Oregon was about to vote on the Woman Suffrage Amendment. On an April morning, I saw C. W. Fulton's name in the list of arrivals from Astoria, and, knowing that he was a friend of the cause, I drove directly to his hotel. Stepping to the counter, I inquired of the clerk:

"Has Mr. C. W. Fulton breakfasted yet?"

I heard chairs moving behind me, and Mr. Fulton's voice saying:

"Yes, Doctor, I am here. And don't you know these three gentlemen?" He, with Col. John Adair, and his two brothers, were all having breakfast at the same table, and they urged me to join them. We made a jolly party, all talking Woman Suffrage, as we partook of the morning meal.

I had not seen any of the Adairs for years. General Adair and my father had been warm friends, as Kentuckians can be; and when I was thirteen, John was a large, handsome boy of his age, with the most beautiful curly auburn hair imaginable. I admired, and was quite fascinated with him, then. He came to my home occasionally with his father. I had attended school with his brothers, S. D. and William Adair, in the sixties.

For General Adair, their father, I always had the most profound admiration, and when, years later, I looked upon his noble face for the last time, as it lay in the casket, I thought I had never seen so beautiful a countenance. To me it was a true index of his honorable and upright life, and it was then, and must ever be, a comfort to me to know that he was always my friend.

> "Friend after friend departs;
> Who has not lost a friend?
> There is no union here of hearts
> That finds not here an end."

Colonel Adair and I were married July 24, 1884, in the First Congregational Church of Portland, Oregon."

The church was filled by the invited guests, a number of whom were from Roseburg, 200 miles distant.

When we left the church, the street was lined on both sides with friends and uninvited people, and when the carriage rolled away, many called out: 'Goodbye, Doctor, goodbye!"

We drove to the home of my sister, Mrs. Hyman Abraham, who had prepared a reception for us, after which we boarded the boat for Astoria, and from there to San Francisco.

After a month's absence, we returned to Portland, and I took up my work where I had left it.

More than twenty-one years have passed since I plighted my marriage vows. Many sorrows have been interspersed with the pleasures of my married life, and during all these years, I have been as active and determined as in former days. I have never flinched from any undertaking, and I hope I never shall, to the day of my death; but during these later years, I have often looked back over my past life, not with a shudder, but to gain strength and courage to meet the financial difficulties that had accumulated, and threatened to engulf me.

My yearly income at the time of my marriage was fully $7,000.

Colonel Adair is an optimist of a happy and cheerful disposition, and, as I have frequently said, he is usually among the clouds, and rarely gets down to *terra firma*.

There were no dark shadows in his pictures, and my love for him knew no bounds. Soon after our marriage he induced me to invest in a large property, neat Astoria, in which he saw millions in the near future.

A large portion of this was unreclaimed tide land. Reclamation at that time was very expensive, and little understood. I was earnestly advised not to invest in the proposition.

At the age of forty-seven I gave birth to a little daughter; and now my joy knew no limit,—my cup of bliss was full to overflowing. A son I had, and a daughter was what I most desired. For her my plans were all made. She should be my constant companion. With her nurse, I would take her on all my rounds. She should imbibe the love of the profession not only from her mother's milk, but by constant association, as well. She should have all I possessed, and all that could be added.

But ah, how little we mortals know what is in store for us! And how well it is that we do not know. God's ways are not our ways, and they are past our understanding. For three days only, was she left with us, and then my treasure was taken from me, to join the immortal hosts beyond all earthly pain and sorrow.

> "There is no flock, however watched and tended,
> But one dead lamb is there.
> There is no fireside, howsoe'er defended,
> But has one vacant chair.
> She is not dead, the child of our affection,—
> But gone unto that school
> Where she no longer needs our poor protection.
> And Christ, Himself, doth rule."

My grief was so excessive I felt it was more than I could bear, unsupported by the companionship of my husband, who, with the aid of twenty-five Chinamen, were trying to reclaim the tide-land, a task which did seem, as his brother once said, "Like fighting the Pacific Ocean."

So I said to him: "I will go to Astoria, where I can be near you. I can have a practice anywhere, and I cannot endure our separation, now that our baby is gone." I rented a pretty home there, for two years, and money came as usual, until the two years were nearly past, when I was stricken with typhus fever, due to defective

94

drainage. Believing that my time had come, I said: "Bring me an attorney, that I may make my will while my mind is yet clear."

My will was made, but my time had not yet come, and I recovered slowly. My husband now urged me to go to the farm, saying:

"Your health absolutely demands the change. In that pure, fresh air you can soon regain your health and strength. In less than two years railroad trains will be running across our land, and our fortunes will be assured, and you will never need to work again."

In my weakened condition, I consented, and July 1st, 1888, found us on the farm, where we remained eleven years.

Now, as I look back, I realize that that move was one of the greatest mistakes of my life. I soon, however, recovered my health, and accustomed vigor and energy, and was ready for business. During all those eleven years, I carried on my professional work as best I could, in that out-of-the-way place; and at no time did I ever refuse a call, day or night, rain or shine. I was often compelled to go on foot, through trails so overhung with dense undergrowth, and obstructed with logs and roots, that a horse and rider could not get past; and through muddy and flooded tide-lands in gum boots.

A few cases will better illustrate the nature of much of my practice, and the hardships which were entailed upon the physician in that locality. One day a Mr. William Larsen came, saying: "My wife is sick. Come at once." There was a most terrific southwest storm raging, and we had a mile to go on foot over the tide-land before reaching the Lewis and Clark River. The land was flooded, the mud and slush deep, and the swollen sloughs had to he crossed on logs and planks. Nearly the whole distance was overgrown with enormous bunches of wire-grass, many being three feet across. This long, intertwined grass was a great obstruction to walking, and I fell prone, again and again, before reaching the river. My boots were filled with water, and I was drenched to the skin. The wind was howling, and dead ahead. Mr. Larsen was a powerful man, and a master-hand with the oars. He sprang into the boat, throwing off his hat and two coats, and began to remove his outer shirt, saying: "You must excuse me, Doctor, but if I ever get you there, I shall have to strip near to the skin."

I thoroughly understood the situation, and well knew that the odds were against us; and I fully expected that, notwithstanding his uncommon strength and skill, we would be compelled to land far below our starting point on the opposite side, and be forced to make our way over tide-lands many times worse than that we had already crossed. However, before we had gone many rods from shore, the shrill whistle of his little steam milk-launch was borne to us in that on-rushing storm, and she now came shooting out of the big slough leading to his house, with the terrible storm at her stern forcing her onward.

In his anxiety and distress, Mr. Larsen's first thought was that his wife was dead, and in the anguish of his heart, with tears streaming over his face, he cried out:

"My God! My God! My wife is dead!"

"No, no! Your wife is not dead," I said. "Captain Johnson has returned from Astoria, and knowing you could not get me there, has come for us." Which proved to be the fact. As soon as the launch was in hailing distance, he called out:

"How is my wife?"

"A-l-l-r-i-g-h-t," instantly came the cheering reply. The sudden reaction of relief came near being too much for that strong man, who had a heart to match his powerful frame.

I had most of the practice in that section, and made many trips to that neighborhood.

One warm day, Mr. Irving Jeffers came rushing up to the house, hat in hand, his forehead and face bathed in perspiration. He said: "My wife is sick; can you come at once?"

He had been running nearly all the way over that same road. The ground was now dry, but the tangled wire-grass was about as difficult to get through as it was in winter. His anxiety was so great, I found it hard to keep up with him, and I fell several times before

96

reaching the river. When nearly there, he ran ahead, and had the boat ready for me to jump in without a moment's delay. It did not take him long to cross that beautiful river, which was then as smooth as glass; then up the Jeffers slough, and to the landing, at the boat-house. The lovely boat-trip had rested me, and I was ready for the short run to the house. As soon as we came in sight of it, however, we saw his mother, Mrs. Elijah Jeffers, on the front porch, who waved her hand and called to us not to run. He forged ahead, however, and was soon at the bedside of his beautiful wife.

His mother came to meet me, saying: "I expect Irving has run you nearly to death. I told him not to hurry you, but he is half beside himself."

The worst storm, without exception, that I ever experienced on Clatsop occurred one dark winter night. It had been raining and blowing fiercely all day, but that night was truly fearful! The wind howled, and shrieked in fury; the house trembled, shook and swayed; the rain fell in a deluge. We could not sleep. "This is such a night as I might expect a call from Seaside" (fifteen miles distant), I said; "and I feel as if I should be called any minute."

"Well, you'll not go. I'm sure of that," said my husband.

I made no reply.

Sure enough, at four a m a lantern-light flashed across my window. (It was my custom to raise my window-shade on retiring.) I was out of bed in an instant, hurrying on my clothes. The door-bell rang, and the man said: "The

Doctor is wanted at Seaside. I left there at ten last night. The storm has been at my back all the way, but I could not get here any sooner. There are trees down all through the woods. I had to leave my horse half a mile back, and come on on foot. We shall have to cut our way out."

Colonel Adair said: "It is simply impossible for my wife to attempt this trip. It is really dangerous for anyone to be out in the woods in such a storm, with the trees falling all around."

"I promised to go, and I must go," I said. "There is no other doctor nearer than Astoria, and after this storm they might not be able to get one from there sooner than twenty-four to forty-eight hours; so saddle the horse: I will be down to the barn by the time you are ready."

I succeeded in reaching the barn without being blown off my feet, by taking the driveway under the hill. After I was in the saddle, a blanket with a hole in its center was drawn over my head, and its corners, sides and ends made fast to the saddle and cinch. Thus, in true Indian fashion, my wraps were held in place, and I could not be blown off. The messenger and my husband armed themselves with axes and lanterns, and we started for the woods. We found five trees in the road, and after two hours' hard work, we got around and past them. After we got out of the woods, the horses found great difficulty in facing the storm, and my good, sensible old horse wanted to go home. I was so bundled and tied up, I had little control of him, and the messenger had to come back and lead him for some miles. After daylight the storm began to abate, and by ten a m it was over, and the sun was shining. We found man) more trees across the road, but we finally reached our destination, at eleven a. m., and found the folks anxiously hoping for our arrival, and fearing they would have to dispatch a messenger to Astoria, which would have been a serious undertaking, as the railroad track was, in places, completely blocked with fallen timber.

I quickly relieved their anxiety, and was ready to return as soon as my horse was fed, and I had had my dinner, not having had any breakfast.

In addition to my professional duties, I worked early and late, in the house, and on the farm. There was little on the farm that I could not do.

In the winter of 1892-3, during which time my husband made two trips to New York in the interest of the Astoria Railroad, I had full charge of the farm; and often spent from three to seven hours in the day in the saddle looking after the stock. But in time that terrible mental and physical strain began to tell upon me. Rheumatism, which is hereditary in my family, had taken hold of me, and was fast undermining my health.

In the winter of 1898 my husband became alarmed, and begged me to go to North Yakima, Wash., and spend the holidays with my son and his family, in the hope of benefitting my health. I went; and that high altitude, and dry climate acted like magic. In but a few days, I was relieved of rheumatism, and felt twenty years younger.

I now confided my troubles to my son, who said:

"You will die, or be a cripple for life, if you do not get out of that wet climate. Let the old farm go, and come up here. I am sure you can make $150 a month, and that is better than going behind that much. You ought never to have gone there." All of which I well knew was the truth.

I said: "I will come," and he smiled, for he knew that meant decision.

"Well, mother, I will look out for a house and office for you. Spring opens here by the first of April, and you ought to be here by that time."

"I will be here," I replied. "But I want you to secure me living-rooms in connection with my office. Help cannot be depended upon, and the expense of a separate house would be much greater, and more than I can afford. I shall do my own work, which will be play beside that which I shall be leaving."

My mind being made up, and my plans formed, I felt more buoyant, happy and hopeful than I had for years, for I felt confident that I could now save at least a portion of our properties. I wrote to Colonel Adair saying: "I shall be home soon, and I want you to be prepared for a revelation."

Upon reaching home, I told him: "I have decided to move to North Yakima. We will rent the farm, sell off all the stock, and pay off as much of the debt as possible. We have three months in which to accomplish this." He regarded me with perfect amazement!

"Well, my dear, I earnestly advise you to think seriously of this before taking such a step. It is a terrible thing to give up our home at our age."

"I cannot feel that in reality we own anything that is covered with mortgages," I answered. "A $24,000 debt at eight and ten per cent interest will, at no distant time, leave us without a house or home. I shall soon become a cripple if I continue to live in this wet climate. Death, to me would be preferable. I shall make money, and you ought, with your education, to be able to get into some kind of paying business."

My wishes were carried out to the letter, and April 6 found us in North Yakima, Wash., where, in one week, we were comfortably settled in four lovely rooms.

Three days later I performed a surgical operation for which I received $100. I found many persons who had seen and heard of me as a physician, and so business came, as in former days.

On the last day of June we started overland to Seaside, Clatsop, Ore., to spend the two hot months near our Sunnymead home. I at once opened my office at this popular summer resort, which brought me in several hundred dollars.

Upon returning to North Yakima, the first of September, I found another $100 surgical case awaiting me; and thus my business increased.

The following summer, instead of going to Seaside, I went to Chicago, and entered the Chicago Clinical School, for physicians only, and received a post-graduate degree. I found it exceedingly hard attending lectures and clinics from nine till six, and from eight to nine p m., in that intense Chicago heat, where people were dying frequently from sunstroke. I left home July 1st, and returned September 11th, feeling well repaid, and equipped for going on with my professional work. I had reviewed my past work, and been brought up to date, just what I needed, after those eleven years on the farm.

After another prosperous year, the summer found us again at the seaside, with my sign out. That vacation proved the most profitable of any preceding it, from a money point of view. I was, of course, compelled to remain at my office, except when on professional duty.

As my business increased, I found that my professional, social and household duties were pressing me very hard. I said: "Colonel, I cannot attend to my professional work which *must* not be neglected, and keep house any longer. You are in no business here, and I think you had better take John and go back to Sunnymead. John's health is poor here, but he will get strong on the farm, for which he's always grieving. If you cannot get into business clown there, you can certainly see that the place is kept up. I will stay here until the properties are made self-supporting, and we have a sufficient income to enable us to live comfortably on the farm, and then I shall be glad to retire, and return home."

In June, 1902, he and John went to Sunnymead, and established themselves in our home there. Our renters were living in a cottage at the foot of the hill. I have spent my vacations with them since that time. My mother and niece were with them nearly a year.

Thus, for three and one-half years, I continued on, each year bringing increased rewards, but I was growing tired of that constant, grinding treadmill, not that I was not physically and mentally competent, however. I had more time for reading and writing than I had ever had before, and I improved it. I still took my cold bath every morning, following it with vigorous physical exercise, which kept me in perfect health, and I had a large country practice, which I greatly enjoyed. I had a good horse and buggy, and always did my own driving. It was nothing for me to drive twenty to thirty miles at a time, day or night. I was not at all timid, and I never took my age into account, but my son and good daughter-in-law did. She would say: "Mamma, you are getting too old for that sort of work, and I do not like to see you do it."

"But I am not old, Hattie, mentally or physically. I am strong and healthy; my stcp is quick and active; and you know I can endure more now than most women of forty-five, and if everybody here did not know I am Dr. Hill's mother, I would not be thought any older."

"But then we know you are."

"Oh, yes, and according to Dr. Osier I ought to have been chloroformed five years ago." "But, mamma, you have been struggling and toiling all your life, making thousands and thousands of dollars, and denying yourself all the comforts and pleasures of life, when you ought to have been living off the proceeds of the money you have earned, instead of slaving to pay off miserable debts."

"Yes, that is all true, but what is done cannot be undone. Two years ago I set my stake, as I did in early life, saying: 'When I reach those figures, I will stop. With continued health and strength, I shall be ready to retire in 1906,—perhaps sooner. Then the properties will be self-supporting, and my investments here will return me sufficient income to assure a comfortable support on the farm.' "

That time came, sooner by several months than I had expected, and so, on October 10th, 1905, I closed my office door in North Yakima, where the community had so generously shown their confidence and friendship by giving me their patronage, and paying for my services a sum which amounted, approximately, to $25,000.

After having received the kindest appreciation from friends, the public and the press, I bade the fair city adieu, and with my good horse, Pride, started in my carriage for The Dalles, much desiring to make the trip overland once more. I took dinner with my esteemed friends, the Hardisons, of Parker, reaching the Simcoe Mountains that evening, where I was kindly entertained by the Jensens; reached Goldendale the next evening, and enjoyed a visit till the afternoon of the following day with my friends, Mr. and Mrs. John Hess. Reaching The Dalles, I took passage for myself and horse on the steamer, enjoying once again that wonderful trip down the Columbia, amid scenery acknowledged to be among the grandest in the whole world. Reached Portland, the metropolis of Oregon, at four p m. Enjoyed dinner and a short visit with my sisters and nieces, and then boarded the Potter, which landed me in Astoria at seven a.m. Driving to Senator C. W. Fulton's, I breakfasted with them, after which I drove on over to Sunnymead, and reached there well and happy, having made the journey in four days, collected $10 of bad debts, and made $20 more on the way, and having enjoyed the trip exceedingly, notwithstanding the earnest counsel of many that it was too late in the season to cross the mountains,—[was sure to have breakdowns, etc. I knew my good horse, Pride, and I had confidence in myself. It was simply undertaking what I had been doing for years, and was to me a stimulant and rest, away from responsibility, sickness and pain. After two months on the farm with Colonel Adair and John, I embarked on the steamer Roanoke, *en route* for National City, San Diego County, California, where I now am with my old and much loved friend, Mrs. Inez E. Parker, in January, in her cosy little "Wren's Nest." In this the most beautiful of climates, amid the singing of birds, and the fragrance of flowers, I at last find myself free to take up that work which, for so many years, I had planned to do after my retirement,—write a book on medicine from a woman's standpoint. During the last few years, however, by the advice of friends, and after due reflection and consideration. I have decided that my first effort at book-making should be one of reference to, and records of early events, together with short sketches of the lives of various pioneers of Oregon, especially those of Clatsop County, which was my first, and is to be my last home, and, in addition, a short, plain, truthful story of my own life. In rehearsing it, I have purposely stripped it of the sentiment, love and romance with which my nature has always been super-charged, and which has cheered me on and given me health and happiness throughout a long career. Such are and should be bright and sacred spots in any woman's life, the memories of which can never be obliterated. I have preserved hundreds of pages filled with sentiment, and overflowing with love and adoration, to which I can turn and drink again at the fountain of youth, and mature life. A deathless love for spring-time, the youth of animal and plant-life, is perennial in my heart, and in that sweet season, Sunnymead shall put on her gorgeous robes of beautiful blossoms and shrubs and flowers. The old house shall be renewed and re-dressed, inside and out, and made ready for our friends. My husband loves to entertain; the latch-string of our Sunnymead home shall always be found outside, and plentiful pot-luck within.

In 1888, Dr. Hills' wife died, and I received my then only grand-child, Victor Adair Hill, into my heart and home. Years after, when Dr. Hill married again, I prevailed upon him to allow Colonel Adair and myself to adopt Victor, making him our heir-at-law.

In 1891 I officiated at the birth of a boy whose mother gave me her child. I took the little orphan to my bosom, and gave it a share of my mother-love, and, with my husband's consent, I called him John Adair, Jr. Colonel Adair and I have perpetuated our family name through a plot known as Sunnymead Addition to Astoria. Through the farm and plot run three beautiful streams, one of which we have named Adair Creek, another Mattie Belle, and the third, Vera Creek.

The longest street is Hill Street; another is called Victor Street.

I hope to live to see my grand-son, Victor Adair Hill, my boy, John, and my grand-daughter, Vera Owens Hill, all grown, and settled in life, before I take my departure.

Having been requested by a number of the passengers of the Roanoke to give the Oregonian an account of her late perilous trip to San Francisco from Portland, I respectfully submit the following:

At three p m., November 27th, 1905, Captain Dunham, master of the steamship Roanoke, attempted to cross the Humboldt Bar at Eureka. There was a heavy sea, and the bar was very rough. When nearly across, a tremendous breaker caught the ship, driving her out of the channel, and carrying away her rudder. The Captain endeavored to swing her back into the channel, but, finding she would not obey her rudder, promptly backed her. At this moment the next huge on-coming breaker, gathering force as it came, struck her with a stupendous force that, combined with the skillful maneuvers of the Captain, swung her completely around, with her prow toward the sea. Had this mighty wave moved against, instead of with his efforts, we should have inevitably been lost, as the ship was heavily laden, and would have been speedily ground to fragments on that seething sinuous bar. Then, with added steam, she was forced across the spit, on which she struck three times as she passed, with such violence as to cause her to shiver from stem to stern, with a noise like the roar of a cannon, into deep water.

Now she rent the air with piercing signals of distress, and calls for help. Meantime she was vigorously struggling, so far as was possible, in her disabled condition, to escape the bar, and reach the open sea. Finally, she succeeded in reaching comparative safety, and soon afterward a tug from Eureka came out, losing one of her life-boats on the bar in crossing, to our assistance. She stood by all that night, in case her help should be needed. The barometer then indicated fair weather.

The whole of that night was occupied by Captain Dunham and his crew in rigging a jury rudder, which was put in place about eight a m. Between six and seven, Captain Dunham had dismissed the tug, directing its master to telegraph to the company at San Francisco that he would proceed under jury rudder, and requesting them to dispatch a tug to meet him, which would find the Roanoke about twenty-five miles from shore.

Almost immediately the new rudder broke, and was rendered useless, after which each day was employed in constructing and shipping new rudders, all of which soon met the same fate as did the others. About ten a m a southeast (off-shore) breeze providentially sprung up, which materially aided us in getting out to set; for, as the ship revolved in her rudderless condition, each time her bow was pointed seaward, the full force of the engines was exerted to force her forward, thus, in seaman's phrase, "kicking" her ahead; the favoring wind helped hold her to her course till the maneuver was accomplished. This continued till between eight and nine that evening, when a terrific northeast gale set in, lashing the sea into a raging fury, and lasting till three the next morning.

And now, for the first time in my life, I realized the full and awful import of that much-used expression, "Like a ship at sea without a rudder."

Lying prone on my back; clinging desperately to the bars of the berth above me to prevent being thrown violently from my own, and, perhaps, crushed to death, my ears filled with the pandemonium overhead, and all around,—furniture banging from side to side, crockery smashing, everything movable in constant and violent collision, the wind shrieking, and tons of water crashing down upon us, even, filling the smoke-stack,—every awful plunge of the vessel threatening to engulf her,—so the long hours dragged on. In the midst of all this, a life-boat was wrenched from its davits, and smashed into kindling-wood; and two immense iron life-rafts were torn loose, and raked the deck back and forth with every movement of that laboring ship, adding their distracting uproar to the dreadful din. As if this were not enough, the jib-sail, by the assistance of which the Captain was vainly endeavoring to guide his distressed vessel, was torn loose, and came thundering to the deck, the boom barely escaping his own and his first officer's heads, and forcing its way through a deck window. In the expressive language of Rev. De Witt Talmage, "God, in His infinite mercy, snatched us from the jaws of death, and delivered us out of the regions of hell."

About three a. m., Wednesday, the 29th, to the joy of all on board, the fearful storm ceased, but the waves, lashed by its jury, still ran mountain-high, but gradually calmed down. On Thanksgiving morning the sun shone, out like the approving smile of God upon us: and warmed us back to renewed life and hope. On Wednesday morning the Captain had said to me at the breakfast table: "We shall be in San Francisco on Thanksgiving"; for he had great faith in the rudder then under construction; but unfortunately, it, also, was carried away almost as soon as it was in position. Nothing daunted, another was promptly begun, and in the form of what is called a "log." made of two spars lashed together. This not proving a success, i: was hoisted on board, and a boom lashed between the spars, and a 500-pound anchor attached. This, as last, proved the successful rudder which enabled us to make four or five miles an hour.

Our Thanksgiving was spent on board, where an excellent dinner was enjoyed by every passenger. While at times obliged to hold to the table to preserve equilibrium, all were only too glad to exchange deadly danger for such slight discomfort.

Late in the evening the doctored rudder was lowered, and the staunch ship began to assert her normal power. Friday morning was bright and beautiful, and we kept on our course rejoicing. At three-thirty Saturday morning, December 2d, the tug Reliance, sent out by the owners to our assistance, arrived from San Francisco, and stood close by till after daylight, when she was attached to the stern of the Roanoke, where she acted as a rudder until we had passed through the Golden Gate, after which she came alongside the steamship, and assisted her to her pier.

On Friday we had seen several ships, and at ten p m., a Seattle steamer spoke us and threw her search-light upon us; then steamed away to San Francisco, where she reported our safety. Saturday, after getting well inside the harbor, marked excitement was seen. First came a little tug belonging to the company, whose crew and ours seemed to be friends, and their joyful greetings of "Hello, Jack," or "Jim," or "Charley," and "Harry," showed where the heart was. But what pleased me most was the greeting from a young boy on the tug to another on the Roanoke. The expression of happiness on the face of that young lad was a sight to be remembered. He seemed to see no one but his friend.

A score of boats were soon around us, making fast to the Reliance, and climbing from her to our decks, were reporters and men galore.

An officer of the company came out in a small boat, and climbed over the Reliance to us, leaving his boatman in the skiff. By some movement of her propeller the tug upset the small boat, which glided off like a shot. The occupant, who had jumped clear of danger, swam for his upturned boat, and scrambled up on her bottom, where he held on pluckily. There was a strong ebb tide, and the boat was floating off rapidly. Our crew threw him a life-buoy, which he could not reach, he began at once to divest himself of clothing, while our crew were hastily lowering a life-boat, which was soon in the water, and off to the rescue. Meantime, a beautiful little steamer,—a Government boat, raced out under full steam, and rescued the man, while the life-boat went on, and picked up the empty boat, and the sailor's coat, vest and hat. After this delay, we proceeded to the dock.

Lt was a singular, and not at all pleasant sensation, which we felt, as we read our names in the published death-list, well knowing what that must have meant to the loved ones at home.

One young man, on his way to Arizona for his health, said to me: "Think what my poor mother must have suffered! But I have telegraphed."

There was a general rush to the telegraph office, the moment we could leave the steamer, to send our already-prepared messages home. It seemed almost like being resurrected, to be again on solid ground. There was one passenger, booked for Eureka, worthy of mention,—a fine, handsome $1,000 thoroughbred horse. During the storm his fastenings were broken, and he was pounded about most unmercifully, and finally thrown to the deck, where, m order to save his life, he was lashed down on his side. Thus he lay till Friday afternoon, when the sailors raised him with block and tackle, supporting him in a swing, with mattresses around him, to prevent further injury. On reaching the dock, he was gotten ashore, and a veterinary surgeon called at once. The first thing he did, before taking him to the hospital for horses, was to open three abscesses. He also found one more, to be opened later. He pronounced the prospects for the valuable animal's recovery good, though the blemishes he must always carry would be reminders of that memorable voyage. There were many interesting and characteristic occurrences on board the Roanoke during our eventful trip, in addition to those included in my report to the Oregonian and the Yakima. Republic, which might make good reading. I will mention only a few.

During the beginning of the storm, a lady was thrown violently to the floor, and sustained a severe scalp wound. Her son, a young man, rushing to his mother's assistance, was pitched with such frightful force against the piano that one of its legs was broken completely off. With great difficulty mother and son were carried to the nearest stateroom, to receive needed attention.

With a steady barometer, the appearance of the sun, and a calming sea, our heart-felt Thanksgiving was ushered in, bringing with it a hope and happiness which shone on every face. Nowhere, perhaps, in the wide world are attachments and friendships more quickly formed than on shipboard.

We had an intelligent company, and talent, as well, and excellent music, both instrumental and vocal, was furnished, that crippled piano being kept busy sending out sweet and melodious sounds, while the young folks never seemed to tire of coon and love-songs, in which all would join in the chorus, with hearty good-will.

The Captain allowed a young man in the steerage,—a gentleman in education and manners,—to come to the first cabin to add to our entertainment. He made the piano "talk" eloquently by the hour.

Countless jokes and puns were indulged in, at the expense of the Roanoke, and, in this way, we learned that we had a real, live poet on board, Mrs. Bancroft, of Portland, Oregon, as the following will attest:

> "Dear Santa Claus, send us a rudder;
> We need one awfully bad;

109

We lost our own on Eureka bar;—
Made another with a rotten spar;
And now we don't know where we are,
Our plight is very sad.
This is a dreadful thing to be bumped
Around in a stormy sea.
We've asked the Captain to stop the ship;
Have given all the crew the tip;
But it's all no go,—they don't care a rip,
So send us a rudder, C. O. D."

The first persons I met, on boarding the Roanoke at Astoria, were Mr.—and Mrs. A. T. Webb, pioneers of Portland, Or. They had seen my name in the passenger list, and were looking out for me. I was delighted to find friends, and especially so to find we were all booked for San Pedro. The next morning after our belated arrival in San Francisco we embarked on the beautiful steamer Santa Rosa for Southern California. This delightful trip acted as a soothing balm to our wearied minds and bodies. It did not seem possible that we were on the ocean. It certainly is the most lovely sea-voyage any person could ever expect to take. We were in sight of the shore almost the entire distance of over seven hundred miles; and, with the aid of Mr. Webb's field glasses, and sometimes without them, we could see herds of horses and cattle feeding on the hillsides, and get excellent views of the farms, villages and cities, as we glided on so smoothly.

At Los Angeles we reluctantly parted company, to meet in San Diego a few weeks later. I reached San Diego early in the morning of December 5, where my life-long friend, Mrs. Inez E. Parker, met me at the depot, and we were both happy to meet on this earth once more. We were soon on our way to her cosy little home, "The Wren's Nest," which to me will be a quiet haven of rest. I hope the beauties of this pretty little suburb will inspire the muse to come to my aid, that I may use the golden pen, even as Captain Lemon said I would do, on the occasion of its presentation by Syringa Chapter,—"For the good of humanity."

With an extract from a letter from my friend, Miss Mary Wherry, I will close this chapter:

Toppenish, Wash., Dec. 4, 1905.

My Dear Friend—You will never know with what anxiety we watched for reports of the Roanoke, not knowing whether you sailed on her or not, but believing you did. If you were aboard, allow us to congratulate you on your safe arrival. It must have been a dreadful experience. I'll bet you helped the crew to fix the jury-rudder, if they would allow you. At any rate, you will have some more valuable matter for your book. It did not seem possible now that you are just getting through your struggle,—just getting ready to live,—that you could meet with such a dreadful death.

I hope you will live many more useful years yet; and I truly hope that all your undertakings will be crowned with success, and when you start on your final voyage that you may enter the Golden Gate as safely as you did this time.

CHRISTMAS OF 1905

WHICH BEGAN SO HAPPILY, AND CAME NEAR ENDING IN A TRAGEDY

The sun rose in all his effulgent glory. The birds were singing their early Christmas anthems, while the flowers were adding their sweet fragrance. The morning was filled with many and varied Christmas blessings. Mrs. Parker and I were up on time, adding our congratulations for all the beauties and blessings which surrounded us.

We were to take our Christmas dinner, by invitation, with our mutual friends, Mr.—and Mrs. Pitman Parker, of San Diego. Mrs. Parker had said, "Be sure and come early, so we can have a good visit," and we had decided to leave "The Wren's Nest" at 8:30 a m., so as to catch the nine o'clock train to town. In the midst of our preparations a good neighbor appeared with one hand full of holly and a live chicken in the other,—a "Merry Christmas" for Mrs. Parker, who was profuse in her thanks, but said, "I am afraid I shall never be able to kill it."

"Don't worry," I said; "I'll attend to that. Better let me kill it now." "No, the poor thing shall have one more day to live," she said, and started off with it as I supposed to shut it up in a little chicken house at the back. But in a few moments, to my astonishment, I saw Mr. Chicken marching around in a small enclosure which had recently been planted with great care to vegetables, the peas just beginning to make their appearance.

"For goodness sake! What did you put that chicken in there for? There won't be a pea or anything left by the time we get home," I exclaimed. Back she went to catch the chicken, but, having good wings and no mind to be caught again, he was outside in two seconds. Then we both sallied out in the deep, dewy grass and tried to drive him back into the yard, but I soon gave up the chase and returned to prepare breakfast. At last she got him headed toward a neighbor who kept chickens, where she hoped to recover him later. Coming to a thick cypress hedge, he took refuge in it, and wedged himself as far in as he could, where he was captured. I saw her coming, stroking and talking reassuringly to the chicken. I went to meet her, and said:

"You had better let me kill the chicken, and be done with it."

"'Well, perhaps that is the way to give the least suffering to the poor thing," she said, with tears in her voice. She ran for the hatchet, but it was all over before she could get back, and in fifteen minutes more it was dressed and in the cold safe, ready for our next day's dinner. We were at the station ahead of time, each carrying a huge bundle of roots, cuttings and flowers, as Christmas offerings to our hosts. Strange! We heard no train coming; we could always hear it twenty minutes before it reached our station. At last it dawned upon us that, as the "9" was a freight train, with only an accommodation car attached, it had been laid off for the day, and we were not very sure of a ten o'clock train, either, so, as it was only three and one-half miles to our destination, I said, "Let us walk; the road is so beautiful, with the mountains on one side and the bay on the other," and off we went, enjoying every step of it. After a delicious dinner and a delightful social time we concluded to walk home, as the train did not reach our station till 5:30. We started about 4:30 p m. The oiled road was smooth and level, the scenery of mountains, bay and islands grand, and the day was like "a day in June."

"What is so rare as a day in June?" We had gone about half way when we were overtaken by an elderly couple in a light spring wagon, who urged us to ride. We accepted with thanks, and proceeded to get acquainted with our new friends, whom we found intelligent and congenial, and the time passed rapidly till we were near our station. When opposite a small house on an elevation, and surrounded by trees, some 250 feet from the road, we heard loud cries. Mrs. Wellington said, "What is that?"

"Children having Christmas," I answered, and Airs. Parker said: "That is where an old lady, ninety-three years old, lives all alone."

Then came a terrible scream, followed by continuous shrieks, and I said, "That's a woman's voice! Let's go quickly," and Mrs. Parker said, "Yes, something dreadful is the matter with the old lady. Let us go and help her." I' naturally thought the old lady was dying, and some hysterical woman was frightened by being alone in the presence of death. Mr. Wellington was seventy-three, and very deaf and heard nothing. His wife soon succeeded in making him understand, and he drove up to the gateway, about fifty feet from the house, which stood between three hundred and four hundred feet from the station. The moment the conveyance stopped Airs. Parker and I jumped out from the back and ran to the house. Mrs. Wellington, who was a large, tall, fleshy woman, said, "I'll go, too"; but we soon distanced her. The front door was open and a bright light shone from the door and two windows, one being near the front door.

The frightful screams had been kept up until now. Looking ahead I saw shadows. Airs. Parker and I were running side by side. Being next to the wall I stopped a second to glance into the window, while Airs. Parker sprang in at the door. We both saw an old lady on the floor, across and in front of the doorway which led into the back room, and directly opposite the front door. Her face was covered with blood, and a big, burly man in his shirt sleeves was bending over her with his back to us, apparently jamming her down on the floor. Mrs. Parker cried out:

"What are you doing to that woman? Let her alone!"

By this time I was inside the door, and called out: "Let that woman alone, you brute!"

Instantly he whirled, and bellowing out, "What are *you* here for, meddling in my business? *I ll* fix you!" he sprang for me savagely. I knew then what to expect, and turned to dart out of the door, calling loudly: "Run!" But he had cleared the twelve or fifteen feet between us and grabbed me.

I felt the grip of his hand on my shoulder, but I wore a loose jacket, and I threw my arm back and let it slip off, and was out of his reach in a second and speeding down the hill. As I ran I saw Mrs. Wellington about ten feet from me. She had heard my warning voice and had started for the wagon. The next moment I heard her scream, and, glancing over my shoulder, I saw her on the ground—

114

the villain was there, kicking her. At the same time I saw Mrs. Parker rushing by them, toward the station, screaming. "Help! Help!" I knew she was on her way there, for the train was just passing us. I rushed down the hill and around to the wagon, which was about six times the distance necessary, but it was now so dark I could not see the direct course. I had just succeeded in getting Mr. Wellington out of the conveyance when Mrs. Wellington *came running up to us, and on looking around I saw the brute coming and making straight for me. I snatched the whip from the socket, which was heavy and loaded with an iron rod, and when he was within ten feet of me I rushed at him and dealt him a blow on the side of his head with the butt of the whip with all the strength I possessed. It was sufficient to break the whip and to stagger him; but the next instant he struck me with his closed fist over my right ear, and dropped me as if I had been struck with a bullet. As I fell he snatched the whip from my hand. Mr. Wellington now rushed at him, attempting, in his feebleness, to defend me, but he received a similar blow from the ruffian, which laid him on the ground. The villain now began beating him over the head with the broken whip handle. This gave me a chance to spring to my feet and run toward the station. I had not gone more than thirty feet when I saw through the darkness the outlines of three men with Mrs. Parker. I called out, "Run, run, or he will kill us all!"

They quickened their already rapid pace, and as soon as that miserable wretch saw the men he straightened up and became as meek as a lamb he came right up, saying, "My name is Farrel. I haven't done anything." We then all went up to the house and found the old lady standing in the middle of the room with her face streaming with blood. She assured us that Farrel had not intended to hurt her, but was after a Mexican woman, who had made a shield of her to protect herself. She said she would be all right, and requested us all to go home and leave her alone. She is a spiritualist, claims to live with the angels, and to talk with God, face to face, and she expects to be transported to heaven as was Elijah.

It developed later that Mrs. Wellington had started to run, and, stepping into a hole, had fallen down, and before she could get up the ruffian left off his pursuit of me and rushed up and gave her a most vicious kick, with all the force he could put into his heavy boot, in her abdomen; but, as I have said, she is a powerful woman, and returned his kicks with vigor. As she was still on the ground he caught her feet and started to drag her down the hill, and in so doing he stepped into a hole and fell down backward himself, thus giving her a chance to regain her feet and reach the vehicle by the shortest route, which was not more than fifty feet. Mrs. Parker had screamed to Mr. Wellington as she passed him, but owing to his extreme deafness he had sat holding the horses, in blissful ignorance of the whole occurrence until I screamed into his ear to get out and help us.

All this was begun and ended within ten minutes, and in that short time the brute had injured five women and one old man, the combined ages of the persons attacked by him amounting to over four hundred years, namely: Mrs.,

93; Air. W., 73; Mrs. W., 57; Mrs. P., 60; Mexican woman, 37; myself, 66, and the assaulter himself past 50. As Mrs. Parker said, it was an "old folks' party" (or "scrap"), and the liveliest one she ever attended, especially as our party of five had never met one of the participants before.

I went over early the next morning to see the old lady, as I feared the shock might have been too much for her. I found her up, and "O. K." She showed me her bruises, and I examined her face wound and said, "You will come out all right, and will only have a scar to remind you of the affair."

"Oh, no, there will never be a scar," she responded; "I am engaged in a great work. I talk with God, face to face."

She told me that the man Farrel was drinking and got into a row with the Mexican woman over a cow, and the woman ran to her for protection, throwing her arms tightly around her and making of her a shield from the man's blows. "He swore that he would kill her," said the old lady, "and he would have done so if you had not appeared just when you did, for he had knocked us both down."

"Where was the Mexican woman?"

"When he left us for you the Mexican woman slipped out and ran home."

Farrel went to her and the Mexican woman the next morning and begged forgiveness, and claimed that he had no recollection of anything that happened the night before. They forgave him. Mr. Wellington was badly hurt, and so was his wife. I treated my head to poultices and hot-water bags for two weeks. Mrs. Parker was the only one of us who had not felt the power of his fist or foot, but she suffered more from nervous shock than I did from my "knock-out."

The man declared afterward that "someone hit him with a rock." The supposed "rock" was the butt-end of that loaded wagon whip, and I am free to say that I greatly regret that it had not been a rod of iron with which I could have knocked him down and pelted him over the head with it, as he did poor old MV. Wellington after he had knocked him down. The wonder is that any of us escaped alive in such an encounter with an alcoholically-crazed brute.

My grandson, Victor, wrote: "I read in the papers about your terrible trip on the *Roanoke*, and saw your letter about your fight with the drunken man. It seems to me California is not very healthy for you."

Mrs. Hill writes: "We received your letter, and enjoyed every word of the description of how you spent your Christmas. Doctor said, 'Well, mother has plenty of the Owens grit left yet'; but my opinion is that a few more such experiences like your trip on the Roanoke and your Christmas adventure and you will be brought home in a box. In the language of the schoolboy, you are certainly 'having the time of your life!'"

MATTIE'S DIARY: A PICTURE OF SUNNYMEAD HOME LIFE

Sunnymead Farm, January 1st, 1890.

This has been a stormy beginning for the new year. There has been snow, rain and hail at intervals, interspersed with sunshine. 9:30 P. M.—It is clear and cold. To-day we have had the first snow of the winter, except enough to cover the ground yesterday morning. The

117

cattle are all doing well. Dr and Col have Devon up to-day. We expect a calf in a few days. I prophesy that she will have a heifer. (Devon was the cow that Mattie liked best, and Dr. Adair had given the cow to her.) All the members of the family have been busy, and consequently there has been considerable work of different kinds accomplished. Sallie and I ironed and baked this morning, while Victor amused us with his pranks and mischief. We had a nice little dinner alone, and enjoyed it, too. This evening Col has been reading Edward Bellamy's "Looking Backward," and the papers. Sallie and Victor had a romp before their bed-time. (Sallie is the doctor's niece, about 12 years old.)

January 2—There was about six inches of snow this morning and it kept coming down all day, at times. I have been sick to-day and have not noted many events. This afternoon Victor came into the sitting-room looking very sober, and said: "Well! I think *everybody's* out of humor to-day."

I had told him a short time before not to climb over the back of my chair, and his grandmother had sent him out of the kitchen. Sallie and Victor gave a performance from "Little Lord Fauntleroy."

January 3—Weather is still clear and cold. Temperature at Skipanon 22 degrees above zero. Dr.—went to town this morning, expecting to go to Portland to-night to attend the meeting of the stockholders of the Oregon Prohibition Pub. Society, which will be held on the 4th. This afternoon Col brought up one ewe with two lambs.

January 4—Clear and cold. Have been sick to-day, and Victor wanted to start this morning to bring his grandmother home. He only wished he was a big man. Then he would go at all hazards. He is remarkably affectionate and sympathetic for a child only four years old.

January 5—Sallie cooked a nice breakfast all alone, which we all enjoyed. About noon Dr walked in on us, much to our surprise and delight. Victor has been a good boy ever since his grandma went away. I have been sick to-day.

118

January 6—Clear and cold. Col found Devon with a red heifer calf this morning. Am sick to-day, and Victor assisted in bringing up my breakfast. I also poured and creamed my coffee, and assisted in eating the toast. I let him carry all the things down, not excepting my new cup and saucer. Of course he was delighted to find himself of so much importance.

January 7—Victor helped to bring up my breakfast and entertained me while I ate. Then he drank all the cream. Said he was a great lover of cream; also knew all about taking care of sick people. "Just call me if you want anything." Then he was off to the barn.

January 8—It is still clear and cold. Sallie and Victor have been having a merry time sliding and "kating," as Victor says. Dr got a nice dinner to-day. I did some darning, and mended Col.'s gloves while he read. He began reading Bryant's United States History.

January 15—Victor jumped on his grandma's back while she was putting pies in the oven, and pulled her down on the floor. He did the same when she took them out, and upset a custard on the floor. He was held to be in disgrace by all of us, but the punishment was not so severe as to interfere with his enjoyment of the piecrust, which he said was nice. Victor sat in his grandpa's place at dinner, said grace, and served the plates. He was excited, and amused us all very much with his performance. We had fried tripe, and there happened to be one piece at least six or eight inches long, which he took on the fork and insisting on passing to each one of us in turn, asking if we would have it. At last he helped the plates very nicely, but undertook to pass his grandma a piece of bread with his fingers, which I fear were not very clean, and his face did not appear to have been washed for an indefinitely long time. However, he was the picture of health, and embodied lots of sunshine for so small a personage. I'm sure we would hardly be able to get along without him, with all his misdeeds. He wheeled in lots of stove wood to-day and filled the box. Dr is cutting out a dress for Sallie. Victor is having his romp, and Sallie is practicing. Here is a panic! Victor comes and says he has some popcorn up his nose! He said: "I didn't put it up there, it just went up itself." By blowing hard he got the corn out. He went to sleep at 7 o'clock, delighted with the idea of sleeping with his "dear grandma."

January 16—Cold rain, with S. E. and S. W. winds alternating all day. Col is not at home yet, so Dr and Jim went out to see about the sheep this afternoon, and found a ewe with two dead lambs. Victor has played with one all evening, and insists that it is not dead, "for it moves its head, wiggles its tail, and has one eye open," which in his opinion is positive proof of its being alive. This morning Victor asked his grandma if he might pour his tea into his saucer. She found that Ralph Dawson did that. She told Victor that he had stored it up in his memory for future use. Then she gave us a beautiful talk about how important it is that we should improve our minds by storing up beautiful thoughts, and using correct and ornamental language. Sallie and Victor, and each of us are trying to gather the precious things in our early life, so that when the summer and autumn time shall come, we will be the possessors of caskets filled with jewels of priceless value, not only to ourselves, but to those around us, as well.

January 17—Today has been cloudy, with some rain; the snow is melting slowly. Dr went to town, and Col came home this morning. Sallie and Victor buried the little lamb, but Victor's dear, tender little heart was almost broken. He said that he could not see it buried, and turned away crying. It reminded him that his mamma was buried too, so we sent him and Sallie to the barn to play with the live lambs. He has been a dear little boy all day, and anxiously expected his darling grandma to come, for he expected marbles. Suddenly this afternoon he turned into a brown hear and frightened me so! Finally I found that the bear was quite tame. Then I felt very safe. The Dr was late getting home, as the boat did not reach the landing till six o'clock. Sallie started to meet her at three-thirty, so we were very much worried for fear something had happened to them. Col and Jim set out at half past six, with lanterns, and at nine o'clock brought home the lost ones. Victor set the table alone, all but two dishes, and did it nicely, too. We had a nice supper, fried chicken, with rice, etc., with nice gems and gravy. Our little boy went to sleep on the lounge immediately after supper.

January 18—Clear all day, and the sun was warm as spring this afternoon. We ate dinner, with the dining-room windows open. Dr made a call to Mrs. Jeffers; was back by two o'clock. Victor has been good and sweet all day. He has been carrying a piece of calico rag for a handkerchief. He can't keep a good one, but has had this for nearly a week. We call him our "Little Lord Fauntleroy," but I scarcely think the title and handkerchief are suitable companions, so tonight I gave him a clean handkerchief, which I found on the floor after he had gone to bed. Jim went to town to-day to get his New Year's outfit, so we did the farm work. I milked Bonny and Devon, the two nicest cows, and Dr fed the calves and lambs. Col read and we spent a pleasant evening. Our evenings are always enjoyable, when we are all at home. We are learning many instructive and beautiful things pertaining to life.

MATTIE'S LAST LETTER

Sunnymead, Ore., Oct. 10, 1893.

Dear Mother—We are all so glad when your letters come! Victor's eyes get big, and John says, "Hurrah for mamma and the big fair," as we have taught him, and always adds "Hurrah for Cogo." This morning, while he was being dressed, Victor taught him a new word. It was "Of course." So, at breakfast, someone said, "Where is mamma?" and he said "in Cogo, of course." You would be surprised to hear him talk. Victor says "It is 'stonishing." We all talk of you, especially at the table, and keep a bouquet of choice flowers at your place, and of course the children think that is fine. They smell them every time, and when they fade they' pop the leaves and have lots of fun. Then we put fresh ones on.

Colonel received a letter from George last night, written on September 30. He said that he and Hattie's brother had bought a farm the day before—140 acres—at $20 per acre; did not say what kind of a farm it was, but that it was six miles arid a half from town, and the cheapest farm in the county. Colonel answered the letter this morning. Colonel told you that we are sending nineteen rolls of butter to town, but there are twenty—all made within ten days—and fifteen and a half pounds was churned this morning from cream since Saturday. It is beautiful, sweet butter.

You must see the lovely butter in the Dairy Building; and don't fail to see the "Great White Horse Inn." It is near the Stock Pavilion. You will wish to see it, as it is a facsimile of the inn made famous by Dickens' "Pickwick Papers." Also the Big Tree Restaurant, with a tree for a counter, or long table, through the center. It is in the southern part of the grounds; I can't give its exact location. The tree, I think, is from Washington.

The cliff dwellers is a very interesting place. The Blooker cocoa house is not far off. See the hairy elephant in the Geological Building; also mound builders' relics, etc. Pewter plate, from Mayflower, in Ohio exhibit, in the same building. Must close. With love,

MATTIE.

The following is from "The Oregon White Ribboner," in which it appeared at the time:

IN MEMORIAM

My adopted daughter, Mattie 15. Palmer, died at our home, Sunnymead, near Astoria, at one o'clock, on the morning of October 10, 1893. Her death was unexpected, after a very brief illness, and was a grievous affliction to our home circle. Her loss will be sorely felt by a large number of warm friends in both Washington and California, as well as in Oregon.

Miss Palmer was a self-sacrificing, earnest worker for good all her life, and she especially gave much time to work with the Young Women's Christian Temperance Unions of Portland and Astoria.

In both these cities she endeared herself to many of their most worthy people by her cheerful readiness at all times to do real Christian work. Many a poor sufferer in the hospitals of those cities has been cheered by her visits.

She was born in Indiana, September 23, 1861. Her parents removed from Indiana to Oregon in 1862, and settled near Fort Vancouver. While Mattie was yet a little girl her mother was brought to my house, an invalid, for treatment, where she remained till her death, and, becoming attached to me, she asked me to take one of her three little daughters. Mr. Palmer soon after gave me Mattie, and she proved as loving and faithful as my own child could have done from that time to her death. She leaves a brother and two sisters living.

It gave me great pleasure to educate and do for her. She obtained a degree of Doctor of Medicine from the Willamette University, of Oregon, having graduated in the class of 1886. She was so fond of home that she was never willing to leave us to take up the practice of medicine for herself. Indeed, she was such a home-body that we were hardly able to persuade her to visit the Columbian Exposition in June last, and even up to within a few days of her starting she would say: "Well. I am not gone yet, and I am not sure but I will give up the trip at last." She was in tears most of the day before leaving us for Chicago. She was absent six weeks, her very longest visit from home, going East with my son and his wife, and, with them, had an opportunity of visiting her native state. She devoted one month to the great fair, and was full of the wonders of the beautiful exposition, declaring frequently that she could not have learned so much of the world in years of travel.

Early in life Miss Palmer united with the First Congregational Church of Portland, and remained a consistent Christian throughout her life. She was a member and active worker in the Young People's Christian Endeavor, as well as in the W. C. T. U.

She had a fine mind, a most honest and loving nature. Her disposition was so pleasant and sunny that her presence in our home was always most agreeable, and her loss can only be obviated by the years that must come and go. We miss her every day and hour, and can hardly reconcile ourselves to believe that she will never again occupy her vacant chair.

Dr. Palmer was a great and exceedingly good reader. I mean that she read only choice matter, and read it well, and having a most excellent memory, she was good authority on almost any subject. Appreciating her abilities, we anticipated especial pleasure to be derived from her visit to the great White City. But the ways of God are not our ways, and He has taken our dear girl from us while she was yet in the prime and vigor of her young life. His will be done.

We have received many letters of condolence from highly esteemed friends, who knew our good child well, both professionally and socially. These letters contain heartfelt sympathy for us, and well-deserved tributes of friendship to our dear girl. I will only quote a few expressions from those who had especial opportunities for knowing Miss Palmer intimately. Mrs. A. R. Riggs, our State W. C. T. U. President, writes: "Dear Friends—I know not how to express the feelings of sadness and sorrow which at first overwhelmed me on hearing of the death of dear Doctor Mattie Palmer,—our Mattie, as we so often called her when she was so closely associated with the work of the W. C. T. U. in Portland, before your removal to Astoria. It was in this work that I learned so much of the value of her really fine character, always quiet and unassuming; she needed to be well known to be appreciated. Truly, this world has lost one who would have done much to lift it to a higher and better plane. Why she should have been called when she was approaching a mature and well-rounded womanhood, we cannot tell; only He knoweth who is able to heal your sorrow and fill the sad vacancy in your hearts. May 'He who woundeth and His hands make whole' be your consolation in this, your hour of trial."

Mrs. M. E. Hoxter, of Forest Grove, writes: "I know how much you loved and trusted her, and I want you to feel that you have the sympathy of Mr. Hoxter and myself."

Mrs. Dr. G. J. Hill, of North Yakima, Wash., says: "One great comfort to us all is that we know dear Mattie was a true woman, and may God help us so to live that we may meet her in heaven."

Mrs. C. O. Hosford, of Mount Tabor, Ore., says: "How sorry we are that we could not have been with you in your time of great sorrow, to help and comfort you."

Mrs. R. B. Brenham, of Portland, writes: "I cannot forbear the expression of my sincere sympathy with you and your husband in your sad bereavement. It teaches the solemn lesson that we, too, must prepare for death."

Ex-Governor Chadwick, of Salem, Ore., says: "Mrs. Chadwick and I feel this blow very seriously. Poor Mattie; a noble-hearted woman, always so kind to us, we can never forget her." Hon. Wm. D. English, of California, writes: "We were all terribly shocked to hear the sad news of Mattie's death. You and your good wife must feel the loss very keenly, as it came so unexpectedly that it is hard to realize that the vacant chair will ever be without its occupant. Mattie was a self-sacrificing, truly good woman, and she will surely meet her reward in the other world. All my family join in heartfelt sympathy for you and yours."

Miss Jane Weeden, of The Temple, Chicago, writes: "Is it possible that our Mattie Palmer has gone across the river whose thick mists veil the eye from the other shore? If so, I am sure she has gone to a better world than this, but this world sadly needs her, and thousands more like her. I had a great esteem and love for Mattie. She was a thoroughgoing, conscientious woman, and, like Julia Ames, in another department of the world's work, she gave great promise of future usefulness. It is well with her, and we must still face the battle of life."

MRS. OWENS-ADAIR,
Astoria, Oregon.

A TOUCHING LETTER

North Yakima, Wash., Jan. 25, 1904.

To the Editor:

In looking over my old letters I find the following from the late H. S. Lyman, which comes like a message sent back from the heavenly half of the circle to those whom he, too, has so lately left behind. Some of the thoughts are so fine that I herewith submit a copy forwarding the original to his sisters) to your judgment as to whether it should or should not be given to the public.

The Miss Palmer, of whom he speaks, was given to me when a child, by her dying mother, and she received from me the careful training and education of a daughter, which she returned with true filial love and faithful devotion. -She was all that Mr. Lyman says of her, and her death was, indeed, a grievous loss to me, and our home.

(The Letter)

125

Astoria, November 1, 1893

Col. John Adair and Dr. Owens-Adair:

Dear Friends—The sadness I felt, as I learned the evening after her burial, of the death of Miss Palmer, has made me wish to say something comforting, if I could, to you. Your sense of loss—your actual loss—of her out of your home and your work, and your plans for your family and the community, you will not get over, and would not wish to. The place of an one we have really loved is never taken, and never filled. Perhaps it is a comfort that it is so. It may be that the place we have in our hearts for such is like the place, spoken of by Jesus,—one of the places prepared, so that when things are made up again, and each returns to his own, they will find the same place in our affections and the same part in our lives.

Certainly, though we part, none of us, either those that go or those that remain, are outside of God's providence.

> "I know not where His islands lift
> Their fronded palms in air;
> I only know I cannot drift
> Beyond His love and care."

So our mourning is not without hope, and the hope is the main thing for us.

As for her,—one who in this world was fitted to serve, and do good,—and who found her life in making things better and brighter, will not be left without happy ministry anywhere. God, who found her her place here, will find it for her there.

It is with you, as with the rest of us, half our life on this side, and half on that. Our circle—even our family circle—not complete except as it takes in a part of heaven,—half here, and half there, out of sight, but all in God.

I am wanting to see you, but accept, this until I can.

Very sincerely yours,

H. S. LYMAN.

SKETCH OF SARAH DAMRON OWENS

PIONEER OF 1843

Mrs. Owens was born in Kentucky, January 8, 1818. She was the first daughter of Moses and Jennie Damron. Her father was of pure English blood, and emigrated from England with two brothers, Lazarus and Richard, and settled on the Big Sandy River. Mr. Damron was a great Indian fighter, and was employed by the Government as a scout and spy during the war with the Shawnees and Delawares. He performed notable deeds of daring and bravery, which were recognized by the Government. Among them, and worthy of record, was that of rescuing a woman and five children. The Shawnees had scalped her husband and carried off herself and six children. The Indians soon tired of the babe, and tearing it from its mother's arms, beat it to death against a tree and hushed the mother's screams by rubbing her face with her husband's scalp!

Mr. Damron volunteered to go in pursuit of these Indians, and, with eleven men, he followed thirty miles, coming up with them just after dark. There were twenty warriors. The leader was standing before the fire. When the men saw the twenty warriors, ten of them turned and fled. Mr. Damron, nothing daunted, instantly shot the leading savage, who fell into the fire. Damron gave the warwhoop to charge, and the Indians, thinking an army was upon them, fled. Mr. Damron and his one faithful comrade rushed in and rescued the woman and children and carried them across a mountain and returned to the trail, well knowing that the Indians would soon be on his track. He secreted himself under an old stump having an overgrowth. Soon two Indian scouts came along, striking their flints and lighting their punks. They stopped close by the stump, so near that Damron might have touched them with his hand. He often said that he thought then the scouts might have heard his heart beats.

They did discover the tracks of the retreating white men, and on they rushed, whistling to their comrades to follow. As soon as they passed Mr. Damron lost no time in returning to his charge, and, with his comrade, took the woman and children to a settlement in another direction.

For this feat of bravery our Government presented Mr. Damron with a splendid rifle, richly mounted with silver, and valued in those days at $200. Mr. Damron also killed the noted Indian terror, Big Foot, shooting him in a pass of the Cumberland Mountains.

During those dreadful times of Indian wars Mr. Damron, in 1812, married Miss Jennie Mullins. To them were born six children,— Moses, Sarah, Louisa, Elizabeth, William and Solomon.

In 1826 they moved to Illinois, where they lived two years, but, not being satisfied there, Mr. Damron started to return to their old home in Kentucky. They reached Posey County, Illinois, on the Ohio River, where they stopped to rest. Here Mr. and Mrs. Damron were attacked by what was then known as the "milk sickness," and within six days they were both dead and buried. During their illness the father called the eldest son and daughter, Moses and Sarah (the object of this sketch), twelve and ten years old, and told them many times, describing in the minutest detail every turn and cross-road on their long journey home. He marked out their whole route, and made them promise that they would' continue steadily on till they reached their relatives in Kentucky. In those days children without parents were often "bound out." To provide against this, Mr. Damron called in his Masonic brethren and exacted a pledge from them that they would see to it that his children should not be "bound out." He then made all arrangements for their journey. After the burial of their parents these six children started on their sad journey in a light, one-horse wagon, or carriage. They reached home in one month, including all stops, never once losing their way or having to retrace their steps, so well had the wise father impressed his own accurate knowledge upon the minds of his young son and daughter, but, sad to say, this trip was the means of rendering this twelve-year-old lad a cripple for life. While ascending steep hills he often had to put his foot under the wagon wheel to keep it from sliding and thereby bruised his foot and ankle, which brought on a disease of the joint, making him a cripple, and finally causing his death.

The children were overwhelmed with kindness throughout their trip. One night they stopped at the house of an old bachelor, who, upon reading their letter from the Masons, made up his mind to adopt the children. He kept them for nearly a week. He seems to have been a good, but very eccentric, person, for he had provided himself with a coffin, in which he kept his jug of whisky. The sight of the coffin thoroughly frightened them, especially Sarah, who ran, screaming, down the stairs.

The old man was very kind to the children, and loaded them with good things to eat. One day he went to town, leaving them with an old negro and his wife, telling the children he would not be gone long. As soon as he was out of sight the children hitched up their horse and slipped away, the old colored people pretending not to notice them. They traveled with all haste, for fear the old man would follow them, but they never saw him again. Sarah and Eliza had the ague, and shook every other day. After several days' traveling they came to the Widow Hopkins', a wealthy woman, who was known far and wide. She kindly took them in and cured the girl's ague.

Widow Hopkins had a large plantation and a hundred slaves. Her two widowed daughters lived with her. The hearts of these wealthy and good women were warmed toward these orphaned children, and they begged them to stay with them, offering to raise and educate them. But Moses, that honest and faithful boy, said: "No. I promised father on his deathbed that I would take the children home to our people, and I must obey."

After they reached home they were divided among their relatives. Sarah went to live with her maternal grandmother, then eighty years of age.

After her grandmother's death Sarah went to live with an uncle and aunt, who were very kind to her and taught her to spin and weave and do all kinds of work. Her only sorrow was her separation from her brothers and sisters. The nearest was thirty miles away. When she would get homesick to see them her aunt would tell her to visit them. Then she would take her shoes and stockings and a change of clothing i n a handkerchief and start early in the morning. She would walk and run thirty miles, easily, in one day, wading a creek called Shelby thirty times.

I have often heard mother say that when she started on these trips she felt as if she could fly, and she did run for miles at a time.

Thus passed her young life until she reached the age of sixteen, when she met and married a Mr. Thomas Owens, then sheriff of Pike County, Kentucky. Mr. Owens was the son of a wealthy planter, and was a tall, handsome, athletic young man, and for six years had been sheriff of his county. He knew neither danger nor fear. They settled on a farm on the forks of Big Sandy, about seven miles from Piketon. Here their first child was born, who survived but a few weeks. Also their first daughter was born here. After two years they emigrated to Missouri. For this trip my father, Mr. Owens, built a flat-boat, in which he moved his family and effects down the Big Sandy to the Ohio, and up the Ohio to Cincinnati, where he sold his boat and traveled by steamer to Van Buren County, Missouri, where their second daughter, Bethenia (the writer), was born, February 8, 1840. My father built a log cabin, and made rails and fenced in some land, and the following spring he bought five yoke of oxen and broke twenty acres and planted it in corn. He fixed a little chair on the plow, in which the oldest child, the late Mrs. John Hobson (mother of Mrs. Ada Fulton, wife of Hon. C. W. Fulton, the present United States Senator from Oregon), would ride, while mother, with her baby (myself) in her arms, walked behind and dropped the corn, which was covered up by the next furrow. The corn was planted in every third furrow, and this planting produced a fine crop without any further attention.

Father and mother lived here only about a year and a half and then moved to "Platte Purchase," Missouri. This move was due to the continuous affliction with the ague. On February 22, 1842, a son was born,—the late Hon. W. F. Owens, of Douglas County, Oregon. In the spring of 1843 my parents moved to Independence, Mo., and there joined the emigration of that year for Oregon.

MY MOTHER'S STORY

The first day everything went along finely, and for several days thereafter. Our wagons were loaded with provisions, and everybody was happy until we came to a creek called the "Blues." Here we camped, and about midnight a fearful wind-storm blew down our tents, and the rain fell on us in torrents. The next morning we found that about half our cornmeal was wet. Then my husband said to the company: "At least half our meal is wet, and unless it is converted into bread it will he lost, and my advice is that we make fires and at once make it all into bread." This advice was, unfortunately, followed only by myself and a few other women. Thousands of pounds of meal were left by the roadside. Had Mr. Owens' advice been taken and economy practiced as it should have been no person in that emigration need to have suffered from lack of food.

That day was principally devoted to getting dried out, ready for a new start. From here we moved on without special occurrence till we reached the Platte River, where we camped, while the men found a good ford which seemed to be about a mile across. Then the wagon-beds were raised about six or eight inches, and from forty to fifty wagons and teams were fastened together with long chains. Horses were attached to the first wagon and oxen in the rear. The men went ahead on horseback with ropes tied to the front team. Upon reaching the other shore the men would pull in the ropes, in this way keeping the front team in the right course, while each man sat in his wagon and directed his own team.

In that way we all crossed in safety. Thus we journeyed until we came to Sweetwater, in the buffalo country, where Mr. Owens was made Captain of the hunters. I then took charge of the oxen and drove them throughout the buffalo section. While the hunters were killing game other men with pack-horses were sent out to bring in the meat. As soon as it reached us the women set to work cutting it in thin slices and stringing it on ropes, which were fastened to the bottoms of the wagon-beds. Within three days this meat would be well cured and ready to pack away in sacks.

This was a jolly train. We had music, singing and dancing nearly every night. In the evening, while the men were attending to the cattle and horses, their wives and daughters would be carrying buffalo "chips" in their aprons, making fires and preparing supper, which was eaten and relished with appetites that only out-of-door life can give.

During all this time we never saw an Indian to annoy or molest us, and not until we reached Independence Rock, where Dr. Whitman met us, and we got our first scare. Our hunters here saw a band of Indians, and notified the train. This brought the only non-social member of our company into close relations. This Englishman, by name Evers, was a very unsocial and disagreeable man. He usually camped a quarter of a mile away from the company, but the Indian scare brought him into line. After this guards were stationed every night.

Dr. Whitman traveled with us until the Blue Mountains were reached, and then went ahead and blazed out our route.

We proceeded on till we reached Chimney Rock (Three Rocks), where we camped and sent out the hunters. They found the buffalo very wild.

There our first serious accident occurred. While the hunters were approaching the buffalo through the tall grass, a gun in the hands of one of them was discharged and shot a Mr. Goodman through the hand, which crippled him for life. The hunters were successful, and coming in with their game, we proceeded on our journey.

The next evening, after camping, we had quite a scare from a band of at least five hundred buffalo that were apparently coming down on us; but fortunately they were swerved from their course sufficiently to pass us, while had they continued straight on we would have been trampled to death.

The next crossing of the Platte we found very deep and swift, detaining us three days, preparing to cross this turbulent stream. To do this we tacked buffalo hides on the bottoms of several of the wagon-beds. In these novel boats was placed our portable goods, ropes were then fastened to them, and good swimmers carried them over and pulled the boats across, while other men swam alongside to steady them and keep them from upsetting. In this way our goods and families were all safely landed on the other side. The wagons were then taken apart, and ferried over in the same way, after which the stock was driven in and made to swim across. It required two days after this to prepare for our onward march. From this to Fort

Hall we subsisted principally on antelope meat and small game, the buffalo having become very scarce.

At Fort Hall those of the company who had become almost destitute of provisions procured some, and here Mr. Owens sold his buffalo gun for $50.

A few days after leaving Fort Hall we had another "scare" when some fifty or sixty warriors of the Osage tribe came in sight. We stopped at once and prepared for battle, making a square enclosure with the wagons by placing the tongue of each wagon on the back of the one next to it. In this corral the stock was placed. Fortunately the Indians did not molest us.

When we reached the sage-brush country our Captain, Mr. Jesse Applegate, divided us into platoons of four wagons each, in order that each platoon might take turns for one day in the lead, breaking a road through the high sage brush. It would have been impossible to have proceeded otherwise, as the sage brush was from two to six feet high. After passing through this section we reached Snake River and found a ford, which we all crossed safely, except Mr. Evers. Our wagons were hitched together and a man went ahead with ropes to guide the foremost team. Mr. Eyers' family were afraid to cross with him and begged to go with the company, and so were landed in safety. Mr. Eyers would not heed the protestations of the company, but persisted in driving his fine mule team in by himself. The mules soon became unmanageable, turned down stream, and soon Mr. Eyers disappeared from sight—lost his life and everything he had. The company brought his family through.

Coming to the Powder River, our troubles began in earnest, for, owing to carelessness and wastefulness by many in the company, starvation began to stare them in the face. Captain Nesmith, with a part of the company, were a few days in advance. We found many dead and disabled cattle along the road, which were used for food by those who were in need. Thus we proceeded to Salmon River, where we bought some dried salmon and dried berries from the Indians. In the Snake River country we met the old mountaineer, "Peg-Leg" Smith, and did considerable trading with him and his squaws, who were very friendly and represented quite a tribe.

133

From here we went on to the Blue Mountains, where Dr. Whitman left us, proceeding homeward to send us provisions. We toiled on till we reached and passed the summit of the Blue Mountains. One night we were overjoyed to receive supplies of wheat, corn and peas from Dr. Whitman. Then the parching of wheat and corn and the grinding of coffee mills made sweet music to our ears, bringing encouragement and happiness to us all. In the midst of this pleasure and feasting I was called to the bedside of Mrs. Ollinger, and soon was ushered into the world a girl baby,—the first child born to the emigration of 1843.

(The writer is disposed to add that eight years ago she met a tall, handsome lady of education, who said: "Doctor, are you any relation to Mrs. Thomas Owens, of the emigration of 1843?" "Yes, I am her second daughter,—the eldest now living." Then the lady said: "I would rather see your mother than any woman on earth, for she attended my mother at my birth, on the Blue Mountains." This lady's name is unfortunately forgotten.)

In the morning the mother and baby were placed in the wagon, and all proceeded merrily on the road that was being blazed and cut out by the young men who preceded our wagons.

We soon reached the Grand Ronde Valley, but before reaching it we had to descend a long and very steep hill. Here trees were secured to the back end of the wagons, then the wheels were securely locked to prevent injuring the horses and oxen. In this way every wagon was safely landed in the valley below. Mr. Owens drove almost every wagon from the top to the valley. There we camped by a beautiful stream of water, with plenty of luxurious grass for the stock.

The next day we reached Dr. Whitman's, where we rested for three weeks, preparatory to embarking in canoes for Vancouver. We left our stock and wagons with Dr. Whitman. We bought canoes and took one Indian guide. When we came to the impassable portions of the river, the women and children would leave the canoes and walk around on the river bank while the men and Indians took the canoes safely through the rapids. A few days after embarking Mr. Applegate, his son and hired man, with several other men in the boat, ran against a rock and upset the boat. Mr. Applegate's son and one hired man were drowned.

Several days later our next accident occurred. A Mr. Sterman and family were in their own boat, which upset, and their son was drowned.

We had many amusing incidents as well as sad ones on our way down the river. One might be mentioned to prove that human nature is much the same the world over. We had been out of salt for some time. Mr. Owens had succeeded in getting a little sack for which he paid fifty cents. It was our custom to build one large fire sufficient to accommodate all of our now reduced company. We were all seated about the fire near the river bank, eating our supper. There was one couple who never seemed to tire of quarreling, especially at meal time. The little sack of salt had been passed around, that each might be helped, when, as usual, the surly couple began their exhibition. The wife, becoming enraged, threw her cup of coffee at her husband; he retaliated by slinging the sack of salt at her head. She dodged it, and the sack went into the river. Mr. Owens, seeing the precious salt disappear, sprang to his feet and exclaimed: "Now, sir, you dive in there and get that salt, or I will pitch you in after it!" Without a moment's hesitation the man dived in over his head and brought the salt out so quickly that it hardly had time to get wet.

That chastisement seemed to have a good effect, for we had no more exhibitions from this source.

We continued on down the river without further misfortune until we reached Fort Vancouver, where Mr. Goodman's boy died. We here met Dr. McLoughlin,* who was a friend to the emigrants. We remained at Vancouver three weeks, while Messrs. Owens, Hobson, Simmons and Holly, procuring a boat from Dr. McLoughlin, went down to Astoria, and on to Clatsop, where Mr. Owens took up a land claim. They then returned to Vancouver, and Dr. McLoughlin furnished my husband with provisions and seed, and we then proceeded to Astoria, where we landed safely on Christmas day, 1843.

*Dr. John McLoughlin (1784–1857) was a Chief Factor and Superintendent of the Columbia District of the Hudson's Bay Company at Fort Vancouver from 1824 to 1845. He was later known as the "Father of Oregon" for his role in assisting migrants to the area and promoting the American cause in the Northwest. In the late 1840s his general store in Oregon City was famous as the last stop on the Oregon Trail.

The next day we crossed the bay to Clatsop, landing at "Tansy Point," now "Flavel." Here we were met by Rev. D. L. Parish, and Messrs. Trask and Perry. These were the only three men who had white wives then living on Clatsop, Dr. Solomon Smith and Mr. Tibbets having native wives. Messrs. Trask and Perry took us and all our effects in a wagon, by the way of the beach, to their home, the present Taylor farm.

Mrs. Trask had, only a few days before, given birth to a pair of twins.

Here we remained until Mr. Owens built a log cabin on his claim, just south of and adjoining the Trask farm, our houses being only about a half mile apart. We moved into our Clatsop home in the midst of winter. I gathered dried ferns and mixed them with clay to chink our cabin. My husband drove in four posts by a big hole left in one end of the cabin and between these we built a fireplace and chimney with sods, the posts acting as supports, the sod part being carried above the roof. The roof was weighted down with poles, which were tied down at each end to keep the clapboards in place, there being no nails in those days. As soon as we were settled Air. Owens proceeded to make rails averaging two hundred per day, from the wild forest. Soon we had land fenced and everything far ahead for a spring crop. Dr. McLoughlin exchanged four fat steers with us for lean oxen, at Walla Walla, in 1843. Then, in 1844, we sold the fat steers to Dr. McLoughlin for a supply of provisions. My husband was gone over a month getting these provisions, in the summer of 1844. When our husbands were away from home Mrs. Perry and Mrs. Trask always insisted that I should stay with them, as they were too timid to be alone. One night we were awakened by scratchings and whisperings at the door. I insisted on getting up and investigating. Mrs. Trask and Mrs. Perry protested, until at last I could stand it no longer, and opened the door, to find two Indian women, who begged to come in. They said that the Indians were all drunk at the lodge, and their husbands had run them off. I let them in, and they laid down by the fire, and we were all soon asleep.

I think the most unhappy period of my life was the first year spent on Clatsop, simply for the want of something to do. I had no yarn to knit, nothing to sew, not even rags to make patches. We had very little to cook. Salmon and potatoes were our principal diet. One of my greatest needs was a cloth for a dish-rag. One day Mrs. Parrish gave me a sack half full of rags, and I never received a present before nor since that I so highly appreciated as I did those rags. There were quantities of berries, and during berry time Mrs. Trask, Mrs. Perry and I spent much time in gathering berries. We would start out early, taking our children, and stay all day, coming home loaded. The only way we had of preserving these berries was by drying; we seldom had sugar. After 1845 cranberries brought from $10 to $12 a barrel in San Francisco, and I gathered from ten to twelve barrels for market yearly for several years.

During the summer of 1845, my husband was from home most of the time. Messrs. Owens, Trask, Perry, Marlin and Tibbets were building a grist mill on the Ohanna creek, just below where the Astoria and Columbia River Railroad now crosses that stream, near its mouth. That was the first grist mill built in Clatsop county. It was built in the fall of 1845.

An Indian called Spuckem, claiming to be a sub-chief, came to our house during our absence, and, climbing down the chimney, robbed us of nearly everything we had. The wheat and potatoes stolen were to have been returned to Dr. McLoughlin to pay for those he had loaned us when we came to Clatsop. Next spring this same Indian came to our house, with two young women, daughters of the head men of the tribe. He wanted to come in and stay all night. I told him he could not, and then I shut and bolted the door. Not hearing them for some time, I supposed they had gone, and opened the door. Soon after this, Spuckem rushed into the house, seized a brand of the fire, and started to build a fire in some shavings against a pile of boards. I told him if he burned those boards I would tell Owens.

He said, in a jeering way: "Owens is a 'Kloochman' " (meaning he is only a woman).

He moved his fire, however, to another part of the yard, and helped himself to our woodpile. He then sent the women to ask for potatoes and salmon (boiled), and they ate their supper. They then made their bed in the chimney corner, outside, and, after carefully putting out their fire, went to bed. They lay talking and whispering till long after midnight, excepting when the dogs would bark, when they would be very quiet. During all that time I stood guard with the rifle and shotgun, not knowing what might happen. The two younger children were fast asleep, but the two eldest were much too frightened to sleep. Just before daylight, the Indians took up their effects, and quietly slipped away. The next morning several Indians came to the house tracking the runaways. I showed them where they had made their fire, and that I did not allow them to stay in the house, and the pursuing party went on. This sort of behavior made the young sub-chief very unpopular. Soon after this, he came riding up with several Indians, and attempted to ride right into the house. I saw them coming, for some distance, letting down top bars, so they could jump their horses over. I sent one of the children quickly to tell Mr. Owens to come. As he came running into the yard, Spuckem saw him, and turned his horse to run, but Owens caught his axe from the block and hurled it at him with great force. The axe turned over in the air, and the poll of it struck Spuckem between the shoulders, nearly knocking him off his horse. Fortunately, it was not the blade of the axe that struck him, or it certainly would have killed him. This was the first chastisement Spuckem had ever received, and he swore vengeance against Mr. Owens, though he was afraid of him.

This Spuckem had now become a "terror" in the neighborhood. Both whites and Indians were afraid of him, for he had quite a following, especially among the young braves.

The Indians warned the whites, and said Spuckem was determined to kill Owens. Early in April, the settlers, being anxious about their safety, called a meeting for the purpose of electing a sheriff. This meeting was held at Capt. R. W. Morrison's. Mr. Thomas Owens was placed in nomination by Mr. Tibbets, and Mr. Jerry Teller seconded the nomination. As no other person was placed in nomination, Mr. Owens was unanimously chosen, thereby becoming the first sheriff of Clatsop county.

Spuckem, nothing daunted, made a practice of riding through the fields, letting down fences, and allowing the stock to get in the crops, merely to show his authority. He continued to get bolder and bolder, until one day—I think it must have been in July—he went out with his lance, and killed an ox belonging to Mr. Tibbets, and gave a great feast to all the Indians. He knew that Mr. Owens was sheriff, and would attempt to arrest him, so he pretended to have gone to Tillamook, and kept in hiding for some time. One day Mr. Owens was cultivating potatoes with a plow for a near neighbor by the name of Lewis Taylor, who had an Indian wife. Spuckem knew that Taylor did not know him, and thought he was safe from detection, but Taylor's wife saw him coming, and told Taylor whom he was. Spuckem walked in, and set his gun inside the door. Taylor went out into the field, and told Owens that Spuckem was in his house. Owens replied:

"I have nothing but a pocket-knife, and I know Spuckem always carries his gun. Could you manage to get it out for me while he is talking to your wife?"

Taylor replied: "I think I can."

They went to the house, Owens keeping out of sight, till Taylor got the gun and handed it to Owens through the door.

As soon as Spuckem saw Owens, he ran and hid in a clump of willow bushes, Owens and Taylor following.

Owens approached the willows, and saw Spuckem crouching down by a large tree, on his knees. He called to the Indian, in his own language, to come out and give himself up, and he would not be hurt; that the whites did not want to kill him, but that he must pay for the ox. Spuckem replied in good English: "You have got my gun, and I will kill you with my knife!" and rushed upon Owens, with a long, sharp dirk-knife.

Owens receded several paces, with the gun leveled at the Indian, telling him he would fire, hut on he rushed, till the muzzle of the gun he had himself loaded almost touched his breast; then (he fatal shot was fired, the bullet passing through his lungs. Spuckem dropped his knife, and ran across a little hill, to his lodge, where he died, after a few hours of agony.

Although the Indians were in reality glad that Spuckem was dead, they demanded tribute, and made many threats if it was not forthcoming.

The whites sent them word to meet them at our house in the morning of a certain day, that the matter might be amicably settled. All the white settlers came to this council, and waited all day, but no Indians came. Late in the afternoon, when the last white man with his gun had gone, the chief, with about fifteen or twenty warriors, in full warpaint, feathers, and equipments, came over the hill to the house. My husband, with his rifle in his hand, walked boldly out to meet them, while I stood in the door, with the shotgun in my hands.

The chief said: "We don't want war; we want blankets."

They told how many they wanted, and Mr. Owens told how many the white people would give.

After a long pow-wow, the terms were settled, and the pipe of peace smoked. Thus ended what might have been a bloody massacre.

Mrs. B. C. Kindred, always a very bright, thoroughly reliable lady, says, in referring to the killing of Spuckem:

"I remember all about it, just as though it were done yesterday. Air. Owens brought your mother and the children (you a very little girl then) down to spend the day with me, while he was plowing, or cultivating, for Lewis Taylor. The killing was in the afternoon, for your father came down for dinner. We heard the gun sometime after he returned to work, and feared that something had happened. I was so scared that I would not stay at home, so we all went with your father, in the wagon, and on to Captain Morrison's. Your mother and I went out to the place where Spuckem was shot, and saw blood on the grass. I think I could go to the place now. Lewis Taylor's squaw told me that they were afraid to stay at home, and so slept out in the brush all that night."

During the winter of '44 and '45, Mr. Owens put in most of his time making rails for Rev. J. L. Parrish, in exchange for provisions.

Among other things, was a little pig, which we kept in a flour-barrel for some time. For this pig, 300 rails were made.

During all this time, the only bread we had was made from wheat parched in a skillet, and ground in a coffee-mill. This bread consisted principally of potatoes, cooked and mashed, and then mixed with the ground wheat.

During the winter, our son, Josiah Parrish, was born.

In the spring of 1845, Mr. Owens sowed about six acres of wheat, and an acre of potatoes. Up to this date, none of the family had either shoes or stockings. We had moccasins, however, which I made from deer-skins, obtained from the Indians. My husband made his shoes from the skins of the elk he killed, which he cured and tanned himself. These shoes were made on a wooden last, the soles being put on with wooden pegs.

The first flax raised in Clatsop county I planted in the spring of 1844. I dug up a little garden-spot with a hoe,—the only garden tool we had. In order to reach the sub-soil, I cut through the sod with an axe, and removed the sods in squares. Then I cultivated the sub-soil with the hoe and my hands. When thorough pulverized, I planted my handful of flax seed, which I had brought from the States. It was the custom in Kentucky to plant flax on Good Friday, and I followed this old custom. I never saw such fine flax before, though I had been accustomed to flax culture all my life, as well as to the spinning and weaving of the fiber. I harvested this little crop with great care, saving every seed, which yielded about one quart. I pulled the flax up by the roots, and tied it in little bundles, and laid it in a small lake nearby, to undergo the rotting process. I then dressed my flax with tools roughly made by my husband.

From this crop, I obtained enough floss to pad two quilts, and a large hank of the finest fiber I had ever seen. Out of this I spun shoe-thread, that was used in making the first pair of shoes I ever wore on Clatsop. My spinning-wheel was made by Mr. David Ingalls, who had never seen a flaxwheel, but made it from my description.

The shoes, made of elk-skin, prepared by my husband, as mentioned above, were made by Mr. Samuel Hall, who also made the 'last for them.

The Indians soon discovered the treasure I had produced, for it filled a long-felt want, in making their fish-nets, as it was greatly superior to the twine they manufactured from cedar bark. They watched the growth of this flax with great interest, and were crazy to get it, engaging it all ahead. I found that I had quite a profitable business in flax, having ready sale for all that I could raise, at from fifty to sixty cents a pound. I was only required to take it through the rotting process, and remove the woody fiber; the Indians would use every thread of it by hand-twisting it over their knees. This crop averaged me from ten to fifteen barrels of fine Chinook salmon every spring, worth $9 to $10 per barrel.

About 1847 and 1848, salmon-fisheries began to make their appearance, in a way, and I received employment in making shirts, which the fishermen sold to the Indians for fish. These shirts were made of a very strong fabric called shirting. There being no thread in the country, I ravelled out the chain, which I doubled and waxed, making very good thread. I made from five to six shirts a day, receiving for them twenty-five cents each. With this income I was able to procure shoes and clothing for the children, and assist in getting food for our rapidly growing family.

I made one garment worthy of special mention, it being for the old chief, "Katata." He brought me ten yards of bed-ticking, from which he wanted me to make him a great overcoat, or robe, that would touch the ground. I put all the stuff in the coat, and it greatly tickled his vanity. He would strut about in this royal robe, amid his admiring subjects, and I doubt if ever any king upon his throne in his regal purple and ermine, felt his importance more than did this

142

old chief, Katata, wrapped in his bed-tick. For making this garment, I received ten Chinook salmon.

In 1846 or 1447, Mr. Owens procured a herd of Spanish cattle from Robert Shortess,—about sixty or sixty-five head. From these we were to have one-third of the calves, and give Mr. Shortess ten pounds of butter a year from every cow we milked. A woman had never attempted to milk one of these vicious animals until I tried it, while my husband stood by with a club. Up to this date, he had never learned to milk a cow, but he soon learned to milk. We broke and milked ten cows the first year, and obtained 50 cents to $1.59 for every pound of butter we made. From this time on, we made money easily.

About 1847, Mr. Owens being desirous to have some sheep, took an Indian and went to Vancouver, and brought home two ewes and a buck. These were the first sheep landed in Clatsop, and they proved very profitable, both in wool and increase. We readily received 50 to 60 cents a pound for wool.

I have good reason for remembering those sheep. Father said sister and I might each have a ewe. I was more enterprising than she and more selfish and at once selected the fine handsome ewe, leaving her Hopkins' choice of the inferior looking one. Sister complained, hut I would not yield. When spring came her ewe presented her with a pair of twin ewe lambs, while a buck fell to my lot. That almost broke my heart, and to add to my discomfort, I was told that it was a just punishment. Next year this was repeated, giving sister five head, four ewes, while I had but three head, one ewe. This was a lesson that served me well through life, and brings forcibly to mind what the earnest and late Judge Cooly, president of the law department of the University of Michigan, once said: "If our children could only profit by our experiences, what a grand world this would be, but it seems to be a law of Nature that everyone must learn through his own experience."

In the spring of '48, Mr. Owens, with Messrs. Trask, Perry and Tibbets, built a little two-masted Schooner at Skipanon, which they called the "Pioneer." They loaded this schooner with dried and salt salmon, potatoes, butter, cabbage, carrots, cranberries, and a few skins. Mr. Robert S. McEwan was made captain, and with all the owners for a crew, the little vessel made a fortunate trip to San Francisco, where the vessel and cargo were sold at a great profit. All the owners and captain returned home safely, excepting Mr. Tibbets, who died on the way back.

From this time on, we found our herds so much increased, that we began to look for a better range. Air. Perry had moved to Southern Oregon, and settled in Roseburg, Douglas county, and was urging us to come out there, where there was plenty of water, grass and game. So, in the summer of '53, my husband built a 'large flat-boat, and in the fall we rented our Clatsop farm, transported all our cattle, horses and sheep in the flat-boat (requiring several loads and trips to do so), to St. Helens, from where they were to make the remainder of the journey overland.

Then he returned with the flat-boat and brought his family and goods to Portland, from which place they continued their journey in wagons. They were to meet and join the men with the stock farther on, which they did in North Yamhill, one of the garden-spots of the Willamette valley, about twenty-five miles from Portland. Here was situated the fine farm of Mr. Burton, father of Mrs. Richard Hobson, of Astoria, Oregon.

The remainder of the journey was delightful. Water and grass were found in abundance for the stock. The trip was successfully made, and, in less than a month, we reached Deer creek, and were given a hearty welcome by our old friends, the Perrys, who were overjoyed at seeing us again. They had a home provided, and we moved our household goods in at once, and were soon ready for the winter, then near at hand. Mr. Owens at once took up a land-claim just across the South Umpqua river from Roseburg, and established a ferry. Roseburg then consisted of perhaps a dozen families. Mr. Owens set to work at once to build a boat, and get his material on the ground for a house. In the spring our new home was completed, and we moved in. It was soon followed by barns and all other conveniences. Here my husband found ample range for his cattle, and fine horses, and accumulated wealth as rapidly as he had in Clatsop, county. From here he furnished large supplies for the

Rogue River Indian war troops, getting his pay in scrip, but not a cent in coin. The war-scrip gradually became valueless, causing my husband, as well as other patriotic men, serious loss.

At this time, deer were very plentiful in that locality. We often saw herds of the soft-eyed beauties, feeding upon the beautiful grassy hill, just back of our barn. Indeed, they often came within gun-shot of the house.

After getting settled in our Roseburg home, our pioneering may be said to have ceased, for we then, and ever afterward, had all the comforts and conveniences around us, including excellent schools for our growing children. We lived here in peace and plenty fourteen years, with little to give us trouble or anxiety, until about 1867, when my son Pierce's health became very poor, and my husband's strength, also, began to fail.

In order to find relief for both husband and son, we moved to Trinity county, California, and located at Piety Hill. Here we found a delightfully mild and uniform climate, giving us hope that our two invalids would recover their health and strength. Our hopes, unfortunately, were doomed to disappointment, for we buried them both in that balmy, southern country.

Shortly afterward, I returned to Oregon, and began living with my children, always keeping a little home of my own, in which I have spent most of my time. For several years past my home has been in Empire City, Coos county, near my daughter, Mary McCully, one of whose twin girls I took at birth, and have raised as my own. This child was lately married, and, with her husband and infant daughter, are now living with me, thus enabling me to enjoy life, daily reminded of childhood's happy years.

(My mother is now nearing her eighty-eighth birthday. She still enjoys excellent health; is strong in body, and vigorous in mind, having still a very firm hold on life.)

A WESTERN WIFE

She walked behind the lagging mules,
That drew the breaker through the soil;

Hers were the early-rising rules,
Hers were the eves of wifely toil.
The smitten prairie blossomed fair,
The log home faded from the scene;
Firm gables met the whispering air;
Deep porches lent repose serene.
But withering brow and snowy tress
Bespeak the early days of strife;
And there's the deeper wrought impress—
The untold pathos of the wife.
Oh, western mother, in thy praise,
No artist paints, or poet sings.
But from the rosary of days,
God's angels shape immortal wings.

—Will Chamberlain.

MRS. ASENATH GLOVER HOSFORD

The late Mrs. Hosford, of Mt. Tabor, wife of Chauncey Osburn Hosford, was one of "Old Clatsop's" pioneer women, of whom any county in the state may justly be proud. Mrs. Hosford's maiden name was Asenath Glover. She crossed the plains with her brother, Aquilla Glover, and his family, in 1846. They were of that ill-fated Donner party, but Mr. Glover left the party, and pushed ahead with his family, a few days in advance, and reached the valley of the Sacramento in safety.

In the days of "forty-nine" there were very few women in California. Miss Glover was one of the five unmarried American young ladies in San Francisco at that time.

Rev. C. O. Hosford crossed the plains in 1845. The following year he became a student in the Willamette University, and was licensed to preach by that institution in 1847, being at that time twenty-five years of age.

.In 1848, he, with nearly all of the men of Oregon, went to the California gold mines, he going under license from Elder Roberts, and preaching in San Francisco, at "West's boarding-house."

Then he organized the first Methodist class-meeting west of the Rocky mountains, which became the nucleus of the first Methodist church in California. Mr. Hosford was of excellent English blood, and when a young man chanced to be in a ship that visited the island of St. Helena, at the time the remains of the great Napoleon were removed from the island, and saw all the ceremonies of that impressive occasion. This is only one of the many most interesting incidents in this good old pioneer's remarkable life.

In San Francisco, in 1849, he married Miss Asenath Glover, the woman who proved to be more priceless to him than could have been all the gold of the earth, and who remained his faithful help-mate, even unto her death.

Mrs. Hosford came to Oregon soon after her marriage. He was a circuit preacher, and for a time their home was on Clatsop plains, and here it was that Mrs. Hosford's admirable character first began to be known to the people of Clatsop county. She was possessed of a strong individuality, and great force and decision of character. She was what is termed "a level-headed" woman; being a frugal, active, economical, and thorough housekeeper, and, withal, a most excellent cook. She was an energetic, cheerful, consistent Christian mother, and an ever faithful, able, and watchful wife. Her husband, being a preacher, had many calls upon his charity, and had often to rely upon his clear-headed, industrious and thrifty wife for advice, which prevented their impoverishing themselves, and forgetting the essential adage that "Charity begins at home." It was the writer's privilege to know Mr. and Mrs. Hosford intimately. I knew them while they were hewing out their home from the Mount Tabor fir forests, as well as later, when Mrs. Hosford had made her yard literally blossom with beautiful shrubs and flowers of almost every variety. She delighted in flowers, and 'with all the care that fell upon a mother with a large family, she was always able to find time for the recreation and pleasure of cultivating her much-beloved flowers and rare plants.

Their beautiful home was enhanced within and without, by the presence of lovely and fragrant flowers, and in her last delirium, she talked of them: "Beautiful white flowers; how beautiful! And they are always used at funerals."

Yes, and they were used in profusion, at her burial. Even her casket was filled with the "beautiful white flowers" she loved so well.

No one could have been missed more than Mrs. Hosford, not only by her devoted family, but by her legions of friends, who loved and appreciated her, and will cherish her memory throughout their lives.

Mrs. Hosford had great executive ability, and was scrupulously just. When she was stricken down in her last illness, she knew that death was near, and at once called in her attorney, and proceeded to divide her property among her children, thus finishing up her last work, and setting her earthly house in order.

It had been Mr. Hosford's invariable habit to preach at least once each Sabbath, which habit he most industriously and faithfully continues, in storm and sunshine, sometimes going so far that he is not able to reach home for the usual Sunday afternoon family gathering. This happens less often in these days of steamboats, railroads, and electric cars, than in the days of canoes, blind trails, and cayuse ponies. When Father Hosford promises to preach, he is sure to be there.

For forty-eight years this worthy couple fought the battle of life together, shoulder to shoulder, and heart to heart. To them, marriage was the greatest gift of a merciful God.

Mrs. Hosford died at her Mount Tabor home, December, 1896, surrounded by her affectionate and devoted family and friends. Her strong, self-reliant nature enabled her to overcome all the trials and privations of an eventful pioneer life, and her later life was made happy by her loving family and faithful friends. Her irrepressible cheerfulness brought happiness to her home, and all with whom she came in contact. She left the world much better for her having lived in it.

> Bring fragrant flowers, and let them sweetly tell
> The story of her gracious life; she loved them all so well,—
> So much she loved the dewy children of the sod,
> Her own soul grew into a perfect flower for God.

—Inez E. Parker.

Mrs. Hosford was the mother of eight children, and seven grandchildren; two sons, Captain Olin and Perne Hosford, of East Portland, and four daughters, Mrs. Peterson, wife of a prosperous fruit-farmer, of Mt. Tabor; Mrs. Harkins, wife of Superintendent Harkins, of the Southern Pacific shops; Mrs. Field, wife of L. R. Field, superintendent of the Oregon Southern Pacific lines; Mrs. Cora Grout, wife of Prof. D. A. Grout, of the Park Street school, of Portland, Oregon.

All these living children are well settled in life, and worthily enjoy the esteem and friendship of a large circle of friends.

FRANCES O. GOODELL ADAMS

Frances Olivia Goodell was born October 5th, 1821, near Monson, Maine. Her mother's maiden name was Betsy Newell. Her father, Deacon Abel Goodell, was a worthy scion of the old Puritan stock. Industrious, scrupulously honest, though poor, his neighbors honored and trusted him, and relied upon his advice, in their troubles. It was often said of him that "Deacon Goodell is so honest he always cheats himself in a bargain, for fear he will cheat the other man"; and, for my part, I would rather deserve to have that said of me, than that I was a king of finance, and worth a billion dollars.

Deacon and Betsy Goodell had eight children, of whom Frances was the fifth. When she was twelve years old her parents moved to Henderson county, Illinois, nine miles from Galesburg, the seat of Knox College, where she was a bright pupil under Professor Locey, and President Blanchard.

She taught her first school at the age of fourteen years, and was quite successful. She "boarded around," and always afterward spoke with affectionate gratitude of those motherly women who were so kind to the young school- mistress, and who remained her friends through life. A former pupil of hers, now living in Eugene, Oregon, says: "She had the sweetest disposition of anyone I ever knew."

She *was* amiable, almost to a fault, since a total lack of resentment and self-assertion is sure to cultivate arrogance, and a domineering disposition in those to whom its habitual deference is given.

Yet, in her ease, her superior intellect, and exceptional conscientiousness commanded respect wherever she was well known.

She was a member of the Washingtonians, the first temperance society in the United States.

On the 28th day of August, 1844, she was married to William L. Adams, in the log house where her parents first lived in Illinois. They were both graduates of Knox College, but Mr. Adams had taken an additional advanced course at Bethany College, Va., under President Alexander Campbell, with marked proficiency in Greek

150

and Latin, for which he had a special taste and gift. His wife was equally fond of literature, and her reading embraced a wider scope, since he despised all fiction, thereby losing some of the finest literature, and best thought of the world.

Both were ready writers, but she was modest, retiring, and self-distrustful, while he was the exact opposite, being bold, self-assertive, and self-confident. He wrote and published much, in a keen, witty, and forcible style, and was an excellent ortheopist, but it was upon his wife he depended always, when not quite sure of a word.

"Frances, how do you spell..." he would ask; well knowing that she would answer promptly, and that she was infallibly correct.

She also wrote well, when she could find time from the cares of a large family—for to them, also, were born eight children, three sons and five daughters. She wrote excellent logical essays for the neighborhood lyceum, and poems of real merit for the albums of her friends; and her letters were a source of enjoyment to her relatives and friends. She read much, and rapidly, retaining and digesting all she read, and was, therefore, well, even marvelously well-informed, not only as to all current events, and concerning all the prominent characters of her own day, but she was an encyclopaedia of information regarding the world's history. I used, as a child, to wonder how mother could remember so much; for I noticed that no name or circumstance in history was ever mentioned in her presence that she did not know apparently all about it, and have intelligent ideas of her own oh the subject.

Though so extremely shrinking and dependent in action, she was, notwithstanding, a most clear and independent thinker.

She was of short stature, but sturdy frame. Her hair and eyebrows were dark brown, her eyes blue-gray, and her brow high, full and broad. Too timid to lead in any important undertaking, unless driven to it by conscience,—if she trusted her leader she could, and would, follow him to the death.

When her first two children were two and one-half, and six months old, she, with her husband, started, May 1st, 1848, on the long, long journey across the plains to Oregon, the land of moist, mild winters, green grass, and good and abundant water.

Their household goods, provisions, and babies were conveyed in a wagon, drawn by one yoke of oxen. They had one cow, old Rose, of blessed memory. She well deserves mention here, for when one ox mired and died on the Cascade mountains, it was she who, beside furnishing milk for the babies all the way, bravely took her place beside the remaining ox, and brought the wagon and little ones safely into the Willamette valley. She lived ten years after that (over twenty years in all), giving us an abundant, and almost constant supply of milk,—the pet and companion of the children, who climbed all over her, and rode on her hack when she was lying down, or standing and walking, unresented by the dear old beast, who loved us all as much as we loved her.

My mother walked more than half way across the plains, to spare the tired, faithful oxen.

The Indians were friendly then, and grass for the cattle better than it was later, after more emigrants had passed over the road.

Once, in the Cascade mountains, we come to a long slope, so steep that the wagons had to be chained together to get them safely down. Mother carried her baby, now nearly a year old, down first, and setting her where she thought she would be safe from harm, she came back up the mountain for me. I was then nearly three, and can remember the scene. On her way up, she was passed by a dozen or more Indians on horseback. Alarmed for her infant, she hastened on to bring the older child as quickly as possible. To her terror, she saw that the Indians had stopped exactly where she had left the child, and were apparently trampling it. Breathless she ran, to find that they had only formed a close circle around it, to guard it till she came. With tears, she motioned her thanks, and they understood, nodded, smiled, and rode away.

"Right here," Dr. Adair says, "I want to add a few words to this sketch of my dear, departed friend, whom this picture so vividly brings to my mind; for, had the precious life of baby Helen been thus nipped in the bud, what, an incalculable loss it would have been to humanity. Few women have done more for their country than this same saintly Helen, whose whole life has been filled with Christian deeds, and duty to her husband, family and neighbors. (In the full scripture sense of the word.)"

She has given four splendid sons and two beautiful daughters to her state. All were welcomed by their devoted mother, who, by precept and practice, has faithfully trained and guided them into paths of usefulness and honor. Her first two sons are successful and able ministers of the Gospel, Herbert, the eldest, being pastor of the Warren Avenue Baptist church, Boston, Mass., and the second, Virgil (whom I call my boy), is pastor of the First Baptist church in Claremont, New Hampshire.

The third son enlisted, at the age of sixteen, and went with his company on the first transport that left San Francisco for the Philippines. He was in the battle at the taking of Manila, and remained in the islands six months. On his return, he re-entered the University of Oregon, where he is preparing himself for a literary career.

The fourth son is also still in the university. He is all a mother could desire, and will not be found wanting whenever and wherever his country needs him, when his majority is attained.

The two daughters are happy wives and mothers; and, though both took the college course with their brothers, they are mistresses of the culinary art, and of housekeeping, and home-making; and are following in the footsteps of their intellectual, yet domestic mother.

What prophet could have foretold the future blossoming and fruitage of the dormant seeds of posterity that lay folded away in that tiny, blue-eyed, fair-haired human bud, around whom those stalwart savages were mounting guard? What more beautiful eulogy can be bestowed upon her than that of sacred writ? "Her children rise up and call her blessed; her husband, also, and he praiseth her."

My parents came to a final halt in Yamhill county, Oregon, six miles northwest of the present city of McMinnville, and spent most of the first winter (we reached Oregon October 1st, 1848) in the hospitable home of Dr. James McBride, father of Representative John R., Judge T. A., and Senator G. W. McBride.

These great-hearted people took in the wayfarers with kindliest good-will, though their house then consisted of but three moderate-sized rooms, and a spacious "loft"; and they had, at the time, all at home, eleven children of their own. I never heard a quarrelsome word, or saw any but the kindest, jolliest behavior in that house during our stay, nor in all the years in which we were constant associates, as neighbors and schoolmates. My father used their back room as a school-room that first winter, and the families of Dr. McBride, his sister, Mrs. Woods, and Mrs. McBride's sister, Mrs. Shelton—all living near each other—made a full school. Here I, early in my fourth year, received my first, and lasting lessons in geography and United States history, from hearing the others recite.

Two governors, a representative to congress, four prominent physicians, an eminent judge, and a United States senator, came from those three families, arid all save the senator, who was born later, came from that school. *They* managed to fit themselves for exceptional success and usefulness in life without the aid of any "machine" whatever.

In the spring of 1849, my father went to the California gold mines, and my mother taught the neighborhood school, in a little log house, built by the settlers for' that purpose, boarding at the home of Zebedee Shelton. "Aunt Vina," his good wife, was a sister of Mrs. McBride, or "Aunt Mahala," as we all affectionately called her.

Never can I forget Mrs. McBride, a small, but executive woman, dark-haired, blue-eyed, with intellectual brow, and keen, commanding glance, who sat in the wide chimney corner, almost always with a baby in her arms, ruling and directing her family with a wise, firm, but kindly hand.

No dishonorable act, or even thought, dared to meet that penetrating eye! But sorrow and need never sought succor in vain from that generous hand; and her husband was her fitting mate, revered, trusted, loved by the whole countryside. They had fourteen children, all exceptionally intelligent, amiable, yet spirited, witty, forceful; and all thoroughly trained, and ingrained in the cardinal principles of integrity, industry, and hospitality. The daughters, as well as the sons, possessed strong mentality, and self-respecting independence, and, as all Oregon knows, have been leaders, wherever they were, in all that was worthy, elevating and helpful to the community and to themselves.

They were, all told, the most loyal family to their friends, and to each other, that I have ever known.

My father returned from the mines within the year, with $900 in gold-dust and nuggets. With this sum he purchased a farm of 640 acres, of a Mr. Carey. They had a black woman, a former slave, living with them—the first negro I ever saw—and I well remember how terrified I was to see her take my baby sister in her arms. To me she was like some strange, wild creature, who might devour children. I soon found, however, that she was even kinder than white people were to children, and that my fears were groundless.

Here we lived five happy, busy years. My mother worked with my father laying rail fence, making garden, milking, and aiding him in any way she could, between her household duties, which she never neglected. Our first bushel of seed potatoes cost $5 in gold. "Small potatoes," they certainly literally were; but they soon yielded noble returns, for that was ideal soil for them; and in those five years we had made a pleasant and comfortable home. Also two more children,—a son, William H., and a daughter, Julia Frances, were born.

My father's mother, and her two youngest daughters, and his eldest brother, O. H. Adams, and his family, had come to Oregon in 1852, and his younger brother, S. C. Adams, had arrived the year before. They all settled near us, and Uncle

S. C. Adams married Dr. McBride's eldest daughter, Martha, a noble woman, whom he worshiped to the day of her death, over thirty years later.

My father's sister, Eunice, was also married to John R. McBride, the eldest son of the family, who afterward represented Oregon in congress.

My grandmother was a strict Presbyterian of the old school, and it distressed her to see any relaxation of the old time rigid rules, especially those of Sabbath observance. But I now thank her for many requirements that I then thought too strict.

Mother had us commit to memory the Proverbs, many of the Psalms, and nearly all the Gospels, but we never thought that a hardship. She lived, and taught to us, her religion in a way that constrained us to love and absorb it into our very physical, as well as mental fiber, so that our love for her and God seemed one.

My father, having a live interest in the political affairs of his adopted state, and a facile pen, had already become known for his contributions to the Oregonian, then edited by Thomas Dryer, and, in 1855, he purchased the "Spectator," a newspaper published in Oregon City, Oregon, and we removed to that place in the spring of that year, renting the farm.

We remained in Oregon City four years, and here a second son, Gaines M., was born. Mother did not like city as well as country life, but she made the best she could of it for father's sake.

We attended good schools here, and my sister Helen and I, at the ages of nine and eleven years, respectively, entered the office of "The Argus" (during two years), of which our father was the editor and proprietor. The office, also, was an excellent school, especially as the foreman, D. W. Craig, was a scholarly young Kentuckian, to whom we owe much for the sterling training he gave our minds, as well as our fingers. He presented us with carefully-chosen books, which, under his advice and assistance, we read, and treasured, and it is to these, and to his wise suggestions as to our future choice of reading, that whatever we possess of sound literary taste is largely due. He could not have been kinder to his own little sisters, and his unfailing interest in, and affection for us, is today, after fifty years' duration, one of our priceless possessions. Who shall dare to say that such a friendship, lasting for fifty years on earth unbroken, can be ended by death?

In 1859 my father moved back to the farm, where he built a handsome new home, and remained two years, during which time a twin brother and sister, Arthur Craig, and Amy Cecilia, were born.

In 1861 father was appointed collector of customs at the Port of Astoria, where we lived the next four years, and where our youngest sister, Claribel May, was born. My mother disliked the responsibilities of official social life, yet she recognized its just claims, and endeavored to discharge its necessary requirements to the best of her ability. Her eldest two daughters were now of an age to assist her in this, so far as their school duties permitted.

It was in this school that they first met Mrs. Owens, afterward Dr. Owens-Adair; and, in their close association as classmates, learned to respect, appreciate, and admire her many fine qualities.

I, the eldest child of our family, was married, during our residence here, to Wilbur W. Parker, of Washington, Vermont, July 4, 1863, and made my home there with my husband until his death, January 9th, 1899.

Here, also, my sister Helen was married, July 3d, 1865, to Prof. W. Johnson, afterward president of the University of Oregon. And here, too, our brother Arthur, the twin, died, at the age of four years.

My mother was not sorry, at the end of father's four years' term of office, lo return to the farm, where she felt happiest, and most at home.

But she was not permitted to end her days there, for eight years later—twenty-five years from the time it came into his possession—my father sold the dear old place to R. R. Thompson, of Portland, for $25,000—just $1,000, beside our living from it, for every year we had owned it.

All the family, save mother and I, were glad it was sold, that they might remove to Portland, but we grieved for the old farm.

Father purchased the property then on the corner of Eleventh and Harrison streets—now Thirteenth and Harrison, in Portland.

Mother was quite contented in her Portland home. Her eldest two daughters were now happily married; her third daughter teaching the Portland public schools; and her eldest son was an attorney and police judge of the city. My father had taken up the study of medicine, and, after taking his degree in Philadelphia, was then practicing his profession in Portland.

Mother always loved gardening, and her Portland home was soon made beautiful with shrubs and flowers. She greatly enjoyed her church, the First Christian, corner Main and West Park streets, within walking distance.

There were no street cars in those days, and many residents of the city, not in its outskirts, either, walked regularly one and a half to two miles to church. It was a genuine Christianity that induced a regular attendance then, through winter's storms, and summer's heat; and our mother's was genuine. ' Her flesh had very greatly increased, and she was somewhat lame from an old ankle-sprain, so that a walk of ten blocks was no easy task for her, but she and her family were always in their places, at the morning services, at least.

In the country, when far from any church, she always dressed us with unusual care on Sundays, and, after the dinner work was done, she would gather us about her for an hour's reading, and instruction from the Bible. All of us who were old enough read a verse in turn, and mother talked to and with us about its meaning. We loved that hour, for one thing because it was the one hour in the week that mother was not busy, and could give herself entirely to us. Often, in summer, we spent it under the trees, beside a lovely mountain stream which flowed near our Yamhill home—Glen Avoca, as father had named it. She never "preached" to us. She was not strict. Indeed, grandmother thought her almost dangerously lax in her religious training and family discipline, but, though we might sometimes be slow in doing her bidding, we absolutely never did anything she told us not to do; and her teaching and example made lovers of God and righteousness of us all; and her influence for good reached beyond us, to the hired men, and even to the wild Indians, who were then all around us.

After a few years, my father purchased the place where he now lives, in Hood River, and mother spent about a year there, returning to Portland for a short time, but soon moved to Eugene, Oregon, for the educational advantages for her two younger daughters. After their graduation, two years later, they both engaged in teaching, and she was free to visit her married children.

Her eldest son, William, was now married to Miss Olive Paget, of Portland; her daughter Julia to Dr. W. J. McDaniel, an esteemed physician, and her son Gaines to Miss Anna Pasley, of Idaho. All her five married children were comfortably settled in life, and greatly enjoyed her visits, and urged her to prolong them. Her health had always been exceptionally good up to her sixty-fourth year, when it failed rapidly, and, while spending the last New Year of her earthly life at my home, she one day said to me: "I feel that I have done my work, and I dread becoming sick and helpless, so, if it the Lord's will, I would like to go soon. My children do not need me now, and I am ready to go.'* "Oh, mother," I said, "we *do* need yon. All your sons-in-law love and respect you, and are as glad to have you in their homes as we are. You can enjoy your life, now, with no more anxiety or hard work."

"Yes," she said, "you are all good to me, and I know I am welcome, but I shall never be well again, and I am praying to God to take me soon, without my knowing it. I do not dread the change,—only the physical pangs of death, which I would like to be spared, if it is right."

Dear mother's prayer was granted, and the following summer, after a terribly hot day, she was suddenly stricken with apoplexy, and, after lingering unconscious but twenty-six hours, she entered into her rest June 23d, 1886, at the home of her youngest son, Gaines, at Cedar Mill nine miles west of Portland, Oregon, aged sixty-five years and eight months.

"Still let her mild rebuking stand
Between us and the wrong;
And her dear memory serve to make
Our faiths in goodness strong.
"And grant that she, who, trembling, here

Distrusted all her powers,
May welcome to her holier home
The well-beloved of ours."

NANCY IRWIN MORRISON

A part of this sketch of that remarkable woman, Mrs. Nancy Irwin Morrison, was furnished me by her second daughter, Mrs. Mary Ellen Carnahan. The remainder is from the pen of Hon. John Minto, husband of Mrs. Morrison's eldest daughter, Mrs. Martha Ann Minto. Mrs. Carnahan says:

"My mother was born April 27th, 1809, in Anderson county, Missouri. She was the mother of nine children, thirty-one grandchildren, and eleven great-grandchildren.

We crossed the Missouri river en route to Oregon, May 2d, 1844, and reached Astoria, January 19th, 1845, after a nine day's trip down the Columbia, in an open canoe. The rain continued during the entire trip down the river. The family never slept in a house from the time we started for Oregon, until we reached Astoria, nine months later; and I have often heard mother say that when she took the beds up from the floor the first morning in Astoria, the floor was wet where they had lain, so saturated was everything, from the continuous rain.

Prior to coming to Astoria we camped at Linnton, opposite Oregon City, until father came down to Clatsop to see the place, and get a canoe to move us. He rented a part of the late Solomon Smith's place and a part of their log cabin.

We landed at Skipanon, January 20, 1845, and camped in a hole, dug for a cellar, where Mr. Wirt now lives.

To reach the Smith place we had to cross a swamp, through a perfect thicket of brush and crab-apple trees. This swamp was between two and three hundred yards across, and only a trail had been cut through, and there were no bridges.

In some [daces the water and mud was from two to three feet deep in the winter, and as it had been raining steadily for nearly two weeks the swamp was flooded. So there was no other alternative but to wade and carry all our effects over. Mr. Eldredge Trask met us at the swamp, and, taking my youngest sister and a brother, one under each arm, he went ahead. Father followed with my youngest brother,

161

and mother with the rest of the children brought up the rear. I think I can see my mother's face now, with such a discouraged expression on it. She said then that she would have "sold out for a picayune" (6£ cents).

Mother brought a little flax wheel, a bunch of flax and a sack of wool, but no cards. We children picked the wool, from which she spun yarn, and we knit stockings. From the flax she spun sewing thread.

When father went to the Cayuse Indian war, and was gone from December till May, mother managed everything, putting in crops, making butter, and doing everything there was to be done. And, in addition, she did anything she could get to do for the support of the family.

I remember that she worked for many days, with the help of two of the children, untying a net that had been too coarsely woven, for which she charged only twenty-five cents a day. I also remember that she paid the taxes for one year by knitting socks.

At the eighteenth reunion of the Oregon Pioneer Association Mr. Minto read the following interesting sketch of Mrs. Morrison:

"It is a labor of love on the part of the writer to attempt thus to convey to others the character of this estimable woman, as seen in the toilsome action and the trying inaction, the sleepless vigilance and constant readiness to meet and overcome or endure the trials in which her duties as a wife and mother placed her, as an emigrant to Oregon, and as a settler in that new country, upon her arrival.

"My point of observation was as a member of the family, at first by temporary adoption as an assistant during the journey to Oregon, and subsequently by marriage to her eldest daughter three years after arrival.

"I state this to show the reader that I had excellent opportunities to know what manner of woman this was who crossed the plains and mountains with ox-teams, when the entire distance, from the Missouri to the Willamette rivers, was in possession of the Indian race, to become, with her husband, a home-builder in Oregon.

"My task is grateful to me because Mrs. Morrison was, I think, an excellent representative of her class; there were many her peers, and some more than her peers, in artificial acquirements, while some might fall below her, so that I think, all things considered, she was a good representative. The same was true of her husband. They were both descendants of pioneer settlers of Kentucky, where they were born, in the early part of this century, grew up, married, and moved west to Missouri with the frontier settlement.

"Here I wish to speak of the acquirements of this worthy pair of representative Americans, of a class whose work is done on this continent. Neither of them were much indebted to the school teacher. He could read, which he did, on the subject of political economy, studiously, at every opportunity. He could write, also, but with such difficulty that it was never a congenial employment. She could read with difficulty, but rarely attempted it in the prime of her life, when her children claimed her attention. Later in life it was a source of great comfort to her, the New Testament being her favorite book.

"Of course she was versed and very expert in the domestic labors, which in her early life involved cooking, dairy management, spinning, weaving, and soap boiling, as well as the rougher preparation of flax and hemp for the spinning process. She brought with her across the plains a flax wheel, flax seed, bobbins, weaving sleighs, etc., necessary for the manufacture of clothing. She had another acquirement not usual to womanhood. She could use a rifle with effect. As a frontiersman's daughter, left in early girlhood her father's housekeeper by the death of her mother, she had been taught the use of the rifle, but she never affected it in mannish ways. I have heard her tell of killing a hawk, in defense of her poultry, but never saw her handle the rifle we called her gun, although I did overhear her asking where it and its accompaniments were, one night when the camp was in alarm, expecting a night attack from the Indians.

"At the time I first saw Mrs. Morrison, in her Missouri home, I made up my mind it would be very stormy near her when domestic matters went wrong, supposing I saw signs of a very high temper. I believe yet the temper was there, but it has never been my lot to know anyone who had more self-control, or who laughed so often when someone would rail and scold. I will give an incident which occurred within the first hour of my becoming a member of her household.

"It was yet early in the morning when Wm. H. Rees, subsequently a representative man in early Oregon, and I reached Mr. Morrison's farm, having left the camp of intending emigrants upon information that he (Morrison) wanted two assistants for the journey. We found him just leaving the house, after an early breakfast, as he was much pressed for time for his preparations. In less time than I can write it we had agreed to serve him in any way we could to get him and his family and effects to Oregon. He was to board us, do our washing and mending, and haul our trunks of clothing, etc., for such service. Learning we had not breakfasted he took us into the cabin, introduced us and our need of breakfast, and went himself and saddled a horse, and, as we arose from the table, put money (gold coin, a rare money at that time) into Mr. Rees' hand and told him to ride to St. Joseph, nine miles away, and buy nine barrels of flour, and so much cornmeal, for the journey. Mr. Morrison took me with him to bring a tongue, or pole. Mrs. Morrison came to the door and said: 'Wilson, you'd feel queer if that man should serve you a Yankee trick, and go off with your horse and money.' It was evident to me that such a thing had not occurred to Mr. Morrison. He was speechless for some seconds, and then quietly remarked: 'Well, all I can say is, if he does he had better not let me catch him.' The lady laughed and returned to her household affairs; and these, from the time I became a member of her household, were certainly very laborious.

"Here I wish to note a fact which I presume was true of a large majority of the wives and mothers who crossed the plains as pioneers. The movement was against the judgment and feelings of Mrs. Morrison. She told me so, in so many words, but never alluded to the subject again until she had been several years in Oregon, and then she told me she was satisfied with the change, on her husband's account; but she believed that he, himself, was not.

164

"No person seeing Mrs. Morrison in her daily routine of duties would have supposed she was engaged in an enterprise her judgment did not endorse. She was no complainer. While sociable, she was not an excessive talker. She was at this time in the prime of life, and, thinking for words to characterize her in her relations to her family and others, those of Proverbs xxi:25, come to mind:

'strength and honor are her clothing.'

"Her neighbors and friends must have been very numerous, for during the last two weeks of her residence in Missouri there was an almost incessant stream of visitors, many of whom came from a distance, and all the shifts of frontier life were brought into play to provide beds for all.

"The reason firm, the temperate will,
Endurance, foresight, strength and skill;
A perfect woman, nobly planned
To warm, to comfort, and command;
And yet a spirit still and bright,
With something of an angel light."

Sara Hurford Jeffers, widow of the late Joseph Jeffers, was born September 21, 1808, near Worcester, Ohio. The following incidents of her life were given to the writer by this wonderfully active and worthy lady, in April last, while visiting at the home of her son, E. C. Jeffers, whose beautiful home is very appropriately named "Grand View." She said:

"We were married in Wheeling, West Virginia, November 29, 1829. My parents were both natives of old Virginia, my father dying when I was quite young. My husband's parents were also born in Virginia, and his grandfather was a soldier of the Revolution, and the war of 1812.

"In 1837 we moved to Burlington, Iowa, then a little town with many stumps and much ague, but there we made our home for ten years. In 1847 we started on our long journey to Oregon, with our three children, John H., Elijah C., and Cara L. We had already lost five children, and my husband's health had not been good in Iowa, the cold weather not agreeing with him. To obtain a home in a healthy country was the chief cause of our coming to Oregon. After arriving here my husband looked around for the healthiest part of Oregon, leaving me and our children in Oregon City. He finally located here in this place, in Clatsop county, where we have, indeed, had excellent health. Here my husband died on January 2, 1867, since which time this has been the home of my son Elijah and his family. I think my husband's life was prolonged considerably by coming here.

"At this date (April 11, 1897) we have two living children of all the eleven born to us. The survivors are my son Elijah, and daughter, Mrs. Cara Hibbard, of Portland, Oregon. I still enjoy, thanks to Almighty God, excellent health, and feel that I have had many blessings throughout my long life. I have endeavored to lead a Christian life, having united with the Methodist Church when a girl, in Wheeling, West Virginia.

"I attended the Methodist Church in Oregon City the first Sabbath after our arrival, and heard the Rev. Mr. Roberts preach from the text, 'As for me and my house, we will serve the Lord.' "

Mrs. Jeffers is spending the evening of her life with her son Elijah, on the place selected by her husband, half a century ago. Here this good lady is surrounded by her grand-children and great-grand-children, and, at nearly ninety years of age, she still reads for several hours a day, and occasionally writes, with extraordinary ease for one so old. Her mind and memory are bright and reliable. She is a great blessing to the household and bids fair to live to be a hundred.

I might cover many pages in writing of this worthy Clatsop county pioneer, but she has already a prominent place in "The History of the Pacific Northwest," Vol. 2, page 389.

While time lasts and memory exists Grandma Jeffers will live in the hearts of many people as an illustrious example of the pioneer mother, grand-, and great-grandmother, who followed the golden rule, "Do as you would be done by," throughout her long and eventful life.

"Servant of God, well done."

The parents of these beautiful children, Irving Jeffers and wife, their grandparents, Elijah Jeffers and wife, and their great-grandparents, Joseph Jeffers and wife, pioneers of Clatsop county, Oregon, were all particular friends of Dr. Adair, who officiated at the birth of both children.

Their great-grandmother, Mrs. Jeffers, was a woman of rare nobility of character. Dr. Adair attended the party given by her son Elijah to celebrate his mother's 90th birthday. All the invited guests were pioneers—friends of her first years in Oregon, and tried friends of succeeding years.

Mother Jeffers sat at the head of the table: and said a feeling and appropriate grace. She was bright and animated, and enjoyed the social communion with her old friends greatly, declaring that evening that it was the happiest day of her life.

Before they all parted she requested the privilege of praying with them, so all knelt together and listened to the most beautiful and touching prayers from her lips that they had ever heard. The scene made an impression on the minds of those present never to be effaced.

At the age of 93 she attended the pioneer reunion in Portland, Oregon, and Dr. Adair, seated near the speakers of the day, saw her sitting in the front of the audience. The Doctor stepped down, and, taking her by the hand, led her to the platform and seated her well forward, where she could hear and see everything, thus adding much to the dear old lady's enjoyment, besides giving her a deserved place of prominence, for she was truly one of the grandest of pioneer women, a noble and devoted Christian heroine, a queen uncrowned.

She kept up her correspondence with her old friends and was constantly busy, mending, knitting, reading much in her Bible, and assisting in the care of her grandchildren. She retained her faculties to the very last, calmly, nay, joyfully awaiting her summons, and passing peacefully and painlessly away at the ripe age of 94, universally honored and beloved.

"Oh, sweet, calm face, that seemed to wear
The look of sins forgiven!
Oh, voice of prayer that seemed to bear
Our own needs up to heaven.
"How reverent in our midst she stood,
Or knelt in grateful praise!
What grace of Christian womanhood
Was in her household ways!"

Very little more than a century has elapsed since our beautiful Columbia river was seen by other eyes than those of savages.

Just three hundred years from the eventful 1492, when Columbus demonstrated to the unbelieving world the existence of another continent toward the setting sun, beyond the ocean that had hitherto bounded their lives, in 1792, on the 11th day of May, a ship from Boston, commanded by Captain Robert Gray, discovered and entered the mouth of this, the third great river on the American, continent, giving it the name of his ship, the Columbia.

From this time attention was directed to the Northwest coast, and vessels frequented the river until March, 1811, the present site of the town of Astoria was selected and occupied by the Pacific Fur Company. This was the beginning of the settlement of Oregon, but it spread no farther for about twenty-five years. In response to the touching appeal of the four Indians who came from their home beyond the Rocky mountains to St. Louis in 1834, asking for the "White man's Book," telling about the "white man's God," and a teacher to explain it to them, the hearts of Christians were aroused, and two of the missionary societies took measures to answer the call—the M. E. Society of the United States, and the American Board of Commissions for Foreign Missions, at Boston. The company of missionaries sent by the American Board were Rev. Samuel Parker, and Dr. Marcus Whitman, who established a mission station among the Nez Perces, at Walla Walla. When the location was decided upon, Dr. Whitman immediately returned to the East to procure associates to carry on the mission. On the strength of his report, the American Board resolved to enter upon the work, and instructed Rev. H. H. Spalding and Mrs. Spalding, with Dr and Mrs. Whitman, to proceed the next year to Oregon to labor among the Nez Perces. At the solicitation of the board, Mr. Wm. H. Gray, of Utica, New York, accompanied them as secular agent of the expedition, and, in September, 1836, the party reached Walla Walla, on the Columbia river. The following year Mr. Gray -returned to the East to procure supplies and reinforcements for the mission, and in both respects was successful. While there he sought in marriage and won the hand of Miss Mary Augusta Dix, of Champlain, New York, a choice in which he was signally guided by the good hand of God upon him. Miss Dix was a young lady of refinement and education, and of unusually lovely person, manners and character. In addition to these she was a humble, consecrated Christian. She came to the wilds of the unknown Territory of Oregon, not as many came in later years, drawn by the stories of the wonderful attractiveness of the climate and soil, but the word went to the East that there were human souls under dusky skins calling for "the Bread of Life," and, actuated by a desire to teach the Gospel of salvation to the heathen on our own shore, she came with her husband, in the second party of missionaries, under the direction of the American. Board, to join the four who had preceded them, and formed the advance guard of the grand army which founded a new civilization on the Northwest coast. The party arrived at Whitman's station, Waiilaptu. September 1, 1838. Mr. and Mrs. Spaulding had established another station at Lapwai, and thither Mr. and Mrs. Gray proceeded, remaining to labor with them among the Nez Perces.

Mrs. Gray entered heartily into the work of teaching the Indian women and children at Lapwai. She commenced her labors immediately, with from fifty to one hundred children, which she taught under a pine tree during the fall, and until a log schoolhouse was built. This is described as a "puncheon" (log hewn flat) seated, earth-floored building; and here she taught her pupils until March, 1839.

One especially interesting fact in connection with her labors there has been handed down to us. She had a remarkably sweet, well-trained voice, and when, on the morning after her arrival, she joined in the singing at family worship, Mr. Spaulding felt that it would be a power in their Sabbath services, and requested her to conduct that part of the worship. When the Indians heard her sing, they were visibly impressed, and afterward spoke of her as "Christ's sister." (The above is related and told by some of the older Indians and Hudson's Bay men.) Whenever she sang they would gather and listen with rapt attention as if to heavenly music.

In the fall of 1839 she left for the Whitman Station, with her husband and infant son, in a Chinook canoe, paddled and steered by two Nez Perce Indians. They remained there, Mrs. Gray assisting Mrs. Whitman in teaching, until 1842, when they came to the Willamette valley. Later they removed to Clatsop Plains, where they resided several years, and finally settled in Astoria.

Wherever they went they strove to advance the Kingdom of Christ, and exerted a decided influence in the cause of education, temperance, and benevolence. In 1846 they assisted in forming the first Presbyterian church in Oregon, with Rev. Lewis Thompson and Mr. and Mrs. Condit, of Clatsop Plains (Clatsop Church, organized September 19, 1846). Seven of their children survive them. They are: Judge J. H. D. Gray, of Astoria; Mary S. (Mrs. Frank Tarbell, of Tacoma); Caroline A. (Mrs. Jacob Kamm, of Portland, Oregon); Sarah F. (Mrs. Wm. Abernethy, of Dora, Coos county, Oregon); Captain Wm. P. Gray, Captain Albert W. Gray, and Captain James T. Gray, of Portland, Oregon.

While visiting at her mother's, a few months before her death, Mrs. Kamm said to her one day: "Mother, I have often wondered how you, with your education and surroundings, the refinements of life you were accustomed to, and your own fastidious personal habits, could possibly have made up your mind to marry a man to whom you were a total stranger, so short a time from your first meeting with him, and going with him such a terrible journey, thousands of miles from civilization, into an unknown wilderness, across two chains of mountains, and exposed to countless dangers. Mother, how could you ever do it?"

While Mrs. Kamm was recounting all these, to her, insurmountable objections to a young lady of delicate sensibilities, and native modesty, her mother sat with her eyes intently fixed upon the carpet, and then, after a few moments' pause, replied with great earnestness: "Carrie, I dared not refuse. Ever since the day when I gave myself up to Jesus, it had been my daily prayer, 'Lord, what wilt Thou have me to do?' and when the question, 'Will you go to Oregon as one of a little band of self-denying missionaries, and teach those poor Indians of their Savior?' was suddenly proposed to me, I felt that it was the call of the Lord, and I could not do otherwise."

And her daughter saw and felt the power and love of Christ that had been the governing principle of her mother's life, and owned the sweet and sacred influence.

Among Mrs. Kamm's first recollections were the little missionary and maternal meetings which were held in their house. She distinctly remembers these meetings, as it was her lot to "take care of the baby," while her mother conducted the simple services, and afterward wrote the minutes in a spare copy-book. The collection on missionary day was never forgotten. These early records would be of the deepest interest now, but they cannot be found.

In 1870, after an absence of thirty-two years, Mr. and Mrs. Gray returned to New York for a visit, going by steamer to San Francisco, and thence, by rail, to New York. One can imagine their sensations, as they were whirled along rapidly over the ground which they had crossed so many years ago, so slowly and laboriously.

On the 8th of December, 1881, Mrs. Gray died at her home on the Klaskanine farm, aged 71 years 11 months and 7 days.

She had taken her seat at the breakfast table, as usual, but, feeling quite unwell, retired to her room. She was seized with severe vomiting, which could not be stopped. She was evidently sinking. Her husband said to her: "Mother, are 'you going to leave us; are you prepared to go?"

"Yes, if it is the Lord's will. I have endeavored faithfully to serve Him, and He will not forsake me now." From this time she appeared to be relieved, and with a little more conversation on family matters, she ceased speaking. Soon after, with an earnest prayer that her children and friends might join her in her Father's House, "not made with hands," there to dwell with her Lord and Savior, Who had been with her through all life's journey, she passed peacefully into her rest.

One who knew her well, writes: "The death of Mrs. Gray calls forth regret from a large circle of friends, who have long known and loved her, and we add our testimony to the valuable life of one whose friendship we valued so much. She came as a missionary, filled with a desire to devote her life and earnings to the cause of Christ, and well did she fulfil that promise, bravely facing all the dangers and deprivations of a pioneer's life—no light thing for one who, like her, had sacrificed high social culture to such a life among Indians, in a wild, far-off, unknown country. Leaving all behind her, she turned her face to the setting sun, laying her life down on the altar of God without regret. She was one of the few women who grow old gracefully. Time only seemed to add sweet grace of manner, and the lines of age on her face showed only kindness, and the extreme patience, of her daily life. 'she hath done what she could.' Who can count the influence of her life and example? A large family, who have gone out into the world, will miss her sweet counsel and admonition. The beautiful description of a good wife, by Lemuel, in 'the prophecy that his mother taught him' (Proverbs, xxxi:10-31), finds a perfect verification in Mrs. Gray's daily life and character: 'The heart of her husband doth safely trust in her; she shall do him good, and not evil, all the days of her life. She layeth her hands to the spindle, she stretcheth out her hands to the poor, and to the needy; she openeth her mouth with wisdom, and in her tongue is the law of kindness. She looketh well to the ways of her household, and eateth not the bread of idleness; her children rise up and call her blessed; her husband, also, and he praiseth her. Give her the fruit of her hands, and let her own works praise her in the gates.' "

Mr. Gray survived his wife about eight years. He spent the last seven weeks of his life at the house of his son-in-law, Jacob Kamm, Esq., of Portland, and died November 14, 1880, aged 79 years 2 months and 6 days.

Besides his missionary duties and the other labors consequent upon his engagement to the American Board from 1836 to 1842, Mr. Gray found time to keep a minute detail of the occurrences of their daily life; and in 1879 he published a "History of Oregon." He had also published lesser works, but quite important, and did much to establish the fact that Dr. Whitman's purpose in his now famous ride across the continent in the winter of 1842-1843, was to save Oregon to the United States.

A handsome monument of Italian marble marks the spot in the Astoria cemetery where they lie. It was prepared as a memorial of love and respect to Mrs. Gray from her husband. "For if we believe that Jesus died and rose again, even so them, also, which believe in Jesus will God bring with Him."

The above sketch is from the pen of Mrs. Amory Holbrook, of Portland, Oregon, a devoted friend of the late Mrs. Wm. H. Gray. Mrs. Holbrook is herself a pioneer of Oregon, widely and highly esteemed. She has devoted her life to her church, and to benevolent works. No one person in Portland has done so much for the First Presbyterian church as has Mrs. Holbrook. She has always been wide awake and energetic in keeping fully abreast of the times in all the work of charity and benevolence. Time brings to her only beauty, homage and love.

Judge McCown, in his "occasional" address of 1884, stated, on page 21 of his address: "No woman ever turned back."

An incident related by Judge J. H. D. Gray, showing the strong character of his mother while living on Clatsop Plains in 1846, just after Mr. Thomas Owens had killed the bad, vicious Indian, "Spuckem," while, as sheriff, he was attempting to arrest him. The Clatsop Indians put on war-paint, and a large number of them rode by Mrs. Gray's house in hostile Indian fashion. Mrs. Gray, at first sight of them, sent her children out into the brush, warning them to keep out of sight. Judge Gray distinctly remembers how they were urged, and finally persuaded to remain peaceful by the eloquent and forcible language of Mrs. Helen Smith, the Indian wife of a white settler, whose great influence over her people is elsewhere referred to in these sketches. Here we have another of the many occasions where a woman's influence saved a whole settlement from destruction by Indian massacre.

> "Take up the white man's burden—
> Send forth the best ye breed—
> Go, bind your sons to exile,

To serve a brother's need;
To wait in heavy harness,
On fluttered folk and wild—
Your new-caught, sullen peoples,
Half devil, and half child.
"Take up the white man's burden,
In patience to abide;
To veil the threat of terror,
And check the show of pride;
By open speech and simple,
An hundred times made plain,
To seek another's profit,
And work another's glain."

—Rudyard Kipling.

CAROLINE CHILDS VAN DUSEN

Mrs. Caroline Childs Van Dusen was the daughter of Lloyd and Amy Childs. She was born September 3, 1825, in Wayne comity, New York. Her father was a farmer. When she was about 6 years old her parents moved to, and settled in, Michigan, then a new country. In 1845, at the age of twenty, she was married to Mr. Adam Van Dusen, who was of German descent.

Mr. Van Dusen's health not being good in Michigan he decided to emigrate to Oregon, and his young wife, being of pioneer stock, was pleased with the idea. Judge Aaron E. Wait, a cousin of Mrs. Van Dusen, then a prominent young attorney, had made up his mind to go West, so they joined forces, and provided themselves with a wagon, five yoke of oxen, one horse and a good milch cow. This wagon differed from most wagons, in that it had a deep bed in which was placed all their provisions for the six-months' trip. Across the wagon-bed projections were placed, widening it out sufficiently to admit of beds being made crosswise of the wagon. Judge Wait's bed was in the front end; there a curtain formed a partition. On the center cross-piece was placed a little round sheet-iron stove, about the size of a three-gallon bucket, with a little tea-kettle, boiler and frying pan. On this little stove cooking was done with great ease and satisfaction. Mrs. Van Dusen says that many times she sat in her cosy kitchen on wheels and cleaned and cooked a bird while the wagon moved along. On cold nights their little stove made their house very comfortable. They had also a little churn in their kitchen. The milk was placed in the churn each morning, and the motion of the wagon churned it, so that every evening they had fresh butter. In this way one cow furnished them with sweet milk, buttermilk and butter, daily. Mrs. Van Dusen says she really enjoyed the trip very much indeed. Their old friend, the late Judge Columbia Lancaster, had an outfit similar to theirs. These two teams left Michigan March 4, 1847, to join the emigration of that year at St. Joseph's river. On leaving St. Joseph's their company consisted of forty-eight wagons, with Wm. Meek employed as a guide. Our wagons were called the "steamboat wagons," on account of their having the little stovepipes passing up through the top covers. We also had a tin reflector for baking bread. There were many excellent people in the company, two young ladies of which I remember especially, a Miss Clum, and a Miss Rollston. Miss Rollston's step-mother, Mrs. Rollston, gave birth to a baby boy while crossing the Platte river. The baby was named Platte. Unfordable rivers were crossed in the usual pioneer way, by turning a wagon-bed into a ferry-boat. Strife and dissension occurred in the company, causing it to break up into sections that would separate, and occasionally unite again as we traveled along until we reached Fort Hall. Here a part of our section decided to go to California, the other part to Oregon. Judge Lancaster and family were our only traveling companions from Fort Hall to Oregon City.

As we progressed our oxen grew thin, grass being scarce. Some days we were compelled to travel all day without finding any feed for our cattle, but we pushed along, finally reaching the Cascade mountains. In climbing a very long, and steep mountain in the Cascade range, our team was, as usual, doubled up with Judge Lancaster's, to take his wagon up first. This left my husband and myself alone at the foot of the mountain. Shortly after two Indians came riding up at full speed. They stopped beside our wagon and looked us over, talking among themselves. We were much frightened, but pretended to be very brave, Mr. Van Dusen having his pistol and knives in his belt and plenty of guns strapped on the wagons, which we examined, walking around and talking: At last the Indians turned their horses and rode away at full speed. In about an hour they returned and went through the same performance, and left us again. To our great relief we saw no more of them. Shortly after this Judge Wait returned with the teams to take our wagon up the mountain.

On the Barlow road, in sight of Mount Hood, we had several heavy rains, making the road very slippery. Late one evening our wagon upset for the second time that day, and as our cattle had found nothing to eat all that day the men had to leave the wagon on its side and go ahead with the cattle in search of grass. We got out a few bedclothes, made a big fire, and sat up nearly all night. We could hear the brush crackling and the wild animals screaming during the night. I suppose our fire kept them from attacking us. The next morning the men brought the cattle back without having found anything for them to eat, and we pushed on until late in the evening, when we fortunately found grass.

We soon reached Oregon City, and put up at the Barlow Hotel. Having arranged my toilet and put on a new calico dress, I went in to supper, and everybody declared I could not have just crossed the plains, for I was not tanned a bit. After a few days we went to the private boarding house of Mrs. Hood, and soon after that we found a house which we rented for the winter. Early in the spring of '48 we prepared to move down the river. About this time our late governor, George L. Curry, was expecting to marry Miss Boone. Mr. Van Dusen sold Mr. Curry his dress suit, and I sold Miss Boone my wedding bonnet, a lovely little bonnet of the gypsy style. They were married, and took our house for their first home.

Mr. Van Dusen had already been down to Astoria and taken up a land claim on the Wallacut river, now owned by Mr. H. S. Gile. When we reached Astoria we decided to give up the Wallacut claim, and take up one on the west side of Young's Bay, in Oregon, and we located on the place now known as "sunnymead" farm, and owned by Colonel and Dr. Adair. Their home stands just where our little log cabin stood in 1849. We lived on this place one year, planting and raising a garden, principally potatoes. The winter of 1849 was extremely long and cold. Adair creek, in which we kept our boat, which was a large one, became frozen up, and we did not see a human face for six weeks.

Early one Sunday morning our dog barked, and Mr. Van Dusen got up quickly, to find the old chief, Walluski, standing at our door. Chief Walluski was then living on Smith's, or Taylor's, Point, just across the bay from us. He came across in a little duck canoe, to the west side, and walked up on the ice. He told us that he had been watching for smoke from our cabin for several days, and, seeing none, thought we must be "memaloosed" (dead), so he came to see. We invited him to breakfast with us, and showed him every respect. I remember this happened two weeks before Christmas, and the chief said that if the ice remained until Christmas he would come and take us to Astoria.

He came, as he promised, and took us across the bay in his big canoe. We remained in Astoria two weeks and then our friends took us safely home in a large boat.

This one year was long enough for us on the land claim, so in the spring of '49 we moved to Astoria. At this time there were but two frame houses in Astoria—Mr. Welch's and Mr. David Ingalls'. We moved into one of the Shark houses, that stood near where the Parker House now stands, in Astoria. These houses were built by the men from the wrecked vessel "Shark."

Mr. Van Dusen had to split out boards for roofing and chinking this house. We had no furniture, except what we made ourselves. Our bedstead was made by boring three holes into the logs of the wall into which end and side rails were driven and fastened to one large log on the floor. We were very thankful, however, for this humble home, and soon made it cosy and comfortable.

About this time Mr. and Mrs. Truman P. Powers arrived in Astoria, and we gave them house-room for the use of their cook stove. We partitioned our house by the use of "clisquises" (mats), purchased from the Indians. These mats were very nice and pretty, being made from dried tides, from three to five feet wide and varying lengths.

Many Indians were camped on the hills near our house, and they seemed to keep up an incessant howling. As Sally, their queen, was very sick, they constantly made night hideous with their medicine performances. The queen's slaves were in mortal terror lest she should die, and they be buried alive with her, according to tribal custom. I became so familiar with their peculiar and varied music that I might have excelled as one of their magicians. Our house stood near 'a little bay, the front of the house being three or four feet above the ground; frequently a number of Indians would come over from Chinook, landing in the bay, then, coming up to the house, stand around the fire to dry out and get warm.

They often slept under the house, and one night an Indian baby was born under there.

The following incident might be of interest: I was always very handy with my needle, and had made me a pretty hood, quilting it very nicely. Mrs. B. C. Kindred was visiting me one day, and, seeing this hood, offered me five pounds of butter if I would make her one like it. I made the hood. Butler was then 25 cents a pound. Time passed, and we built us a comfortable home in Uppertown (Adair's Astoria), and here, in 1852, I was keeping boarders. By this time the California gold mines had made money very plentiful, and produce of all kinds very high. One day Mr. Kindred called and said: "Well, I think it is about time we were paying for that hood. How much is it?" I said, "Five pounds of butter." He replied, "Well, butter was 25 cents a pound then, while it is worth a dollar and a half a pound now." "Yes," I said, "but the price was five pounds of butter." He laughed, and paid the five pounds of butter.

Mr. Van Dusen was the first person in Astoria to sell goods from shelves, the Hudson's Bay Company always having sold their goods from boxes.

My first child, Seth, died in infancy. The next was Florence, born November 6, 1851; then Cara, born January 20, 1851; Brenham, April 16, 1856; Hustler G., October 3, 1858; Lloyd, August 29, 1860, and Mary Amy, May 2, 1863.

Mrs. Florence Westdahl and Mrs. Mary McIntosh live in Oakland, California, and Mrs. Cara Trenchard, Brenham, and Hustler G., and their families, live in Astoria, Oregon.

The above story is given as told by Mrs. Van Dusen, and is of great interest, as coming from one of the very few living actors in the tragic times of our state's pioneer history. In later years, about 1862, Mr. Van Dusen moved his family down to their beautiful modern home, built a little east of the original Fort Astor. This delightful home at once became the most prominent house in Astoria, and here this worthy family cordially and generously entertained their hosts of friends, including many prominent visitors to this Far-Western city.

Although Mr. Van Dusen's hospitable and genial presence is missed from around the family table, his charming widow still lives in her lovely home, surrounded by children and grandchildren, as well as hosts of friends, who appreciate and delight to do her honor, for her true and inestimable worth. Her days are much occupied with her children and grandchildren, yet she finds time to devote to church and charity, and is a pillar of strength in all good works.

"Her air, her smile, her motions told
Of womanly completeness;
A music as of household songs
Was in her voice of sweetness.
"An inborn grace that nothing lacked
Of culture or appliance—
The warmth of genial courtesy,
The calm of self-reliance."

Mrs. Esther D'Armon Taylor, daughter of Esther and Samuel D'Armon, was born in Lancaster county, Pennsylvania, July 17,- .1823.

Her parents moved to Ohio when she was but a child, and there, in 1839, she married James Taylor. They made a home in Kalida, and two children were born to them there, the eldest dying when but two years old. In 1844 there was much talk of the great country on the Northwest coast, and Mr. Taylor decided to join the emigration of the next season, and to take the long trip across the plains. This he did for the love of adventure, and also for the benefit of his health, which at that time had been greatly impaired. He expected to leave his wife and infant daughter in Ohio until his return, or at least until he had seen what this far-off land was like; but Mrs. Taylor would not listen to this plan, and insisted that she was quite as able and ready to go as he. So they made all arrangements, leaving Lima, Ohio, March G, 1845, for Independence, Missouri, where their company was forming. They left Independence May 10, and arrived in Oregon City on the 10th of the following October, after an exceedingly pleasant journey across the plains.

Mrs. Taylor was then just 21. They experienced many hardships and privations, but Mrs. Taylor was always cheerful and hopeful, and quite enjoyed the long journey.

She was often heard to say in later years that the months spent on the road were among the happiest of her life. The last week of their journey came near being a very disastrous one. They were caught in the snow in the Cascade mountains and feared that they would not be able to get their teams through that winter, so it was decided that Mr. Taylor should take the women and children of the party and push on through to Oregon City. They were to take a shorter trail, where the wagons could not pass, and expected to get through in two or three days. But it took them much longer, and their provisions gave out, leaving them for several days almost entirely without food. Fortunately they reached the settlement before they suffered more than severe hunger. The most discouraging time for the pioneers was after they had reached the end of their long journey, when they expected to find some of the comforts of civilization.

Mrs. Taylor was often heard to say that she was more homesick that first winter than at any time on the long journey, or in all the years afterward, and that many times she wished herself out on the plains again.

That first year was spent in Oregon City. In 1846 Colonel Taylor bought a tract of land on Clatsop Plains, and early the following spring he moved his family there. They built the first frame house in that new settlement, and it was their home till the breaking out of the Cayuse Indian war, in 1847, when they went back to Oregon City, and Colonel Taylor, leaving his family there, pushed on and joined the volunteer troops then in the field. They continued to live in Oregon City for a number of years, but returned to their home on Clatsop Plains in 1850. Then their eldest son, the third child, died.

Mrs. Taylor was always energetic, and interested in every good movement. Although not a member of the Presbyterian church at that time, no one was more interested in the building of that little church on Clatsop, which was really the first Presbyterian church in Oregon. After Astoria became a port of entry Mr. and Mrs. Taylor moved there, where they resided until Mrs. Taylor's death, October 23, 1893.

Mrs. Taylor was a thorough pioneer, fond of excitement, and ready for any emergency. Although suffering much from ill-health, and with many family cares and privations incidental to pioneer life, she was always ready to help others and to make and enjoy every pleasure to be gotten out of life.

The above sketch was, at my request, furnished me by one of Mrs. Taylor's daughters, and, though it is true in every particular, I feel that much more should be said of that beautiful, and in every way excellent woman—so well do I remember her myself in my early girlhood.

How ardently I admired her then! Tall, slender and graceful, with dark, sparkling eyes, and rich, black hair, her every movement was grace itself. Her home was always the perfection of order and neatness, and she was hospitable and generous at all times and under all circumstances. I speak from personal knowledge, as our pioneer homes were adjoining farms on Clatsop Plains. Her daughter has truly said: "Mother was always energetic in all good movements." She was, indeed, a type of noble American womanhood, an admirable" example most worthy to be imitated.*

After moving to Astoria, Colonel and Mrs. Taylor's home became the center of attraction for the best society in the land. They entertained much, Mrs. Taylor always presiding with a vivacity, dignity and grace of manner that made their home altogether delightful to her family and a large circle of friends.

This eminently worthy couple lived to celebrate their golden wedding, an event long to be remembered, especially by their pioneer friends.

She died, as she had lived, respected and honored by all who knew her. Surrounded by her loving husband and cherished children, she breathed her last in her beautiful Astoria home. Some months before her death, feeling that her lease of life was uncertain, with her husband she selected the spot that should be their resting place—in the beautiful "old Clatsop cemetery," near where stood the first Presbyterian church in Oregon. Here Mrs. Taylor was laid to rest by tender and loving hands. She was soon followed by the devoted husband, who had honored and blessed her throughout her long and useful life.

There, side by side, these noble old pioneers sleep the last sleep, within sound of the grand old Pacific, whose never-ending music they loved so well.

> "Her queenly form was such an one
> As painters love to trace,
> With raven hair, and deep, dark eyes,
> And steps of royal grace.
> "An inborn charm of graciousness
> Made sweet her smile and tone;
> And glorified her simplest dress

184

With beauty not its own."

The surviving children of Colonel and Mrs. Taylor are Ione E. White, widow of the late Captain J. W. White, of the United States revenue service, Oakland, California; Edward A. Taylor, ex-collector of United States customs at Astoria; Judge F. J. Taylor, present mayor of Astoria, and a prominent attorney of that city; Mary, wife of Mr. Fred. R. Strong, so well and favorably known as a leading lawyer of Portland, Oregon; and Kate, wife of Mr. George Taylor, one of Portland's most worthy merchants, of the firm Taylor, Young & Co.

MRS. NANCY WELCH

Yesterday afternoon at two o'clock all that was mortal of the late Mrs. Nancy Welch was laid to rest in the family vault in Hillside Cemetery. The funeral cortege was the largest ever assembled in this city, over one thousand persons paying this last tribute of respect to the lady pioneer of Astoria.

The funeral took place from the large family residence, corner Fifteenth street and Franklin avenue, and the extensive grounds which surround the house were packed with mourning friends. The services were conducted by the Rev. E.S. Bollinger, pastor of the First Congregational Church, of which Mrs. Welch had been a member for many years. The genuine sorrow at the loss of this pioneer lady defies description. After a useful life of 78 years, Mrs. Welch has now reached the home on high, lamented by an entire city.

The following gentlemen acted as pall-bearers: Mayor E. J. Taylor, W. W. Parker, C. S. Wright, R. C. Carruthers, John Montgomery, S. T. McKean, John Davidson, Dr. A. L. Fulton, Frank L. Parker, Captain Hobson, H. G. VanDusen, J. H. D. Gray and William B. Adair. The members of the Oregon Pioneer and Historical Society attended in a body, and the following beautiful address was delivered by request by Judge Gray, which was written for that organization by Mrs. Oliva R. Welch, wife of Hon. James W. Welch, of Astoria, the eldest son.

Again we are called upon to perform the last solemn duty that the living owe the dead. It is hard for us to realize as we now look upon the serenely peaceful face of the dear mother pioneer, whose hands are quietly folded upon her breast, that her life work is finished, her toils upon the earth are done. But it is true we behold for the last time all that is mortal of the faithful, loving wife, mother, friend and neighbor.

Nancy Dickerson Welch, who at 6:30 p m on Tuesday evening, February 11, 1896, surrendered this life to the God of her fathers, and her body returns to earth from whence it came.

Of her we may truthfully say she was indeed a typical pioneer woman. Born in the then western wilds of the State of Ohio, in Washington county, on the second day of January, 1818. She was inured to the privations and hardships, the toils and dangers of the Ohio pioneers. She lived with her parents until about twenty years of age, who in the meantime had moved into Iowa, and was then left an orphan with nine brothers for whom she thereafter took upon herself the duties of mother and housekeeper. We have heard from her own words how she performed the manifold duties for that numerous family of young brothers, washing, ironing, cooking, and with her own hands weaving and fashioning the necessary garments that constituted this wardrobe, and primitive though they were, she would sew until far into the night, by the light of tallow candles. Sewing, mending, knitting and darning were the necessary employments that occupied her winter evenings, and finding the days too short to encompass the many more active physical duties and labors that fell to her lot. So her busy life ran along until March 12, 1840. At Bloomington, Iowa, she was married to James Welch, and early in 1843, they with a number of families, who had heard of the wonders of the far off land of Oregon, started across the plains with the slow, steady teams of oxen that then took the place of the beautiful palace cars of today. They were compelled to temporarily stop at St. Joe, Mo., during the winter of 1843 and 1844, on account of Indian depredations, until the spring of 1844, when they again resumed their journey. After long, tedious months of journeying, they finally arrived at Oregon City, Oregon, in October, 1844, and in the spring of 1840, Mr. and Mrs. Welch came to make a permanent home in the then trading post of Astoria. And thinking of the Astoria of that time, we can but wonder at the physical courage and fortitude, the serenity and happy contentment that enabled her to at once set to work to help her husband make a home on the banks of the Oregon, within sound of the roar of the Pacific Ocean, with only a few companionable people, surrounded by dense forests, wild beasts and Indians. Her life must, for many long months, have been often desolate and lonely.

To more fully illustrate the indomitable courage of Mrs. Welch we will relate the following incident:

It was the custom of the Indians on the death of a chief or Indian of note to bury their slaves with the dead. On such an occasion, soon after the arrival of the Welches in Astoria, a slave who was to be buried with her master came running to the Welch home for protection. Mrs. Welch took her in and stood guard over her and bravely refused to surrender the refugee, after repeated demands of the Indians thereby forever breaking up that barbarous custom of sacrificing human life to a superstitious custom of the Indians at the mouth of the Columbia River.

Many of the necessaries of living were either procured at the Hudson's Bay trading post at Oregon City, or at Vancouver, which was also a Hudson's Bay trading station. And when we remember that the journey to these trading stations at that early date was made in Indian canoes, which were hollowed out from large cedar trees, and it took from three to four weeks to make the journey, purchase supplies and return, we may be enabled to have a slight conception of the many vicissitudes, trials and hardships this pioneer mother was called upon to endure. Surrounded by her young family of small children, spending the weary days and nights alone, while the father was away on those periodical journeys, getting such necessities as flour and general provisions. Oregon City then owned the only flouring mill in this part of the Northwest, being contiguous to the grain fields of the French Prairie, the only portion of the great Willamette valley settled at that time. On one of the periodical journeys made by Mr. Welch to Oregon City, he was detained many days beyond the time he intended staying, and from much hard work and exposure, Mrs. Welch was taken suddenly ill, having as a companion her only white woman friend and neighbor, Mrs. Ingalls, at whose death bed Mrs. Welch happened to be last fall in the city of Los Angeles, Cal., and along towards midnight, notwithstanding the exertions of Mrs. Ingalls, Mrs. Welch sunk away into a comatose condition. Just at this critical juncture, Mr. W. H. Gray, the honored pioneer, being the only acting physician at the mouth of the Columbia, there being no other physician nearer than Vancouver, came, whether by accident (to stay over the night with his friends as was the custom in those early times) or not, the writer cannot now call to mind; but at all events Mr. Gray had with him his medical case, and after being informed by Mrs. Ingalls that her friend was gone across that bourne from whence no traveler returns, Mr. Gray immediately went vigorously to work with the stimulants he had at hand, and with the aid of hot applications and much rubbing of the feet and hands, they were at last rewarded by returning consciousness. Mrs. Welch has related this incident to the writer, and spoke with much feeling of gratitude of the manly, noble pioneer who saved her life to her family, for many years after he was laid away to rest.

Mrs. Welch was possessed of a rare physical and moral courage, traits that many of those hardy pioneers were endowed with, a moral courage that was so great that it precluded any shadow of cant, hypocrisy or deception. She wore upon her brow throughout a long life of arduous duties trials and temptations, the insignia of moral worth and womanly purity, the brightest jewel in the crown of life. She was a woman who was true to herself, and it naturally followed, as the night follows the day, she was true to others. In relating the many hardships incident to her early life, there was never a shadow of self-pity, never a thought of what might have been, only a womanly, noble, self-reliant feeling that her duty had always been done as best she knew.

I cannot close these necessarily few and meager reminiscences without alluding to her eminently patriotic love for her own adopted Oregon. In the fall of 1894 Mrs. Welch, in company with her youngest daughter, for the first time in all these years visited the scenes of her early life. Visited her only surviving brother in Iowa, and attended the great world's exposition in Chicago, which she greatly enjoyed. But she returned to her dear adopted home in Oregon, happy and grateful in the thought that her home, as she expressed it, was in the best part of God's world. She saw no place, that she thought equalled the evergreen carpeted Oregon. In October last she went for a few weeks' sojourn to her sister state, California, and although she appreciated the many beautiful semi-tropical scenes of Southern California, she again returned to her home, filled with thankful gratitude to her Maker that her life had been spared to again enjoy the dear loved scenes, every one of which the tendrils of her heart were closely woven about. She spoke to us of the great enjoyment it was to again behold the beautiful green grasses and the evergreen trees of Oregon.

So we will lay her to rest 'midst the scenes that she loved, near the beautiful evergreen trees that will evermore sing soft, sweet requiem lullabys as they wave their arms gently to and fro, as though showering heaven's best blessings o'er the beautiful earth which is the mother of us all. And those of us who are left behind for a little while can have a grateful comfort in knowing that the spirit that erstwhile illumined this body has gone again into the loving arms of the Father of us all.

> "A full, rich nature, free to trust,
> Truthful, and almost sternly just,
> Impulsive, earnest, prompt to act,
> And make her generous thought a fact,
> Keeping, with many a slight disguise,
> The secret of self-sacrifice."

Nancy Dickerson Welch Cabin No. 6, Native Daughters of Oregon, was organized November 9, 1899, at Astoria, Oregon, with twenty-two charter members.

MRS. POLLY HICKS MCKEAN

Polly Hicks McKean was born April 24th, 1798, in Delaware county, New York. She married Samuel Terry McKean March 9th, 1817.

After living a few years in New York, they moved to Ohio, where they lived till the summer of 1832, when they made another start west, at the time Illinois was first open to settlers. They stopped on the Illinois river, and laid out a town, calling it Chillicothe, after the town they came from in Ohio.

In 1847 they made another move, west, in company with their two married sons. They had eight children born to them—five boys and three girls. Two boys died while they lived in Ohio; the rest all lived to be grown and married. They left their old home in Illinois April 15th, 1847, with four wagons and a good many cattle and horses, to start on the long and tedious journey across the plains to Oregon. They stopped the first winter at the falls of the Willamette, opposite Oregon City, where they arrived in November, having stopped at Vancouver, which was then in the hands of the Hudson's Bay Company, for a couple of weeks. In February, 1848, they moved down the Willamette to a place called Linton, where there were a few little houses. In September of the same year they put what household goods they had left, after the Indian Whitman troubles, on board a scow-schooner, called the "Calapooia," and came down to Astoria.

Resided in Astoria until 1864, when she, her husband and youngest daughter, then unmarried, moved to San Jose, California.

Her two married sons had preceded them to California, and for a number of years she resided with one or the other of them at or near San Jose.

After the death of her husband, which occurred near San Jose, February 12th, 1873, she continued to live with her eldest son for a time, and afterward with her son-in-law, Mr. J. M. Battee, of San Jose. She survived her husband four years, and died April 15th,

1877, while on a visit to her daughter, Mrs. Eliza Hustler, at Astoria, Oregon.

It is difficult to describe or estimate such a life and character as hers. So quiet and unassuming, creating no stir in the world, not differing greatly from thousands of women, especially during the early and middle part of this century, and yet she possessed strong individuality and independence of mind. Never robust in body, with limited education and opportunities, she was looked up to and loved, not alone by the members of her family, but by all with whom she came in contact. She had no patience with cant or hypocrisy in any form, did not believe much in secret societies, her creed consisting principally in doing good when and where and to whom you can. As a parent she was devoted and self-sacrificing, perhaps too indulgent, but always endeavoring to instill in her children habits of industry, temperance and independence. She seemed to realize more fully than most persons the futility of looking to others for help in the various difficulties of life, and that to attain success at all one must be self-reliant and persevering.

Withal, she was very charitable toward others' faults, and no child or person in trouble ever went to her in vain for sympathy or such help as she could give.

"For all her quiet life flowed on As meadow streamlets flow,

Where fresher green reveals, alone,

The noiseless ways they go."

MRS. RACHEL MYLAR KINDRED

Mrs. Rachel Mylar Kindred was born in Kentucky in 1821, and is the great-grand-niece of the celebrated Daniel Boone. Like her illustrious ancestor, her life has been filled with deeds of courage and endurance. And now, at the advanced age of 76, she is still vigorous, both in mind and body. Her household and farm are under her immediate direction and control, and are well and systematically managed.

While a young girl, Miss Rachel Mylar moved, with her parents, to Missouri, and there met and married Mr. B. C. Kindred, in 1841. Mr. and Mrs. Kindred, with their baby boy, Henry (since so well known as Capt. Henry Kindred), joined the emigration of 1844. Mr. Kindred's team became nearly exhausted before reaching the summit of the Blue Mountains, and Mrs. Kindred was compelled to complete most of the remaining journey on foot. Her shoes and stockings soon gave out, and her clothes became thin and ragged. Thus, with bare feet, bruised and swollen, and with sunburned face, arms and hands, she toiled on, always preparing the meals, and assisting her husband in every possible way. This long and tedious journey was completed December 24th, 1844, when Mr. and Mrs. Kindred reached Oswego, on the Willamette river, near Portland, Oregon. Here they pitched their tent and unloaded their scanty provisions. The next evening Mrs. Kindred was presented with her first Christmas gift in Oregon—a fine, large, healthy baby boy, whom she called James. This son is still living, and has been a blessing to his mother in many ways. At the death of his first wife he gave his mother his baby girl, Gussie, whom

Mrs. Kindred has reared from babyhood. She is now a strong, healthy woman, and a devoted and loving granddaughter.

During the winter of 1845 Mr. Kindred proceeded down the Columbia river to Clatsop, and bought the improvements on the land now known as Gearhart Park, from a Mr. Jerry Tuller, for which he gave one yoke of oxen.

On New Year's eve Mr. Kindred and family reached Capt. R. W. Morrison's on Clatsop plains, where they remained a few days, and then removed into their new home, a little log cabin 10 by 12. There they lived till November, 1846, when they sold their improvements to a Mr. Motley and moved upon their donation land claim, now known as New Astoria, and Kindred Park, where they have since continued to live. Here Mrs. Kindred began in earnest to assist her husband in building their future home. Mr. Kindred was occupied in freighting between Astoria, Portland and Oregon City, and of necessity was compelled to be absent from home most of the time.

Their home was in the midst of a large settlement of Indians, whose burial grounds were nearby. To Mrs. Kindred these were days long to be remembered, with three small children, one a babe, and only two or three white families for miles around, yet she never faltered. During these early and lonely days of toil and hardship she had many and varied experiences, among which I will mention two.

Going down to the beach in front of her house one day, she found a man, cast away on the shore, in a helpless state, apparently about to die. She got him home to her house, after which she recognized him as a discharged soldier who had been living with the Indians. According to their custom, they had cast him away when they thought him dying. Mrs. Kindred nursed him back through a long illness. He had no money, but gave her a shotgun in payment for her services. After his recovery, however, he went back to his Indian friends. He soon began to want his gun and, forgetting the kindness and debt of gratitude he owed his kind benefactress, he went to her house, in her absence, and stole the gun. Mrs. Kindred soon discovered who had taken the gun and, taking her little son and a little girl who was staying with her, she went straight to the chief and laid the case before him. The chief commanded the man to deliver up the gun, which he did at once. The chief then reprimanded him severely for what he had done.

Later on, the schooner Woodpecker, loaded with flour, was wrecked on Clatsop Spit. The settlers, knowing that she must soon go to pieces, set about trying to save the flour, which was at the time worth $12 a barrel. The weather was unsettled, and they could work but a short time during the last part of the ebb tide, as the water was breaking over her most of the time. On the second day they had only succeeded partially in cutting away the hatch, when driven away by a strong wind and incoming tide. They found it impossible to make a landing on the beach and were forced to take refuge in Tansy creek. Mr. Kindred and his two sons were of the party, and were congratulating themselves on having secured seven sacks of flour, and were contented to wait till the turn of the tide and wind late in the evening. Mrs. Kindred, becoming worried about the non-arrival of her husband and boys, went down to the beach to look for the boats. Meantime the flood tide had completed the work begun by the men and had broken up the deck and floated out the entire cargo of flour. When Mrs. Kindred reached the beach there was not a boat in sight, but she saw what she said looked like a large flock of white birds. The tide was bringing the Woodpecker's cargo ashore. Mrs. Kindred understood the situation at a glance, and did not hesitate one moment, but removing all unnecessary clothing, she waded in up to her armpits, meeting the incoming flour, and bringing it to shore, and then carrying it, sack by sack, to a place of safety, beyond reach of high tide.

Hour after hour passed; still she worked, not realizing fatigue, so stimulated was she by her success. Late in the evening Mr. Kindred and the boys landed with their valuable cargo of seven sacks of flour, to find 360 sacks landed and stacked on the beach by Mrs. Kindred, who was still watching for any stray sacks that might come within her reach.

Mrs. Kindred is a pure blonde, below medium height, with small hands and feet, and when young was quite slender. She is a woman of strong principles, upright and just. She has, all her life, strictly attended to her own business, and now, at the age of 76, her mind is clear and active. Both her and Mr. Kindred's memory of early events is good.

Six years ago Mrs. Kindred sold her half of their donation land claim—320 acres—to a syndicate for $25,000. It was platted and named "New Astoria." Two years ago Mr. Kindred bonded his half (after reserving two blocks upon which their home stands) for $35,000.

Mrs. Kindred is the mother of twelve children, thirty-eight grand-children and twelve great-grand-children, all of whom are residents of Clatsop county excepting two.

MRS. HANNAH PEGG PEASE

Mrs. Pease says:

"I was born in Staffordshire, England, September 16th, 1825, and came to America with my parents when I was four years old. We were eleven weeks crossing the Atlantic Ocean. On reaching New York, my parents settled in New Jersey, where we lived eight years. Then we moved to Illinois and settled in Jerry county, where I met and married David E. Pease, March 16th, 1845. Owing to ill-health, we decided to move to Oregon, and therefore we joined the immigration of 1849, and started on the first day of March. We had a good trip, and no difficulty with the

Indians, due to the fact that they had heard that there was a company of soldiers just behind us on their way to Oregon.

"We arrived at Mr. Foster's, at the foot of the Cascade Mountains, on the 6th of September, 1849. Mr. Foster took a crowd of us out to his corn and potato field, and we all helped gather corn and potatoes. Then we went back to our camp and cooked them, and we thought we had never tasted such good corn and potatoes before.

"After reaching Oregon City we embarked in an Indian canoe for Astoria, with Mr. and Mrs. John Minto, Mr. Judson and a young man named Legrand Hill. On the way down I became so frightened that we got on board a vessel at Oak Point and came on it down to Astoria. From there we went up the Lewis and Clarke river to Hunt's mill, that was being built by Hunt and Judson. Here Mr. Pease was employed by Mr. Judson, as were also Mr. Legrand Hill and Mr. Isaac, who crossed the plains with us and continued with us through the winter. Mr. Pease received $75 per month. In the spring of 1850 we moved to Lexington, near Skipanon, and rented a log house— 24x18—with an upstairs, where we kept boarders. This house was built by a Red river Indian, on the bank of the Skipanon river, near the landing, which was then used by all the Clatsop people, and within fifty feet of where the schooner Pioneer was built the year before by Owens, Tibbetts, Perry and Trask, and commanded by Capt. Robert McEwan, who now lives on Clatsop.

197

"The Pioneer was loaded principally by the Clatsop farmers, and taken to San Francisco in 1849. The vessel and cargo was sold at a great profit to all concerned. This brought a great deal of money into Clatsop, and people were going and coming to and from the mines, which made money plentiful, and everything brought high prices. So we opened our hotel at this thoroughfare. Butter cost $1.50 per pound, $6 per bushel for potatoes, and 50 cents a pound for sugar of the poorest quality that would not be used at all nowadays, and 25 cents a pound for meat. We received $1 a meal and $16 per week for board.

"Later, we bought the block on which we lived—one acre—from Mr. Wirt, for which we paid him $1200.' In 1853 we took up a donation land claim, on which a part of Warrenton now stands. We lived in a little log cabin near where Mr. D. K. Warren's handsome residence now stands, five years, then moved back to Skipanon and bought Jerry Tullen's donation land claim, and built the house in which O. B. Wirt now lives, and kept a livery stable for twenty-two years, running teams to and from Seaside with freight and passengers.

"My husband was the first postmaster at that place. He received his appointment while from home. He was in Oregon City, disposing of his teams, and was present at the hanging of the murderers of the Whitman massacre. He held the office of postmaster about fifteen years, and at his recommendation the office was called Skipanon, and as time went on the little town dropped its old name of Lexington and adopted that of the postoffice. In June, 1850, the first general election was held at our hotel, and Mr. Pease was elected sheriff. Also the first court, as far as I know, was held in September, 1851, by Judge Strong, in our house. We sold our old home and part of our buildings to C. A. McGuire in 1879, and built us a comfortable little home, where I now live with my adopted daughter and granddaughter. Here Mr. Pease and I celebrated our golden wedding anniversary in 1895. My husband died in June, 1896, and was laid to rest in the old Pioneer cemetery, near the first Presbyterian church of Oregon."

Mrs. Jerusha Brennan Wirt was born in Indiana in 1822, and was married to Mr. A. C. Wirt in 1840. Mr. Wirt was born in Lancaster county, Pa., in 1814.

Mr. and Mrs. Wirt lived in Illinois until 1843. Their first child, Andrew, was born in October, 1842.

In the spring of 1843 they started for Oregon. They traveled as far as Missouri, and there they wintered. In March their daughter, Annie, was born. A month later they joined the emigration of 1844, under Capt. Gilliam, at Independence. The company was a large one, and after a few days a section of twenty-five wagons moved on ahead, Mr. Wirt and family among them. They elected a Mr. Bunton captain. No deaths or serious accidents occurred.

On the Sweetwater between two and three hundred Indians surrounded them, with drawn bows and arrows, but the courageous pioneers were ready for them. They had already secured their stock within the pioneer corral of wagons, and every man stood, with rifle cocked and revolver and knife at his side, ready for the attack. No shots were, however, exchanged, as the Indians concluded it was the better part of valor to withdraw, which they did.

This small company pushed forward and reached Portland on the 10th of November, fifteen days in advance of the main company.

Mr. and Mrs. Wirt wintered in Oregon City. Mr. Wirt was a tailor by trade, but the only job he got was to make one blanket coat.

During the winter Mr. James W. Welch, Mr. Barton Lee and Mr. Wirt hired an Indian canoe and came down the river to Astoria and Clatsop to look for a place to locate. Mr. Welch located in Astoria, but Mr. Wirt found Mr. Perry, an old friend, on Clatsop, and Messrs. Perry, Trask and Morrison offered to give Mr. Wirt a portion of their claims if he would locate and be neighbor to them. This generous offer was accepted, and he at once set about building his log cabin, on the same spot where later the Rev. Lewis Thompson built his residence.

Early in the spring of 1845 Mr. Wirt employed Samuel Smith, better known as "Tickey" Smith, to move his family and effects to Clatsop in his plunger. Smith landed them at the Indian settlement where now stands Fort Stevens. From that place Mr. Trask moved them to their new home on Clatsop by an o t team. "Tickey" Smith lived on Smith's Point, now known as Taylor's addition to Astoria.

Smith took up his land as a claim, and when the donation land law came into effect he married the Indian woman with whom he lived, to make good his title. Later, Colonel Taylor bought this land, for which he gave about $700. Two children were born to Mr. and Mrs. Wirt in their Clatsop home. In the fall of '49 Mr. Wirt left his wife and four small children with Mrs. James Welch in Astoria, and he and Mr. Welch went to the California gold mines. They embarked in the old brig "Henry," which sailed from Astoria the last week in September. They lay in Baker's Bay (in sight of Astoria) till the 7th of November, over a month, unable to get to sea owing to bad weather. Mrs. Wirt wrote to her husband begging him to give up the trip, but he would not. There were 125 passengers on board, booked for California, but twenty-five, including Captain Kilborn, became discouraged and deserted the ship and returned home while she was yet in Baker's Bay. Then the mate, Mr. Ray, took charge of the ship, and after a terrible trip of seventeen days, succeeded in reaching San Francisco with no loss of life. They encountered a fearful storm, in which the sails were blown to shreds, and the deck load was all lost, including many wagons and 30 barrels of flour. In the midst of the storm Captain Ray gave orders to throw everything overboard except the two barrels of water. Mr. Wirt said that Mr. Welch, who was a giant in strength, being six feet tall and weighing over 200 pounds, tossed those barrels of flour overboard with greater ease than an average man could have thrown over a 50-pound sack.

Mr. Welch and Mr. Wirt went to the mines together and in' the following May Mr. Wirt returned to his Clatsop farm with $3000 in gold dust. In the summer of '49 he traded his Clatsop farm to Sam Gardiner for his Fort Clatsop farm. But Mrs. Wirt was not willing to move so far back in the woods with her four small children, so Mr. Wirt bought a block—about an acre—in Lexington (now Skipanon), for which he paid $700. This townsite was laid out and platted by Mr. Jerry Tuller. This was the block on which Mr. Wirt now lives. Mr. Wirt moved his family into a log cabin. The Wirt cabin, and a board shanty, with a lean-to, for a blacksmith's shop, belonging to a Mr. Swazey, who had a Kanaka for a wife, constituted the city of Lexington.

Mrs. Wirt gave birth to her fifth child, Philip, in February, 1850, and died one week later of puerperal fever, and was one of the first to be laid away in the old Clatsop cemetery. Mr. Wirt sold his block of land in Lexington to David Pease in 1850 for $1200. In August, 1850, Mr. Wirt married Miss Susan M. Kimball, of the Whitman massacre fame. They began building their present home in September of that year. They paid $165 for the three thousand bricks to build their chimney. These bricks came around the Horn as ballast. The lumber cost $75 a thousand, in the rough, at the mill. This mill stood on the east bank of the O'Hanna river, just north of where the A. & C. railroad crosses it, near Seaside. The mill was built by John Moreland. A Mr. Walker took the contract for $900 and board to build their home. He was nine months completing his contract. Everything was done by hand, and done well. The house was thirty-two feet square and two stories high, with eight rooms; ceilings, nine feet, and parlor sixteen feet square. Mr. Evans plastered the house throughout, and it was the first plastered house in Clatsop county. The house is in a fine state of preservation at the present time. All the early pioneers especially remember this house for the many dancing parties and good suppers they enjoyed within its hospitable walls in early days.

Mrs. Susan Kimball Wirt was born in Frankland county, Vermont, in 1831 and crossed the plains in 1847, reaching Clatsop in the spring of 1848. Her first child, John, was born in, November, 1857. Hattie (Mrs. Rieman) was born in December, 1852; Ione, July, 1854, and O. B. Wirt in 1856. Mr. and Mrs. Wirt kept a hotel and horses and wagons for hire for twenty-five years. They are now enjoying a quiet life in the old home where they have lived for fifty-two years. Mr. Wirt, now 89, is a hale, hearty man. He can plow and sow and reap and mow as fifty years ago. He drives to the beach, several miles away, for his winter's wood. He cultivates and tends several acres of ground, and always raises a fine garden, and plenty of roots for his milch cows. He and Mrs. Wirt especially enjoy the present mode of reaching Astoria by the railroad. Mr. Wirt greatly enjoys the annual reunion of the pioneers, and never fails to attend the meetings of the Pioneer Association.

OBITUARY OF MRS. SUSAN KIMBALL WIRT

DEATH TAKES A SURVIVOR OF THE WHITMAN MASSACRE

One by one the pioneers of those stirring days of Oregon's early history are passing to the unknown future, and as each death is recorded, memories are revived of the part they took in exciting events.

There are few of the survivors of the famous Whitman massacre of 1847 alive. The last to be taken by the hand of death was Mrs. Susan M. Wirt, of Skipanon, Oregon, whose demise occurred on February 29th, 1905.

At the time of the massacre Mrs. Wirt, then a girl of sixteen, was accompanying her parents, Mr. and Mrs. Nathan S. Kimball, across the plains from Indiana to the territory of Lewis and Clarke. The family were natives of the State of Vermont, where the subject of this sketch Was born in 1830. Three years later they journeyed to Indiana, where they remained till the spring of 1847. After untold hardships the family reached Whitman Mission, near Walla Walla, where they decided to remain for the winter.

The day before the massacre Mr. Kimball tried to convince Dr. Whitman that the Indians were planning a raid, but the doctor would not believe anything was wrong. The following afternoon the Indians began the awful attack, which resulted in the death of thirteen men and one woman, Mrs. Wirt's father being one of the number. The Indians stole all that was of any value to them, and left the sick and almost helpless women and children at the mission. For some time Mrs. Wirt remained with her mother at the mission, but finally came to Oregon City.

Later the mother of Mrs. Wirt remarried and the family settled on a farm on Clatsop Plains, where Mrs. Wirt resided until she was married and moved to Skipanon, Oregon, where she died.

Among the many honored pioneers of Oregon, and one well known in Clatsop county, is the name of Mrs. Harriet Kimball Jewett. She was the second daughter of Josiah and Sarah Sanborn, her mother's maiden name being Shepherd. These two families were pioneer people of Northern Vermont, and plainly showed what stock they were made of during the Revolution.

Harriet Sanborn was born in Richford, Vermont, February 26th, 1809, and was married to Nathan Schofield Kimball February 21st, 1830. In the winter of 1833 they moved to Indiana, where they lived until the spring of '47, when it was decided to move to Oregon, not only for the good things promised, but for health. I have often heard my mother say, at this time, that she seldom thought of going to bed without first giving a dose of quinine to some member of the family. Consequently, that spring father sold everything but what was needed on the trip, and on April 14th, 1847, began the long journey across the plains. The family consisted of seven children, the eldest a girl of 16, and the youngest a baby of three months.

They had what was called a good start; two wagons, four yokes of oxen, a brood mare, two cows, $1500 in gold, and last, but not least, the children's pet dog. The money was in $5 pieces and was sewed in three belts, father, mother and my eldest sister each wearing one all the time. Nothing more than ordinary events happened on the trip until we reached the Platte river country. There a little sister of three years did. As it was in the heart of the Indian region, it was necessary to make her grave in the road and drive all the teams over it in order to obliterate all traces of it, otherwise the Indians would have desecrated the grave for the clothes. When crossing the Snake river my oldest brother, aged 14, caught a severe cold from getting wet, and after a week's suffering, he died September 26th, 1847. It was late in the fall when we reached Whitman Mission, near Walla Walla, and there my father concluded to stay for the winter. There was plenty of work, a good school for the children, and fine pasturage for the tired, worn-out cattle. But my father's suspicions of the Indians was aroused by their removing a lot of wheat from the upper room of the big house in which they lived, where they had it stored. I have often heard my mother tell that just the night before the massacre father talked about it to Dr. Whitman till 1 o'clock a m., but he would not believe anything was wrong. The measles had broken out at the mission, and Dr. Whitman treated all alike, but the white children got well while the Indians died, because they would jump into the water when they were burning up with fever, so they were made to believe that Dr. Whitman was poisoning them and curing the whites.

The massacre occurred on the afternoon of November 27th, 1817. Lather was only wounded at first, and ran to the Whitman house, where he staid till the next day, when he tried to slip home, but the Indians saw him, and just as he was climbing the fence at the back of our house he was shot and killed right before our eyes. Although I was only six years old, I can remember seeing him fall down by the fence.

The Indians were not satisfied with killing alone, but cut open the bodies, took out the hearts and burned them. After this the Indians were at liberty to come in and out, as they pleased, and help themselves to what they liked. What my mother endured then can never be told—her husband killed, two boys that were likely to be killed at any moment, and a daughter that might receive treatment worse than death. One woman, thinking she would be good to the Indians, and thus get their favor, gave them cake and pie till they were sick, then all the other women had to eat some, to show that it was not poisoned, or they would have killed her, too.

My mother always firmly believed that the massacre was at the instigation of the Roman Catholic priests, for they came there the following day and buried the dead, and all the Catholics were sent from the mission, on one excuse or another, a few days before the massacre, and returned as soon as it was over. We remained at the mission a month longer and were then brought to Oregon City, but there was nothing left of the good start but the money, which we managed to keep securely secreted. Even the dog that had followed all the way, had to be left on the bank of the river.

The Indians had taken everything else, even to almost all our clothing.

April 15th I had a new father and seven more brothers and sisters.

My mother married John Jewett, and then we came to Clatsop county, where we lived and grew to man and womanhood. Our first home was near Seaside, but even there the Indians were not to be trusted, and we moved to the farm now owned by Josiah West, where we lived till we separated to homes of our own.

My mother lived to the good old age of 83, and died in Astoria at the home of her youngest daughter, Mrs. F. H. Surprenant, leaving seven sons and daughters, seven grandchildren and fifteen great-grand-children.

The above was related by Mrs. Sophia Kimball Munson, second daughter of Mrs. Jewett by her first husband.

Mrs. Almira Raymond was born in West Troy, New York, in 1827. She united with the Methodist denomination at the age of fifteen. Married W. W. Raymond in September, 1839, and with him joined the Methodist mission then forming in New York City for the purpose of sending missionaries to the Indians of Oregon. The Lausanne was chartered, and fourteen families and five single women sailed in her on the 29th of September, 1839. After a long and stormy voyage of eight months, during which Mrs. Raymond was almost continuously seasick, they crossed the Columbia river bar in May, 1840. The Lausanne passed up the river to Vancouver, reaching there in June. From there the missionary party went up the Willamette in canoes, and settled at Salem, where Mrs. Raymond's first child was born, a little girl, that died at birth.

From Salem Mrs. Raymond removed to The Dalles (then Wascopum), where her second daughter, Martha, was born, in 1842. In that year Mrs. Raymond returned to Salem and remained there till 1846. During this time two more daughters were born. The third died at birth. The fourth, Aurelia, was born in 1845.

The winter of '45-6 was especially severe. Mrs. Raymond passed this winter in a tent. The snow had to be cleared from the roof of the tent every few hours, it fell so fast. The principal part of their diet was dried peas.

In the spring of '46 they removed to Clatsop Plains, where Mrs. Raymond lived until 1849. On the plains two children were born— William, her first son, in 1846, and the fifth daughter, Annie, in 1849.

This year Mrs. Raymond removed to Upper Astoria, and was living there when the Sylvia de Grasse was wrecked. There a second son, Nathan, was born, in January, 1850.

Late the next spring, or early in the summer, Mrs. Raymond moved to Tansy Point, where she resided until 1855. At 'Tansy Point two children were born, James, in '52, and Zilpha, in 1855.

While Airs. Raymond lived at the Point, Dr. Dart made the famous treaty with the Indians at Tansy Point, and during this time the Indians had the smallpox, which carried off so many of them. In one camp (Terwent's) all were down at once, and not a scrap of anything to eat. They were not allowed to go near any house, and were dying of starvation as much as from the disease. One of the Indians got into a canoe and came to Mrs. Raymond for help. She took the half of all her provisions and put them by the canoe for him. He got back to his camp with them, but died that night. (Smallpox in 1852-3. Dr. Adair.)

In 1855 Airs. Raymond moved to Tillamook. This was during the Indian war, and Mrs. Raymond and her children, with all the other settlers, were shut up in Trask's fort, awaiting an attack that never came.

While in Tillamook another son, Louis, was born.

In 1850 Mrs. Raymond moved to the Indian reservation known as the Grand Ronde reservation, and was there when the hostiles, under Chief Limpy and Old John, were brought there, and it was there that her last child was born, a little girl, who lived to be but four years and a few months old.

The next year Airs. Raymond spent in traveling, going to The Dalles for a few months, then back to Clatsop, then down to Tillamook again, remaining there until November, 1858; then back overland to Clatsop. It rained the entire trip, and Airs. Raymond was swept from her horse by the surf, in rounding one of the capes of the short sand beach, and nearly drowned. This was one of her most disagreeable trips. As, however, the trip at that season of the year was of her own wish, she could not well complain.

Mrs. Raymond lived at 'Pansy Point until 1802, when she moved to Astoria. In 18(: she procured a divorce from her husband. She then returned to the Point for a time and then went back to Salem. While in Salem she sold her half of 'Pansy Point (now Flavel) to John Loomis, her son-in-law, who promised to pay her $1000 and provide her with a home during her remaining life. However, she received but $100. This money she soon spent in church work and then went in debt. Her daughter paid her mother's debts many times. Finally, not being able to collect the remaining $(00, she went to live with her daughter, Mrs. Martha Loomis.

Mrs. Raymond hated trouble of any kind. She "took no thought for the morrow," but put her trust in the Lord, and got cheated in all her transactions.

Mrs. Raymond was a very pious woman, who thought taking care for the future showed a want of trust in the Lord, and was therefore a sin.

An instance of this was given when the new Methodist church at Salem was built. Aurelia Raymond sent her mother ten dollars every month expressly for the rent, sometimes more, but never less.

When Aurelia went to Salem and asked what was owing, she found, among other debts, $50 for rent.

"Why, mother, how is this?" she asked. "I sent you the rent money every month."

Mrs. Raymond said a man had promised to give the Methodist church $10,000 if they would build a finer church than the Presbyterian church in Portland, and she said she felt the Lord had opened a way for her to assist in that great work, so she gave the money to the church and let the rent go.

"But, mother, that money was for the rent, and it should have been paid."

Mrs. Raymond's answer was: "The cattle on a thousand hills are His."

Dozens of like instances could be given, showing Mrs. Raymond's unworldly character. No woman, in truth, could have been more unfitted for the privations of a pioneer life, for she was not strong, and naturally took no care for the future. That natural trait was intensified by her religion, which made her think she committed a sin if she took any care for the things of the future of this life. Then, her religion was so entirely a matter of emotion that unless she was in such a state of mind as to be regardless of everything in this world, she felt that she had lost faith, and was unhappy. Mrs. Raymond suffered much from ill-health the last years of her life, as well as from the loss of sight. She died in 1880. A woman, kind-hearted, peaceful and sincere, she obeyed literally the command: "Take no thought for tomorrow." She could not but suffer more than the ordinary privations of the pioneer.

(The above sketch was prepared by a daughter of Mrs. Raymond. Believing it to have been conscientiously prepared, having known Mrs. Raymond well myself, I give it as prepared.)

Mrs. Raymond was a benevolent woman, kind and generous to a fault, but entirely without thrift or economy and, as her daughter has said, utterly unfitted for the privations of pioneer life. She was always placid and unruffled, leaving all her trials and tribulations to the Lord. And, in the midst of want and confusion, she could sing praises to the Lord, never seeming to realize that the Lord required anything of her except the worship of mouth and spirit. The following are the names of the passengers who sailed on the ship Lausanne from New York September 29th, 1839: Rev. J. L. Parrish, wife and three children; Kane and wife; Dr. Richmond, wife and child; J. II. Frost, wife and two children; A. F. Waller, wife and two children; L. A. Judson, wife and three children; Hamilton Campbell, wife and two children; Oley and wife; Henry B. Brewer and wife; W. W. Raymond and wife; Abernathy and wife and two children; Jason Lee and wife, Miss Phillips, Miss Phelps, Miss Clark, Miss Ware, Miss Langton.—(Dr. Owens Adair.)

Mrs. Margaret C. Gearhart, widow of the late Philip Gearhart, was born in Pennsylvania in 1812. Her parents moved to Ohio in 1814, and in 1835 Margaret C. Logan married Philip Gearhart in Decatur, Indiana. Immediately after her marriage, they moved to Iowa and made their home in Henry county until 1843, when they moved to Jefferson. Here their eldest two children, the late John W. Gearhart and Mrs. Annie E. Stout, were born. Mrs. Sarah L. Byrd and Hayden Gearhart were born in Jefferson county, Iowa. They fanned in both of their Iowa homes.

In 1848, after a persistent effort to continue their home in a fever and ague country, Mr. Gearhart determined to try the far-off Oregon country, which then began to be known as a wonderfully healthy region. With a young family of four children, the youngest five and a half months and the eldest a girl only seven and one-half years old, Mr. and Mrs. Gearhart left Iowa April 10th, 1848, for Oregon. They joined a train in Iowa of thirty-three wagons, known that year as "the Star-Belknap Company," and with it crossed the plains. They celebrated the Fourth of July at Independence Rock.

The prime cause of the Gearhart's start for Oregon was to find a healthy country, he and his family having so grievously suffered with chills and fever in Iowa that Mrs. Stout remembers having ridden a horse to plow corn when she was only five years old, the plow being held by her brother John, then only eight, the rest of the family being down with the ague.

The Gearharts had the usual trials of pioneers crossing the plains. At North Platte Mr. Gearhart fell back one day, joining a party of nine wagons, and with them reached Oregon City. September 28th, 1848. Here Mr. Gearhart found the late Joseph Jeffers, who had reached Oregon in 1847, settling in Clatsop county. Mr. Gearhart's first question on meeting Mr. Jeffers was: "Where is the healthiest part of this country?"

Mr. Jeffers replied: "If health is what you are after, go down to Clatsop." And down to Clatsop the Gearhart family came.

Mr. Gearhart bought the donation land claim, as filed upon by Mrs. Marion Thompson and husband, paying therefor $1000. On this place Margaret Gearhart assisted her husband in making one of the most comfortable homes in Oregon. A portion of this Gearhart farm has been improved, and is now favorably known as "Gearhart Park."

Within six weeks after reaching Oregon Mr.* Gearhart succeeded in locating his family and his effects in his Clatsop home. He had four cows, two calves and two fine American mares, as well as a lot of twenty-one cows, obtained in exchange for his plains team of oxen and wagons. Mrs. Gearhart at once began the dairy business, with a good supply of milk, but no pans or buckets. Mr. Gearhart, however, soon made spruce "keelers," or small tubs, that were very good for holding milk, but which required close attention and much washing and scalding. On this Clatsop farm Mrs. Gearhart became the mother of two more children, Maggie, now Mrs. Charles Butterfield, and Pierce Gearhart, of Idaho. Mrs. Gearhart has five children and twenty-two grand-children and great-grand-children now living.

Among many incidents of pioneer life this, as related by Mrs. Byrd (Sarah L. Gearhart), ought to be remembered. She says:

"I remember, in 181!), an Indian, by name 'Whatcom,' came to my father's house on Clatsop Plains and stole a pair of new wool socks. Mother had carded the wool, spun the yarn on a little wheel she brought across the plains, and knit the socks. Father sent word by Mr. Robinson, an old pioneer living near us, for the Indian to bring back the socks. The Indian came, but not to bring the socks, and not alone. He had only thirteen more Indians with him. They came as far as our barn and sent my older brother, who was there thrashing out wheat with the cows, to tell my father to come down to them; they were going to kill him. My father loaded two muzzle-loading rifles, which meant just two shots, put some balls, caps and powder in his pockets, took up a large walking staff, said good-bye to mother and the children, and walked out in view of those fourteen Indians. To win or die was the question. I can remember so well just how it all looked to me. When the Indians saw my father coming toward them their leader utter just one word 'Clatawa' (run), and they did run, for over two miles, to a neighbor, Mr. Thomas Owens. Afterward Mr. Owens told my father that the Indians said Gearhart was after them and was going to kill them all, and asked me to save them, somehow.' Mr. Owens was at this time sheriff of Clatsop county, and while the Indians had a proper respect for him as an officer, they also had confidence in his ability to protect them when necessary, and afterward appealed to him for protection when they had trouble with the settlers."

Mrs. Byrd further relates that in crossing the Deschutes river some Indians rode up to them, threw rawhide ropes over the heads of the oxen, and, after helping them across, asked pay for their services, and her mother paid them in biscuits.

(SISTERS)

Mrs. Ann Perry, daughter of Mr. and Mrs. William Abell, was born December 18th, 1818, in Tippecanoe county, Indiana, in sight of General Harrison's home. She married William T. Perry July, 1839. They left Indiana April 1st, 1842, and crossed the plains that year. With them came a sister of Mrs. Perry, a young widow, having a baby girl, Rosalthie. They journeyed as far as Green River in wagons. There they left their wagons and completed their long trip on horseback. On Platte river they met a Mr. Eldredge Trask, a young trapper, and he traveled on with them to Oregon City. He soon fell in love with the young widow, and upon reaching Oregon City they were married.

This little company while on the plains fell in with Fitzpatrick, an old trapper, who rendered them invaluable service, he being familiar with the Indian character and language, thereby preventing serious trouble while passing through the Sioux country.

The Perrys and Trasks spent their first winter in Oregon City and, as far as I can find, lived in the first frame building in Oregon, built by Mr. Perry, who was a millwright.

Early in the spring of '43 Messrs. Perry and Trask moved their families down to Clatsop Plains and took up for themselves farms about the middle of that then beautiful flower garden. They built themselves a home on the Perry farm, which both families occupied. On October 15th, 1843, a daughter was born to Mr. and Mrs. Perry. This little girl was named Mary, and she has the honor of being the first white child born in Clatsop county. She is now the wife of Mr. Fred Shrowder, a wealthy farmer and dairyman of Coos county, living on the banks of the beautiful Coquille river. Mr. and Mrs. Perry lived and prospered in Clatsop county, but he was of a migratory nature, and not contented to stay long in one place. In 1851 he moved, with his family, to Douglas county, locating in Roseburg, and buying a large tract of land on Deer creek. Roseburg now stands on part of this land. In 1852 Perry built at Roseburg the first grist mill of Douglas county. In 1859 he again moved, this time to Coos county, and settled on the Coquille river, about two miles below Myrtle Point, where Mrs. Perry assisted her husband to build their third and last home in Oregon.

At this home Mrs. Perry died in June, 1872, at the age of 54 years and 6 months, surrounded by her husband and children.

Mrs. Perry was a true pioneer, and never objected to giving up a comfortable home, which had taken years to acquire, and going uncomplainingly with her husband to begin again in a new and unbroken region the toil and struggle of building another home. She was a good neighbor, a true and faithful wife and helpmate, always carrying her full share of the burdens of life. There were five children born to Mr. and Mrs. Perry—Vale, Mary, Emily, Dora and Vela. All are married and have families, and are now respected residents of Coos county.

In December, 1843, a pair of twin girls were born to Mr. and Mrs. Trask on Clatsop Plains—Harriet and Martha. After these, in due time, came Bertha, Jane, George, William, Charley and Ada. Mr. and Mrs. Trask remained in Clatsop county until 1852, when they removed to Tillamook, settling on a river since known as Trask river. They were among the first settlers of Tillamook county, and did their share in opening up that part of our state. Mrs. Trask lived, as did other pioneer women, devoting her time to her husband, her children and her home. She was especially noted for her happy and good-natured disposition, as well as for her benevolence and whole-heartedness. She lived to a good old age, seeing her children grown and settled in life. She was respected and appreciated by all who knew her. In gathering pioneer data I find that Mr. Eldredge Trask did more to assist the early settlers to reach Clatsop than any other one person. He was a large, strong man, with a big heart and good, generous nature. For several years he assisted every family, meeting them either at Tansy Point (now Flavel) or Skipanon, and taking them to his own home, or whatever place had been provided for them.

Later on, in Tillamook, during the Indian war of 1855-6, Trask built a fort, in which all the neighboring settlers were protected for five or six months, known as Fort Trask. He thoroughly understood the Indian character, and was a tower of strength in any time of trouble with them.

Philipina Veith, daughter of Christian and Frederica Veith, was born in Rheinpfalz, Bavaria, and came to America in 1831, with her parents, when 13 years of age. She married Mr. Conrad Boelling in Cincinnati, Ohio, and soon after went to Peoria, Illinois, to live, but, owing to the malarial climate, concluded to come to Oregon in search of health. They arrived in Astoria in 1819, and have made their home there ever since that time. Her mother, Mrs. Frederica Veith, now a widow, came with her, and made her home with her until her death, which occurred in 1878.

Mr. Boelling died in Astoria February 1st, 1885.

Mrs. Boelling is the mother of eleven children, only five of whom are now living, eleven grand-children, eight of whom are living, and fourteen great-grand-children, nine of whom are living at the present time. She lives in her own home, well cared for by her children, two sons and two daughters being yet at home.

She has seen Astoria grow from a few houses at the edge of the water, with a dense forest behind them, to a busy little city, with all the modern conveniences and comforts, and from traveling in Indian canoes, as the only means of travel, to seeing large ships from all ports lying in the harbor, and having fine steamers and later, hearing the whistle of the locomotive in town; from having the mail brought around the Horn in a sailing vessel and getting it once a year, to having it left at the door by a mail carrier several times a day.

(The above sketch was furnished me by members of the Boelling family, with the request that it remain without any changes.—Dr. Owens-Adair.)

JOURNEY TO PORTLAND, VIA PANAMA

FORTY-SEVENYEARS AGO

Mrs. Holbrook was a personal friend of Dr. Adair and she takes pleasure in giving the following interesting article by her a place in this volume.

That Mrs. Amory Holbrook was an easy and pleasant writer is well known among all her friends. Whatever came from her pen was stamped with that bright and sympathetic humor that was so marked a characteristic of her speech and manner.

In the present year of 1899 a little booklet came into print for private circulation, giving an interesting account of the exodus of the Couch and Holbrook pilgrims from Boston to Portland, Oregon in 1852. This makes charming reading, even to the uncaring stranger who feels no special interest in the pioneer experiences of the early Oregonians.

The little company, eleven in all, who made the journey by way of Panama, consisted of Amory Holbrook, United States attorney for Oregon Territory (which then comprised the three states of Oregon. Washington and Idaho, with a part of Montana), his wife and two children and nurse; Mrs. Caroline Couch and her three daughters, and Mrs.

Eliza Ainsworth, of Cincinnati. B. F. Goodwin, of Marblehead, was also a member of the company. As an illustration of Mts. Holbrook's sparkling sense of humor, the following incident that occurred while the boat was delayed at Havana may be quoted from her booklet:

"The staterooms opened out upon a passage-way leading to the guards, the doors facing each other. Those in the rooms across from ours were Mr. and Mrs. Grimes. Mr. Grimes was a wealthy Honolulu merchant, whose wife was in the very last stages of consumption. She was very seasick, as were also Mrs. Ainsworth, Mrs. Couch and I and many others. During the night she was very ill and her moans were most distressing. Miss Carrie went in and endeavored to relieve her sufferings, soothing her in every possible way. When we learned in the morning that poor Mrs. Grimes had paid the penalty of her own folly in eating immoderately of cucumbers, etc., in that tropical climate, by her death, in the early morning, we were not surprised.

"A peculiar feature of Mr. Grimes' sorrow at the loss of his wife was his going to the staterooms of the ladies with whom he had become acquainted, telling them of his loss, and concluding with a kiss, saying: I know you sympathize with me.' The husbands of these ladies were differently affected by this. Some' laughed, as though it was the funniest thing they ever heard. Others were of the same mind as Mr. Holbrook, who, when he came into the stateroom, asked me if I had heard the sad tidings. When he heard of the singular manner in which Mr. Grimes claimed my sympathy he was too indignant to be silent and he exclaimed:

"'And you let him!'

"'Why, yes,' I replied, "the poor man was so full of sorrow.'

"The journey across the isthmus was made on mules, and occupied nearly three days. They traveled by night in order to avoid the heat, stopping at ranches by day to rest."

"One incident," she wrote, "greatly amused us, and whenever it came into our minds, made great laughter and fun. At intervals along the road were large tents spread for the refreshment of travelers—restaurants.

"To our great astonishment, the mule carrying one of our elderly ladies, the dearest and sweetest of the whole company, and the most demure, suddenly started up a hill to the right, making straight for a saloon, at which he had evidently been accustomed to call, and not content with stopping at the door, rode right in, coming out at the other end. The dear little lady, somewhat chagrined at having been compelled to make such a call, turned her head back as she came out, to join in the laugh of her companions, when the pole supporting the end of tent caught her bonnet, and the mule galloped off by himself, leaving her seated on the ground, quite unhurt, but a little startled. The gentlemen rushed to her rescue and she was soon reseated upon her subdued steed."

After arriving at Panama Mr. Holbrook decided to remain at the isthmus ten days, the time being spent on a pleasant little island in the bay, where the mountain breezes strengthened them for their voyage on the Pacific. Shortly after arriving at San Francisco they embarked for Oregon on the steamer Columbia.

"We arrived off Astoria Friday morning, and just above, a few miles, we met the steamboat of which Captain John J. Ainsworth was master, the Lot Whitcomb, as fine and hand' some a passenger boat as any in eastern waters at that time. He came on board to welcome his mother, and we all remarked how much they looked alike, and after we had gotten started again we learned to our amusement that she was his stepmother.

"We arrived at Portland at daylight Saturday morning.

During the day we had a call from Miss Mary Dryer, daughter of the editor of The Oregonian, a very pleasant young lady."

They did not remain at Portland, but went on to Oregon City, which was to be their home for several years. After touching on the* many changes, marriages, births and deaths that had occurred in the forty-seven years that had elapsed since that historic journey, Mrs. Holbrook concludes as follows:

"It may fall to a younger hand than mine to make the record of the succeeding years, but I shall be satisfied with the granting of this one petition: that the blessing of God—Father, Redeemer and Comforter, the Name which is above every name—may be upon us, and upon our children to all generations."

ADDRESS BEFORE THE PIONEER SOCIETY OF OREGON

(By Hon. Charles W. Fulton, Astoria, United States Senator from Oregon)

"The last of the Mohicans" is the title of one of Cooper's most interesting tales. The hero of the story, though a savage, is pictured as possessing many noble and admirable traits of character, but his heart is heavy, and dark forebodings cast a shadow over his pathway, for he has witnessed the downfall and dissolution of his tribe, and he realizes that ere long none will remain to recount the achievements or perpetuate the legends and traditions of his people.

I come before you today to speak of the last of the pioneers. They, too, were among the noblest of their race; but their lives were not disturbed by any fears for the preservation of their posterity. On the contrary, animated by that confidence which is born of the lofty courage, fortitude and strength of character necessary to the successful prosecution and consummation of all great undertakings, they felt and knew it was given to them to reclaim the wilderness from savagery and lay the foundation for future states—states destined to be peopled with millions of their countrymen, if only they should plan the foundation wisely and build it deep and strong.

That they did their work ably and well, all generations following them will testify. Under them the trackless plains and primeval forests were converted into productive fields and fruitful gardens. "Where rolls the Oregon," who once "knew no sound save his own dashings," was soon heard the echo of the ax, the hammer and the saw, and the wilderness became "quick with life." The wigwam and hunter's lodge gave way to the settler's cabin, the school house and the church; and amidst this "solitude of centuries untold" was now heard the laughter of children and the "sweet and solemn hymn of Sabbath worshipers." Settlements widened into communities, and communities broadened into states, all under the shadow of the Stars and Stripes, and dedicated to human freedom, religious and political liberty.

Such, in brief, was the work of the Oregon pioneers. I have said that they were the last of the pioneers, and in a sense they were. True, since then many others have gone out into the wilderness and builded for themselves homes, but they have followed in the footsteps and camped on the trail of the Oregon pioneers.

The conditions under which the Oregon Country was occupied and settled differ widely from those attending the settlement of every other section of our country. All previous frontiersmen had located within reaching distance of support and supplies. Even the Pilgrim fathers and early settlers on the Atlantic Coast could, in a comparatively short period of time, by ships return to the old world, or send for food and protection, but when the Oregon pioneer had crossed the Missouri river and turned his face to the setting sun there was in front of him two thousand miles of wild, unsettled, practically unexplored and unknown country. At the end of his proposed journey, and inspiring him to undertake the passage, was the surf-beaten shore of the Pacific, where the warm winds from the tropic currents keep the flowers in perennial bloom and clothe the earth ever in the garb of spring.

Between were trackless plains, wide belts of treeless wastes, affording no protection against the all-penetrating alkali dust, the blistering heat of the summer sun, or the freezing blasts of the winter winds. Lofty mountain ranges interposed their rocky sides to the passage of the weary, foot-sore beasts of burden and heavily laden wagons; and as if these difficulties were not sufficiently great to cool the ardor of the most enthusiastic emigrant, this wide, wild region was nowhere inhabited by a civilized people, but throughout by numerous tribes of the most cruel, crafty, bloodthirsty savages this world has ever known. Such were the conditions attending the migrations of the Oregon pioneers.

We have been accustomed to hear of the hardships and dangers endured by the early settlers of the Atlantic Coast portrayed and described in poetry, prose and song, their sufferings commiserated, their courage extolled. And that too much has not been said, may not be said on either behalf, I most freely admit. Yet how small the obstacles they faced, how few the dangers attending their migrations, how inconsiderable the hardships they endured, compared with those of the Oregon pioneers of the '40s and early '50s. The early pioneers of the Atlantic Coast reached their destination in ships. Their real dangers and deprivations commenced at the end of their journey, while those of the Oregon pioneers began at the crossing of the turbid waters of the treacherous Missouri and continued, with every possible variation and addition, throughout their long, trying journey of two thousand miles, and when their destination was reached were probably not greatly less than those with which the early settlers on the Atlantic Coast had to contend.

In all the annals of history there is no story more thrilling, more romantic than that of the Oregon pioneers. No feature is wanting to lend to it all the intense interest of the most absorbing works of fiction. No hero of Cooper, or of the Western border, ever faced a situation so pregnant with dangers and hardships, or gave such proofs of the highest order of courage and strength of character as was evidenced by our pioneers in making the journey from the Missouri to the Pacific. In truth, the Oregon pioneers were by nature molded and designed for the great work they accomplished, and which only such as they could have accomplished. They were, as a rule, born and bred pioneers; were the product of generations of the best pioneer stock. The task which they so willingly undertook, and so splendidly performed, would have been impossible for the passengers of the "Mayflower," or any people less acquainted with and inured to the hardships and vicissitudes of border life. The Oregon pioneer was strictly *"sui generis'* His education, while not deficient in book knowledge, covered a wide range in that school of experience which peculiarly and especially fitted him to meet and successfully contend with the difficulties and dangers incident to frontier life. He could frame an excellent code of laws for the government of a community or state, shoe a horse or mend a broken wagon wheel, as the occasion required. He could solve a problem in mathematics, shoot a grizzly, set a broken limb or match a red devil in cunning, as the exigency of the case might demand.

That they were men and women of exceptional resources, fortitude and courage is evident, though, for the matter of that, such is usually the character of the pioneer. The coward does not venture amidst the dangers and discomforts of such a life, and the sluggard prefers slumber and repose to toil and hardships. Only the enterprising and brave are actuated to become pioneers. Particularly is this true where the point of destination is distant and the hardships and dangers to be encountered exceptionally great. Such were the conditions attending the early settlement of America: hence the remarkable mental and physical vigor, energy and progressiveness of our colonial ancestors, and hence the unparalleled progress we have made as a nation. The isolation of our territory, the great distances between it and all thickly populated countries, the dangers and difficulties necessarily encountered in reaching it, and the hardships to be endured in subduing it, all contributed to its being peopled with a hardy, energetic, self-reliant and resourceful race.

Much has been said and written on the question of to whom credit is due for turning the tide of immigration to the Oregon Country in the first instance, and thereby saying to the United States this great and splendid domain. The question is deeply interesting, but too wide to be discussed fully here if reference shall be made to any other topic. Originally our claim of title to the Oregon Country was based on discovery, exploration and settlement. The sources of our title may be broadly stated to be (1) the discovery of the Columbia river by Captain Robert Gray, a citizen of the United States, in 1792; (2) the visit and exploration of Lewis and Clark in 1805-6; (3) establishment of a trading post by John Jacob Astor at Astoria in 1811; and (4) occupation and settlement of the territory by citizens of the United States.

That the discovery and naming of the Columbia river by Gray and the explorations of Lewis and Clark were necessary and vital links in our chain of title all will admit, and here I may add that while we could not properly base any claim of title to this territory on our purchase of the Louisiana territory, yet that purchase is inseparably associated with, and in a sense, resulted in our acquisition of the Northwest Territory, for had we not acquired Louisiana it is improbable that the Lewis and Clark expedition would ever have been undertaken; and not only did their visit constitute an important link in our chain of title, but the interest excited by their report and the publication of their journal did more, probably, than all else in directing and attracting attention to the marvelous resources and natural advantages of this section, and ultimately in its settlement by citizens of the United States.

Certainly Astor and the missionaries Whitman, Lee and others are entitled to much credit for what they did, both in the matter of strengthening our title by occupancy and inspiring immigration. While it is true that Astor came here primarily and avowedly for the purpose of engaging in the fur trade, there is evidence that he, also, hoped thereby to assist in strengthening the title of the United States to the Northwest Territory. Indeed, Irving in his "Astoria" directly states that such was -one of the motives that inspired Mr. Astor to the undertaking. The missionaries probably had little, if any, thought of promoting American settlement and possession when they first located here, but they subsequently did much to encourage and assist such immigration.

The actual settlers, however, the pioneers of 1842-3, were the final and concluding factors in securing this great domain to the United States.

The cause of their coming cannot fairly be credited to any particular individual, company or association. In truth, the real cause was that mysterious, resistless force that has been in operation throughout the centuries. It has impelled the migrations of mankind with a power as unyielding, as continuous as that of gravity itself.

It carried the civilization of Greece to Rome; of Rome throughout Western Europe; of Europe to America; and of America to the islands of the Pacific seas.

Professor F. G. Young, in an exceptionally able and interesting article published in the Quarterly of the Oregon Historical Society, December, 1900, truly says: "In a sense the Oregon movement was in preparation from the time when, in 1636, Puritan congregations were led by Hooker and others from the vicinity of Boston westward through the forests to the banks of the Connecticut."

The statement is true, but I think he might with equal truth have said that the movement was then in execution, as it had been for thousands of years before. For centuries the tide of emigration has set westward, due, doubtless, to the love of adventure ever dominant in courageous, hardy, restless natures, but evidenced, I submit, most pronouncedly, most strikingly, in 1843, by a thousand men and women voluntarily quitting comfortable and secure homes and dwelling places and, unattended by any military escort, boldly plunging into the very heart of a wild, unknown, practically unexplored region, inhabited only by predatory bands of merciless savages, and entering upon a journey of two thousand miles through such a region—a journey they knew would be attended with hardships and dangers that no tongue can describe, no pencil can picture. The undertaking was without precedent, and it will remain without parallel. In conception and execution, those wonderful, marvelous journeys rise to the grandeur of an epic, worthy of commemoration by a Homer or a Virgil.

The immigration of 1843 may be said, I think, to have been the real substantial beginning of the permanent occupation and settlement of the Oregon country. Like a mighty wave from an exhaustless sea breaking over or sweeping aside every barrier, came the great human tide of that memorable year. Exhaustless, in truth, was the sea, and the tide never ebbed, and the wave never receded, but flowed steadily, resistlessly onward.

Memorable, indeed, was that year. It witnessed the sovereignty of this republic indelibly stamped upon the Oregon Country. After that immigration there might be discussions, debates, diplomatic storms, boundary commissions, even war, but the firm tread of a thousand American settlers on Oregon soil was the stamp of fate, the seal of sovereignty.

Memorable, also, is that year, because of the great names it saw added to Oregon's roll-call of heroes—James W. Nesmith, Jesse Applegate, John G. Baker, Daniel Waldo, Thomas G. Naylor, Peter H. Burnett and many others who became distinguished in the early history of the Northwest. The greatest of these were Nesmith and Applegate, both men of exceptionally strong character and conspicuous ability. Nesmith was the stronger, completer man of the two. He will ever he remembered and honored in Oregon for the splendid support he gave to the Union cause during the civil war. Though elected to the Senate of the United States as a Democrat, he gave to President Lincoln and his policies earnest and loyal support, and, being a man of exceptional ability, his support was of great value to the administration and reflected luster and honor on our state.

No matter how often or in what distant years the roll of Oregon's great and honored names shall be called, the name of Nesmith will ever be found in the list, for his name and fame will only grow grander and brighter as time wheels onward in its unwearied, unending flight.

But should you ask me who of all those heroic hosts are entitled to the highest praise and admiration, whom, above all others, we should reverence and honor for exceptional courage and fidelity, my answer would be: "The women, the pioneer women of Oregon." History furnishes no record of more genuine heroines than were they.

That men should willingly subject themselves to hardships and dangers such as the pioneers were compelled to face and endure, though sufficiently remarkable, is not incredible. But that refined, cultivated, delicately-reared women as readily undertook the journey, as calmly faced the dangers and endured the hardships, will be deemed a myth in ages to come, and some future poet may be expected to picture them as an Amazon race.

Picture in your own mind, if you can what must have been their trials and sufferings on that long, weary, trying journey. Children were sometimes born on the way. How terrible must have been the physical and mental suffering of a mother, nursing her young babe in the fearful heat and dust of a long wagon train, crossing an alkali desert with the bed of a freight wagon for a mattress, and harassed by the knowledge that merciless savages might be lurking about the trail seeking an opportunity to attack.

And then the women had their work to do, and plenty of it, cooking at the campfires, with little to cook, and less wherewith to cook it. But there were hungry mouths to fill; little folks were tired, fretful and impatient, and all called on mother for help. Mother must do this, and mother must do that. Mother! What a world of love and gentleness does that word, that sacred name, imply. Mother must cheer up all. Teach patience here, encourage there, and minister everywhere. And when the long journey was ended, and the pioneer homemade, how much need then of domestic sunshine; and was it not the little wife and mother who supplied the most of it? Then there were clothes to make, yarn to spin, and cloth to be woven in the loom, new stockings to knit, old ones to mend, and all this, also, must mother do. At the same time, she must be chambermaid, housemaid, cook, milkmaid, and maid of all work. Yet it is marvelous what cheer she provided with so little, so very little oftentimes, wherewith to provide it.

Would we evidence our appreciation of the highest courage, the purest patriotism, the most profound devotion to home and country of which history has any record, we would erect on some historic spot in this, our beloved state, a monument—a splendid monument of whitest marble—and dedicate it to the memory of the world's greatest heroines, the pioneer women of Oregon—they who did, dared and suffered more than all others to reclaim the Northwest country from savagery and the wilderness and preserve it as part of the domain of this republic.

But for their courage, their sacrifices and their devotion the towering peaks of Hood, St. Helen and Rainier would this day stand as the silent sentinels of British sovereignty and the British flag. Yet what monument can we erect to them that will endure as long as their memory will be honored and revered? Their glorious achievements, their noble lives and characters constitute an imperishable monument to the highest type of American womanhood.

Many of them have already passed over to the last grand camping ground. Those who yet remain with us are even now entering the darkening shadows of the falling night, yet above and beyond the shadow and the darkness they behold the gathering dawn of a new and a grander day. For whatever reward is given in the future life for duty faithfully discharged here has surely been earned by them in full, rounded and heaping measure. As they pass from amongst us we will place their sacred forms at rest on the banks of the noble rivers which their fidelity preserved to this people. There they shall sleep throughout the centuries, lulled by the murmuring waters as they flow "onward and past us forever," while the snow-capped dome of Hood, emblematic of their purity, elevation and sublimity of character, shall stand and be known as their monument throughout the ages.

From that lofty summit will look down upon them and the vast domain which their devotion secured to this nation, not forty centuries only, but eternity itself.

CLATSOP PIONEERS

In selecting these six names from the roll of honored Clatsop pioneers who materially aided in the upbuilding of Astoria, the first city founded on the Northwest Coast, "the Venice of Oregon," I would not convey the impression that there were not many more equally worthy. But these were my friends. I knew and loved them for their many lovable qualities. Differing widely from each other, they all possessed in a marked degree qualities worthy of admiration and love.

Love has countless sources from which to spring, countless roots through which to feed and flourish. There is the love of parent and child, of family and friends; the love of sex; hero worship, or love; the love of intellect and soul; of fame, wealth and power; the love of the grand and beautiful in nature; and last, but by no means least, the love of God and humanity.

It is time the world ceased giving but the one narrow sex definition to that mightiest and broadest of all words—*Love.*

JOHN HOBSON

Mr. John Hobson was born in England in 1824, and came to the United States in early boyhood.

With his father, sisters and brother, the late Richard Hobson, he crossed the plains in 1813. They and my father's family were in the same division, which brought the two families very closely together, an association which grew into a lasting friendship and later resulted in a permanent relationship.

John was a strong, healthy lad of 19, who, by his faithful, untiring, unselfish labors in camp and on all the long, tedious and unbroken road, won a place in my mother's heart which he never lost.

Soon-after reaching Oregon, his father and mine located on Clatsop, but a few miles apart, and both within the sound of the mighty music of earth's grandest sea.

Here John at once set about assisting his father in the support of the motherless younger members of his family. This brought him into our family much of the time, until his marriage with my beautiful sister Diana.

As a boy, Mr. Hobson was honest, faithful, truthful and industrious, never shirking any duty, and as "the boy is father to the man," so he grew into a clean, pure manhood.

In all my association with him, which extended over fifty years, I never heard him give expression to an oath or a foul word, which was the more remarkable, considering early rough customs and contaminating influences. He was quiet and unassuming and, withal, one of the most modest men I ever knew, so much so that it became the subject of ridicule with people by no means his equal. There was no roughness or coarseness about him. He went right on, attending strictly to his own business and meddling with that of none. He never forgot his early time of struggles and privations, which fitted him for a life of thrift and frugality. He was in truth, a "self-made man," having had less than one year's schooling in his boyhood.

I have frequently heard him relate how he learned to read, spell and cipher in the old pioneer way by the light of a tow string in a mug of dirty grease; but he had a most remarkable memory, particularly for names and dates, and, in fact, for everything. Like a sponge, he absorbed information, and then stored it up for future use, to be called up at will.

I well remember that after his and my sister's trip to Roseburg in 1858, when I returned to Clatsop with them, he could not only recall every man and woman he met going and coming, but he could give their names and all the details of what they had said and done. His eyes were ever open to all that went on around him. No one could have written the history of Oregon in detail with more accuracy than could he. Many a time have I said to him:

"Oh, John, what a shame it is to let so much of Oregon's history die with you! Do begin now and write down all those early facts before it is too late."

But he never had any confidence in his own literary ability, and he always under-rated himself in all respects, so it was never done. He was a good and constant reader, and was unusually well informed. He had even a remarkable knowledge of geography, and always kept posted on what was being done at home and abroad. In reality he was educated in all the essentials of life, through his thorough digestion of his extensive reading, though, of course, deficient in the rudiments. He could have made a fine linguist, as he had no trouble in picking up any language with which he came in contact. He acquired the Indian jargon then so much in use so quickly and thoroughly, imitating the difficult guttural sounds so perfectly that a listener out of sight of the parties talking could not distinguish his speech from that of the Indian with whom he was conversing. In addition, he also learned much of the native Indian tongue, which the Indians were greatly averse to using in the presence of the whites, and by this knowledge he more than once obtained information of great value to our people.

After the tragic death of the wife of Governor Gaines Mr. Hobson, by the advice of my father, purchased the governor's farm, as he and my sister Diana were shortly to be married. Here they lived for many years, making their home the most beautiful on Clatsop at that time, and here, surrounded with luscious fruits and the sweet fragrance of flowers they passed the springtime of their wedded life. Here all their five children, except baby Maude (now Mrs.

Clyde Fulton, of Astoria), were born, amid the singing of birds, the humming of bees and the sweet breath of gorgeous and beautiful blossoms.

My sister's home was a model of neatness and sweetness, made charming by all that nature, intelligence and industry combined could create and provide.

Later they removed to Astoria, where Mr. Hobson and Mr. D. K. Warren became partners in the grocer's and butcher's business combined. I have often heard Mr. Hobson say that during all their business relations not one unpleasant word ever passed between them. With two such upright, unselfish and conscientious men there arose no occasion for unpleasantness, and there was none, notwithstanding one was a Republican and the other a Democrat. How well if all men would emulate their example!

Mr. Hobson was appointed Collector of Customs at the Port of Astoria under the administration of President Cleveland, and filled the position with credit to himself and "his constituents at large.

After my sister's death, which occurred in 1874, Mr. Hobson, several years later, married a second time, continuing to live at the family residence in Astoria, where three more children were born to him. There, in 1896, he died, surrounded by his good wife, Anna, and all their children, and was lovingly and reverently laid to rest, with the wife of his youth on his right, and a vacancy on his left which was filled within the year by the faithful mother of his three younger children, who are now all grown and taking their part worthily in life. The relations between the two families have always been, and still are, most harmonious and pleasant.

COLONEL JAMES TAYLOR

Colonel James Taylor was born in 1809, and came to Oregon in 1844. He was a man of education, refinement and courtly bearing, yet possessing in full measure those sturdy qualities of forceful energy, determination, bravery and perseverance indispensable to the successful pioneer. He began life as a farmer, in which occupation his cultivation and refinement was no bar to his success.

Later, removing to Astoria for educational advantages for his children, he built a beautiful home, where he and his charming wife dispensed the most delightful and generous hospitality, not alone to his fellow-townsmen, but to the whole state, whose best people felt honored by its bestowal.

Colonel Taylor was an ideal husband and father, an ideal citizen, and a noble "epistle to be known and read of all men." His chivalry and sympathy were so great that to him no human creature was too poor or mean to be treated with consideration and respect, and his salute to a poor, mixed breed woman was as courtly as if she were the highest lady in the land. I have seen him take the child of a poorly dressed woman from her arms and assist her off the unsteady boat to the slippery landing with not only the grace of a Chesterfield, but what is better, the true kindness of a Christian gentleman. He seemed to see the angel in every human "house of clay," and do it homage. He was such a lover of home, country and humanity that he was as truly the loyal, chivalrous, hospitable gentleman at home as abroad. I believe he was never guilty of a dishonorable thought or act. There was in him a reverent regard for the individuality of every human being such as I have rarely seen equaled in any other, and it was the root of his profound consideration for even the humblest, a quality which, to my mind, adds a charm to personal independence. Indeed, it is true nobility. All this, and more, Colonel James Taylor proved himself to me during my early struggles in Astoria. He always met me with a gracious smile and a warm shake of the hand.

During the early days of the civil war a company of United States soldiers was stationed at Fort Canby, fifteen miles from Astoria. As usual, the officers were ready and anxious to entertain, especially as they had handsome quarters. They had only the town of Astoria from which to draw for guests, and, being strangers to all, they were obliged to depend upon some resident to fill out a list of guests for their invitation. Naturally their choice for this duty fell upon Colonel Taylor, who, in fulfilling it, did what only an unusually broad-minded man would have done in those days of strife and hatred, and showed his good judgment and magnanimity (being himself a strong "Union" man) by including in the list members of both political parties. Nor did he forget the lowly widow, and it was to him that I owed my passport to the charmed circle of "Brass Button" society. Many were the brilliant, and to Astorians, then, unexcelled entertainments given by those esteemed officers at Fort Canby, and in return the citizens and heads of invited families did their utmost to reciprocate their attentions in kind by social 'functions in their own homes.

Colonel Taylor had the misfortune to break his leg by the fall of his horse when he was past 80 years of age, yet he recovered from this injury quickly and without deformity, which is very unusual at that time of life. His uniform kindness and politeness never failed him during those trying weeks of enforced idleness and weariness. Truly he was, beyond all question, one of "Nature's noblemen."

CAPTAIN GEORGE FLAVEL.

Captain George Flavel came to Astoria at a very early date in its history and identified himself with its seafaring interests continuously, directly or indirectly, up to the time of his death in 189..

Little is known of his early life, as he was of a proud and reticent nature, which repelled any inquiry into his private affairs; not that there was, presumably, anything to conceal, for during the whole of his long life in Astoria, which was open to all, his honor was unquestioned, and he invariably showed the greatest scorn for hypocrisy or meanness of any description. But there was a dignity and reserve in his demeanor which even those nearest him did not venture to attempt to break through.

He was not unapproachable, however, for any worthy object, as many solicitors for aid to deserving charities can testify, and he could and did give excellent advice when asked for it. He never offered it unasked, for his business acumen was of the best, as exemplified by his own success in acquiring an independent fortune by his judicious management, as well as by his personal industry and daring. For in those early days the only pilot boat on the Columbia bar was a small schooner, and the life of a pilot, which was for years his occupation, was anything but a safe or easy one.

Many were the hair-breadth escapes of the seafaring men of that time. On the occasion of the loss of the steamer General Warren, in 1853, Captain Flavel was on board of her as pilot, but the ship's captain insisted on crossing the bar in the evening, against the judgment of the pilot, and she went aground on a sandbar. Captain Flavel, with two other men, embarked in a small boat on the desperate and only chance of obtaining assistance. They battled with the waves and in the darkness for hours, guided only by the seaman's experience and instinct and, finally, when almost exhausted and despairing, they succeeded in making a successful landing at daylight on Clatsop Beach through the surf. They were the only souls saved, the rough seas of the turning tide having beaten the doomed ship to pieces and drowned all on board before aid could reach her.

I stood in great awe of Captain Flavel in my early life. I did not even dream that he ever thought of or even noticed my struggles until 1872, when I was en route to Philadelphia to enter a medical school.

He then said to Mr. Hobson, who was a close friend of his: "That woman deserves great praise. She has accomplished more through her own efforts than any woman I ever knew."

His voluntary, eulogy I have always treasured and prized far more than gold. I knew from that time on that Captain Flavel had been and was my friend, and the knowledge was a tower of strength to me.

In later years, when I no longer feared to approach him, I saw more of him and knew him better, especially after I went to live at Sunnymead farm and he had purchased Tansy Point and other property adjoining, now known as "Flavel," where he so loved to sojourn and work during his declining years. We often met at this time, going to and from Astoria, frequently engaging in conversations which afforded us much pleasure, and he often invited me to his home.

The following incident illustrates the character of the man. When he sold his Tansy Point property for $350,000 he was to receive $100,000 down, the payment of which was made in the form of a check. I was told that he received it, glanced at it, crumpled it in his hand and thrust it down into his pantaloons pocket. Then, taking up the mortgage for $250,000, he strolled leisurely down to the court house to have it placed on record. Later, when the proprietors of Flavel were trying to "boom" their newly-acquired purchase, they gave a grand clam-bake, which was held on their grounds.

Residents of Astoria and Clatsop were out in full force, with waving banners, decorations and archways, to receive and escort the speakers and the poet of the day and the several hundreds of guests from Portland as they came steaming up to Flavel, amid the flutter of flags, the screaming of whistles and inspiring strains of music by the band. It was indeed a great day. Before leaving for home. Captain

Flavel came to me and said: "Well, doctor, this is truly wonderful! You and I never expected to see this day."

"No, captain," I said, "but I hope we may live to see the realization of all the prophecies that have been made today."

Captain Flavel had a will of iron, with which he did not fail to control himself, as well as others. He was a born commander, but a magnanimous one, and working men were eager to be employed by him, for, if he exacted the best of service, so, also, did he pay the best of wages, with most gratifying promptness, adding generous commendation when deserved. Astoria bears the impress of his master hand on almost every corner, but never for ill. He was loyal to the little city of his adoption, and made his interests largely hers. Her finest buildings were erected by him, and much of the money he made was put into the place where it was amassed.

Beneath a sometimes brusque exterior he carried a noble heart, which appreciated the fearless, disinterested spirit who dared to appeal to his generosity, and many times he made such spirit glad by bestowing five-fold what was asked for a worthy cause.

It almost seemed that not even disease could conquer that indomitable will, and he resisted long before he succumbed to the "Fell Destroyer."

"Even Death itself stands still,

And waits an hour, sometimes, for such a will."

W. W. PARKER.

Mr. W. W. Parker came from Vermont to Oregon, via California, in the spring of 1852.

He engaged passage on the steamer Panama (built by the Aspinwalls), the first steamer that ever left New York for the Pacific Coast by way of Cape Horn. The steamer started with only two passengers, but before she reached San Francisco she was crowded with gold seekers from all along the western coast, the news of the discovery of the California gold mines having only been made public since she had rounded the Horn.

237

Mr. Parker was then but twenty-four years of age. He had educated himself, after gaining all the village school could give him, at Norwich University, Vermont, where there was also a military school, at which he took a three years' course in addition to his other studies. His father objected to his having more than a common school education, saying it would be of no practical use and, though well-to-do, declined to assist him. However, his desire for knowledge overcame all opposition, and he, with his elder brother, Freeman, worked their way through the university, living on the plainest fare, earning their books, fees, food and rent by sawing wood, and literally "sleeping on a board" during the three years in the military school, that being a part of the military training in those days. At the end of the course, there being no war in prospect, Mr. Parker decided not to continue in the military line and, as he was offered an excellent situation in the copper mines of Lake Superior as a civil engineer, civil engineering being a science in which he especially excelled, he accepted it, and spent two years in those world-famous mines in Northern Michigan, where, according to a record kept b)' him, thirty-six feet of snow fell one winter.

Returning to New England, the Western fever seized him, and, as before said, at the age of twenty-four years he started from New York to the then practically unknown Pacific Coast in October, 1848, the same month of the same year in which his future wife arrived in Oregon.

On his arrival in San Francisco, then but a village of tents on a sandy beach, he rolled out from the hold of the steamship his only possession in the world (beside his trunk of clothing), a half barrel of hardware, consisting of dirk knives, saws, hammers, shovels, axes and like useful articles ill a new country, in which, with true "Yankee" thrift and foresight, he had invested his last $50 after securing his steamer ticket.

These he "auctioned" off on the spot, receiving from the sale over $600. After spending less than a month in the mines (making $20 a day every day he was there), having no taste for mining, he returned to San Francisco and engaged in hotel keeping, his first hotel being all of cloth excepting the necessary wooden corner supports. Men thronged to the mines from all parts of the United States, and his business was immense. He paid his cook $600 per month and his baker $400. "Saleratus" was $16 a pound, and other food supplies were correspondingly high, yet in one year he had cleared $20,000.

This he put into a better hotel, and soon after lost it all in one night by fire, with the exception of $1000 in the bank.

Mr. Parker was a member of that first famous "Vigilance Committee" organized by the law-abiding citizens in San Francisco, in the absence of legally established courts, to deal with criminals and stamp out crime, which was becoming rampant. After a few of the murderous thugs were summarily strung up to lamp posts by this committee comparative law and order was restored.

And now, at the age of twenty-eight, Mr. Parker went on a sailing vessel to Astoria, Oregon, where he cast his lot, identifying himself with and laboring for the interests of his adopted home city and state until his death forty-seven years later.

He was always public-spirited, giving much time and thought to the civic welfare of his city and state and, indeed, to that of his whole country.

He was active in establishing the first public schools in Astoria; though then without a family of his own, and though not himself a church member, he believed in churches, and aided in building and supporting them, he helped organize the first temperance society in Clatsop county and afterward, when he was representing his county in the Legislature he worked hard for the temperance bill, a petition from the citizens in favor of which was contemptuously voted to be "thrown under the table" by a majority of that honorable body.

He served as postmaster of Astoria at one time and later was elected mayor of the city. He was twelve years deputy collector of customs for the port of Astoria, serving so ably under one collector that he was retained for two more terms by the two collectors following.

It was he who was mainly instrumental in securing the construction of the splendid system of water works of which Astoria is so justly proud, and which will ever stand as a monument to his memory. He was for years, up to his death, president of the Water Commission, and his name is carved above the stone entrance to the great city reservoir, placed there by his fellow-citizens in recognition of his gratuitous services so untiringly given to this arduous work till its successful completion, from first to last.

He was of a most equable temper, and uniformly kind and genial in his home life. A staunch believer in equal rights, he put his views into daily practice in his domestic relation-, thus showing that he possessed one of the main essential attributes of the ideal husband.

He was married in July, 1863, to Miss Inez E. Adams, my old schoolmate and lifelong friend.

He used neither intoxicants nor tobacco, and he preferred simply-prepared food to that highly seasoned with condiments. He was a man of pure life, as an incident in my own experience will go to prove.

About the time I was moving to Astoria, our boat on one occasion landed in the lower part of town, and as I was walking up the street next to the water toward the business center I met Mr. Parker going toward his home, his gaze directed downward, seemingly unconscious of his surroundings.

"Why, how do you do, Mr. Parker," I said.

He was passing on without reply, when I raised my voice, thinking he had not heard me, and repeated: "How do you do, Mr. Parker?"

He kept his head down, made some indistinct sound, and tried again to pass me, when I placed myself directly in front of him, saying:

"How do you do, Mr. Parker! Don't you know me?"

He then for the first time looked at me, and exclaimed:

"Well, well, doctor, how do you do? I did not expect to see you *here*"

"Why not here?" I asked.

"Well," said he, smiling, "we don't often meet ladies on this street."

"Why, what is the matter of this street?" I queried.

"Well, this neighborhood is called 'swill-town,' " he answered.

I laughed heartily, saying: "So you thought I was one of the denizens of the 'demi-monde/ did you?"

I was not then as well acquainted with the town as I afterward became, but had I been and business had required it I should not have hesitated to pass through any neighborhood in order to reach my destination.

CAPTAIN J. W. MUNSON.

Captain J. W. Munson was born December 25th, 1818, in Washington county, New York, where he spent his boyhood.

He came to Oregon in 1853, by way of Panama, and located first at Oak Point, where he was employed as a millwright for one year, during which time he never lost a day, besides working many nights. On the completion of this job, as he often laughingly told, he had "a hat full of $20 pieces and didn't know what to do with them."

When he first reached Oak Point he had remaining just one $-5 piece, hearing date of 18-10. This he kept, and afterward presented to his wife, who wears it attached to her watch chain as a souvenir.

After the completion of the Oak Point mill Mr. Munson came to Astoria, working at the carpenter's trade. He built Dr. C. J. Trenchard's residence, which was the first house of consequence in Astoria at that time, and it is still a good house, although over fifty years old. Mr. Munson said that during the time he was working on that house he often saw bear and elk come down and drink from the small stream running past nearby. That portion of Astoria was then covered with tall, dense timber.

In 1857 Mr. Munson went to Oysterville, Wash., where he remained six years, engaged in the oyster business.

In 1859 he was married to Miss Sarah Sophia Kimball, of Clatsop Plains. In 1865 he was appointed light keeper at Cape Disappointment (now Fort Canby), which position he held till 1878, after which he moved to Astoria and built the steamer Magnet, which he ran in his own interest until 1881, when he received the appointment of keeper of the light at Point Adams, which he occupied till October, 1898, when lie' retired on account of ill-health, and died at Skipanon, Oregon, March 22nd, 1899.

Mr. Munson might well be called a "diamond in the rough." He had a big heart, a hilarious, jovial disposition, and loved company and a good social time.

He was a tall, broad-shouldered, powerfully-built man, with a large, square head. He was a natural musician, and loved the violin, on which he could play by the hour, day or night, and never tire. I have heard him say, "I believe I could play in my sleep if I tried." I have seen him play and laugh and talk at the same time, never missing a note or losing time or expression.

Dancing was the popular amusement in those early times, and to dance well was an admired accomplishment. For this good music was essential, and if Mr. Munson could be secured for any party its success was assured.

I have seen him, when the dancing set became entangled, raise himself to his full, commanding height, dropping his violin by his side, with his hand holding his bow uplifted, with a broad smile on his face, and vigorous stamp of his foot, call out in a stentorian voice: "Hold on, now, and get straightened out!" Then, with an energetic and artistic stroke of his bow, accompanied by another stamp of his foot, he would start them on again. If they failed a second time, he would exclaim:

"Here, now, just change off! Some of you old dancers come over here and help these new ones out!" In the end he was sure to bring order out of confusion, and in such a joyous, hearty way that everyone laughed at his own mistakes and no one felt hurt.

He was as much a captain in the ball-room as on board his steamboat. He was a most excellent mechanic and a fine machinist, and he could make anything, from a steamboat to a violin. Like the traditional "busy bee," he was never idle.

I have in my possession a piece of his handiwork which I greatly prize. It is a large window curtain pole, made from a piece of black walnut picked up from the drift near Point Adams. On this are eight large brass rings, fashioned by him from brass obtained from the old British bark Cairnsmore, bound for Portland, Oregon, from London with 7500 barrels of cement on board. The Cairnsmore was cast ashore on Clatsop Beach September 28th. 1883, her commander, Captain Gibbs, having lost his reckoning during a spell of very foggy and smoky weather. The ship came ashore at 11 p m at high tide, in a dead calm, on a heavy swell, which landed her high and dry on the beach, where she may still be seen, a dismantled wreck of a once stately ship.

Mr. Munson manufactured a number of violins, some of which were valuable. One of these he made from a piece of hardwood which he found several feet below the surface while digging a drain in a swamp near the lighthouse. No hardwood grows anywhere near that vicinity, and this fragment must have drifted ashore long years before and been covered with the debris, it may be, of a century. Thus with his skillful hands and fertile brain he was able to bring sweet music from the very bowels of the earth with which to charm the senses and make glad the heart. He did his best, and did it well. Who can do more?

D. K. WARREN.

My first personal transaction with Mr. Warren, as I now recollect it, was in June, 1886. I called on Mrs. Warren to obtain a lease of her house, her former home, which was surrounded by beautiful shrubs and flowers, and was then one of the handsomest residences in Astoria. She was uncertain what price to ask, saying: "I think a great deal of my old home. What do *you* think it ought to be worth?"

"I will give you $30 per month upon a lease for two years," I replied.

"Well, we will see Mr. Warren," she said, and we went.

"Do you think I ought to let the doctor have my house for $30 a month for two years?" she asked him.

He smiled, and said in gentle, reassuring tones: "Well, if I were you I should think I was very fortunate to get $30 a month for two years with Dr. Adair for a tenant."

When I see a man show such gentle consideration toward his wife he is sure to find the way to my heart and win my admiration and confidence ever after. I lived neighbor to Mr. and Mrs. Warren for thirteen years, and I think he was' never once in my house, yet I knew him well, as did all his neighbors, through his strictly upright and quiet yet forceful daily life. He was a man of few words, but he thought deeply and well (which reminds me of what a lady once said of my Mattie Bell): "When Mattie does open her mouth, you may be sure something good will come out, for she never gives utterance to a silly thought."

Mr. Warren was a lover of the artistic and beautiful, as his lovely home and model farm attest. I might liken him to a perfect housekeeper, in that he "had a place for everything, and everything in its place," showing especially in his case that fine object lessons are of vastly more worth than words.

Mr. Warren was quiet, unassuming and industrious, with an exceptionally clear head and reflective mind, through which he acquired a fortune, every dollar of which was honestly accumulated. He lived a laborious, honorable life from day to day, battling with and overcoming the hardships of early Oregon life for the good of both his family and the community in which he dwelt.

He once said to me: "I believe that every man should settle property on his wife early in life, and allow her to manage it herself, that she may become accustomed to business, for women are often superior to men, and I think they ought to be encouraged."

I shall take the liberty here of referring to a conversation I had with Mrs. Warren a few years ago. We met on the train. She was in somewhat low spirits, saying that her son George was soon to finish at the Portland Academy and that it was her special ambition that both her sons should have a university course, but that George was not willing to take it. I said:

244

"Mrs. Warren, when your sons have finished the academy course they will have a better book-education than their father had, and book-learning, after all, is but a small part of the education essential to success in life, and if your sons prove themselves the worthy equal of their father you may well take pride in being their mother."

Mr. Warren showed his superior forethought, generosity and gratitude by doing what every right-minded man should do—providing bountifully for his faithful and worthy wife, who was the joy and comfort of his life.

He has gone from our mortal sight. "Being dead, he yet speaketh." His protecting kindness yet guards the hearthstone of his loved ones, "at twilight's hour and dewy morn," and still sheds a beneficent influence over the whole wide circle of his former activities.

Mrs. Warren can be found in her beautiful home, surrounded by her worthy and devoted children, dispensing help and comfort to the afflicted with wise and liberal hand, the "Lady Bountiful" of the community at large.

STEPHEN FOWLER CHADWICK

(By L. F. Grover.)

There is no country in the world, and especially no state in the Union, whose approach to civilization, and whose original occupation by cultured people came through more romantic mystery or through greater hardships and dangers than accompanied the first settlement of Oregon by the American pioneers.

This settlement was accomplished by exceptional people, under exceptional circumstances. No one undertook the long journey to this far-off land who had not in mind a vision of the broad prairies, of garden richness, the grassy hills, the snow-clad mountain peaks and the deep and silent forests of stately trees, "where rolls the Oregon," and, withal, the Eden-like climate. The charm of taking part in a new and fruitful life, where the Government gave, everyone a homestead of broad acres, and where an opportunity offered of taking part in organizing new society, and building a new state, with its thousand chances of success in public as well as in private life, was at the foundation of the impulse that brought the early migration of thousands to Oregon.

Added to the sturdy pioneers from the valley of the Mississippi, with their numerous families, came also many highly educated, talented and brilliant young men from the Atlantic states, who joined the moving panorama westward to the *Ultima Thule* of American colonization and American destiny.

Among those who were drawn by these attractions from his home in New England was the subject of this sketch.

The Chadwicks came from England with Governor Winthrop's colony in 1630 to Massachusetts Bay. They settled at Charlestown and Malden.

A branch of this family removed thence to Connecticut, on the earliest occupancy of that region by the English. The descendants of this name have furnished many notable instances of distinction in the learned professions and the army and navy. They have been a stalwart race, and noted for business capacity and honorable life.

Stephen Fowler Chadwick was born in Middletown, Connecticut, December 25th, 1825, so that, at the time of his death, he was approaching the Biblical span of life of threescore and ten years. After receiving a preliminary education in his native state, of that thorough kind usually given in New England, he entered upon the study of the law in the city of New York, where, after due course of studies, in which he exhibited notable proficiency, he was admitted to the bar by the Supreme Court of the state.

Early in the spring of 1851 he started for Oregon by the isthmus route and on his arrival settled at Scottsburg, in Southern Oregon, where he commenced the practice of his profession. At that time there was but few white settlers in the territory. Scottsburg, was at the head of tide-water navigation on the Umpqua river, and was the nearest available port of supply to the mines of Southern Oregon and Northern California, then just discovered, so that shortly a brisk trade sprung up, calling for shippers, merchants, pack trains, mechanics and all the concomitants of a smart mining business.

In all this new life young Chadwick took a full part. He became the first postmaster of Scottsburg, and a leading citizen. But not long afterward Roseburg, the county seat of Douglas county, becoming a more important place, he removed to that town, where he was elected the first count)judge of that county.

Showing evident aptitude for public work, official honors and trusts began to cluster about the name of the rising young attorney. He was appointed prosecuting attorney for the Territory and deputy United States district attorney for the Southern District of Oregon.

In 1857 he was elected a delegate from Douglas county to the convention called to frame a constitution for the new State of Oregon. In that body he was a member of several important committees, and in particular he served on the committee on the schedule, which had the important and delicate duty of engrafting the territorial upon the state government, and of settling the slavery question, which was thrown into the convention as a fire-brand from burning Kansas, at that time in the throes of discord and bloodshed on account of the same subject. This committee was selected from the most conservative members, noted for ability and sound judgment, and in exercising this duty Judge Chadwick took his full part in the work before him with credit and honor.

In 1864 and 1868 he was elected on the Democratic ticket as presidential elector, and at the latter date he was designated by the Oregon electors as their messenger to take the vote of Oregon to the electoral college at Washington. He there delivered the vote of this State for Horatio Seymour for President.

In 1870, on the ticket headed by L. F. Grover for Governor, he was elected Secretary of State for the term of four years, and in 1874 the same ticket was re-elected.

On the resignation of Governor Grover in February, 1877, to take his seat in the Senate of the United States, to which he had been elected by the last preceding Legislature, Secretary Chadwick became Governor of Oregon by virtue of the provisions of the State constitution. In all his duties as Secretary of State his work was marked by clearness, soundness and honesty.

His administration as chief executive was characterized by promptness and strength in the exercise of public duty and a care for the public good, giving ample proofs of a high class of executive ability. While he was Governor, in 1878, the Indians of Eastern Oregon made their last struggle against civilization, rising in arms against the white settlers in a threatening and murderous manner. The Governor went in person to the front, and succeeded in securing the co-operation of the United States military forces and of the friendly chiefs in that quarter, and procured the surrender of nine of the ringleaders of the outbreak, who were indicted in the state courts for murder and were convicted and hanged.

At the close of his executive term Governor Chadwick delivered a message to the Legislature, which was a public document replete with valuable suggestions and wise counsel.

No one of positive qualities in public place is ever free from the shafts of criticism and detraction. Governor Chadwick received his share of such attentions. But correct history and public opinion have cleared the field of his public life from all aspersions, and his public record stands out without a blemish.

At the close of his administration as chief executive of the State he resumed the practice of his profession, and gave attention to his many business interests.

For twelve years Governor Chadwick was a member of the original board of directors during all the construction period of what is now the Southern Pacific Railroad, and gave material aid in the completion of this first of Oregon's railway enterprises.

It was in the mystic rites of the Masonic fraternity that the high personal and social qualities of the subject of our sketch shone out in their clearest tone. He was a Scottish Rite Mason, of the thirty-third degree; was Grand Master of the Grand Lodge of the State, and for over a quarter of a century he acted as chairman of the Committee on Foreign Correspondence of the Grand Lodge of Oregon. He had filled every position in the offices of the order, from the lowest to the highest.

As a lawyer he was able and cogent, in his discussions before the courts, clear in the presentation of his subjects, and most careful and honorable in the protection of the interests of his clients, so that success at the bar was easy and natural to him. In his later years he retired from professional work. As a public speaker he was attractive and interesting and often eloquent. Among his occasional addresses was the one at the laying of the cornerstone of the State Capitol at Salem in 1873. He also delivered the principal address at the annual meeting of the Oregon Pioneers in 1874.

In 1855 Governor Chadwick was united in marriage with Miss Jane A. Smith, daughter of Judge Richard Smith, of Douglas county, formerly of Virginia. The issue of this marriage was two sons and two daughters—Stephen J., a prominent lawyer of Eastern Washington, late mayor of Colfax; Ella P., wife of William T. Gray, a prominent citizen of Salem, Oregon; and Mary and P. F., yet unmarried.

In his home relations his life was most genial and happy, and he was much given to social entertainment. He was a member of the Episcopalian church, to which he imparted many beneficial influences.

The death of Governor Chadwick took place on the 14th day of January, 1895, and came suddenly and in a startling manner.

He was entertaining an invited guest at dinner and in the midst of pleasant conversation at the table he was suddenly attacked by a stroke of apoplexy and died almost instantly. While medical aid was at hand, Dr. Owens-Adair being the guest at the dinner, no human power could recall his life from the hand of the fell Reaper.

The news of his death soon spread through the halls of the State Capitol, where the Legislature and Supreme Court were in session, and where his stalwart form was but the day before a familiar figure. All public business was interrupted and the public bodies adjourned out of respect to the deceased statesman.

The funeral was conducted in the highest obsequies of the Masonic fraternity, every lodge of the state being represented in full regalia. The members of the Supreme Court and of the Legislature and the state officers, with the mayor and city council of Salem and a large concourse of citizens joined to pay their last respects to the honored dead. He was buried in the Rural cemetery, amid the oak-covered hills south of the city, where all that is mortal of him rests in

"The low couch of everlasting sleep."

Of Stephen Fowler Chadwick it may be truthfully said:

"His life was gentle, and the elements
So mixed in him, that Nature might stand up
And say to all the world: "This was a man!""

PRESS REPORTS. F. CHADWICK DEAD

Salem, Oregon, January 15th, 1895.—Ex-Governor Stephen F. Chadwick died suddenly tonight, having been stricken with apoplexy at his home in this city just as he had nearly finished dinner, and was entertaining an old-time friend, Mrs. Dr. Owens-Adair, of Astoria. Dinner had progressed to the interim preceding dessert. His daughter Mary had been to the kitchen a moment, and upon entering the dining-room uttered a cry of dismay, pointing to her father, whom she had left in his happiest mood. Mrs. Chadwick and Dr. Adair, turning toward him, beheld the aged statesman lying back in his chair, purple in the face, and gasping for breath. Dr. Adair exercised her professional skill quickly and applied restoratives, but to no purpose. The aid of Drs. Byrd, Smith and Morse, who were hastily summoned, was also unavailing. The ex-Governor was dead.

Governor Chadwick was on the streets of the city and around the State Capitol today, showing no signs of the approach of the awful visitor. He passed away without apparent pain or struggle, and a number of friends who flocked to his residence, with the dismal hope that the report was not true, found the benevolent features in their usual placidity.

Salem, Oregon, June 29th, 1895.

My Dear Dr. Adair:

I have thought of writing you, oh, so many times, for mother and I think of you every day, and upon our return from Southern Oregon Ella told us someone was at her house inquiring for mother, and from the description of the maid we thought it must be you, knowing you had been in Southern Oregon. We regretted very much we did not see you, as a good long talk would have done mother lots of good. We were gone about ten days. The trip did not benefit mother as much as I thought it would. She isn't very strong, and feels our loss more every day. I assure you, life is very blue and lonely, and it seems pretty hard to keep up at times, but we must.

We were out to the cemetery this evening, and took some flowers. There is so little comfort in going.

Steve and family are on the Sound, and will probably remain there most of the summer. Ella is pretty well again, but was miserable for months after pa died. We were so uneasy about her. Pitzer, too, had a long sick spell. We hear from him every week. He is still in Colfax. I enclose you an article Governor Grover wrote, which we think a great deal of. We would be pleased to hear from you at any time.

Mother joins me in kindest regards to the Colonel and yourself.

MARY CHADWICK.

Salem, Oregon, July 2d, 1880.

251

Mrs. B. A. Owens:

Dear Madame—Mr. and Mrs. Chadwick take pleasure in acknowledging the receipt of your last letter, containing the important announcement of your success, and we assure you it is a pride to us.

We thank you for this mark of esteem, and trust you will advise us of your progress. Our good wishes shall attend you always.

Your many friends will rejoice to hear of your good fortune. You certainly deserve great praise and rich reward for your individual efforts and final success. That you will have them there is no question. We shall be pleased to see you, and welcome you to your field of labor. That you should have maintained yourself so well abroad is another matter of pride to your friends. With great respect for you, we remain

Very truly your friends,

S. F. CHADWICK.

For self and wife, Mrs. Chadwick having read this letter with approbation.

LETTER OF HON. S. F. CHADWICK TO DR. OWENS

Dr. B. A. Owens:

My Dear Madame—You are such a stranger, and so far away, that I had almost looked upon you as lost; lost, indeed.

But, if I had thought a moment, I should have known that you are among those who cannot be lost on this earth.

While not hearing of you, or rather from you, for some time, I have seen excellent notices of you, which have made me very proud of your good name and character. I talk about you to your friends. Only a few days ago Dr. Glenn was speaking of you. In fact, it was on the day you were to sail for Europe. The impulse to do you justice on all occasions is very strong in me, hence I often think of you and your career as a heroine, for such you are. Now I will say your letter of the 7th of April is before me. So far as the duties on instruments and apparel are concerned, I fear that I am not able to advise you correctly, but hope that the kind Providence that has prospered all your ways will protect you in all your undertakings, especially in this, and return you to your friends and professional usefulness after you have enjoyed the pleasures of the anticipated visit to your friends in Europe. I believe your visit to Europe will help you. After all, I believe you are the first woman in the United States who studied medicine regularly. In this I may be mistaken, but I think not. When you borrowed books of Dr. Hamilton so many years ago to read up in your profession, I wondered at the step you had taken. So did others. While I was hopeful of you, and encouraged you, others were disposed to question the propriety of such a step.

Time rolled on, and you came out of the trial with honor.. Who could have done more, or as much? No lady stood higher, and none more deserved to. All your life you have been marked for decision of character, excellence of purpose, and great ability in all you have undertaken, and today you have the respect, confidence and praise of all your acquaintances, who have watched and admired you. This is no flattery. You need none, for you are as far ahead of it as the day is from the night. Put all this together with the fact that you were the first lady on the Pacific Coast, if not in the United States, whoever took a medical work into her hands to master the medical profession, and you will not wonder at the honor I bestow upon you.

From your standpoint now, look back and see how many ladies have since gone into the profession of medicine. You know many, but when you began you did not know one. To maintain that honor, and make your life a further mark for the respect and confidence of your friends will be your constant care.

You may not like to be called the "mother of all the lady doctors." but in one sense it is so, and they should be considerate enough to bestow upon their "alma mater" that love and esteem due you from those who have but followed the example you were firm and resolute enough to set them. You broke down the barriers of prejudice, defied the scandal that followed the profession when woman aims to assume its functions, and said to the world: "This delicate and sympathetic office of a physician belongs more to my sex than to the other, and I will enter it, and make it an honor to woman." You have done all these things, and more, for the cause you espouse.

I hope your visit will be pleasant. I know it will be. It is the desire of my life to take such a trip. No one will appreciate it more than you will. Local news is scarce. My family are well. Mrs. C. did not get that paper you sent. I want to read the article. Perhaps it will come yet.

We look for a large immigration this year. You will return in good fruit time, and we are to have an abundance of it. You are fond of such seasons.

You did not mention whether George is with you. May God bless you and keep you from harm. We send our love to you.

I remain your friend.

S. F. CHADWICK.

In a letter to Colonel Adair, Governor Chadwick said:

"I trust the doctor is well. I am indebted to her skill and kindness. These things I shall treasure, for they have given me better health than I had a year ago, far better, and your joint attentions last year, are very pleasant memories. Would that I could return them. May you both enjoy a year of prosperity in everything, to be followed by prosperity through all coming years."

Salem, Oregon, April 24th, 1890.

Mrs. Dr. Owens-Adair:

Dear Madame—I notice you are having natural gas at Warrenton. I don't mean real estate agents, though the country is full of that kind of gas. I want to tell you something you may know. Mr. William Perry, whom you knew when he lived on Clatsop Plains, in the '40s, also at Roseburg, told me that the Indians often brought to his place, and no doubt to your father's too, in small cans, "Barba-does tar" (petroleum).

They got it from a mountain, where it ran out of the side. While the Indians could not tell exactly where it was, they said it was down the beach toward Tillamook. Perry always said he could find it. I kept at him to do so, but he never found time to go and see to it. He sent Vail about fifteen years ago. He went over to Tillamook, and up the mountains, until he was lost, and finally returned home without finding it. The Indians reported plenty of tar.

I have thought this: If some petroleum could be put into a can and shown to the oldest Indians along the coast to Tillamook, they may remember where it can be found, for there are Indians living who knew all about it. They may be found on the reservation, but Clatsop Indians would know, from the oldest down to their descendants. It was not worth much then.

If this story of Perry's is true, and I believe it, that flow of petroleum can be found. Now you will ask: "Why don't you borrow an oyster can and come down and find it?" Well, I will tell you why.

Five weeks ago today I was at Roslyn, Washington, and when about to leave I slipped on an icy patch and fell on my ankle, spraining it badly. Why I did not break a bone I cannot tell. I have not walked since. I went to Ellensburg and George, your son, attended to it for me, and I am doing very well. Can walk, with the aid of a chair, though I do not do much of it yet. I think in two weeks I shall be out once more. I could not walk with the chair support a week ago. When I get well, and the season is suited to it, I will be on hand, with sample boxes, or bottles of petroleum, in search of this mountain, or hill, that contains the precious stuff. It is there, and maybe it will stay there; who knows?

I see your "Union" party is quite respectable. The names, so far as I know, are of our best citizens. Great credit is due you for the name. I think they will poll a large vote. They are men who mean business.

Give my regards to the Colonel. Ask him if he wants to be a partner in a mountain of tar. Yours truly,

S. F. CHADWICK.

I forgot to say we are all as well as usual, except my case, already reported.

Salem, Oregon, April 30th, 1890.

Col. John Adair:

My Dear Sir—Yours of yesterday came duly to hand. I see that you have secured your railroad. I am so glad. The Coos Bay and Roseburg will be built, also. What will become of this country? Old Major Tucker, whom, perhaps, you knew, when a boy, used to say that "Oregon was the extenuation of a great country," and when he was "full" he was rather interesting. But he never dreamed of a railroad then. A reader of Irving's "Astoria" could not find the place now. I presume there is a dispute as to where old Fort George stood. I was on the spot in April, 1857.

But you are to have the "boss" residence property, as well as for business, with a railroad whistling through it all. I have great faith in the doctor's long head and good luck. She has made no mistakes in her judgment in going to Astoria. You are going to be very rich. Now I feel sure of the "Barbadoes tar." We shall find it, as sure as we live. It will follow the doctor's good luck.

Silas B. Smith I do not now remember. His mother was not the wife of Miller Smith, of Roseburg, was she? If so, I was acquainted with him. Had I taken Miller Smith in those early days, we could have found the tar. Never thought of him. I tied to Mr. Perry all the time, and did nothing. This Smith boy was quite a lad then. I hope you will find the person you want. It will be on Government land, no doubt. If found on school land, we can buy it. If otherwise, we will have to get it the best way we can—preempt or homestead. We must look into this before the thing is made public. I have looked over all the mineral works I have, and find no mention of petroleum. You are the authority on that point. We must be sure that we have the thing certain, if it is found. I am now going about the house with crutch and cane. My inside ankle, on right side of foot, is quite sore, but improving. This is near the last of it. Better, otherwise. I will be ready for that excursion to the mine in about a month.

With kind regards to the doctor, I remain, yours truly,

S. F. CHADWICK.

Jesse Applegate (1811–1888) was a pioneer who led a large group of settlers along the Oregon Trail to the Oregon Territory. He was an influential member of the early government of Oregon, and helped establish the Applegate Trail as an alternative route to the Oregon Trail.—Ed.

My excuse for making public the letters from my dear and honored friend is that they show the depth of his pure and sensitive nature, and I believe that Oregon is entitled to all that enhances the greatness and goodness of this, one of her noblest sons, who served her for so long, so faithfully and well.

He nursed me as a babe, and carried me on his brawny shoulders for many miles over those rough, almost endless emigrant trails. He and my father were devoted friends, and to the day of his death he was to me as a true and affectionate father, his habit being always to address me as "My child."

Ashland, Oregon, April 23d, 1872.

My Dear Friend—I returned here yesterday from Sacramento and San Francisco, and will commence operations in the field as soon as Dan joins me from home and my party is equipped.

If you still wish your son to make a campaign with me, I shall be pleased to please you in that matter, hoping to make the campaign as pleasant as possible to the young gentleman himself.

I find that I am not the only old man who has fallen desperately in love with you. Colonel Hooker is even (if that were possible) more deeply smitten than myself, and I am satisfied, from the strong expressions he uses in your praise, that if the colonel had not an "encumbrance" already, A. would have to look to his laurels, for he would have a persevering and most gallant competitor for your favor.

Not knowing when at Yreka that I would meet orders at this point, I promised to deliver for the colonel his very high regards, which he clothed in most knightly phrase, saying that he "failed to call upon you when last at Roseburg, not because his heart did not prompt him to do so, but because, covered with mud and dirt, with no means of improving his toilet, his vanity stood in the way of the promptings of his tenderer feelings. In a word, the colonel has formed a very high opinion of you, and says he does not think that in his whole life he has met a lady who combined so many personal charms with so bright an intellect. Nor must I forget to thank you for the words of kindness in which you expressed yourself to him concerning me.

If your son is not ready, or he by any accident misses Dan,

I will in a week or ten days complete a part of my work that must be immediately reported at Portland. This may enable me to make a flying visit home, when I can take your young gentleman in my own charge on my return, and if I come no farther north than Jacksonville, to which point I *must* come,

I will telegraph to you for your boy to meet me there.

With most sincere wishes for your health and happiness,

I am, as ever, your sincere friend,

JESSE APPLEGATE.

P. S.—My work commences at the south boundary of the State, on the western shore of Little, or lower Klamath lake, and extends north. A much pleasanter country than I expected to be in when I last saw you. Broken rest and hard work has rather prostrated me. Such things seem to tax my physical powers more than formerly. Perhaps you are soon to lose a friend who hopes for your happiness with the unselfish yearnings of a father. Let him have your kind remembrance. J. A.

Yoncalla, Oregon, June 22d, 1872.

My Dear Friend—When I arrived at home from the south I found one of my two bundles of blankets open in the stage. I gathered up such things as I could find, supposing that George's pillow and Dan's carpet-bag were in the other bundle, but both bag and pillow are missing. I did not arrive from Portland until this morning, or I would have instituted inquiries after them earlier, with better hope of recovering them. As George will know the carpel-bag, tell him I will thank him very much if he will inquire at the stage stable and of the drivers respecting the bag and pillow. I will write to Oakland about them today.

The bag (Dan's) is a common (and as well as I can remember) red and white carpet. It contains, besides some clothes, his watch. I wish George to write to me and let me know what he is studying, for if I cannot always have him with me I would like to have him for a correspondent. Perhaps it was love for the mother that first warmed my heart toward the son, but that could only have produced a prepossession in his favor, soon to pass away, had there been no quality in the boy to keep alive and increase the growth of my kindly feelings; but I like the boy for himself. For, of hasty temper and quick to like or dislike, he also readily forgives. His heart is too full of love and tenderness long to afford room for the baser passions of malice and revenge. For though of the thoughtless age of youth, and sometimes suffering from both pain and fatigue, he always showed for me not only respect, but tenderness and thought of my comfort before his own. At night, when we were under our blankets, and, as it were, alone with each other, he would nestle close to me and caress my hands or face with the gentle touch of woman, and make the kindest inquiries after my comfort. Once, I remember, when our bed was made upon a rough rock, I complained of its hardness. He was so determined I should sleep on his pillow that he would not use it himself, and said if I did not want it, it might lie on the ground unused. It was not until after the perverse child was asleep that I could arrange his bedding so that he could rest comfortably. If, sometimes, when in the moonlight, as I looked upon the pale face of the sleeping boy and anxiously studied his future (when neither his modesty nor his manhood would be offended by the liberty), I kissed his cheek or his forehead, I am not ashamed of the weakness. It is not to alarm you, but if possible to avert the fate that seems to threaten the poor boy, that I disclose the anxious fears I have respecting him. His frame, I fear, is far too weak long to support his ever active intellect and ever active spirit. "The over keen blade soon cuts away the scabbard."

As I said to you at Roseburg, you have done your part in his parentage by imparting to him your own bright intelligence and warm affections, but his father was not himself sound, or from some other cause, has not given to his son a strong, enduring body, or at least one not equal to the strain put upon it by a mind as active as that of George.

George is also full of courage, which, united with a hasty temper, is always a tax on a weak constitution. My sons, if not markedly intellectual, are, at least, strong, robust, enduring men, of much firmness and persistence and, of course, animal courage—the result of these fine bodily qualities. They owe these hissings to healthy parents, who lived in the simplicity of nature, unvexed by the turmoils, artificial cares, hate and jealousies of so-called civilized life.

About hatred and jealousy I have only to say: They are base passions, which we have in common with the lower animals. Besides the evils they work to others, they are a continual punishment to those who entertain them. They cannot long remain the tenants of a pure and innocent heart. They will soon drive out innocence and corrupt purity, or be themselves driven out. I write knowingly upon this subject, because in the course of my life I have been afflicted with both.

But I have earnestly struggled against them, and no struggle in a good cause is entirely barren of good results. Toleration and charity for the faults and failings of others, I am *sure,* may be cultivated until they will create in our souls desire for the good of all, and a sense of being at peace with all the world. Perhaps no degree of cultivation will save us from anger when provoked by deep or sudden injury, but we need not suffer it to degenerate into hatred and revenge.

Sincerely your friend,

JESSE APPLEGATE.

Linkville, Oregon, November 20th, 1873.

My Very Dear Friend—Your letter was brought to me at my sheep ranch, more than fifty miles from any postoffice. I read it sitting upon a stone, with the broad expanse of solitude spread around me, while I watched and herded another man's sheep for a living! When you also consider that I am between sixty and seventy years of age, and poor, and have won no distinction of any kind, it seems to me the oracle you consult is a frail one indeed. But as I do love you, dear, as the "bone of my bone, and flesh of my flesh," my great partiality for you may lead me to hope more from your remarkable intellect than you will realize. If you had the means (and if I had them you should have them) your plan is just such a one as I would form for you, as your inclinations lead you in that direction.

You are right in deciding that your mind was not given you to be frittered away in frivolity. I was right in deciding that marriage and motherhood were not intended for you by the Creator. He designed you for a higher destiny, and you will attain it. Let your motto be "Excelsior." Avoid love, marriage and all other entanglements and relaxations until you have attained to the high distinction to which you aspire. Fame and fortune will then await you, and there will still be time to indulge in the tenderness of your heart and the warmth of your affections.

It is not probable that you and I will ever meet again. I am old and continually receding into a deeper and darker obscurity, perhaps shortly to die in some solitary desert, where even my bones will not again be seen by any human being, while your course will still be onward and upward, with a fame probably as wide as literature and as enduring as Time. I feel, however, that the mystic cord of affection has drawn us together; that the love and sympathy between us has been pure and chaste as the virgin snows upon the lap of Diana, and that it will endure to the end, whatever end we shall reach.

At a time of more leisure I will try to write again.

God bless and prosper you in all your undertakings.

JESSE APPLEGATE.

Clear Lake, Colorado, January 5th, 1874.

261

Dear Friend—Your short note of "farewell" was received yesterday. While I am comforted and pleased with the earnest expressions of the love and sympathy of one so much above the common, both physically and mentally, I feel it to be my duty to disabuse you of some errors respecting myself. And though the confession will probably lower me in your esteem, which of all things I would like to retain, yet, as an honest man, I cannot retain your love, highly as I prize it, if given under a false impression. Intellectually, I fall far below the standard you seem to have set up of my measure. Not from a lack of a clear, discriminating mind, but from a lack of that indomitable courage and perseverance that inspires you to great undertakings, and will bear you forward to great results. Too easily discouraged and turned aside by obstacles, and influenced by strong passions and appetites my advance in the path of knowledge has not been that of a traveler determined to reach the end of his journey, but a loiterer, who follows the path for the beauty and grandeur of the scene and the rich abundance of the flowers that strewed the way.

My mind led me in the pursuit of science; it was to me an easy road to pursue. Those things difficult and abstruse to most minds presented no difficulties to mine. My remarkable progress attracted the attention of the learned. Rich men offered their patronage, and money freely tendered was not wanting to bring me forward on the road I seemed so easily to follow. But I was too proud to be dependent on any man's bounty and too poor to prosecute my studies without first procuring the means of support. Since then I have only been able, at periods few and far between, to review what I so rapidly acquired in youth. It is too painful to recount, even to you, my sympathizing friend, my further history. Suffice it to say that, like many others, the promise of my youth was not realized in manhood. The struggle for competence brought me in contact with the world. I yielded the lofty but lonely pursuit of science to its seductions. I have committed many follies and some vices. All the ills that beset me I owe to myself. All the pleasures of my life I owe to others. The love and respect I receive from those near to me by the ties of blood rise up before me as a continual reproach. It was a great folly, almost a crime, that has brought them into the world, and it is owing to my non-improvement of my opportunities that they are left to struggle with it in the humble vale of poverty and ignorance. It is but a poor atonement I can make for all the ills I have brought upon them to devote the few remaining days I have to living entirely to their service. And it would be a pleasure I do not deserve longer to enjoy your love and sympathy under the false impression that I am either a martyr or a hero. God bless you. Good-bye.

JESSE APPLEGATE.

Clear Lake, Colorado, November 5th, 1876.

My Friend—When you told me the pecuniary success you had gained and the social standing you had reached by making yourself, a physician, and I suggested to you that a further success was in your reach by making yourself eminent in the scientific departments of your profession, you asked me the question, "Do you really believe me capable of reaching so high an eminence?"

Upon an examination of this question it presents two aspects. Neither of them are very flattering to me. First, it expressed a doubt of my sincerity, or, second, a doubt of my judgment, and I think I at least have a right to ask upon which ground I am to place the meaning of your question. If there is anything in our past intercourse that implies a want of sincerity on my part, I am not aware of it. True, I have said things of you and to you that were flattering, and intended to be so, but they were uttered in the utmost sincerity, and intended to encourage you in pursuits calculated to elevate, strengthen and refine you intellectually.

I have had no personal end to gain by flattering your vanity, or by misleading or deceiving you on any point. And as you know this as well as I do, I must conclude that you think my judgment, which, you have flattered me by placing a high value on, is now failing me. Is this so? And if so, have I not earned, if in no other way, by always treating you with candor, candor in return?

I have much more to say to you, but it seems out of place until this question is settled. It seems to me that if it is possible for a man and woman to hold intercourse as pure, but kindred intelligences, free from even the taint of passion, it is so for you and me.

You are in the glory of womanhood, endowed physically with perfections enough to excite the admiration of the opposite sex and the envy of your own. You have an intellect strengthened by a powerful will, which has overcome all obstacles to your upward course. Hardest task of all, you have crushed out love and tenderness from your woman's heart.

Are you going to stop in the midst of your career? Are all these sacrifices to be made, and you yet fall short of the goal of your ambition?

Most solemnly and earnestly do I protest against such a termination.

Better to have remained the humble dressmaker and enjoyed the humble but free and independent life that calling afforded you than fail in a higher aim. Let me know how it is with you. Very truly yours,

JESSE APPLEGATE.

Mount Yoncalla, Oregon, June 23d, 1878.

Dear Madam—Your letter of June 9th was received but a few days ago, as I get my mail at Drain, being most convenient.

I am sorry you deem it necessary to go East to study. It will, of course, put an end to your present prosperous practice, and instead of "putting money in thy purse," it will draw upon it heavily. Money is a very handy thing to have. I know by bitter experience that the want of it is not only very inconvenient, but puts a veto on many great undertakings and grand schemes.

The practical (which you call clinical) branch of your profession you can perfect yourself in while at the same time helping yourself and others, while two hours in the day devoted to the study of a specialty of your own choosing may give you the wealth and fame your friends hope you may sometime possess.

But as you promise me a visit, I will defer the discussion of the subject until that time, as there may be reasons for your Eastern journey other than study.

I shall be very glad to see you and have you spend a few days with us, but I think it right to warn you that we are very poor, live very hard, and can promise you none of the comforts and luxuries you enjoy daily in the home you have created for yourself. Truly your friend,

Mount Yoncalla, Oregon, August 14th, 1878.

Mrs. B. A. Owens:

Dear Madam—Since striding over the matter of your contemplated journey in the pursuit of knowledge, and how I could best assist you in your laudable purpose, I have come to the following conclusions:

As your purpose is to raise yourself not only to a higher place in your profession, but also to a higher sphere in human society, a word or two of advice from an old and sincere friend must not give offense. From the moment you step on board the steamer to begin your tour, put on the manners, deportment, dress and address of the class to which you intend hereafter to belong, and never thereafter let yourself down from the highest standard. Even as a subject of conversation avoid politics generally, and woman's rights especially, as you would the plague. In your own person and pursuits you give the highest proof of the equality of the human intellect, and an exemplar as to the branches of human knowledge to which that of the female should be directed. In the broad and as yet unexplored fields of science there is plenty of room for all minds to act without jostling each other, and to labor in the fields of knowledge in which the dress of flesh which Nature has placed upon them is not an encumbrance.

Leave, therefore, the kindred subjects, of war and politics to minds cast in the stronger and grosser molds of man, as inconsistent with the delicacy and refinement that makes woman most attractive to her opposite. This perhaps is as large a dose of nester as I should give until I see what effect it has upon the patient. If the symptoms are favorable I may continue the treatment. Sincerely your friend,

Had I but taken the advice of my dear old friend not to talk politics, woman suffrage and kindred subjects, I might have saved myself worlds of trouble and fountains of tears.

But, with my impetuous and willful nature, it seemed impossible for me not to battle for what I considered to be right and to denounce that which I believed to be wrong. And thus, through my life I have acted in accordance with my nature, and doubtless will to the end of the last chapter.

B. A. O.-A.

Ann Arbor, April 25, 1879.

My Dear Friend—I shall do what I should have done, six weeks ago—answered your valued letter. I thought when I left home I should have an abundance of time to devote to letter writing; but, alas, I find I have been obliged to drop most of my correspondents; have only saved a few choice ones, and am sorry to say that they have been sadly neglected; but when I tell you I am crowding three weeks' work into two, you will not censure me. You know I have never had early training. I find it hard work attempting such a science, with so little preparation; but I would have you understand that I am not in the least discouraged; to the contrary, I am greatly encouraged. My health is excellent, and I have accomplished far more, thus far, than I had expected, and I look forward to when I shall be fully fitted to enter upon the life-labor of my choice.

In fifteen months from now I hope to be on my way to Europe, where I contemplate spending one, perhaps two, years. Then for home, and friends. You are right when you say I am seeking high position in the medical profession. I am. And who but you, my dear, honored friend and father (for you have been a father to me in the true sense of the term), first said to me, "You must occupy a professor's chair; I would have no other place for you." God knows how often I have blessed you for that encouragement, though it did then seem an impossibility. The road was so long; the height so great; and withal, I had so little faith in myself.

' Not so now. I feel that I am on the right road, and sometimes I fancy I can almost see the glimmer of rays in the not far distant future. And thus I am urged on and on, receiving new strength every day.

I know your ambition for me is in another direction, but I feel there is too much risk involved in it, and it would prevent or delay the consummation of other plans by which I believe I can do more good with no risk to health or life. I feel that the time for that has passed now. I must look for the crown in another direction. I must sacrifice one, and I have chosen that one which to me seems fraught with less danger, and more success. True, the longings of my heart reach out toward the other, yet I must be content with that which is within my reach. Circumstances and regulations forbid the one, at present, and may never favor its development, but I shall strive to make up for the loss by a life well spent; this I promise you.

Please write when you find time. Your letters always encourage me. They are filled with beautiful thoughts and sentiment, which I treasure with care by copying in a blank book, with other valuables. Someday they will be utilized. They must not decay.

B. A. O.

June, 1879.

Dear Friend—Yours of the 25th ult was received yesterday. If I could believe all the flattering things you say of me, I should be very vain, indeed; but I am no longer a believer in my own judgment, and am a frequent sufferer from mistakes in my own person. It would make me very unhappy to believe that errors that have made my own life a failure extended their baleful influence to those dear to me.

I have of late felt much uneasiness in regard to you, knowing that I most earnestly advised you to the pursuit of knowledge. I have feared my advice had some influence in shaping your life, and that success in your high pursuit would be too dearly paid for, if gained at the expense of your happiness.

This feeling has been painfully increased by a little incident that happened when I was in Roseburg last month.

Since I advised a sacrifice of your heart to your brain, I think your lover, has looked upon me as an enemy; at any rate, he has not met me with his usual cordiality,—and I, as a matter of course, have not called upon him. This time I met him in the street, saluted him pleasantly, told him that I had lately heard from our mutual friend, Mrs. Owens; that you were pleasantly located at one of the best educational institutions in the Union, and pushing your studies with the energy and industry which he knew you always practiced. I said this to him, as I wished to meet the only matter which could cause him to have hard feelings toward me. I saw that he was glad to have the opportunity to talk of you, but I could not then stop, as I was on my way to meet an engagement with my lawyers. But an hour after, in the dusk of the evening, I found him in the same place, and the desired conversation was had.

When you have reached your highest ambition, and are enthroned on your coveted professor's chair, with the approval of those whose approval is fame, it is not probable a higher tribute will be paid to you than by those two earnest men, so widely differing from each other in age, sentiments, and pursuits, but each finding in you qualities to admire, and to love, according to his own standard of excellence. The one estimating you as a bright intellect, eager to drink deeply at the fountain of knowledge; to the other as a bright, beautiful woman, loving, and inspiring love. To the one you are a seraph; to the other a cherub; a goddess to both.

Your medical science informs you that for the health of the body every organ must have full play, every muscle free exercise. So, also, to make happy the mind, a free intellect must be warmed and fostered by the cultivation of the affections.

To gain a high degree of knowledge, it is not necessary, as you seem to think, that all the cravings of the woman's heart must be denied. On the contrary, their continual craving for indulgence will ultimately so engross the mind as to weaken its strength, destroy its activity, and blunt its perceptions. True, if the question of bread and butter was involved, it would make a difference, but this is not your case. You have enough for the present, and may provide amply for the future by accepting the love and protection of one whose long and faithful devotion Ought to soften the coldest heart. If you tell him that after you complete the tour of Europe you will become his wife, I think you will make him extremely happy, and, perhaps fill the void in your own heart. Your friend,

JESSE APPLEGATE.

Ann Arbor, Mich., June 16, 1879.

My Dear Friend—Your valued favor is before me. I am very sorry that you should feel remorse of conscience in regard to what might have been between the person and myself. Now let me forever relieve you of every vestige of condemnation in that direction, and believe me when I tell you that he alone was the cause, and the only cause of our separation. He knows this, and should not blame a living being. He never understood me; never knew how to treat me; and yet he loves me to that extent that he is jealous of the love of all who pay me respect. His ideas of woman's position (sphere) do not run exactly in the groove with my own. I never was born to be controlled by the light of any one's opinion, simply because that person happened to be a man, and I could not be thus led if that person had become my husband. I can never give up my freedom, my individuality; I will not be subjected to whims and fancies. Gold and luxuries do not tempt me. I do not covet an aimless, or fashionable life, made up of dress, parties, dinners, gossip, and little nothings. Such a life would soon bleach my hair, adorn my face with wrinkles, and transform me into a hysterical old woman,—not a very beautiful picture, but one which can be found in many homes of wealth.

I will anticipate you by saying, "Love can regulate and control all these objections."

I admit that it has done wonders in the right direction, but still it has led thousands upon thousands to destruction. The loves of appetite are the greatest of all curses. They may have their origin in hereditary ideas and principles, which, as you know, are not easily eradicated, especially when sanctioned by society, and protected by

269

law. I agree with you that every organ of the body does require exercise for health, but not equally so, one with another. True, the cultivation of the affections is necessary for the healthy and happy mind, but this does not depend upon wedlock. If we are lovable we will be loved. Our daily lives afford ample opportunities for the cultivation of these refining elements.

I have looked this subject over. I have studied its many surfaces and angles. I have divided it into its different elements. I have tested each one. And today I thank God that I had sufficient power to choose the path which I did select. Never will I forget the encouraging words which you, and one other, gave me, when all others opposed. The flesh was weak. I needed a stimulus, and I received it. Perchance it was the workings of a "guardian angel" that sent you. Happy thought!

When I return, should I consent to accept the position which you seem to think I should accept, he would be a happier man than he ever could have been had I occupied that place years ago.

I have preached you a sermon. How do you like it? Am I right, or am I wrong? Talk to me freely. Show me all my imperfections. I will profit by it. Oh, if I only had language, words, to express my feelings and views! I would write you a letter on this subject worth reading. But alas, I have but a conglomerate mass of confusion to select from. My implements are all rough, unpolished.

Well do I know what long years of persistent toil are required to set this house in a systematic, working order. I am equal to the task, if life and health are spared me. I shall succeed.

B. A. O.

Yoncalla, Oregon, Aug. 27, 1883. Mrs. B. A. Owens, M. D.

My Very Dear Friend—Your kind and flattering letter, addressed to me at this place, has been received, and probably your most skillfully prepared prescription never soothed the suffering of an afflicted body more than your kind and affectionate words have cheered and comforted my somewhat drooping spirit. I have so often been the victim of misplaced confidence,—so often by misfortune, had reason to doubt the soundness of my own judgment,—my sincerity doubted, and my motives misjudged by others, that you can scarce conceive how proud I am of your good opinion and kind recollection.

But, my dear friend, you greatly over-rate the little I have been able to do for you. It is true, I gave you my best judgment, and my warmest sympathy, unbiased by a single selfish motive; but it is to your own strong mind, and indomitable energy that you owe your success in life; and to your *merit,* not to luck or accident, is due the favors that fortune is showering upon you. Be true to yourself, and firm in the pursuit of a high purpose in life, and neither men nor devils can prevent you from reaching the goal of your ambition. As I believe it will give you pleasure, I will say of myself that I am in better health, better spirits, and am cheered by a brighter future than for many years of the past. And, should I continue on earth a few more years longer, in this happy condition of mind and body, that I shall not be doomed to a struggle with extreme penury, so crushing to life and manhood.

If years are granted to me, I hope to pass some of them in your society,—to see you daily, and perhaps hold in my arms that paragon of a boy who is in the flesh to transmit your honored name and noble blood to posterity. It will be one of my greatest pleasures to renew the friendly and frequent correspondence that once existed between us. That you should "Tell me all that is in thine heart."

I will rejoice with you in all your successes, sympathize with you and console you in your sorrows and misfortunes, and counsel with you in your troubles and perplexities. All this will I do, because my heart is with you. As ever yours,

JESSE APPLEGATE.

Drain, Oregon, Sept. 16, 1887. My Dear Friend—It would afford me much pleasure to witness your happiness as that of any living person, I think, after your hard struggle, and glorious conquest over adverse fortune, you should enjoy the fruits of your labors, while it is yet time. But when our bodies are worn out, and death is at times

271

hovering near us, it is too late to expect much more from the enjoyments of sense.

But I hear nothing from you about woman's rights. Has the woman of grass prevailed over the woman of spirit? Has a good and loving husband proved to be all that a woman needs to make her happy in this world? I think it is even so. But, as man partakes of two natures, mental and physical, the pleasures of sense are not satisfying. The immortal part craves its enjoyments also. The body seeks relaxation and repose, while the ever-sleepless mind demands change, and must have it. Natures like ours are not to be satisfied with any amount of the good, or goods, of the known, but continually seek acquaintance with the mysteries that surround it. And there are plenty of them. When the little "god" has done *his* work, your mind will return to *its* work, with greater energy and strength for its relaxation and rest. Then, and not while you are in dalliance with sensual love, will your mind and mine be in accord with each other.

Give my best respects to your husband, and assure him that I do not envy him his happiness. Sincerely your friend,

JESSE APPLEGATE.

MRS. B. A. ADAIR.

EXPERIENCE AS A NURSE

1859

In the pioneer days, when the professional nurse was unknown, every willing, capable woman received her training as a nurse from actual experience in her neighbors' homes, as well as in her own. Often no physician was in reach, and she was forced to depend alone on her own observation and common sense.

Long before she studied medicine, Mrs. Owens had proved her great natural ability to care for the sick; and her services were much sought after far and near. When she did accept remuneration, she received the best wages paid to any woman at that time.

She was, on one occasion, employed by a farmer named Kelly, who lived two miles from Roseburg, to nurse his wife during confinement. The babe was born the day after

Mrs. Owens' arrival, and she was expected to take the whole charge of the house;—doing the work of a trained nurse, in attending the mother and child day and night, besides caring for the two older children, and her own four years old boy; and doing all the housework and cooking for the family, which consisted of the man, wife, and three children, four hired men (as it was harvest time), and herself and little boy. She kept the infant with her nights, to allow the mother complete rest; was up at four every morning, after being kept awake by the baby, which always had to be fed at least twice in the night; and attended to the milk of ten cows, and made the butter from them; kept the house clean and orderly; did all the cooking for eleven persons; and washing and ironing for six persons, fed the fowls, and carried all the wood she used up a flight of stairs. All this she did faithfully and well, working hard every day and part of the night. The hired men received $2 per day, and rested on Sundays.

When three weeks had passed, and the wife was able to resume her duties, Mrs. Owens prepared to depart, and the farmer, running his hand down into his pocket, asked how much she was going to charge.

"Five dollars a week," she timidly answered, knowing that it was more than a woman's work was considered worth, but feeling that she had fully earned it. The man's face fell, and he surlily said, as he drew his hand empty from his pocket, "I didn't expect to be asked to pay over three dollars a week, but if you will take it in an order on Heinerberg's store, I will pay you five dollars."

Lacking the courage to assert her rights, she unwillingly accepted the order, which she was obliged to exchange for the poorest quality of goods at the highest prices;—for instance, paying twenty-five cents per yard for calico, which we now get for five cents.

This experience had its part, among many similar ones,, in spurring her on to more determined efforts for freedom of action, and a better recognition pecuniarily and otherwise, of her services and ability; and helped to shape her mind into more independent channels of thought regarding the status of woman, and her rights to equal compensation with man for equal work.

The foregoing experience always rankled in her heart, and she said to herself: "The time will come when that man Kelly will be glad to acknowledge my superiority." For, though an ignorant foreigner, he had looked down on her, and treated her as a servant.

That day did come.

Many years later, when Dr. Owens, was at the zenith of her professional fame and success, she was one day on board the cars, going to the state capital on public business, in connection with the legislative session.

A number of prominent gentlemen, who were her friends and fellow-passengers, had gathered about her seat, engaging in animated conversation when this man Kelly approached, anxious to let it be seen that he also knew her. At first, after all those years, she did not recognize him; and when he was obliged to recall himself to her, she received him politely, but, with his supercilious treatment of the past still unforgotten, she could not find it in her heart to be cordial, and he soon retired, discomfited.

The doctor then realized that Time does, sometimes, turn the tables, and brings compensation to those who have suffered undeservedly.

The "wheel of fortune" *had* turned, and now she was up, and he was down, and she had made her prophecy come to pass, and she reflected upon how true it is that a nature that domineers over anyone in its power, is always ready to play the sycophant to those who are above it.

The following letter so vividly and humorously describes the religious customs and ideas, and so pleasantly pictures the life of the settlers in those primitive days, that it is well worthy of preservation here. Mrs. Owens was, at this time, in San Francisco, learning the milliner's trade.

Roseburg, Ore., Dec. 9, 1867.

My Dearest Friend—I really feel sad to learn that you enjoyed such a rough journey, and being sick at the time it must have been a hard time for you. I hope you are all right ere this will reach you. I did not think that anything could induce you to return, but your flowers, but I see you don't even love them. I really don't know what would induce you now to return. I did think that you thought of your flowers more than anything else. Still, I live in hopes, for all men live so.

I have many good things to inform you.

First is, father joined the church last night. Also Isaac Jones and family. (Southern church.)

Flem (Dr. Adair's brother) was baptized yesterday, in Stevens' creek; also Bent. K. Bent, made a fool of himself by his actions.

Ti. (also her brother) told me if I would give him 50 cents he would pitch him out of the house.

He bawled like a calf. Part of the congregation left, in disgust.

He pitched himself on his back, and lay there for half an hour, and bawled like a fool. Oh, I would give anything, most, if you had been there to witness it.

After going down to the river, C., that sweet bird, was baptized.

They came after Bent., and he refused to go in. Ti told him to either be baptized or leave the place; and, after a long talk, he was put under. (Would have been a good thing if he never came up.)

Ti and father are here, and many talking of church again tonight.

I don't know what I can say to induce you to come home, unless it is that if you don't come shortly, the river will rise, and you can't get home. I hope this will find you in good health; also Jane and babes.

Excuse these mistakes, for Ti has troubled me so much trying to find out whether I am writing to you. I told him "No" half a dozen times. He assures me that the letter I received today is from you. I told him it was from Portland. He is also writing at' the desk to Ann. Why don't you come home? From your ever true friend,

A. M.

P. S.—Do come.

During the first years of the war of the rebellion, Mr. Owens, senior, father of Dr. Owens-Adair, lived near Roseburg, where a goodly proportion of the settlers were, like himself, southern born. Naturally, they sympathized with the South. There was strong feeling on both sides, but the Union men were in the majority.

Some of the young Southern men, in their hot-blooded enthusiasm, offered to furnish the silk, for a Confederate flag, to a young daughter of Mr. Owens, if she would make it. The young girl, a mere child of twelve or thirteen years,—too young to realize the seriousness of the undertaking,—accept the material, sewed the flag (quite a small one), and, climbing a tree in front of her home, hung it on a prominent branch.

This was done unknown to her mother, and in the absence of her father, both of whom would not have permitted the unwise act, had they known of it. As soon as it was known that a Confederate flag was flying in front of Mr. Owens' house, threats were made by the young Union men to tear it down, some of them using violent and abusive language. This was heard by a son of Mr. Owens, a youth of 18 or 19, who ran quickly home to warn his family. Mr. Owens, senior, was still absent from home, but Mrs. Owens, the plucky mother of the family, now first apprised of the existence of the flag, was not to be forced to obey the behest of an angry and insulting mob; and she and her son, armed with guns, appeared on the front porch, where she coolly informed the irate crowd that the first one who dared to lay hands on that flag would be a dead man.

They did not dare, and soon went their ways. The flag remained in its place unmolested until it was worn out by the elements.

Dr. Owens-Adair, who at this time sympathized with her family, was of too just and broad a mind not to see both sides of the question and rise above the strong influences of childhood, hence she was later as loyal to the Union as any Northern citizen.

As a student, Dr. Adair was always painstaking and thorough, but in the beginning, before her mind became trained to its later keenness, she required time to come to a solution of abstruse subjects. Indeed, all she has ever acquired has been by sheer determination and hard work.

On one occasion, at a recitation in advanced grammar, there were several different analyses of a very complex sentence submitted by the young ladies and gentlemen of the class.

Some brought no analysis at all, claiming that it was too difficult for them. But most of the class,—notably the young ladies,—had diagrammed, analyzed and parsed the sentence according to their understanding of it.

Mrs. Owens had a well-defined solution, which she promptly put upon the black-board, and convinced all save one member of the class of its correctness. Miss A.'s analysis was different, and she, also, demonstrated her view of it at the board.

The professor, however, decided in favor of Mrs. Owens' analysis, and the dissenting classmate said no more, though none the less convinced that her own rendering was the correct one.

The next day Mrs. Owens announced decisively in the class that she had been thinking that sentence over and had seen her own error, and it was now clear to her that Miss A. was right in her construction, which Mrs. Owens proceeded to clearly elucidate to the class. The professor (unlike Mrs. Owens), unwilling to acknowledge himself mistaken, merely remarked that "the sentence might be construed either way," and dismissed the subject. Mrs. Owens, however, always stoutly maintained what was the fact, that there was but one correct analysis of the disputed sentence,—that of Miss A.

This incident well-illustrated a fine point in her character. Firm, unyielding, assertive, when consciously in the right, she was also prompt and frank in owning herself mistaken when convinced of it, and always ready and anxious to do justice to her opponent.

This broadness of spirit only from a character in which a sincere and intense love of, and desire for correct knowledge is the very foundation stone. Combined with her exceptional loyalty to her friends it is the solid basis on which some of the most enduring friendships of her life still rest unbroken, after forty to fifty years' duration. It is sometimes asserted that a lasting and disinterested friendship cannot exist between women, but her oldest and most faithful friends comprise quite as many women as men.

With all her literary ability and varied authorship, the doctor frequently compares herself to Senator Conkling, who never could learn to spell even common words. Orthography has always been her bugbear, but she strives steadily to master it.

An extract from a speech by Senator Mitchell, in Portland, Oregon, in November, 1904, is so much to the point that it is inserted here:

"Fellow Citizens: Forty-four years ago this month I made my first political speech in this city and state. That was the campaign in which the candidate of the Republican party was the greatest American that has ever lived in this country since the days of Washington—the great liberator, Abraham Lincoln, of Illinois. That campaign resulted in his election, and for four years that great man conducted the ship of state through the rough storms of the civil war, which tested the strength and durability of every plank of the grand old ship.

"While I never had the pleasure of a personal acquaintance with Abraham Lincoln, I had the honor of sitting in the Senate for a period of five years beside that grand old statesman who was his running mate, lion. Hannibal Hamlin, of Maine, and I shall never cease to be grateful for the many kindnesses shown me by him during the first year? of my service in the Senate. When I first took mv seat in the Senate I was given a seat in what was then called the 'Amen corner' of the Senate chamber. It was on the extreme left of the presiding officer,—the scat now occupied by my friend, Senator Nelson, of Minnesota.

"But, before a year had expired, by reason of the death of Senator Buckingham, of Connecticut, I was transferred to a seat on the main aisle, directly in front of the presiding officer,—the seat now occupied by Senator Frye, when he is not presiding. Senator Hannibal Hamlin sat immediately to my right and Senator Conkling immediately behind me. When I went over to take my seat Senator Hamlin took me cordially by the hand and said: 'Mitchell, I am glad for two reasons that you are coming over here to this seat.'

"I thanked him and told him I would be glad to know the reasons he had for wishing me over there.

"'Well,' he said, 'In the first place, I think I will like you for a neighbor, and, in the second place, you must from this time on do Conkling's spelling for him.'

"I did not know what he meant, and on inquiry he said:

"'Why, Conkling can't spell two words right; I have been doing his spelling for him for the last number of years; I understand you are a good speller, and you must do it from this on, as you are a young man.'

"I was very much astonished and puzzled by this statement, but it is safe to say that in the five years I occupied that seat Senator Conkling asked me how to spell at least five hundred words.

"'Senator Conkling was a man who wrote a great deal at his desk when not engaged in debate.

"One day he leaned over and inquired of me how to spell wagon. I told him I should spell it 'w-a-g-o-n.'

"He then said:

"'I shall immediately proceed to strike out one "g." '

"On another occasion he asked me how to spell 'Czar' I inquired if he meant the Czar of Russia, and he said 'Yes.'

"'Well,' I said, 'generally it is spelled "Czar," and sometimes "Tsar."'

"He then said:

"'I shall at once proceed to prefix a "C."

"He had spelled it 'Z-a-r.'

"Now, ladies and gentlemen, I must not be understood as contending that because Senator Conkling was not a good speller that that is any reason why Mr. Parker should not be elected President, or even a reason why our candidate should be. I only thought that before proceeding to the task before me it might be interesting for some of you to know that it sometimes ' so happens that some of our greatest statesmen are deficient in some of the simplest and most elementary principles of an education."

SCHOOL CERTIFICATE

Astoria, Ore., March, 1863.

I hereby certify that Bethenia Owens is of good moral character, and has passed an examination in the following branches, with the following result:

Orthography 1

Reading 1

Writing 1

English Grammar 1

Mental Arithmetic 1

Written Arithmetic 1

Algebra 2

Modern History 2

Teaching 2

This certificate is good for one quarter.

CYRUS OLNEY, Supt. Com. Schools.

Astoria, Ore., May 1, 1864.

EARLY LETTERS TO HER SON

San Francisco, Cal., Feb. 7, 1868.

My Darling Son—After waiting a long time for a letter from you I can wait no longer. Why have you not written to your mamma before, dear? It has been about four weeks since I received a letter from my little boy; but I hope I shall get one tomorrow. Mary tells me you are getting along very nicely with your studies. Oh, how glad I am to hear of your success, darling! Only study hard, and you shall have every advantage. I know I shall be able to give you an accomplished education, and perhaps more; and all the reward I ask is to see you a great and noble man. I know you will not disappoint your mother. I have too much confidence in my darling boy to ever think of such a thing. Georgie, I have a grand scheme in view for you, and if I succeed your fortune will be easily made. But I cannot tell you what it is now, dear. Wait till I come home. Now I will tell you something of what I have seen in the city. Well, the other day I went out to see the city gardens; but, for fear you will not know what I mean by that, I will tell you. There are ten or twenty acres fenced in with a high-wall fence. We pay 25 cents to get in, then we are at liberty to go all over the grounds and see all there is to be seen, which is a great deal, I can tell you. There are two large towers where you can go up and see all over the city.

There are beautiful summer-houses, and all kinds of flowers and trees; four or five fountains, filled with all kinds of fishes, a nice little lake, and fancy boats for ladies and gentlemen, and boys and girls to ride in when they like; all kinds of swings, where you may swing as much as you please. Then we come to the place where they keep innumerable animals and birds. Oh, how I wished you were here when we came to the cages of animals. I wish I could tell you all about them, but I cannot, it would take me too long. There are all species of bears, a monster grizzly bear, all sorts and sizes of monkeys, in fact, all the animals you could think of. But I must tell you about one large cage we saw called the "Happy Family." When I looked in, there lay, in one corner, the biggest hog I ever saw, and a coon curled up on top of his back; a skunk curled up in another corner, a coyote and a wolf walking backward and forward, while a monkey was hanging on the bars, and two or three chickens and a badger picking around on the floor. Pussy sat up on a shelf, looking down very quietly, while a little black dog went strutting about and seemed to be king of the household.

But, never mind, darling, when you come down to school you shall go out and see all. So now, good-bye, darling; write to me soon. From your affectionate mother,

B. A. OWENS.

This was written while I was learning the millinery trade, after which money was more easily earned.

Roseburg, Ore., Nov. 13, 1870.

My Dear George—I received yours of the 7th inst., yesterday, and am sorry to say have been feeling very unhappy since. Do you ask why? I will tell you. Since your father has been to see you, and you have been going to the city every week, you have been neglecting not only me, but many things you ought strictly to attend to. In the first place, all your letters have been' short, written in a hurry, and' always closed by saying you have not time to write. Now, how can I feel over this, George? Am I not toiling hard to make you a great man, and is this the way for you to repay me? Do you know why you have no time to write longer letters to your mother? I will tell you, George. It-is because you go to the city every Saturday and do not get home till Sunday night, or Monday morning. -You have not told me this, but I well know it is so; and by so doing you miss your church and Sunday school. Is this right? Do you not know that it is your duty to go to church and Sunday school; And then I always knew that between three and four o'clock, you were writing to me, which was a great pleasure, indeed, to know that at least one hour in the week your thoughts were given entirely to your mother, and home. But, how is it now-? When three o'clock comes, I think: Where is my child, and what is he doing? And it makes me very unhappy, indeed.

Now, George, I do not wish to deprive your father of your society, but I do not wish you to neglect me, nor the privilege you now have of improving your mind, your morals, and your manners, and you cannot attend to all these and spend two days out of the week in the city.

Now, what I wish to say is this: If your father wishes your society and desires to have you with him one day out of the week, I have no objection, so he goes after you on Friday evening and you return on Saturday evening; and then, if he wishes to be with you on Sunday, he must go to Oakland and go to church and Sunday school with you, for you must not remain in the city on Sunday; I forbid it; and I know you have too much sense,—also too much respect for your mother, to disobey me. I have perfect confidence in you, and I know you love me too much to make me unhappy. Another thing: I was very much hurt to have you ask me to burn my letters. Why should you wish to destroy your mother's letters, my child? Have you not a trunk with a lock and key to it? Can you not put all your little things in it and lock them up? I wish you to keep your things in neatness and order in your trunk; also, number all your letters, tie them all up neatly in packages, and lay them carefully away. This will be nice employment for you on Sunday,—to put your things all in order, and never leave them in confusion. And when you write, tell me what books you are reading; how you are getting along in your studies; how many years you think it will be before you can be admitted into the university, and write me long letters.

Winter has set in here, and the streets are very muddy. Jake has to bring his beef into town in a cart.

The courthouse is done and fenced in and looks very nice.

Now, dear, I must say good-bye, and may God bless my darling, is the prayer of your affectionate

MOTHER.

P. S.—You can tell your father what I have said about your going to the city.

Roseburg, Ore., Nov. 23, 1870.

My Dear George—I hardly know how to begin this letter, I am so uneasy about you. I have had no letter from you for two weeks, and, though you were well when you last wrote, still I fear something must have happened to you. Two nights ago I dreamed of seeing you drowned. Night before last I dreamed I saw you killed by a snake, and last night I thought I saw you in such low company, with a big, long pipe in your mouth. Oh, I felt so bad, and I thought I begged you, for my sake, never to put a pipe in your mouth again, but you acted stubborn, and seemed to think it was so manly to do as you pleased.

But at last I thought you said: "I can't promise to quit, but I will promise to try."

You know, dear, I do not believe in dreams, and I am thankful I do not, for I should then be more unhappy than I am. I am so anxious about you that when I sleep you are in my mind, and I am sure to dream something horrible. Asher has not received an answer to his last letter, either, and he thinks you have forgotten him.

November 24.

My Darling Boy—Allie Brown came yesterday while I was writing, and I was so busy all day and till ten o'clock at night, that I could not get a moment to finish this. But, thanks to a kind Providence, your precious letter reached me this morning, and drove away all my unhappiness. I was so uneasy and excited last night that I decided to telegraph today, if I did not get a letter this morning, but it came, and my gloomy feelings, since I know my darling boy is well and loves his mother too well to make her unhappy. You will never regret, my darling, sacrificing that little pleasure for your mother. I know it is a sacrifice, and I know, too, that it is for your own good, as you will say yourself after awhile. I fear you have not enough bed-cover to keep you warm. If you still need more, go to the teacher and tell him to get you a pair of blankets and charge them to me. I sent a hundred dollar greenback to Mr. Geo. Tait to pay your school bill, which is $85.50. I told him to give you what is left for your own use. Well, dear, company has come in, and Asher is waiting to post this, so now, my precious darling, good night, with many kisses from your affectionate

MOTHER.

286

Roseburg, Ore., Nov. 27, 1870.

My Dear George—Your welcome letter of the 20th inst reached me yesterday. You do not know how much pleasure it affords me to hear from you, and to know you are happy and progressing so fast. I have never been so happy in all my life as now, and all because I have got such a good and dutiful son, who is willing to do anything his mother asks of him, and I know my darling will never regret obeying his mother, for what more, my child, have I to live for but you? Without you my life would be a burden. I am anxiously looking forward to the time when you will have finished your education and we can travel and see the world together. I know it must be pleasant down there. We have had but little rain this fall, but the hills are looking green, and the roads are muddy. Christmas will soon be here, and then I shall begin to count the days and weeks till I can start to see you. You would hardly know Roseburg now, it is so much improved. Dr. Hoover has built a drug store facing on Main street, and the Plaindealer an office, also. Frink's have painted and fitted up their dwelling house, and have been trying very hard to make that the main, or principal, street. They have built two bridges out this side, and beyond the church, so the travel would come that way. So the property holders on this street have built a fine bridge up the other sides of Barnes', and put a nice railing on it, and cut down the large tree in front of Joe Stevens', and have graveled the street nearly all the way from my house to the new bridge. So you see we do not have much mud on our street. They have moved the old courthouse back of Swan's old house. I can see it as I sit; by the fire and write to you. I have had the walk made narrow in the back yard, and put in new plank, and the garden covered all over, about a foot deep, with manure. It looks splendid, and I guess it will pay me for the trouble. \ wish you were here to see how nice it looks. But when I come down I will tell you all about it. Did I tell you that Annie and Alice Kent have opened a millinery store in Jacksonville? They bought all their goods from me—$300 worth. They are doing very well. I have a splendid business this fall; if J had not, it would have gone pretty hard with mc, fop Mrs. Ralls ran the Oakland business in debt $200. But I must close, dear, as it is time to get ready for Sunday school. So good-bye, darling, with many kisses from

287

MAMMA.

Roseburg, Ore., Dec. 3, 1870.

My Dear Georgie—Your welcome letter of the 27th ult reached me yesterday. It is such a relief to hear from you, and to know you are well and happy. You are very anxious to know just when I will start. I cannot tell you, exactly, now, but I think not before the last of February or the 1st of March, as I wish to be in the city the last of March to get the latest spring styles. I am so anxious to see you and clasp you in my arms and kiss your precious lips; but I must not neglect my business, for that would be neglecting you, and that I shall never do. And, as success depends upon strict application, I shall not leave one stone unturned, for I am determined to make my business here pay.

I saw, a few days ago, that girls were going to be admitted into the university. Is it true? I hope it may be, for I do not think the society of girls is any detriment to boys. I think it always has a tendency to refine and improve their morals. I should always rather you would associate with refined, intelligent girls than ordinary boys, for I am sure you would gain more high principles and fine feelings from them. We have not had any cold weather this winter yet, but considerable rain, and the roads are very muddy. The stages are running on long time now, I cannot think of an item of news worth writing, everything is so dull here. So I will say good-bye to my darling for a few days, when I will write again.

MAMMA.

Roseburg, Ore., Dec. 12, 1870.

My Dear George—It has been more than a week since I had a letter from you, and I fear it will be a week more before I hear, for they say the snow is ten feet deep on Scott's mountain, and the stages have not been able to get over for several days. It rained perfect torrents nearly all last week. They decided to have a Christmas tree yesterday. How I wish you could be here on Christmas eve. I know there will be no stocking hung up by little hands here, and no sweet voice to greet my ears with "Merry Christmas!" But I hope my boy will be happy, and rest assured that I will think and speak of my bright, black-eyed boy many times. Everybody asks of you often.

But I must say good-bye, darling. I hope to see you soon.

MAMMA.

Roseburg, Ore., Dec. 26, 1870.

My Dear George—Christmas has passed, and New Years will soon be here. I hope you were happy and did not feel lonely among strangers. I was not very happy, for it made me feel sad to see all the children getting presents and my darling not here. And as I thought, "Perhaps he is feeling lonely and forgotten the tears forced their way into my eyes, and I wept for my own darling boy. But I hope the time will soon be here when I can be with you a few weeks, or days, at least. I sent you five dollars in a letter, just a week ago, for a Christmas present. I hope it reached you in time. Now I suppose you would like to know what I got for Christmas presents. Well, a large, handsomely-bound volume of Shakespeare's works, a dress, a handkerchief, a handsome bead basket, and a beautiful cushion for the bureau.

We had about ten days of extremely cold weather, but the day before Christmas it rained all night, and is very warm now. I did very well before Christmas, but I expect it will be dull now, as there seems to be so little money in the country.

But now, dear, I must close, so as to get this in the mail. I wish you a Happy New Year, and I hope I may hear that you are happy. So good-bye, darling.

To George, from his affectionate

MOTHER.

Boston, Mass., May 18, 1874.

My Dear George—I have been waiting in vain for three weeks for a letter from you. I have had only one from you since I left home. I expect you will be surprised to see I am in Boston, but I believe I wrote you that I thought of coming here to stay till the fall term of college commences, which will be in October.

Well, I came here the first day of May and rented an office, advertised, and prepared for business. I begin to think the angels must have sent me here, for the next day after I advertised I got two patients, and they have been coming ever since. I have made ninety-five dollars and fifty cents, enough to pay all my expenses and get all my instruments and quite a little stock of medicine. Now, my darling, what do you think of that for your mamma? They think here that I am an old practitioner from the Pacific Coast, and that, for off-hand, has a great charm for people over here. I believe I shall do splendidly; but it keeps me studying, I assure you, for I study up every case, so as not to forget it, which will be of great benefit to me. I do not go out to practice, but do a strictly office business, so all my patients come to the office to be treated. Oh, George, you don't know how much nicer it is than selling goods, and working night and day; and it agrees with me, too. You would hardly know me, I am getting so fleshy, and looking so much better. I like Boston so much better than I do Philadelphia. I know I shall not like to go back. How often I think of you, and wish you were here with me. It seems I am always looking for you in every boy I see. There are about one hundred boys in military dress who parade by here on the Common twice a week. When I hear the drum I run to the window and wish I could see my own dear boy among them. I think this is one of the best cities in the United States for a woman doctor, as there are about forty thousand more women than men here, and they are mostly working women, thousands of whom are afflicted, and the major part of them seem to prefer a woman doctor.

Well, darling, another patient, so I must attend to her, and ask you to excuse me for awhile.

She is gone, and I will proceed. Poor girl, she has been doctoring for more than a year, without relief, and seeing my advertisement as coming from the Pacific Coast, she came to me. I understand her case, and feel confident I can cure her. She says if I can she can bring me four more new patients. I am well pleased with Boston. The people here seem to occupy a higher and broader plane than any I have seen.

My darling, write to me often.. I send you some of my cards.

STORY OF GEORGE

1870

Dr. Adair, then Mrs. Owens, lived at one time near where a house had been burned. Nothing remained of the place but the cellar, which was half filled with dry rubbish.

The neighborhood children played about and in it, and one day they wantonly set it on fire. In a few moments the excavation was a seething caldron of flame. About that time a boy two or three times as large as little George Hill got into a fight with him and tried to throw him into the fire; hut George, who was a wiry, plucky little fellow, and active as a cat, succeeded in whipping the big fellow, finally tripping and throwing him down, hut the big bully fell on top. Driven to extremity, little George seized his antagonist's head by the hair with both hands, and, holding it down, bit his face and nose severely. The other boys, willing to see fair play, then turned them over, so the little boy was on top, where he punished the big bully till he howled for mercy, and the boys parted the combatants.

George had on a long linen duster, and it and his face were covered with blood, making him a frightful looking object, though he was in no way injured. Catching sight of his mother's terrified face, as she saw him approaching, apparently half killed, he considerately called loudly to her: "I'm not hurt, mother! I'm not hurt!" thus relieving her worst fears before she could have time to assure herself of the fact by actual examination. Young as he was, he felt that he wished to spare his mother every possible minute of such agonizing anxiety, thus showing unusual sympathy for a boy-child.

DR. ADAIR AND HER MOTHER, MRS. THOMAS OWENS

1904

I spent some time last month with my mother, Mrs. Thomas Owens, pioneer of 1843, at Seaside, Oregon's great summer resort.

My mother is nearing her 87th mile-stone. We were in the yard one morning as the sun came up in all his glory. My mother said:

291

"This reminds me of what I have not thought of for years. You and I had been riding all night in the stage, and the sun came up, just like this, and the driver asked you to sing a song. You sang 'My Sailor Boy,' and I thought I never heard you sing anything so well; and when you sang the chorus, 'Toral, lal, lal; toral, lal, lay' the whole woods seemed to be full of echoes. The driver and passengers cheered and cheered you. Don't you remember it?"

No, I could not recall one word of it. She said: "Well, that is strange! It has been forty or forty-five years ago, but I can remember the first song I ever learned. It was composed by a preacher on his death-bed, and his wife used to sing it. My father was good to her, and whenever she came to our house he would ask her to sing that song, and that's the way I learned it. That was about eighty years ago!" My mother had a remarkable memory, in her youth, and, even now, it is good for recent dates, considering her age. In pioneer days singing was much in vogue. My mother had a sweet, soft voice, and could sing love songs by the hour. I will here give "My Sailor Boy" for the benefit of pioneer men and women, who, like myself, forty-five years ago, were full to overflowing with love and sentiment, which was ever ready to burst forth in song when opportunity offered.

MISS BARTON RETIRED

1904.

(Extract from The Daily Oregonian.)

"The National Red Cross Society is at last to be reorganized, with Miss Barton left out. This is not as harsh a measure as it appears. An efficient factor in the work of the society for many years, she is no longer able, for reasons not one of which reflects discredit upon her, to longer manage the business affairs of a great organization. She has reached the limit of usefulness; the limit fixed by nature. She is no longer young; is feeble in health, and frail in body.

"Miss Barton is said to be a broken-hearted woman, chafing in her age against what she conceives to be the ingratitude of those who insisted on her retirement from the presidency of the Red Cross Society."

Such cases as this of Miss Barton certainly evoke pity, but it is a sort of pity from which self-respecting pride recoils.

If we must retire, let it be from choice, and not under compulsion. The wise few learn this from keen observation and voluntarily step aside from the midst of the stirring scenes of their arduous and worthy labors and successes, before their work begins to show signs of the inevitable effects of advancing age, instead of waiting until they are crowded out by those younger and more active, and more modern in their methods. And even when, as in the case of Dr. Adair, the health is not impaired and the individual has kept abreast of the age in advanced ideas, the 'enthusiasm and ambition of youth, which nothing else can replace, is gone, or going, and it is, as she says, the part of wisdom to recognize this and bow gracefully to the unchangeable law of Nature.

For it is far better to leave one's bright public record unmarred by later deteriorated work. I say "public record," because the retiring from public life by no means necessitates relinquishing active endeavor in some pursuit, and many years of this may, and should, remain.

It is decidedly pleasanter, as Dr. Adair further remarks, to be sought out in voluntary retirement and to find your services still in urgent request by the public, which is still loth to "lose" you, than to hold on and on, feeling yourself gradually but surely set aside in spite of your best efforts, and be subjected to ill-natured criticism by young upstarts who know far less than you do.

Some seem unconscious of their failing mental powers, while acknowledging and taking pleasure in describing their physical disabilities. But the trained mind of a professional man or woman ought not to be so dull or blind as to fail to notice in itself what is so obvious to it and to all in others.

Such, if not too blinded by self-esteem, perceive even before others discover it the first indications of their own decadence, and prepare to shape their remaining years in accordance.

It need not cause unhappiness to themselves or others. The transition can be so gracefully and gradually made as to be only pleasantly perceptible. We all know a few delightful and lovable old people, whose lives are a comfort and a blessing to all about them, and we can make them and their lovely, unselfish characters ours, by God's help, if we will.

October, 1903

In pursuance of the above views, Dr. Adair has retired from an active and lucrative practice, in her sixty-sixth year, with the purpose of devoting the remainder of her life to literary pursuits, free from the weighty sense of responsibility attending the knowledge that life and death are constantly depending on one, which is the inevitable accompaniment of the conscientious practice of medicine, even more than of any other profession.

CENTENNIAL CELEBRATION

OF THE DISCOVERY OF THE COLUMBIA RIVER

The celebration, on May 11, 12, and 13, 1892, of the one hundredth anniversary of the discovery of the third largest river in the world by Captain Robert Gray was fitly held in Astoria (the second city in size in the state, though the first in point of establishment), situated at the mouth of that noble and historic stream.

Its citizens rose with just pride to the occasion, and prepared to receive and entertain with due honor the distinguished guests they had invited from far and near. Professor John Fiske, of Boston, Captain Gray's home city, who had consented to deliver the centennial address, was the first guest of honor, but there were many other eminent persons present. The managing committee appointed a committee of prominent ladies of Astoria and vicinity to assist them in entertaining and to take charge of the great banquet, which was to be one of the principal features.

Citizens threw open the doors of their homes and warmly welcomed friends and strangers to their hospitality. Routine business was for the time laid aside, while all Astoria gave itself heartily to the entertainment of its guests.

The battleships Baltimore and Charleston were in attendance, and as such warships were not so common with us then as now they were the "cynosure of all eyes." Gaily decorated with bunting, they were constantly crowded with delighted visitors, who were received with unremitting politeness and patience by their officers and men, who kindly and pleasantly answered the questions of the thronging groups of eager people.

At night the scene was even more beautiful and brilliant under the strong, swiftly-moving searchlights—the first ever seen in that vicinity—with the countless lesser lights gleaming on every other craft.

One unique feature was a night race between the fishing boats, several hundred of which took part in it, everyone bearing a bright light at its masthead. The long, sinuous procession on the soft, dark stretch of water looked like a great, waving, swaying chain of glittering jewels, and was indeed a charming spectacle.

The ladies took an active part in their departments. Dr. Adair was first*appointed chairman of the ladies' managing committee, but as she did not reside in the city, she declined in favor of Mrs. Samuel Elmore, and took the chairmanship of the committee on serving and preparing the grand public banquet. This banquet proved to be the unqualified success that was assured when Dr. Adair took command, as she always makes a success of whatever business she undertakes; and no one better understands, not only what to provide for a large banquet, but how to marshal the forces necessary to bring it successfully to pass—as the sequel proved, for the guests universally declared that never had they sat down to a finer dinner.

Dr. Adair first called together the ladies, whom she had carefully selected, and notified of their appointment as her assistants on the banquet committee. *At this meeting she outlined the work and appointed sub-committees on each separate department, with all necessary instructions and powers, and, inspired by her own enthusiasm and energy, they all went to work with a will to carry out her orders, and did their part so well under the efficient chief that the guests who sat down, five hundred at a time, at the long, snow-white, flower-decked tables in the immense, handsomely decorated hall, vied with each other in praise of the appetizing result.

Dr. Adair and her adjutants had decided that as Astoria is a fishing town, all kinds of fish and crustaceans must be served. The ladies to have charge of the five tables, one to each, were chosen by lot, that there might be no suspicion of partiality, and these ladies chose their young lady assistants, who were thoroughly drilled in their duties beforehand.

At each end of the long tables was served an immense Royal Chinook salmon, smoking hot from the oven, accompanied by hot creamed potatoes and all the appropriate accessories. The various canneries contributed these salmon, which weighed from sixty to eighty pounds each, and as no range-ovens or pans large enough to contain them were to be had, roasting pans were made to order, and the salmon were roasted in baker's ovens, and from thence taken directly to the tables and served in the pans in which they were cooked.

It is a literal fact that no fish on earth compares in delicious 'flavor and richness (to say nothing of size) with the salmon, and the Chinook salmon are as far beyond all other salmon, as *they* are beyond all other fish.

These royal specimens of the king of fish were done to a turn, and many were the ecstatic encomiums showered upon them by the guests from abroad. Other fish, shell-fish of all varieties, including oysters, clams, and crabs, in their native shells, with every other dainty of the season and vicinity, appeared on that bountifully-furnished board, the bivalves, especially, prepared in such delicious ways as the dwellers contiguous to their native home best understand, and rarely is seen assembled so rare, so happy and well satisfied a company of diners as partook of them.

The sturdy pioneers were there, attended by the younger generation, who delighted to do them honor. Stories and reminiscences were recounted, and experience compared with experience by the white-haired, but still active and genial, founders of this wonderful Northwest. The entire celebration was most successfully carried out, and has been the means of fixing one of the most important events in our history more clearly and firmly in the minds and memories of the rising generation, and of adding cheer and honor and pleasure to the last days of the revered pioneers, whose work, begun and long carried on in toil and hardship, is ending, even in their own day, in peace, plenty and renown.

FIRST WOMAN COUNTY SCHOOL SUPERINTENDENT

IN OREGON, IN MULTNOMAH COUNTY

("Oregonian.")

"There was silence for a minute or two, when this order of business was announced. Teal whispered to a friend near him, 'Who is a good woman for the office?' 'Miss Sabin; smartest teacher in town (Portland); ought to be city superintendent.' Teal then placed in nomination Miss Ella C. Sabin, principal of the North School. O'Hara asked whether the election of a woman to the office would be legal, and if so, he would be glad to work and vote for the lady. Fenton was called upon to answer. He stated that he was present in Judge Deady's office several days ago, when Mrs. Dr. Owens-Adair called and propounded the same question. Without reflection, several lawyers present were of the opinion that a woman could not hold the office, because she was not an elector. Continued Mr. Fenton: 'The question has never been passed upon by the courts, but if Miss Sabin will allow us we will elect her and Gault will not contest it. If he does I will volunteer my services to defend our candidate's title to the office.' (Applause.)

"O'Hara asked: 'Is Miss Sabin a Democrat?'

"Teal responded that he was not able to say, but he could say she was a remarkably bright educator, and was possessed of splendid executive ability, and that was sufficient to entitle her to the honor.

"Miss Sabin was nominated by acclamation, amid genuine applause."

OFFICE LIFE

1882 and 1905

The office life of a physician is, from one point of view, a series of stories, sad, dramatic, amusing,—sometimes all three in one,—and their graphic recital would, in itself, make an interesting volume.

This is especially so in the case of Dr. Adair, with her strong convictions and antipathies and vigorous expression of the same.

One day in 1882 she had just dismissed a patient at the outer door of her consulting room and passed through the inner door to her office, where she found a number of patients, in waiting, besides two young men with bills to collect, one of whom was Mr. Willis Duniway, with a bill for advertising. He sat quietly awaiting his turn, while the other stood puffing a cigar, and, without removing it from his mouth, he pompously announced:

"I have a bill to collect."

Before replying Dr. Owens threw a window wide open, and then, turning toward him, commanded incisively:

"Take that cigar out of your mouth. I do not allow smoking in my reception-room. Do you not see that there are ladies present?"

The fellow hastily threw his cigar out of the window, and, in a more subdued tone, repeated that he had a "bill to collect."

"Well," said the doctor, "you can come in tomorrow and collect it."

The young man departed, and she then turned to Mr. Duniway, whose refined, gentlemanly manner was in refreshing contrast to the boorish behavior of the other collector, and said pleasantly:

"Mr. Duniway, have you a bill?"

"Yes, madam, for advertising," he replied, and she continued: "I shall take pleasure in' paying you now," which she proceeded to do.

She always paid her bills promptly at the first of every month, and only deferred settling with the first collector to more thoroughly impress upon him a badly needed lesson in deportment.

The patients in the office were all smiling, pleased to observe the difference in the behavior of the two men, and the special treatment each received from the doctor.

A ring at the door. Enter a stranger.

"Madam, I want to show you a fine line of toy balloons I am selling."

Dr. Adair: "I have no use for toy balloons; if you will go down street to Dr. Hill's office, you may sell him one. He is my baby. He is only forty-nine years old."

Exit toy-balloon man, in a dazed condition

CORRESPONDENCE

In the course of her long, active, and varied experience, Dr. Adair has enjoyed the close friendship of many prominent persons, some of whose letters are of public, as well as private, interest, and are worthy of permanent preservation,—and really form a part of her life-history. They are, therefore, incorporated in this volume, together with such of her own replies as seemed relevant and characteristic.

LETTER FROM HON. TILMON FORD

Salem, Ore., Oct. 29, A. D. 1873.

Mrs. B. A. Owens, W. C. T., Roseburg Lodge, I. O. of G. T.

Dear Friend and Sister—I promised to write to you last Friday, but have been unexpectedly and unavoidably so very busy that I *positively* have not had time to do so until now.

Yours in regard to commission is also duly at hand. Your secretary was right in sending the recommendation to Bro. James A. Smith, G. Sec., as I have signed commissions in blank, and placed them in his hands, with instructions to fill them out in accordance with recommendations from subordinate lodges. I did this so that our Grand Secretary would be placed in direct communication with all Lodge Deputies in the state.

I am well pleased to learn that Flem is now Bro. Owens, and that he is to be your Lodge Deputy. I have just written to the G. W. Sec to send forward the commission immediately, and if he has not already done so, it will reach you by Friday evening. Your Lodge Deputy lives at Oakland, or at least I found him there when I was out in August.

It would be well to extend him an invitation to be present at your installation ceremonies. I would like to comply with your very kind invitation and be present myself, but business prevents.

Our circuit court meets here next month, and I am interested as attorney in several cases that will require my personal attention, from now on, till it adjourns.

Shall start on a visiting tour to the respective lodges along the line of the railroad about the last of November or the first of December, and shall probably be at your lodge by the middle of December, and I shall expect (judging from your letter) to find it in a very prosperous condition. Now, don't let me be disappointed in this regard. Am truly sorry to hear that Bro. S.—has gone back to his cups again. I had hopes that he would stand firm in the great temperance reform. Please write me the particulars of his case. Also give me a full account of your public installation, and the continued prosperity of your noble little lodge, which I assure you will be read with interest by me.

With best wishes for the success of your public installation and the continued prosperity of your noble little lodge, I am yours in F. H. and

C. TILMON FORD.

P. S.—I sent you two constitutions; did you receive them?

MRS. MICHELL

THE CLATSOP

Portland, Ore., March 6.

To the Editor:

In an editorial in the Oregonian of February 27 last you refer to the age of Mrs. Michell, a Clatsop Indian woman, "The last of the Clatsops," who lives near Seaside, and whose age is said to be 103 years. Her name is not Michell. Her Indian name is Tsin-is-tum. Her mother's name was Wah-ne-ask.

When Tsin-is-tum came to a marriageable age she married Wah-tat-kum, who died in 1860. Later on she married one Michell Martineau, a Canadian-Frenchman. Wah-tatkum, her first husband, was the last chief of the Nehalem tribe. Her last husband was always spoken of and called "Michell," so she is called Mrs. Michell. Her "Boston" name is Jennie—Jennie Michell.

It is a singular fact that the Pacific Coast Indians never have but one name, and that name is never handed down from the father or mother to the offspring, but ceases to exist when its owner dies. Each Indian was given his particular name, which had no relation or resemblance to that of either his father or mother. Among the Indians it was considered improper, or irreverent, to ever mention the names of the dead.

You were quite right in doubting that she had reached the age of 103 years. In May, 1900, I went with a committee of the Oregon Historical Society, to Fort Clatsop, Lewis and Clark's headquarters in 1805 and 1806, to show them its location. From there we went to Clatsop beach, to see the location of their salt works, which had then been recently discovered.

We had Mrs. Michell brought there to identify the place. In a conversation between the late L. B. Cox, one of the committee, and Mrs. Michell (the late Silas B. Smith acting as interpreter), Mrs. Michell identified ,the place, which

353 her mother had often shown her as the place where Lewis and Clark made salt. Her mother knew Lewis and Clark, and had seen their men at work there.

In the same conversation she said she remembered when Dr. McLoughlin bombarded the Indian village at the mouth of the Columbia River, in 1829, saying that she was only a little girl, and that her father was killed in that bombardment. If she was nine years old in 1829. she would now be 83 years old.

At the time of the conversation above referred to, Silas B. Smith, who was of half-Indian blood, and had known her all his life, said she was about 80 years old. If she was a "little girl" in 1829, she could not now possibly be 103 years old.

Mrs. Michell, Sel-i-kee, and a Clatsop woman living at Bay Center, Wash., who is a grand-daughter of Twilch, an old Indian whom I used to know, and who remembered Lewis and Clark, are all of the full-blood Clatsop Indians now living. The tribe is practically extinct. Few Indians ever lived to be as old as Tsin-is-tum.

P. W. GILLETTE.

Dr. Adair was personally acquainted with fifteen of the Governors of the State of Oregon, namely:

Governors Thurston, Gaines, Lane, Whiteaker, Curry, Slater, Gibbs, Woods, Grover, Lord, Thayer, Chadwick, Moody and Geer.

Eight of these Governors, Gaines, Lane, Grover, Woods, Gibbs, Moody, Chadwick and Thayer, were her warm personal friends.

Governor Gaines had purchased a home on Clatsop plains in her childhood, which her brother-in-law, John Hobson, bought of him after the sudden and shocking death of Mrs. Gaines, on July 4, 1852 or 1853. The child, Bethenia Owens, was an eye witness of the fatal accident.

Mrs. Gaines and the Governor were on horseback, riding beside a wagon containing people on the way to the neighboring celebration. In passing a narrow place in the road Mrs. Gaines attempted to fall back and let the wagon pass first, and her horse backed in between the heels of the team and the wagon to which they were attached, and she was thrown violently upon the tongue of the wagon. As the frightened horses began to run it was several minutes before she could be extricated, when it was found that her skull was crushed. She was carried to the nearest house, where she soon expired without regaining consciousness.

Governor Gaines was a gentleman of the old school, possessing a high sense of honor and an estimable character, without a stain upon his record. During his administration Dr. Adair was but a mere child, but she well remembers his stately figure and courtly manners.

Portland, Ore., July, 1882.

Mrs. B. A. Owens, M. D.

Portland, Oregon.

Dear Doctor—At the annual meeting of the Oregon State Medical Society, held June, 1882, six subjects were chosen for discussion at the next annual meeting.

It being my duty to appoint one person to each subject, I wish to know if you will prepare a paper on retarded dentition, said article to be prepared, ready for publication, by the next annual meeting.

The subject, author, together with the day and hour when the paper will be read, will appear upon a program furnished to each member, not less than ten days before the annual meeting in 1883, as well as in the daily papers at the time. As it is expected these papers will attract much attention, it is hoped you will be present to read the same. Please answer immediately, so that the proper mention can be made in the transactions of this year. Hoping you will accept this honorable office, I remain respectfully yours,

CURTIS C. STRONG,

President O. S. M. S.

225 West Park Street, Portland, Oregon.

Astoria, Ore., June 9, 1893.

My Dear Children, One and All—So today you are on the swift eastward express. I know you are all happy, and that brings much satisfaction to us. Colonel has just left with Oscar for the front— Colonel for town and Oscar to cut and trim for firewood. The opening is gradually widening. Monday and Tuesday we put in all the turnips and garden seeds. Wednesday forenoon I finished up behind the cottage. Had forty nice hills made just behind the house, where the ground was low; set out all the tomatoes, squashes, cucumbers, etc., as it was drizzling. In the afternoon John and I went with Colonel and Oscar to the front, and they cut down six or eight trees. Yesterday Charlie and I finished hoeing the carrots on the hill, so you see we are all well up with our work, and I intend to keep it up, if possible.

The pioneers are to have a picnic tomorrow, at the end of the Bay R. R. If it is nice we will go, so John will have a glimpse of the world.

We received Mattie's letter last night, and it was a real treat. Colonel read it while I was getting supper, and then re-read it after we went to bed. We laughed over the reference to Solie. "How like her," I said. "It is really too foolish for anyone to take offense at, or be angry with anything she says or does, she is so silly."

So they were all delighted with your going, as well as with your style? Mattie, did you tell them that you were to be the lady correspondent of the Astorian? Well, it is drizzling, as usual, and the glass stands at 1.29. Not very bright for tomorrow's picnic. Excuse pot-hooks, for I am writing with John in my arms. Bless his little heart, he sticks to his mamma like a leech, now that we are alone. He is in love with Victor's little bed. He goes to it at night, when we go. Last night we were looking over letters from the drawers, and I came across that doll that I intended to exchange. Oh, he was so delighted with it! This morning he came out while we were at breakfast, and took me by the hand, and led me to the secretary and showed me to open the drawer, saying: "Dol-la." He had not forgotten where it came from. So my Victor-boy has been a gentleman? What good news for his grandma! We know he can be a gentleman if he tries, and he will make us all happy by trying every day. I want his new grandma and his uncles and aunties to be pleased with our boy. God bless his sweet young life, is my prayer always. We received a nice, long letter from Mr. Monroe. He is to visit us the first of July. He and his wife sent messages to Mattie and Victor. Mattie forgot to put in the clippings, for which I am sorry. We can see a' little colt by Juno, but have had no time to go down. Charley has just finished sweeping and washing the floors. He is doing nicely, and is getting almost over his cough and is looking well.

LETTER OF DR. ADAIR TO JANE WEEDEN

Sunnymead Farm, Ore., Feb. 9, 1894.

My Dear Friend, Miss Weeden—We received your kind and beautiful letter in due course of mail. How full of sentiment and sympathy it was,—just like your own dear self. We are so glad to hear from you! And the Millers; so they and their little ones are in Chicago? Had I known it I certainly should have gone to see them. I cannot say how sorry I was not to have seen and talked with you i called at the W. C. T. Q. headquarters several times, trying to find your whereabouts, hut could find no trace of you. When I met you I was going to lunch with an old college classmate, formerly a Dr. Henderson, whom I had just met. How little I thought then that a great sorrow was so near me. I had enjoyed the morning exercises so much, and now that I had found two dear old friends I was perfectly happy, and looked forward with such pleasure to the literary feast that was awaiting me. For twelve years I had been hoping to be able to attend a National Convention, and now I was there in attendance on the greatest W. C. T. U. convention in the world.

But you know the rest; that day of happiness only was mine. The news of dear Mattie's death came, and I left for home the next day.

What a long, sorrowful trip it was. And then to meet poor, dear Colonel with our two boys, Victor, aged 8 years, and John Adair, Jr., 27 months. Yes, we have two beautiful, bright boys.

Mattie died after a very brief illness. Inflammation of the bowels, the doctor in attendance pronounced it; but, as she had not complained for over forty-eight hours, I think perhaps there was a blood-clot. But whatever the cause might have been, it took her away from us. I have prepared a brief sketch of her short life, which will be published in the Oregon White Ribboner, perhaps this month. When it comes I will send you a copy.

Well, my dear old friend, we are here on the farm, somewhat isolated, but not lonely, with plenty of reading matter and plenty of work to keep us busy.

We have several head of horses, cattle, sheep, and hogs. The young ones are coming in all the year, which requires care, and gives us an interest in life. Our boys, too, afford us much pleasure, as well as care. We have a comfortable home. How I wish you could come and make me a long visit. The pure air and fresh farm cooking would give you a new lease of life. I hardly think you would recognize the place, we have made such a change. We are surrounded by flowers and beautiful shrubs. How poor Mattie did love our home, and she took so much pleasure working among the flowers. Her sister came down and spent a week with us and we set out many roots and bulbs on her grave,—flowers of her choice.

Mattie and Victor, my grandson, went to the World's Fair with Dr. Hill and his wife. They went the first of June. Mattie was gone six weeks, and was delighted with her trip. She boarded with Mrs. Johnson—our old W. C. T. U. Mrs. Johnson—of Portland. You will remember her, she used to conduct the singing.

This has been a long, tedious winter, but we have had excellent health. I have not had so much as a cold. Colonel and the boys had colds for a few days only. We have had no cold weather as yet. Indications are for an early spring. Do you think of coming to Oregon again? How time flies! I am 54 years old. I am strong and have excellent health. I think the country life agrees with me.

How are the Millers succeeding financially? I think they would have done better in Oregon. So your headquarters are in the Temple? What a beautiful structure. Mrs. Hosford and I attended service in "Willard's Hall," and saw Mrs. Carse, who had charge of the meeting.

Well, my dear friend, it is growing late, and I must say good night, with kind regards to the Millers and much love for yourself. Colonel joins me in kind regards. Remember, your letters are always welcome visitors.

Very sincerely your friend,

DR. OWENS-ADAIR.

My baby, John, is carrying the bag of pop-corn around, begging me to pop some. You see, the children are celebrating my birthday with pop-corn, raisins and candy.

NARROW ESCAPE

OF VICTOR FROM DROWNING

While living at Sunnymead, Colonel and Dr. Adair, with their grandson, Victor Hill, then between four and five years old, went on one occasion to visit Professor Lyman, at his ranch at the south end of Cullaby Lake, Clatsop Plains.

Near the western shore of this lake is a small island named, like the lake, for Cullaby, an old Indian chief who had lived upon it in the days of Dr. Adair's childhood, when her parents lived not a great distance from the lake. Fine cranberries grew on this island, which she and her mother used to gather, and the Doctor, who had not visited the spot in years, desired to see it once more. Mr. Lyman, therefore, volunteered to take her and Victor in his boat across the lake, stopping at the island on the way, while Colonel Adair went around by the road with the team, and they were to meet him at the north end of the lake, which was about two miles and a half long. Mrs. Stafford, a near neighbor of Mr. Lyman, also accompanied the party in the boat. The shores of the lake are plentifully and broadly fringed with pond-lilies, and seeing some particularly fine ones in one spot, Victor begged to be allowed to gather them, so Mr. Lyman backed the boat up within reach of the coveted blossoms. Dr. Adair was sitting in the stern, with one arm around the child, who leaned forward and grasped a lily firmly by its strong, thick stem, and Mr. Lyman then sent the boat forward, thinking to aid in breaking the stem, but it was too strong, and somehow, in the excitement of the moment, Victor fell out of the boat into the water. The Doctor screamed in terror, for the impetus of the boat had carried it some distance from the sinking child, but Mr. Lyman backed the boat toward him as fast as he could (being a cripple), and Mrs. Stafford, with good judgment and admirable presence of mind, seized an oar and assisted ably, so that they reached Victor just as he was disappearing, and Dr. Adair caught his clothes and succeeded in pulling him into the boat. Though she retained control of herself sufficiently to act promptly and efficiently at the time, the Doctor was so unnerved and agitated afterward that she could not sleep for the three nights following.

It was sometime after this occurrence before they saw Mr. Lyman again, but the moment Victor set eyes on him, as he was approaching their house, he exclaimed: "Grandma Grandma! Here is the man coming that saved me."

Cullaby Lake is very deep and the water in it is always cold. Besides, the place where the child fell in was full of a net-work of the tough roots and stems of the pond lilies, making it doubly dangerous, as a person sinking there is almost sure to be caught and so entangled as never to come to the surface again. Nothing but the most prompt and speedy action saved the life of the child on this occasion, and he never forgot the experience and the manner of his rescue. He was still in dresses, and his skirts probably kept him afloat longer than he would otherwise have remained on the surface.

A few years later Dr. Adair and family, with Mrs. Butterfield and family, spent the day fishing in the Necanicum Creek, near the Seaside House. While preparing, toward night, to return home, Victor wished to go back to the bridge alone after a certain beloved stick which had been left behind. The Doctor said, "No, you must stay with Mrs. Butterfield and her children till we are ready to start." A short time later she missed the boy, and said, "Where is Victor?" "Why," said Mrs. Butterfield, "he was here just a minute ago; he wanted to go to the bridge (a high one), but I told him to stay with the children and not go near the water."

Wild with apprehension, Dr, Adair rushed down to the bridge and beheld Victor, who was now in pants, coming up out of the water through the hushes lining the bank of the creek, dripping wet from head to feet.

In spite of all orders to the contrary he had returned to the bridge and tumbled off it into the middle of the creek and walked out on the bottom through water over his head! Being exceedingly active in mind and body, and correspondingly enterprising, he could disappear in a second, so it was impossible to keep him constantly in sight, and he was always having hair-breadth escapes. The Doctor declares she suffered a thousand deaths in the course of the time he was with them; yet he always seemed to bear a charmed life, and always turned up unharmed and smiling at her, to him, groundless fears, saying: "What's the matter, Grandma? What's the matter? I'm all right. Nothing is the matter with me."

Not only has Dr. Adair delivered many public addresses on hygienic and other subjects germane to her profession, and also most of the living issues of the day, but she has used her pen ably in the same varied lines her articles rarely, if ever, finding a place in the editor's waste-basket, for the reason that she always writes upon timely and vital themes in a vigorous, trenchant style, with great earnestness, and directly to the point in hand.

Being unusually public-spirited, with great pride in and love for her country, and possessing a warm interest in the individual as well as the public welfare, combined with a sound and practical judgment in practical affairs, what she writes is sure to be interesting reading to the general public, and consequently finds acceptance with the editor.

But for the ceaseless demands of a large and successful medical practice which has fully occupied her time for thirty years past, and the additional care of a home and family during the last twenty years, Dr. Adair would doubtless have written some valuable books from her wide experience, extended opportunities for acquiring the latest scientific knowledge, and her own ripened judgment.

Fortunately, however, one's generation is, of the two, often more benefited by an earnest, industrious, conscientious and continuous practice of correct knowledge and elevating ideas than by their written promulgation. But that both have had a worthy part in the life of ,this exceptional woman is conclusively shown in the productions that follow regular order of their writing, from 1871 onward, begin-

They are here presented, as nearly as practicable, Mrs. Owens' first efforts for publication:

THE FIRST ARTICLES I EVER WROTE FOR PUBLICATION— DATE, **1870**

Editor Pantagraph—I beg leave to ask the Plaindealer, through your columns, a few plain questions. Now, Mr. Plaindealer, I am in earnest and want a candid answer. I am a reader of your paper and have been known as a reliable democrat all my life, and I believe it to be the duty of every voter to know whom and what he is supporting, and I ask how you stand on prohibition. I, with hundreds of others, have a right and demand to know. Any politician can see that prohibition is to be the next issue, and you must be for or against; there is no half-way place for you to stand upon. The Pantagraph has come boldly to the front and declared herself ready for the fight, and where are you, I would ask, with your chivalric disposition? Why have you not buckled on your armor and thrown your banner to the breeze. We have given you ample time, and now we demand to know the cause that holds you back. Now is the time for you to strike in order to retain the favor of those already your friends, and gain the respect of your enemies. You have repeatedly been heard to say you were an enemy of rum, but you must remember the tree is judged by the fruit is bears. Therefore I warn you that the ground on which you stand is shaky. Let us hear from you.

Editor Plaindealer—In your issue of February 28 you said to "that inquisitive person" who asked you a plain question that you were not averse to giving your views on prohibition, providing the question was asked by a responsible person, through your own columns. Now, this is where the interesting act comes in, for "now you see" (in the language of General Lish), that knowing you to be a strong anti-suffrager, and I, poor thing, a "f-e-m-a-l-e,"

I knew you would not consider me a responsible person,—and would quietly proceed to light you pipe with my good intentions, and then nobody Would have ever known that The Plaindealer was edited by a temperance man.

But why did you not answer the pointed questions asked by second correspondent? By the by, the Pantagraph made a mistake in saying "Glad to see it" was written by same correspondent. Correspondent number two is really a voter, Air. Plaindealer, and to my certain knowledge has cast his vote for you more than once. I, being a woman, and like most women having tasted the bitter fruits of intemperance, more keenly feel the necessity of securing a strict prohibitory liquor law enacted to protect our fathers, husbands, brothers, and sons, who have not within themselves the power of self-protection against this fell destroyer. You, and all others, know that many of the best and greatest of our nation have gone down to graves of disgrace and degradation from the influence of rum. Then why in the name of all that is good and pure, in your organization, do you not come forward and join hands with the temperance party in this great struggle for life and freedom? Why not each week sweeten the dispositions and strengthen the doubting hearts of hundreds of your readers by a lively article on temperance and prohibition, which you are so capable of writing?

Friends with sincere hearts would flock about you; old men with whitened locks would give your hand a hearty shake of encouragement; fond mothers would look upon their promising sons and with tearful eyes would rise up and call you blessed.

Think, think well upon this great subject, and let the soft whisperings of conscience decide for you, is the wish of your "friend of temperance."

THE INFLUENCE OF A CORD OF WOOD

1870

Dear New Northwest—A gentleman of this place some months since laughed in my face when I asked him to subscribe for the woman suffrage paper. Shortly afterward he attended Miss Anthony's lecture. The next day he met me and asked if we women dealt in wood; if so, he would give a cord of wood for a subscription to the New Northwest. I accepted the challenge, and before morning his name was on the way to your office.

I am happy to say that he not only receives the paper, but reads it, and then, like a true and faithful public servant, reads it to his neighbors, that it may make other converts. This week he surprised me by presenting a petition for a road, asking me,—a woman,—to sign it. This proves the power of The New Northwest in converting its readers to the belief in individual rights. Three months ago he wouldn't have thought of asking a woman's name to such a petition.

If all men who now profess themselves opposed to the movement would read and investigate, rather than sneer and scorn it, they would let reason rule them, and would speedily espouse the cause of justice.

All that we ask; all that we *entreat,* is that our cause shall be investigated, analyzed, sifted, and if it be not the true metal, of solid principle, let it burn, like dross. The right of suffrage is an inalienable right, withheld wrongfully from woman by her brother, man. No human being who will reasonably and conscientiously investigate this principle will fail to become a convert to it.

The other day a motherly, generous-hearted, pure-minded, but simple, old lady said to me: *"You* are not in favor of women voting, are you?" "Yes, indeed, I am," I said. She raised her hands in holy horror. "Oh, no no, you cannot mean it!" "Indeed," I answered, "there is not another principle in the wide world I so dearly cherish, for there is no other power that can be compared with the power of the ballot."

The good old lady sighed and her eyes filled with tears. "Well, well," she answered, "I know nothing about this woman's movement; but I am bitterly opposed to it."

If she would only give a cord of wood for The New Northwest she would soon learn better than to be opposed to truth and justice.

In conclusion I add that the cord of wood which one subscriber in Roseburg has already given for The New Northwest will prove worth its weight in gold in making many new converts, and should any other persons in this community want to pay their subscriptions in wood I am ready to cash their orders.

CO-EDUCATION.

(Professor McLean was the last of the faculty of Ann Arbor Medical University to consent to receiving women students, but as it was a state institution the faculty could not entirely control the matter. When women were admitted Professor McLean positively refused to lecture before a mixed class. Being, however, an eminently intelligent and broad-minded man by nature as well as by attainment, he was soon convinced that women were an advantage rather than a detriment to the school, and he was magnanimous enough to frankly and publicly admit it.)

A LETTER FROM PROFESSOR M'LEAN

1879

To the Editor of The Daily News:

Sir—As a teacher in a school which provides special facilities for female students, and more especially as a teacher in, and an abiding friend of, the Kingston Medical School,

I ask you to grant me the privilege of saying, through your esteemed columns, a few words to your Storrington correspondent, who signs himself, "A Graduate of Queen's."

If that correspondent (who evidently considers himself a gentleman, a scholar, and a judge of "ladies") will divest himself for a few days of his thick covering of conceit and prejudice, and, leaving it behind him in Storrington, will make a pilgrimage to this large and respectable university, I will confidently promise him that he will hear and see and learn many things not hitherto dreamed of in his philosophy.

Unless he is farther gone in either ignorance or prejudice than his letter would indicate (and that is bad enough, in all conscience), I believe that we can send him home to his rural retreat wishing, in the bitterness of his remorse, that a kind Providence had visited him with a felon on each finger of his right hand, so that he might have been prevented from writing such a libelous letter.

If he will only come here I am confident that we can convince him that not merely ladies, but, what is even better, women,—true, noble-hearted and pure-minded women,—do actually seek, and obtain, admission to the medical profession.

He makes the broad statement that no lady seeks admission to the medical profession. We will show him, if he has eyes to see, that he might just as well have said that no lady seeks admission to a dry goods store, or a church. Your correspondent defies Professor Grant

317

or any other man to point to a single instance in which the love of the study of science, or the desire to benefit the human race, has been the main object in prompting females to study medicine, and he adds:

"It is simply a morbid curiosity." I accept this challenge, and I say to "A Graduate of Queen's," come up here, sir and we will make you hide your head for very shame that you have allowed yourself to exhibit so much ignorance and unfairness. Come here, my poor, benighted fellow; you have been too long confined to the solitudes of Storrington; come here and see and judge for yourself. We will admit you to the class-rooms, the dissecting-rooms, and the hospital wards, where our female students are at work. We will allow you to converse with them, and to observe them closely, and when you have done so I am very sure that you will return to your home an humbler and a wiser man. Before leaving, however, we will give you an opportunity of studying the records of former female graduates, from which I should hope and expect that even you would be able to extract some useful information.

Then you will assuredly have your ideas of ladies in general, and medical ladies in particular, completely modified, and I venture to believe, greatly elevated and purified. Perhaps it may not be improper for me to give you some hints in advance of what you will find in these archives. You will find, I must admit, here and there a record of premature death from overwork. In what sphere of woman's life are such records wanting? You will find, also, I must admit, here and there a record of failure in the practical work of the profession. Is there, I ask, anything peculiar in this? On the other hand, you will find a record of many brilliant examinations passed by female graduates. You will find a record of much splendid work performed since graduation, in the capacity of physicians to female prisons and reformatories, orphans' homes, and female lunatic asylums, and in private practice; and, above all, you will find a record of even nobler work performed by graduates of those schools, who have gone to India, Japan, China, and elsewhere, in the capacity of medical missionaries, either alone or with their husbands.

"All very fine," you will say; "but what of the other side of the account? Have you no records of such impurities as I so broadly hinted at in my decidedly prurient letter.-'"

I answer most unequivocally: "No, sir, not a single one." Two or three intermarriages have occurred between our male and female students in the seven years I have been here, but never a breath of scandal of any kind has been recorded, so far, in the history of the university.

Your reference to Mary Walker would have some price if there were no disreputable characters among male physicians; as it is, it only serves to illustrate the inherent weakness and absurdity of your position.

In conclusion, sir, permit me to inform you that "the world moves," and I, for one, am heartily rejoiced to see that my old friends and colleagues of the Kingston school propose to move with it; and I am very sure that in so good and just and wise a step as that they now propose to take, they are not likely to be stopped by a "fly on the wheel," even though it should take the august form of "A Graduate of Queen's." I am yours truly,

DONALD MCLEAN, University of Michigan.

Ann Arbor, Nov. 11, 1880.

Mr. Editor—I cannot permit this opportunity to pass without adding a word of praise to Professor McLean for publishing the able and manly sentiments contained in the foregoing* letter. And when I consider the prejudice against women who seek medical knowledge, I desire to give expression to the cordial thanks of students of this university to this eminent gentleman for his handsome rebuke of a person who anonymously and wantonly attacks the motives and characters of female medical students. The high professional and social standing of Professor McLean makes this letter one of great importance. He was a student of the celebrated Professor Syme, a graduate of Edinburgh.

A Scotchman by birth, he is always kind and attentive to students under his charge, and is consequently beloved by them. As a surgeon, he takes rank among the most skillful of his profession; as a gentleman, his influence extends beyond the wide range of his professional work; and as a citizen, he labors to promote the best interests of society. This letter of Professor McLean is not the property of the university, exclusively, but of mankind generally. "He that causes noble impulses to dwell where prejudice has had sway, lives for the benefit of his race, and his acts become treasures to be highly prized."

How fortunate it is for woman that prejudice and slander are not conclusive against her character. Whenever she steps forward and modestly claims to be heard in the advancing studies of science, she is quite apt to be rudely told that her influence in educational matters is pernicious, and her character about to be injured if she persists in her effort. And why? Because by this course she asserts in theory and principle what the world should accord her in practice. We believe woman should have a knowledge of the science of medicine. She is the natural nurse and physician of the family, and is endowed with a desire to know more and more of those principles which are essential to the happiness and usefulness of her sex.

In her endeavors to become learned and useful in any science, especially the medical, she keenly feels how greatly this prejudice adds to the sacrifices she must make to attain the desired position. Still she pushes onward and upward, and by a life of rectitude and professional success convinces the multitude that she, though a woman, and because she is a woman, is doubly entitled to praise and honor.

No gentleman will seek to make a club of this noble effort of woman to become broadly educated, by which to knock her down.

It is the moral coward only who will resort to the defamation of the character of woman and accuse her of base purposes in her heroic struggle to honor her sex by acquiring scholarly attainments.

The world *is* moving on, and the purer and higher impulses and ambitions of our nature are not to be destroyed by the club of the vindictive, nor the forked tongue of the slanderer, but they are, and are to be, more and more treasured and encouraged by those who love virtue and knowledge, and realize what a powerful shield they are against crime. Intellectual discipline of the mind of woman makes her more rigidly careful of her conduct and less liable to err, even as an experiment.

It is quite different with men.

In fact, education in the sciences makes conscientiousness the leading element in the character of woman, and her honor and her marked individuality become her citadel of strength. After all, how true it is that the fame of the gifted and the noble often derives added luster from their struggle with prejudice and slander.

The career of a professional woman is an ever-present proof of this. Indeed, such a woman is the architect of her own good fortune. From the very nature of herself and her surroundings she can rely on no man for assistance, and must succeed by her own personal work.

A man may succeed by the help of honorable influences, without which he would be a clear failure. But the moment a woman seeks advancement through the influence of personal channels she is made the mark of poisoned arrows. It is by her own intrinsic worth and persistent perseverance that she secures a position in any profession.

How aptly is this illustrated by the true story of Georgianna, Duchess of Devonshire, in her energetic effort to elect Mr. Fox, the leader of the Whigs, over his opponent, Sir Cecil Wrag. Both were candidates for a seat in parliament in 178-i. Mr. Fox was in the minority, but this woman of extraordinary beauty and the highest mental accomplishments became interested in the contest and took the field for Mr. Fox.

She went from house to house soliciting votes. She appeared at the hustings with Mr. Fox. She was denounced ' by the opponents of Mr. Fox, in the ministry, and mercilessly ridiculed. Ludicrous sketches were circulated concerning her, some of which were vile indeed. She was derided as a woman of the people; but, notwithstanding all this, she moved on, and gained more and more heart in her cause every day.

The result was that Mr. Fox was elected by a large majority. In all this opposition to this remarkable woman they could not prove the slightest stain on her character.

This same spirit exists today against woman, if she seeks to elevate herself to positions of honor and usefulness in the professions, and there are many who are ready to commit the forbidden sin of bearing false witness against her motives and character.

B. A. OWENS.

WOMEN AS PHYSICIANS

For lack of space the lecture, "Women as Physicians," which is somewhat lengthy, is omitted, as an excellent abstract of it is included in the newspaper extracts below appended

Salem paper: Mrs. Dr. Owens, of Portland, read a fine essay on the subject "Women as Physicians" before the late Suffrage Convention. It needs hardly to be said (and we have not asked Mrs. Owens if we may say it) that one of the very best evidences of what women can do is found in her own success. We clip the following:

"In asserting that woman is always ready for duty, and always yielding to its exactions, we believe we present her true character. Today the world beholds her, as she takes her stand upon the great field of science, while the flag of victory floats over her.

"Among the foremost ranks of this goodly array we find our pioneer lady physicians, whose lives have been purified and beautified, broadened and ennobled by the strenuous battle that was required to be fought and won in order that women as physicians might be considered even respectable. Today we honor and bless these noble mothers, while the world looks on with a smile that approves.

"These brave women who have hewn down opposition and smoothed the rugged road to science have, for the last quarter of a century, been persistently knocking at the doors of every university and college in this land. Repeated refusals have only acted as a stimulant, rather than a sedative, and these determined women have set themselves to build hospitals and medical colleges of their own, till today these institutions rank equal in standing to any in our republic, which, as a nation, is today the queen of the world. Had I the time and space I could fill pages with accounts of grand successes in the practice of medicine and brilliant surgery, as well as of the scientific productions of our women physicians and surgeons. Woman today works side by side with her brother, man, and we prophecy that the day is not far distant when he will welcome her with pride and honor, and with his own strong right hand will open

323

wide the doors of science, and, with chivalric pride, found only in the highest type of manhood, will cordially welcome his sister co-worker. And may we not say, as a concluding word, that woman, governed as she is by conscious duty, possesses resistless power, and may achieve the highest honor in the professions of medicine and surgery?"

Dalles Mountaineer: "Our readers may have noticed abstracts published in several journals from the essay upon 'Women as Physicians' read by Mrs. Dr. Owens at the Suffrage Convention held in Portland not long since. We can but look with favor upon this evidence of the opening up of a legitimate work singularly adapted to woman's best efforts—a field for the unlimited development of woman's energy, truth, earnest sympathy, power of inspiration, and ability to make it available in sustaining this great department of human economy, and at the same time, advancing and ennobling her own position in her race and generation. In our own city we have one lady physician, Mrs. Dr Avery, who, we are informed, has a large and satisfactory practice. There is room for all."

"From the many notices given to Mrs. Dr. B. A. Owens' address before the Woman Suffrage Convention in Portland, and which was recently published in The New Northwest, we must infer that she has awakened quite an interest in her subject, 'Woman as a Physician'.

"It is spoken of by the press generally as possessing great merit.

"The lady deserves this praise. Such addresses do much to wipe out the prejudice that usually surrounds the 'woman question, and leaves it open to fair and rational criticism. Many will admire it the more to know that it is from an Oregonian, as well as from a student.

SKATING AS AN EXERCISE

Portland, Ore., Jan. 10, 1882.

To the Editor—I am very much surprised, and I deeply regret to see what I consider very unkind and ungenerous remarks about the skating-rink in the last issue of a Sunday paper.

I, with many others, welcomed the establishment of a skating rink in Portland, believing that it would prove a blessing in many ways to our young people, more especially to our girls, whose delicate health, in the great majority of cases, depends upon the want of proper physical exercise, which fact is well known to every physician. I hold that it is the physician's duty to prevent, as well as mitigate and cure disease.

It has been said, and truly, of the American woman, that her nervous system is developed at the expense of the physical. We have but to look about us to see a host of delicate young ladies, whose loving mothers have taught them the art of plying the needle and thread to the extent that every sofa-cushion and foot-stool in the house is ornamented with cats, dogs, birds, or flowers. But if any one of these young ladies were required to walk briskly a mile and a half she would be sure to have an attack of neuralgia, or perhaps a "nervous chill.

'The doctor comes and prescribes a nerve tonic, a bottle of smelling salts, and absolute rest for a week. This is fashionable, but is it right? Here is a great principle involved, and it is clearly the physician's duty to protect, to strengthen, and to improve the health and vigor of the human race. A strong, healthy brain must be supported and nourished by a sound, healthy body.

I have been consulted by a number of my patients as to the propriety of skating. I have said to all my delicate, nervous and hysterical patients, "Go to the skating rink, by all means, and skate enough to at least start perspiration; it will give tonicity to your muscles, and enable you to sleep without the aid of chloral." I have dropped in several times to witness the skating, and I am pleased to say that I saw no improper behavior. I was pleased to witness the

325

interest manifested on the part of the skaters to excel. I was gratified to note the large number of spectators, especially the ladies, who are among the best families of Portland, and who, I understand, go regularly to the rink with their children. I believe a few accidents have happened, in the way of bruises and a fractured bone or two, but accidents must happen in all vocations in life, and this is no argument against skating.

A short time ago a scientific Englishman said to me: "I am a widower with two children; I should like very much to get married, but I am not wealthy, and I cannot afford to marry a 'doctor's bill.' Your American women are intellectual and fascinating, but among the higher classes it is almost impossible to find one physically well developed. And I believe it the duty of every man, in selecting a wife, to look forward to raising a healthy and vigorous family."

Often, as I have stood watching the skaters, especially the little girls from eight to twelve years old, and seen their happy faces glow with delight as they vied with each other in the race, I have thought that could these girls continue to develop their muscles till they reach womanhood, as do our boys, my English friend would not be in such fear of marrying a "doctor's hill."

This recalls to mind the advice given to a class of young doctors by an old and much honored professor. He said:

"Young men, there are two things which every young doctor needs on starting out in life. First, a wife; second, a microscope. And now, let me admonish you to be careful in the selection of a wife. Do not select one from among that class of dainty girls who are always making cats and dogs in worsted. I can think of but one advantage you would have in marrying one of these 'killing creatures,' and that is, you would always have at least *one* patient, and by and by you will have a houseful of the same sort, which you will find will be all you can manage. Take my advice, and marry a girl physically well developed; one who can dance, skate, ride horseback, and do all kinds of sensible things.

"Indeed, I believe there is no girl that makes so good a wife as what is known as the old-fashioned 'Tom-boy.' who is always ready for a romp. She can run from the basement to the garret, and slide to the bottom on the bannisters. Young man, if you get this girl for a wife, you need give yourself no uneasiness about buttonless shirts, etc., and you can always count on a good, hot breakfast to greet you after a long night's watch, and there will be no sore-eyed poodle dogs with pink or blue ribbons on their necks to receive the first attention."

In conclusion I will say, as regards Mr. Walton, that he is a quiet, industrious young man. All that need be said in his favor is that he labors for the support of his invalid and widowed mother, and he deserves the patronage of a respectable community.

DR. OWENS.

A GIRL WHOM DR. OWENS RESCUED

1882

One Sunday evening between nine and ten o'clock the office bell was rung by a fine-looking young man, who desired the Doctor's attendance upon a sick person.

"What address?" inquired the Doctor, and he replied:

"I will go there with you."

In a few minutes they were on their way, and as they approached the vicinity of Third and Taylor streets, which was then the center of the *demi-monde* in Portland, Oregon, he asked:

"Do you object to visiting an inmate of a house of ill fame?"

"No," said Dr. Owens, "I never refuse to visit any suffering person who desires and needs help. I will go and do all I can for her."

They now entered a building opposite the Taylor Street M. E. Church, and found themselves in a brilliantly-lighted hall. The handsomely furnished parlors were also alight, and groups of beautifully dressed women were standing about, smilingly receiving the men who were thronging in. Music and gaiety prevailed, and everything had the appearance of an evening reception in any private residence.

The young man led the way up the stairs, where they were met by several women, who asked "Is this the doctor?" and took the medicine case from the young man, who said to the doctor:

"I will await you here and accompany you home."

She was then shown into a room where a pale, pretty girl of fifteen lay in bed, very ill, suffering with a severe attack of peritonitis. Questioning the child, for she was but a child [interesting that Dr. Adair would say this, having been married at 14], as to how she came there, she freely told her story,—how her widowed mother in San Francisco had re-married, and how her (the daughter's) home was made unhappy, so that she felt compelled to support herself. How, in the search for work she met a kind (?) woman, who

328

promised her and another girl friend pleasant work and better wages if they would go with her to Portland, Oregon. Unsuspecting, they accompanied her, and on arriving they found themselves inmates of a house of ill-fame, friendless in a strange city, and compelled to live a life of shame, only three weeks of which sufficed to bring her to this pitiable condition.

Dr. Owens had the girl removed to a comfortable room near her, where she could be under her immediate personal care and treatment. She also interested some of the Christian women of Portland in the case, and Mrs. Hurgren later received the young girl into her home until she should be able to be sent back to her mother.

Public interest was thus aroused and enlisted, and plans formed looking toward establishing a Refuge Home for similar unfortunate women who desired to reform. Subscriptions were made aggregating a considerable sum, and one, Rev. , especially interested himself in se curing subscriptions, taking good care to collect his own per cent for this work. Only $40 more than that was collected, as most of the promises of money were made contingent upon the carrying out of the proposed plans of building, which did not materialize. This $40 was deposited in the bank by Dr. Owens, who eventually, some years later, paid it over, with the accrued interest, amounting to some $10, to the management of the W. C. T. U. Refuge Home,—now the Florence Crittenton Home, Portland, Oregon. This was, in fact, the nucleus fund in the foundation of that most beneficent institution.

As soon as the poor girl was able to make the trip a passage was secured for her and she was placed aboard the San Francisco steamer. On board were a number of benevolent passengers, Colonel John McCraken among them, who, besides rendering the child every kind attention, raised quite a s um of money which they presented to her on her arrival in San Francisco. As the trip had been extremely rough, and she had been very seasick, in addition to her weakness from her previous illness, they sent her home in a carriage.

She lingered a few weeks, dying finally at home among her relatives.

The clipping appended below gives additional particulars.

Dr. Adair was always a loyal and powerful champion of her own sex, and no evil surroundings or fear of public opinion ever deterred her from rescuing her erring and suffering sisters.

A WORK OF CHARITY

The young woman who was rescued from a house of ill repute in this city by Mrs. Dr. Owens and others, two months or more ago, was taken to San Francisco, where her parents reside, on the "Queen of the Pacific," which sailed on the 3d inst.

The girl's name has been kept secret in order that she might have all the chances possible for reforming. Her trip down was very severe, and she was very sick. Passengers aboard paid her special attention, and tried to make her voyage as comfortable as could be. When she reached the home of her mother she was so low as to be in a dying condition, and the prospects for her recovery, according to a late private letter, are very meager. She expressed herself as happy and glad to be back at her home, where she could die among her own people, if it was her fate to die. The charitable ladies and gentlemen who took this case in hand have done all they could and accomplished more than was expected of them. By kindness they induced the girl to leave the life that would result in her death in a short time, allowing her all the while to choose for herself, and when she finally made up her mind they threw around her all the safeguards possible. A physician and medicines were furnished, and a good home provided, and last of all, money was raised to send her home. The girl has expressed her gratitude to her benefactors, which was the only re-payment she could make, and which is ample enough, and it now remains to know whether she will pass over the river, the brink of which she has now reached.

The drummer who made such professions of sympathy for her and who, in the beginning, acted as if he meant what he said, has not been heard from since he left here.

1885

Methinks I hear someone say: What has habit to do with heredity and health?

Well, we shall see.

And, to begin with an illustration, I must confess that there is one habit which has grown to be almost universal among the officers of the W. C. T. U. It is this: That each sister believes that her particular department should receive more attention, and is of vastly more importance to the life and health of our great organization than that of any other of the thirty-nine special departments of our work. I do not claim to be an exception to the general rule, and it shall be my purpose in this paper to show as well as I can, the great extent and importance of the influences for both good and evil depending upon habit, which, after all, is one of the prime factors in heredity and hygiene. Too little attention has heretofore been given to this all-important subject.

You may ask, What is habit? Habit is the result of an internal, inherent principle that leads us to do easily, naturally, and often involuntarily, what we do often. Habit may be inherited, or acquired. It may grow and develop through nurture and cultivation, until it becomes the controlling law and consuming power of our whole being. The study and observance of this most wonderful and powerful force should begin, not only with the birth of the child, but with its prenatal life, as well. Parents are responsible, to a great extent, for the moral, mental, and physical condition of their children. I hold that it is the sacred duty of all parents to see to it not only that their children should be properly and well-born, but that the parents themselves shall, prior to marriage, receive suitable instructions concerning that holy and most important duty of this life, the giving to the world children with pure, healthy minds and bodies. With such children, the labor of instruction would be a source of pleasure, while disease and crime would soon become the exception, instead of as now, the rule. We are told by scientists that "we cannot stand still. We must go up or we must go down." This is a universal law to which all nature is subject.

The chemist tell us that the theoretical atoms which give birth to the microscopic molecule are always and must forever continue in motion. On this atomic theory depends the great science of electricity, which was once described as a subtle, imponderable fluid. Today electricity is demonstrated to be *only* a peculiar result, which is produced or developed by a change brought about in the atomic and molecular elements of the medium which is thus acted upon. The various qualities and quantities of this wonderful phenomenon depend upon special forces, operating on special media, which, in turn, give rise to most wonderful and varied phenomena.

The brain, which is the great center of our nervous system, may be likened to the central office of an extensive telephone or telegraphic system, which transmits and receives its communications through this same mysterious agent. Yet the brain, which is the most complicated and highly endowed organ of the organic system, is, as we shall endeavor to show, subjected to the influence of habit.

The old, old saying that "We are a bundle of habits," savors much of truth, and is worthy of our most careful consideration. Each organ of our body has a special function, or work, to perform, which is somewhat independent in its own action. Yet, due to the intimate relationship existing throughout the entire system, the action of one or all of the organs may be modified, or suspended by the abnormal action of one or more members of the great system.

The office of the stomach is to properly prepare the food for the reception of other refining departments for assimilation. Now, if the stomach receives proper consideration and respect, it will, as a rule, return us good and faithful service throughout our natural lives. But that we do treat our stomachs with proper consideration and respect is the exception, and not the rule. The mouth is the receptacle for the crude material, from which must be manufactured bone, nerve, muscle, brain and blood. These, in turn, feed, support, and protect that mysterious something which we call "Life." Our teeth, the most durable and dense of all the human structures, are admirably adapted to the important work for which they were intended—that of mastication. Few persons seem to give this all-important subject a moment's consideration. The great majority of people spend less than twenty minutes at the table. In other words, most people "bolt" their food, thereby imposing much extra work on the stomach, seemingly without a thought of the flagrant injustice done that much-abused organ.

Like the true and faithful servant that it is, the stomach struggles hard under its accumulated task, and for a time, if strong and vigorous, it may succeed in fully preparing the material for the next higher department; but in time this maltreated servant will be found doing the work imperfectly, and the recompense for this culpable injustice will be sure to come in the form of some of the many ills known as "disease," to which all humanity is heir. Gladstone, fully realizing the imperative necessity of thorough mastication, required his children to make forty revolutions of the teeth on a mouthful of meat, before swallowing it. His children will surely form good habits in the observance of one of the essential duties of mankind, that of preserving life and health. English people, as a rule, are much less given to "bolting" their food than are the more nervous, active Americans. Indeed, their movements in all directions are much less impulsive. We have, through the habits of thrift, rush and push, inspired by ambitions worthy in themselves, acquired this national habit of hurry.

This power of habit is a law that holds good throughout the animal kingdom. We see it forcibly illustrated in every avenue of life. It is simply wonderful how susceptible all creatures are to its subtle influence. We are told that the common American swallow, before the advent of civilized man, built its nest in the crevices of the rocks and cliffs. But in time the necessity of self-preservation taught these little creatures the prudent habit of selecting shelter and protection among our chimneys and eaves-troughs. ' This habit has at last developed into a trait which is transmitted to each succeeding generation. Our daily associations have much, very much, to do with forming our habits of thought and action—indeed, in shaping our whole lives. We are constantly receiving from, and giving out to our surroundings. We gradually and often, imperceptibly, partake of the views, manners, and customs of those with whom we associate. This fact was somewhat amusingly illustrated in my own experience during a Villard reception. At that time I attended a meeting of the Y. M. C. A., and listened to short addresses from several eminent English gentlemen. On leaving the building I chanced to meet a very intelligent

English lady, whom I have known since her arrival in the United States, about twelve years before. She said to me: "Well, well, what a brogue! Really, I could scarcely understand them. My -native tongue, I suppose. But it is not *possible* that *I* talked like that when I came to America, is it?"

"Indeed, so potent is this power that almost every organ of our body may be brought under its insinuating influence, for good or evil, thus retarding or developing the growth of our minds or bodies. If you bind your arm to your body, rendering it stationary, it will soon become useless. The joint will anchylose; the muscles grow flabby and helpless. Why is this? Because motion, exercise and labor are necessary to the health, growth and vigor of our organism. A proper knowledge of this fact will enable us to develop and strengthen our bodies as a whole or in part, as desired. The blacksmith's right arm increases in size and strength in proportion to the work he does. If, through ignorance or carelessness, we masticate all our food, with the teeth on but one side of the mouth, we shall soon bring about a deformity of the face, by developing the tissues of one side, at the expense of the other. If a mother lays her infant on one side only for two or three months, its health may not seem to suffer, or its growth be retarded, but its little head will have grown very much one-sided, and, if not forced to lie on the other side for several months to come, it will carry this deformity with it through life. It is remarkable how soon we may accustom ourselves to our surroundings and requirements. If we wish to rise, say at four in the morning, and promptly obey the alarm clock for a few mornings in succession, we may then safely dispense with the alarm, as the habit will have been formed, and it will say to sleep, "Begone!"

This may also be clearly illustrated by the stomach. If you require your stomach to digest four meals a day, as do the Germans, it will remind you of each meal-time by creating hunger, a desire for food promptly at the usual time. But, if you say, through your will power, "I will take three, or only two meals per day," and be resolute and punctual in carrying out your resolve, your stomach will, after a time, cease to annoy you, and accommodate itself to your demands. The longer any habit has been indulged in, the harder will it be to overcome, and the easier it will be to acquire it again, even after the lapse of time.

The will is said to be the controlling power, or balance wheel of our complex mechanism. It is the innate intellectual energy of the human mind. Like a beautiful flower it unfolds itself from all the other forces of the mind, and radiates through the whole sphere of our activity.

It is the purely practical faculty of man. Through a distinct power or energy of the mind, it blends itself with every other power which we possess. It associates itself with our intellectual decisions, on the one hand, and our emotional attachments, on the other. It contains an important element which cannot be resolved into one or both combined.

The other powers, such as reason, conscience, and sensibility, may influence the will, but they cannot constitute it, or perform its peculiar work. Thus we realize the value of a strong, healthy, will-power; also that it should be guided by a pure conscience, a high moral sense, and refined sensibility.

In disease and sickness the will-power is weakened, and is said to suffer more than the other faculties of the mind, as the memory is the first faculty to fail with advancing years.

HEREDITY AND HYGIENE

(1885-6)

To the W. C. T. U. Convention.

Dear Sisters: In the absence of your Superintendent of Heredity, I have been requested to supply a few general remarks upon this important subject.

I will endeavor to show you by relating a little circumstance, how quickly our people take up and understand a subject, when properly brought before them.

Thirteen years ago, when I was made superintendent of this department, I prepared and delivered a lecture on Heredity.

It was announced in the Oregonian. The next morning an article appeared in the local column which read about in this wise:

"I would respectfully ask Mrs. Dr. Owens to define 'Heredity' for the enlightenment of this community, as the word is not to be found in either Webster's or Wooster's dictionaries."

The editor answered this in a line beneath, saying that the word could be found in the appendix of Webster's newest edition.

Today, if there is a heinous crime or tragedy committed, every newspaper of any note in the land begins at once to ferret out the cause, through the channels of heredity.

I presume many of you read the able editorial in the Oregonian a few days ago, on that fearful tragedy in San Francisco, in which the editor showed how, through the law of transmission, for a generation or more, the sins of that great city culminated in this shocking tragedy.

Through our Mother's meetings, Hygiene and Heredity are being taught most thoroughly and properly. I have myself prepared and delivered a number of lectures for these meetings, and today this subject is being brought efficiently into every household, through some of the various channels, especially through the public press, until now we have learned that this is one of God's great laws, and that like a two-edged sword, it will cut both ways, and curse or bless us, as we direct it for good or evil.

Through the knowledge of this law we can and must protect our nation from insanity, epilepsy, and the varied train of abnormalities that follow in their wake.

And today I prophesy that our nation will awake, and arise, as one man, and one woman, and the cleansing work will begin. I believe it will not require more than one century to effectually close the doors of our penitentiaries, insane asylums, rescue homes, reform schools, and all like institutions, under whose burdens we are now groaning, mentally, physically and financially. May God speed that time, is my prayer.

BANDS OF HOPE

My Dear Children:

I am greatly pleased to see so many of you here this evening, and I feel particularly glad to have the opportunity of speaking to all of you. This is your day. Today you are the center of attraction, and your bright eyes and intelligent faces plainly prove that you are aware of this fact. But at your tender ages, you cannot fully realize your great worth to us, your friends, your parents, and your country.

Never was a truth more fully spoken than this: "A home is not a home without children." You are literally our priceless jewels; without you to adorn and beautify our lives we would be dissatisfied, unhappy and lonely indeed.

God created in us this great desire and love for children, and when we look into the faces of our children, we are constantly reminded of our great responsibility to them; and the desire comes to us to live well for their sakes, so that we may train them up to become good and useful men and women.

Every year we value our children more and more, and we are constantly striving to improve them by every means in our power.

You, members of the Band of Hope, have no doubt heard and understand why your society is thus named, but the little outsiders do not know that you are literally our bands of hope. You are just the very children from whom we hope to receive the most good in all the time to come. We hope to see you in the highest places in our land, when you are grown to be men and women. Being our bands of hope, you are also the hope of the liberty-loving men and women of all other countries, as well as those in our own native land. As you grow older, you will understand and appreciate how much good it has done you to belong to one of these bands. You will find the number of these bands and their membership will increase as the years roll by, and while they are growing, each and every child will be doing something to help grown people to put down whiskey and tobacco. We expect a great deal of help from you, and we surely need all we can get; so you must all do your very best to help us.

I hope you will try to get as many of your playmates and friends to join 'your bands as you possibly can. I expect some of you belong to bands of only a few numbers, but do not let that discourage you. Just remember how many very great things have been accomplished by small beginnings. You have all seen a great many big trees, but did you ever stop to think what little seeds they all came from? And some of the very largest came from the tiniest seeds. Now, my children, you are in many ways just like fruit trees. Like them, you need a great deal of care and pruning to make you grow up beautiful and useful. The fruit raiser takes good care of his trees. He digs around their roots, and gives them plenty of rich earth and water, which to them is food and drink. He prunes off all the straggling, ugly limbs, and so makes them grow strong, beautiful and useful.

You, also, need good, wholesome food to make you grow strong, such as good milk, bread and butter, fruit and vegetables; not candy, nuts and sweetcakes. Then you must have all your bad habits cut or pruned off, such as bad temper, saying bad words, quarreling with your playmates, being late at school and many other ugly branches.

When you have gotten rid of all these bad habits, or ugly branches, you will be beautiful and useful, for you will then be full of good which we call gentleness, kindness, truthfulness and nobleness. Then you will not only be a blessing to your fathers and mothers, but everyone will love you. So I say, do not be discouraged; but go right along, pruning off all your bad habits; and remember, just as soon as a bad habit is gone, a good one is sure to take its place. I want you to remember, too, that it is only about one hundred years since the first temperance essay was written in our country; yet now we have numbers of them and of lectures printed every day, and thousands of temperance people in all the towns and cities of the United States. One hundred years ago there were not nearly so many temperance people in all our land as there are temperance children now in Oregon, alone. Perseverance and attention to duty has made our temperance party strong, following your teachers' example and teaching will make each band of hope grow stronger daily'. Many of you are old enough to know why we called the year 1876 our centennial year. Then we celebrated the one hundredth year of our country's independence. Today we commemorate the one hundredth birthday of that most righteous cause of temperance, and, with your help, we intend that many of the children I am now talking to will live to see our country free from the awful curses of whiskey and tobacco. Some of you may never have seen a drunken man. I only wish I could know that you would never see one. But as you grow up, the boys among you will be thrown into the company of the men who drink liquor, and if they take a drink they will sometimes get drunk. Therefore, I say to you all: Boys, the only safe plan in life is not to drink intoxicating liquors at all. Never take the first drink, and you are sure to escape much of the misery that most men suffer. I would also ask you to shun tobacco all your lives. Do not be tempted to smoke cigarettes because some older boys smoke them, even if these bigger boys happen to be your brothers and fathers. Just ask your father if he does not wish he had never learned to smoke; I am sure he will answer, "Yes." It is usually boys and not men, who learn to smoke, and teach little boys to do it, so if you do not begin this filthy habit while you are boys, you are not likely ever to be cursed with the tobacco habit. I have never known a man over thirty years old to begin the use of tobacco; but I have known many above that age to give up the filthy stuff at once, and forever. Neither whiskey or tobacco can do one of you the least possible good, but either will do you a great deal of harm, from the first drink or cigar to the last bottle or pipe. At first, you will think that liquor only makes you a little jolly, and that you will take care not to get drunk. But, my dear boys, this has been the thought and determination of every poor, forsaken drunkard that ever lived. So don't be tempted to take even the first glass. And as for smoking or chewing tobacco, why should you blacken your pretty teeth, make your breath smell horribly, and in addition to all this, make yourself deathly sick? Just for what? Can you tell me? I am sure you cannot give me any good reason. Old smokers cannot tell you what they gain by using tobacco. But they will tell you that tobacco has injured them, in purse and health, and they wish they had never learned to use the vile-stuff, but, having formed the bad habit, they cannot get along without it. The fact is, my dear boys, this bad habit has grown to be such a big, long branch, that they don't think they can stand it

341

to have it cut off. So, now, my dear children, is the best time of all to learn to care for your bodies and minds, while you are growing and developing. In order to do this properly, you ought to learn about your own organism; that is, how you are constructed, or put together; about your different organs', or parts, and for what purpose these different parts of your bodies were given you.

You are each made up of many thousands of organs, or parts, and I want you to remember some of the things I am going to tell you. I want each little boy never to forget that he has just as many organs in his body as the biggest, or greatest man in the world. Each one of you has over 300 muscles, 200 bones, and many thousands of blood vessels and nerves.

All these different organs are your servants, and if you will only learn to care for them, and treat them well, they will do you good and faithful service all your life-time; but if you neglect and abuse them, they will rebel, and render your life very unhappy, so much so that you will be miserable and sick most of the time. For these are God's Holy laws; and if you break them, you must pay the penalty with suffering and death.

Now you know for what purpose your hands, feet, eyes, and ears were given you, and I know you value them so much that you would not sell any one of them for thousands of dollars.

But you could live if you lost all of these. But you have other organs of which if you should lose any one, you could not live. Among them are your heart, lungs, liver, and stomach. To these we have given the name of the "vital organs."

Now it is necessary that you should learn a good deal about yourselves, that you may understand how you should live; what you should eat and drink, in order that you may grow up strong and healthy men and women.

To help you in this purpose, the temperance people have been getting laws made in many states requiring all the public schools to teach these things to every child that attends them. So, next spring, in addition to your other studies, all you children will begin to learn about yourselves, and what you should, and should not, eat and drink.

You will also learn about alcohol, tobacco and opium, Then you will learn that they are poisons, and should never be used, except for medicinal purposes, and as medicines.

My dear children, you cannot yet realize how strongly you will be tempted to use these slow poisons, and do many other wrong things, when you go out in the world. Then your power to resist these temptations—to say "No," will depend very much on your own teachings; just such instructions as you are all now receiving from your parents, your band, and your Sunday-school teachers. Perhaps some of you may break your pledges (though I hope you never will), but many of you will faithfully keep them, and will look back, when you are grown, with pride and gratitude to these blessed teachers, and thank God that through their influence you were saved from man's two greatest foes on earth, whiskey and tobacco.

Tonight thousands of halls are decorated with delicious fruits and lovely flowers, God's free and precious gifts to mankind, and if properly used, they will give us health and strength, but if wrongfully employed, they will bring us only sorrow, sickness and death. Soon you will learn that from many of these delicious fruits and grains, the various alcoholic poisons are made.

The sparkling wine, of which the Bible warns us, is made from the juice of the delicious grapes you see in all our fruit stores. Whiskey is made from corn and rye; ale, beer and porter from barley, and other grains.

But remember this: That in order to make these liquors, these fruits and grains must pass through a rotting process that makes them unfit for food or the nourishment of your bodies. You will soon have a chance to learn all about these things in your public schools. Perhaps some of you children would like to know what a great work is being done by the little people across the ocean. Only a short time since, the United Kingdom Band of Hope celebrated its anniversary in Exeter Hall, London.

Only think of it! One million and a half members reported, and over three thousand young people presented themselves for competitive examination concerning the effects of alcohol, and many more contested for prizes which were given for temperance talcs and essays. During last year they have collected and used in their work, over nine thousand dollars! So you see, children, your Hands of Hope will soon spread over and reach all around the world.

You will soon grow into the grandest army that was ever marshalled into battle for any cause.

We have abiding faith in you and your battle against Rum and Tobacco.

We believe now that you will, in time, drive these enemies from all the civilized world, for you are fighting for God, your home, and your native land.

This is a far-reaching subject, comprising both physical and mental training, upon which volumes might be written of value to the young, and to those fully mature.

I am asked: "When should this training begin?" I answer.

"From the child's birth;" and I might add, with much truth, "From the beginning of its pre-natal life, as well."

You may ask: "How can a child be trained prior to its birth?"

I answer: "Through the discipline of the mother, herself, through the period of gestation."

I would like to say much upon this period of a child's life, which has so much to do with its future growth, health and development.

But the subject is too extensive for this short talk.

Miss Willard says: "The discipline of a child should begin a hundred years before its birth."

Even a bright, vigorous mind must depend much on a strong, healthy body, which, in turn, requires good, nourishing food, warm clothing, soap and water, pure air, and plenty of outdoor exercise. To make my meaning quite clear, I will tell you how I care for a baby, which is somewhat different from the care given to little Miss Cleveland, of which we lately read.

The Oregonian devoted considerable space to her baby-ship a few weeks since, in which I was much interested. I judge that at the time of that writing, Baby Cleveland was between five and six weeks old. The writer stated that she was bathed three times a week; that she was not allowed the luxury of a cradle, but occupied a little basket, set on the floor. That the happy father was not yet permitted to take his baby in his arms, but was granted the privilege of carrying her up and down the room in her basket. Notwithstanding she was at that time represented to be a strong, healthy child, with good lungs, which enabled her to be heard, and to demand attention from her nurses. I judged from this description of Baby C. that she had not as yet had an out of door airing. Nor had she been tossed about in what I considered the rational way to treat a baby. In referring to Baby Cleveland, I would not be understood as criticising Mrs. Cleveland's physician. As a rule, the attending physician has little to do with the newly born infant, which is usually given into the hands of the nurse, professional, or otherwise, who establishes herself immediately as its doctor, in fact, not to be interfered with either by physician or parents. The old adage, "A little learning is a dangerous thing," may, as a rule, be applied to the professional nurse, and no one realizes this fact more thoroughly than does the physician of today.

But we will now return to the new-born infant, where we are to begin our discipline. To better illustrate my views I will outline the case of a baby boy, who came into my care just eight weeks ago yesterday morning. When baby John came into the world, I wrapped him in flannel, and laid him on a pillow that had been warmed with hot bottles, for his reception. I heard nothing from him for half an hour, during which time his mother had been made comfortable. I then examined my little charge, and found a baby boy of seven and one-half pounds, quite thin in flesh. I anointed him with Vaseline, and returned him to his warm nest, where he remained till 7 a m without being heard from—he having been born at 2:30 that morning. Finding that his kidneys and bowels had failed to act, I was compelled to resort to medicine. Since the fourth day his kidneys have performed their normal function, but the bowels still require daily attention. At 9 a m. I undress the little gentleman, toss him about for eight or ten minutes, then rub him thoroughly with my hands. Then relieve his bowels with an enema. Then rub him off with a damp sponge. Again stimulate his body with my hands and he is ready to be dressed for the day. At G p m he is undressed, and thoroughly exercised for five or ten minutes. Then he is laid in his bath, with his head resting on a large sponge, and allowed to enjoy the warm water for five or ten minutes, after which he is thoroughly anointed and rubbed, dressed, and then ready for his supper and a good night's sleep.

You may ask: "Why do you defer the bath till night?" I answer, because a bath produces a soporific effect, by causing a free flow of the blood to the surface, thus relieving the brain, and producing peaceful and refreshing sleep. Night is the time for sleep, and the child should be trained, through such methods, to sleep at night.

Since our baby, John, was four days old, he has been given an out of door airing every day, rain or shine. He has felt the rain drops more than once on his little face, yet he has never had a cold, or the colic up to this writing. You will readily understand that he has inherited constipation, and nothing but persistent and regular attention to this defect will ever enable his system to overcome this weakness.

Whenever the day is fine, he has from one to three hours' sleep in the open air. Before he was one week old, my little 6-year-old grandson, Victor, hauled baby John about the lawn in his little wagon, and carried him across the room in his arms many times. Now, at eight weeks old, we have a strong, vigorous baby, weighing thirteen pounds, able to bear his full weight on his feet, sit bolt upright in your lap, and pull himself up by his hands.

But our ex-president could not be trusted to take his little girl in his strong arms! Children are not so easily hurt as is commonly supposed. Their little limbs are too firmly attached to their bodies to drop off readily, nor are their bones easily broken. Like the young limbs of growing trees, they will bend almost double without breaking. I cannot lay too much stress upon the necessity of exercise, especially out of doors, for babies. It is my opinion that no class of humanity suffers so much for want of proper exercise as do infants, during the first year and a half of their little helpless lives. Children and invalids, above all, should have the benefit of pure air and sunshine. If your baby is fretful, lay aside your work, and take it for a walk. The time will not be lost. Children, like young plants and flowers, thrive in the sunshine. Their little bodies also require vigorous rubbing and manipulation to give their muscles strength and tonicity. The blood is the food of the tissues, and it must obtain oxygen from pure air. Frequent bathing is also necessary, as the skin requires stimulation to assist it to perform its normal functions. The man who works shoveling coal does not for his health's sake, need bathing so frequently as does the gentleman in his broadcloth, who sits all day writing at his desk. The one has strong, active muscles, and perspires freely at his work, while the other lacks vigor and physical strength, for the want of such exercise as will enable his skin to do its normal work. The Emperor of Germany has recently decreed that physical culture shall be taught in all the public schools in his empire, in the interest of good soldiership.

The methods of rearing children today differ greatly from those of Puritan times. Those were dark days for children, and Sunday, of all days, was most dreaded by them, for on that day they were not permitted even to play in the open air, or enjoy any active physical exercise. "Spare the rod and spoil the child," was the rule then adhered to, taken in strictly literal sense. Today Christianity spreads her white wings, and hovers over our little ones with love and sympathy. The most vital question now is how to best care for and train our children; and I am proud to say that this question has been brought into its present prominence mainly by the earnest efforts of the mothers themselves.

In this short talk I can only touch upon some of the most important points that should be constantly kept in mind by those having charge of children, who are verily marvelous little creatures of imitation. It is simply wonderful how fast they develop, and how quickly they contract habits for good or evil. Yes, and how tenaciously they cling to such habits. I consider the kindergarten system for the training of very young children to be one of the best, if not the best, inaugurated. It takes the little ones from the mother's arms, and teaches them, through a most gentle system, how to do a thousand beautiful and essential things, and the charming part of it is that its work is made so like play that the children love it as they do play, which to them is always absorbing, and full of pleasure.

Children fairly drink in their environment, and therefore, they should be surrounded with an atmosphere of refinement and honesty. A child's first impressions take such deep root, and their influences are so far reaching that they form the very foundation of its character. Hence the paramount necessity of saying and doing the right thing in their presence, for your children will do as father and mother do.

It is useless for parents to expect their children to do right, if they do wrong. No amount of counsel will counteract their own bad example. I have heard parents say, "Do as I tell you, not as I do."

The prime secret of controlling children, is to control yourself. They are like mirrors, true reflectors, and this is well, for they often act as a rebuke and a reminder to the parent to keep in the path of rectitude. Parents are, and must ever be examples to their children. It is a law of their being—God's law.

To my mind, no place equals the country for the best growth and development of children, where there are so many sources of instruction and improvement, coupled with innocent enjoyment, and comparatively few of evil. The birds; the flowers; the trees and green grass, the fowls and other animals, are all a never ending source of pleasure and deep interest. Childhood has its dreams, its air castles and ideals.

Children live in a world of their own, and always in perpetual sunshine. Days seem to them as years to us; and when they look forward to man or womanhood, it is almost like looking into eternity.

Give them time for frolic and play, and do not try to make "grown-ups" of them too soon.

It is a noticeable fact that a great majority of our great men and women have been born and reared in the country. It is equally true that country boys and girls carry off the first prizes from our military high schools and colleges. Children should never be discouraged; better say many words of praise than one of blame. Be firm with them, but not stern. Teach them that they are essential to your happiness. Enter into all their joys and sorrows. Take them into your confidence, and make them your daily companions. Children should bask in the sunshine of love. They are sweet buds of promise, and they will blossom and bear fruit according to the soil, and the nourishment they receive from the parent stock.

PHYSICAL CULTURE

Editor Astorian:

In compliance with your request to furnish an article occasionally, I submit the following paper, prepared and delivered before the Mother's meeting, held yesterday in this city:

"This is an age of education and reform, as well as of invention, and it is but fitting that the development and beautifying of our physical being, our bodies, should receive due attention. It has been stated on good authority, that it is an exception to see a thoroughly erect, well-proportioned, graceful man. And the same is true of women. We can partly account for this through the various occupations in which men and women are employed, no one of which will uniformly develop all the various sets of muscles of the body. But the lack of any occupation is most detrimental to both our physical and mental health.

Today, converts to physical culture are numerous, and the idea is fast spreading outside of colleges for boys.

In most of our large cities may be found many classes for physical culture, especially for ladies and girls. Parents, too, are beginning to realize that to rear beautiful children, they must attend well to their physical training, as to the mental. Emerson says: "Elegance of form in the human figure marks some excellence of structure." Any increase of fitness to its end in any fabric or organism is an increase of beauty. Look at the famous the Venuses, the Junos the Minervas, the Helens of mythology and medieval times. All alike have the well-developed arms and shoulders, the full chest, the vigorous, uncompressed body, and the firm, erect carriage. No stooped shoulders, or pinched waists. That same vigorous exercise and untrammeled dress will, without doubt, bring it out again. Less than twenty-five years ago, Sebastian Fenzi, son of a Florence banker, built a gymnasium at his own expense in that city. He preached gymnastics to senators and deputies, to municipal councilors, and also to the crowned heads. He carefully inculcated its advantages on all mothers of families, as likely to increase, to a remarkable extent the charms of their daughters. And as far as his own domestic relations went, his theories were not contradicted, for he was the father of the most beautiful woman in Italy.

From that small beginning the movement has spread from city to city, and is now being extensively studied, practised and appreciated.

I believe that through physical culture women may equal men in bodily strength and endurance. In proof, I might point you to the amazons of South America, the fish-women of Europe, or the Indian women of our own country; or, go to the circus, and observe the feats performed there by the women on trapezes, in all cases equaling those of men. See how their well-developed muscles stand out strong and rigid on their beautifully molded limbs, while they are performing some of their wonderful feats of strength.

We find proof of our statement of this subject in many individual cases. Look at Gladstone, far up in eighty, and note how, in addition to the wonderful amount of mental labor he is daily accomplishing; he finds time to take long walks, and vigorous out door exercise with his ax; for he well knows that upon his physical strength depends his usefulness as well as his life. Gladstone is not the only stirring example. It was the habit of Charles Dickens to walk from seven to twelve miles daily, during the time when he was writing his masterly works. Napoleon sat for whole days in the saddle during his military and strategic maneuvers.

During the walking craze, a few years ago, Mr. Thomas Cary, of New York, aged 61, and Mr. Thomas Marsh, of Connecticut, walked three and one-half days, Mr. Cary walking 211 miles, and Mr. Marsh 209 miles. These men, as you see, averaged sixty miles a day for three and one-half days, thus showing what men can, and ought to be able to do at that advanced age.

Their feat surprised the whole country, and yet it should not have done so.

The main reason why men neglect daily vigorous exercise after middle life, is because they become engrossed in business, giving to it all their time and attention, and forgetting and neglecting themselves.

This neglect soon brings loss of muscular activity; the joints become stiff and uncomfortable, for the lack of lubrication, and will grate and creak as he walks; and the man of from 50 to GO is daily reminded that he is growing old, and must take the best care of himself; to him this means less bodily exertion, and more methodical habits. Therefore he rises in the morning, moves slowly, reads the paper, takes breakfast and goes to his work, to which he gives his undivided attention, often not taking time for luncheon.

He goes home at five or six; sits down to a good, strong dinner; is hungry, and does justice to the good meal that has been prepared for him, forgetting that his neglected stomach should be consulted as to the amount it receives. As soon as the process of digestion sets in, he begins to feel uncomfortable and unbuttons his waistcoat. His children disturb him; he cannot get down and roll over the floor with them and play hide and seek, and he is too uncomfortable to enjoy their little games. He seeks a comfortable position, and reads till ten or eleven o'clock. This mode of life not only brings on an abnormal increase of fat, but is mother to a whole train of ailments.

He does not seem to understand that the human machinery, composed of flesh and blood, and bone, and driven by the human heart, is similar to the iron and steel engine, driven by electricity or steam. If let alone, our joints become stiff and useless. Physicians all know that if the arm is strapped up for only a few months, the joints will become anchylosed, or stiffened; the muscles will become soft and flabby; the arm will lose plumpness and beauty, and become finally useless.

That old adage: "Better to wear out than rust out," should be pasted on every wall, in blazing letters.

The hinges and joints of the human body do exactly the same thing, and serve precisely the same purpose, as do those of the iron and steel engine, and like the engine, they require frequent oiling. But beautiful and efficient as the steel engine may be, it can never attain to the perfection of the human engine. The one was invented and constructed by man, and needs constant oiling and care to keep it bright. But the human machine is the work of God and he has provided wonderfully for its preservation. The membranes which surround our joints secrete, or manufacture their own lubricating fluid; and at each motion this fluid is poured out over the bones and surrounding ligaments. So, unless the manufacturing tissues are stimulated to activity by motion, they will fail to produce the required material; their usefulness will cease, or become impaired, and they will die for want of employment.

And so it is, and ever must be, with every organ of our body, from the brain to the most inferior muscle. All cry out for "Work, work, work. Without work we must die."

The poet, Bryant, was one of the few men who understood and obeyed this law. His daily habit was to rise early, from half past three to four in the summer, and from five to half past five in the winter. He at once began a series of exercises without the encumbrance of clothes. These exercises were such as to expand the chest, to strengthen the muscles, and to lubricate the joints. These morning exercises, while in the city, were continued for fit least one hour; while in the country they were shortened to one-half that time, and walks of from six to ten miles were indulged in. When asked concerning his daily habits Mr. Bryant wrote, at 77: "[have reached a pretty advanced period of life without the usual infirmities of old age, and with my strength, activity and bodily faculties generally, in very good preservation."

Mr. Boggs, who knew Mr. Bryant intimately, says he was a great walker. "During the forty years I have known him, he was never ill, never confined to his bed, excepting on the occasion of his last accident (a broken leg). He always walked from his house to his place of business, even in his eighty-fourth year. He would never wait for the elevator. He was very fond of gymnastics, tie performed various feats on the backs of chairs; hung on his bedroom door, lifting himself up and down many times; skirmished about the room in all fashions, even running under the table." What a grand lesson this great man has left us as a legacy. His life is a shining example of what has been done, and what can be accomplished. Many other worthy examples might be mentioned, but this must suffice for this time.

I cannot lay down specific rules for exercise or physical culture; it would require too much space. The amount and kind of exercise depend entirely upon the person, and his condition; but there is one general rule which may be borne in mind.

"Exercise should begin gradually, and increase daily, never overtaxing the strength."

Out of door exercise is especially beneficial for the various forms of nervous diseases, particularly insomnia. Certain muscular exercises, when properly taken, are soothing to the overtaxed brain, and nervous system. This is easily understood, when we consider how the muscular work aids in equalizing the circulation, quickens and deepens the respiration, and improves the digestion, as well as the functions of all the vital organs. Then sleep, nature's great restorative, "Comes like the benediction that follows after prayer."

I may be asked: "How early should this physical culture begin?"

I unhesitatingly answer: "From birth."

The little infant comes to us helpless and at the mercy of its surroundings. Perchance it may be deformed, its little limbs crooked; but fortunately for the little treasure, its bones are at birth mostly composed of animal matter, and by careful manipulation they can be brought into shape. If all mothers and nurses knew how easily this is accomplished, and were properly educated to the work, we should never see bow-legged, and knock-kneed men walking our streets. Children would all grow up with beautiful and shapely limbs. No set of muscles should be developed at the expense of others; all should have an equal chance, and with this impartial treatment would come a perfect form. Adorn that form with a well-trained heart, and educated mind, and we have God's masterpiece. May that time soon come, is our earnest prayer.

PILGRIM MOTHERS

(Extract from an address delivered by Mrs. Dr. B. A. Owens, at a recent "Liberty Meeting.")

Our pilgrim fathers have been extolled for their heroism, their sacrifices, and their wonderful endurance. Generation after generation is referred to the customs of the pilgrim fathers as examples of industry, economy and sound morality. Two centuries have passed away, and interest in the lives and times of our pilgrim fathers does not abate one jot or tittle. Should we hear of a stalwart New Englander, we are apt to hear further, that he is of the old "Pilgrim stock." This is sufficient to pass him into all respectable society. The pilgrim fathers were masters, and well did they carve out their fortunes. True, these men founded a proper democracy, and made equal laws for the general good, and they well deserve the praise given to them.

But what of the pilgrim mothers? Have their labors and virtues been of less worth to our nation? Yet little, comparatively, has been written of woman. Her position and relation in life are admitted, but seldom praised. It is not a matter of much concern to the world, as it reasons now, if woman is not noticed beyond her domestic relations, though it is generally admitted today that woman is equally as strong in adversity as man. She endures more, and is as patient in her afflictions as in her faith. It seems to be the nature of every true woman to feel that her life is providentially guided. And all the great purposes and deeds of our pilgrim mothers were built on their faith in Divine Providence. It is hardly necessary to picture in detail the privations and persecutions which drove these people from their old world homes. Indeed, these occurrences constitute one of those important events in history that mark the world's progress.

Repression of freedom of thought, and action, especially in matters of conscience, induced the step taken by the pilgrims to better their condition and improve their minds. The world applauds the desire for freedom of thought and speech, which was no more desirable in those days than now. The cunning devices of designing men still cramp and dwarf the intellect of the multitude in some

355

parts of the world, and make superstition oppressive, though it is not so patiently borne now as it then was.

The pilgrims felt this weight resting on them, and were too noble of nature to suffer it. They loved God even more than they feared Him. They desired to live near Him, and no sacrifices were too great to be made for their advancement in their Master's service. When I speak of the principles and causes that forced the pilgrims to seek the new world, I speak equally of both sexes, believing, as I do, that the heroic life-current that coursed through their arterial system was not only morally pure, but was in quality identically the same.

The heroism of these brave women lay, not so much in their privations and suffering in coming to America, as in their determination to be free in body and soul from oppression. Though they saw poverty "Coming upon them, like an armed man," they shrank not. Therefore we regard the pilgrim mothers in no less honor than the pilgrim fathers. If these men framed the work of civil government in America, their wives raised pillars of moral grandeur to sustain it. If the fathers founded an asylum for those who would go to the wilderness for the sake of purity and freedom in religion, it was the mothers who proved the sisters of mercy who, in their lives of self-sacrifice showed the depth and efficacy of faith.

If these pilgrim fathers through want, peril, and every self-denial, found a spot in exile, where all men could enjoy freedom of thought, and liberty of conscience, and the fearless expression of the same, it was the pilgrim mothers who gave to the world those who should perpetuate these virtues to future generations.

And well has this been exemplified throughout our nation's history. We have but to look in any or all the avenues of life, to find faithful and loyal women laboring early and late for the advancement and purification of humanity and their country.

Throughout our nation's history, woman's services and loyalty have been equal to that of man, deserve equal recognition and should receive equal praise.

THE ADVANCEMENT OF WOMEN

SHALL GIRLS BE TAUGHT SELF-SUPPORT? REMARKABLE PROGRESS IN NEW OCCUPATIONS FOR WOMEN. PUBLIC OPINION HAS CHANGED.

By Dr. Owens-Adair.

The mothers' meeting at the Y. M. C. A. rooms yesterday was conducted by Mrs. Dr. Owens-Adair, M. D., who read the following thoughtful paper on the topic, "Shall Girls Be Taught Self-Support?"

The question, I believe, is "shall girls be taught self-support?" In this 19th century, I think the great majority of thinking men and women would, without hesitation, answer in the affirmative. Only a few years ago this was an open question; but the successes which large numbers of women have obtained in various occupations, during recent years, has converted a large majority of the American people to the belief that girls should be given equal chances in the battle of life with their brothers. Witness on our own coast, the Universities of California, both professional and literary, including the grand Leland Stanford, Jr.. University, at Palo Alto. In all of those splendid universities, girls are admitted on the same footing, and have the same chances with boys. And Oregon and Washington are not behind California in opening their doors to their girls.

Less than half a century ago, there were but few ways in which women could earn a respectable living; and those few were hedged about with many obstacles; the question being the supposed greatly superior intelligence and ability of man over woman. College doors and universities were closed against her, but as remarked, recent years have changed those conditions, until now that question is no longer debatable. Experience has taught that girls do make efficient "bread-winners."

It was always held that woman was made for man, but whether or no man was made for woman was not conceded until the Anglo-Saxon woman proved herself as capable, as willing, and as intelligent as her brother. Then the question was solved to the satisfaction of all concerned.

During the last half century, woman has made most wonderful progress. She has successfully dredged out every channel through which the advocates and practicers of self-support may pass on to fame and fortune. She has, step by step, fitted herself to occupy positions of honor and trust in almost every trade and profession now known. She has broken down the bars of prejudice, and drawn aside the curtain of opposition, thus letting in the sunlight of reason,. which has placed her where she justly belongs, by the side of her brother man in the strenuous battle of life. Today there are few obstacles put in the way of women as "breadwinners." Go where you choose, and you will find woman occupying positions of honor and trust. Her hands and her brains are being carefully educated to do that which they "find to do," and to do it well. It seems remarkable, yet it is true, that this great change in woman's condition has been brought about within my own memory.

Less than twenty years ago a little band of brave and earnest women were "rotten-egged" at Bleckley Hospital, in broad daylight, in the old, staid city of Philadelphia. And for what was this done? Their crime was that they were trying to fit themselves for the practice of medicine to alleviate pain and suffering, and thereby earn for themselves honorable self-support. You can readily see that it required a brave woman, even at that recent date, to declare her intention to study medicine. I, myself, studied in secret for several years. To do so openly made a woman the subject of public ridicule, and she was regarded as deserving of severe public criticism. There was scarcely a newspaper in the land that did not delight in holding her up as a "strong-minded nuisance," a "mannish woman" and such-like detestable expressions. How often has it been said, "No modest, or refined woman would study medicine." The doors of all medical schools were closed against her; but slurs and opposition only strengthened her desires, and, with an irresistible will and determination, she rose up in her strength, and builded medical schools for herself.

As in the medical profession, so has it been in all others; and in the various avocations of life, women have won the right to enter them by proving her fitness for them. Thus, step by step, she has paved her way by her good works, to her present position; proving to the world her capability for self-support through the various channels of industry, until today we find thousands of modest, refined, and most honorable women earning their bread in all, or nearly all the callings of honest labor. You find them in our great banking-houses, publishing companies, wholesale and retail stores, telegraph offices, insurance, lawyers' and newspaper offices, and in each and all of these positions, giving full satisfaction;—showing, by their ability as managers or principals in business, by their success, and in earning the esteem and confidence of their superiors where employed, by their zeal, accuracy, and capacity for their work. And yet, woman is not fully educated up to a proper appreciation of the dignity of labor. She is just beginning, however, to learn that to succeed, she must apply herself faithfully and diligently to her work, whatever it may be. The common belief is that certain kinds of labor, especially housework, are degrading, or, to put it more mildly, not genteel; and out of door work is a man's work, and, therefore, objectionable. These are false ideas, and decidedly un-American. Labor should always reflect credit and honor upon its author, and it will do so, if properly performed. Your motto should be: "I will do, and do well, whatever my hands find to do."

Only a very few of the great army of men who graduate in medicine, or law, make eminent doctors, or excel markedly as lawyers, and so it will be with women. Some have capacity for one profession, and some for another. Girls should endeavor, with the aid of friends, to make a proper selection of their "life calling," suited to their tastes and capacities. The worship of money and dress, coupled with the fear of not getting into good society, greatly retards woman's usefulness. She should early be taught the wise lessons that the best society for her is always within her reach. Depending on her calling, she will enjoy the society of those who are the builders and workers in our busy world. But if she has no means of support except that of "catching a husband," she is likely to prove an unhappy wife, although she be a leader of fashion. The Princess of Wales, fully appreciating these facts, has set a most worthy example before the women of Great Britain, in that she has taught her daughters thoroughly the art of housekeeping, in its various departments, including cooking, and butter-making. She has done this, not only as an example to other mothers of her kingdom, but as her duty to her daughters. Both she and her daughters dress much in cotton fabrics. She has always shown much interest in working girls, and one of her strongest desires has been to build a suitable home in London for such girls. From this idea grew the Alexandra House, in Kensington; and from this beginning, many other similar houses have been built in that city. I have seen it stated in print recently that there are several thousand more working women in London than working men. This is also true of the older cities in our own country.

WORK IS HONORABLE

Our girls should be taught that work is honorable, and a real blessing to life. By the way, our boys need large doses of this same medicine. I do not know a more pitiful object than a grown man or woman with nothing to do, and plenty of time to do it in. For such a person, life has no savor, no real enjoyment; they are waifs, adventurers and tramps; a burden to themselves, and a curse to all others..

The bread we earn by hard toil is sweeter far than that coming as a gift or through inheritance. The curse of Eden was, under disguise, a priceless gift from God. By all means teach your girls not to be ashamed of honest labor. Try to study their capacities; their likes and dislikes. Usually what we like to do best we do best. To the mother, again, I would say: "See to it that your girls are fitted for some calling in life, by the use of which* they can earn an honest living, should circumstances require it. I have believed for many years that one of the greatest wrongs parents could inflict upon their children was to raise them in ignorance of self-support."

IMPORTANCE OF HEALTH

As a physician, I cannot close my remarks without a few words upon the all-important subject of the health of your girls. Do not neglect this vital point. Remember that health is their reserve force;—their revenue, to be drawn upon during all their lives. Therefore look to it with a zealous eye.

A few suggestions may not be out of place. To begin, give them good, nourishing food. Provide them with warm, loose clothing, broad, thick-soled shoes, low-heeled. Teach them to breathe and sleep correctly. Breathing, you understand, should be done through the nostrils, and not through the mouth. The most healthy sleep is obtained on the side, and in a moderately straight position of the body. Let them be taught to -work, to run, to skate, and to ride. Give them gymnastic and dumb-bell practice, and, above all, plenty of out-of-door exercise, winter and summer. Thus you will give them health and strength, and prepare them for their best efforts at all times.

NEWSPAPER COMMENTS

The entertainment of the W. C. T. U. last night, for the benefit of the reading-room, was attended by a larger crowd than was anticipated, as standing-room was at par, till a large number of extra seats were brought in.

The singing of Mr. McDonald, of Portland, was excellent; but the principal feature of the evening was the lecture on "Heredity" of that talented lady, Mrs. Dr. B. A. Owens, of Portland. The whole fabric of argument and illustration was so neatly and delicately interwoven that it would be impossible to give the synopsis 'of the lecture, and we are sorry that we have not space to publish it in full.

The speaker fully established that heredity is a law of nature, and that the bad, as well as the good, is transmitted from the parents to the offspring, in both the physical, as well as the mental faculties.

Mrs. Owens is a lady of rare natural talents, and of vigorous mental faculties, and she has taken the advantage of a regular, and special course of medical training, at the medical college of Ann Arbor, and, added to this, several years of successful practice,— much was expected from her lecture last night, and none was disappointed.

Thanks to the W. C. T. U. for securing so popular a lecturer. We hope this is only a beginning of a series of able lectures, a rare means of cultivation, which will render the reading-room popular at once and will be of incalculable benefit to its patrons.

One sentence which the speaker uttered last evening should be placed with those excellent mottoes on the walls of the reading-room, and that sentence is:

"With the mind, as with the body,—to cease to strive is to begin to die."—*Salem Statesman.*

Roseburg, Or., April 2d, 1886.

Mrs. Dr. Owens Adair, Portland, Oregon:

My Dear Madam:

I have just finished your essay in the Prohibition Star. It is excellent. Allow me to thank you, in the name of suffering humanity, for that excellent production. It ought to be read by every man and woman that has entered, or contemplates entering the marital relation, who should ponder well the truths therein evolved, and so ably elucidated.

"No one can stand still." "We must go up, or we must go down." "Gradually, but surely, yet imperceptibly, as time rolls on, we are being molded into new forms,—yea, into new beings."

Noble words, truthfully said. It is the gospel of a "New Dispensation." I thank you most heartily for your views, and trust to hear from you again, in a like lucid manner on that, or any cognate subject. Pardon my enthusiasm, but I felt constrained to congratulate you; therefore, as an act of justice from one who can, and does appreciate such efforts in the cause of suffering humanity.

With much esteem, I am yours fraternally,

W. F. BENJAMIN.

I only inserted these words as samples of the whole, for they are like gems in a necklace of pearls.

Portland, Ore., April 27th, 1886.

Mr. W. F. Benjamin,

Dear Sir:

I received your kind, congratulatory letter by last mail, and I assure you your encouraging words were appreciated, and gratefully received. In my own case, I know that I need just such encouragement to assist me in this work. My inherited diffidence, or want of a proper appreciation of my own ability, has been my own worst enemy to success. All my work in my departments is carried on under great disadvantage, as my professional duties demand my first attention.

Again thanking you for your generous appreciation, I am, dear sir,

Yours sincerely, in this good work.

EXTRACTS FROM AN ADDRESS

BY DR. ADAIR IN DEFENSE OF THE NATIONAL W. C. T. U.

FOR ENDORSING THEPROHIBITION PARTY

This action on the part of the National Union caused some dissension among the local unions, and this the old parties, especially the Republicans, seized upon, and used as a political club.

I wish to call your attention to a few facts to prove that the National Union unquestionably did right in endorsing the Prohibition party.

First The National Union, when organized, adopted the following pledge:

"I hereby solemnly promise, God helping me, to abstain from all distilled, fermented, or malt liquors, including wine and cider, and to employ and to use all proper means to discourage the use of, and traffic in the same."

There could be no broader, or more comprehensive promise than this, and certainly no plainer line of duty could be set them than is set forth by this pledge.

Their actions proved clearly the desire to unite all the state unions, thereby obtaining a concerted movement for good, believing and following the old adage, "In union there is strength."

You have hut to stop and analyze the pledge, and you will be convinced that there was no other course open for the National Union hut to endorse the third party, which to us seems to be the only means through which we can hope to abolish-this accursed traffic. Think of it! The mayor of Portland said the other day: "There are today, in our city, at least 100 alcoholized men, so far gone that they ought to be sent to a home for the cure of inebriates."

My friends, this is truly a lamentable condition; and yet we are no worse off than other cities of like size. It is only natural that we should be shocked by what occurs about us. I realize that it is not known by all men, that the annual drink bill of our people footed up, for the year 188.1, to the enormous sum of $800,000,000.

We are asked: "Is it likely that this great national curse can be strangled by the Prohibition party?" I answer that there is practically but one way of accomplishing any great reform in our country, and that way leads through the ballot-box. Right here, let me tell you that up to this time, there never has been any fair trial of the workings of prohibition—not in Kansas, Iowa, or even Maine: for what have been termed prohibitory laws in these states, have been passed by one or the other of the old parties, and have not been strictly enforced by their officials, who are not in sympathy with the movement, and are too much controlled by the whisky element. I maintain that in order to enforce prohibitory laws we must have public opinion and a party behind the officials, who will see to it that they perform their sworn duty.

The National Union endorsed the third party by 251 votes against 33. Remember that these women came from all over our land, and represented a phalanx of over two hundred thousand homes. Such support cannot be easily appreciated while women do not actually vote, yet they do wield a powerful influence. The truth of this may be shown by the gain of the third party in the last two years. In New Jersey, Maryland, Ohio, West Virginia, Minnesota, Nebraska and Missouri, the Prohibition vote of '86 was three times as great as in

'84: while Texas cast 30,000, as against 3,554 in '84, and Arkansas did even better.

LETTER TO MRS. W. W. PARKER

SECRETARY OF THE LOCAL W. C. T. U. OF ASTORIA, OREGON.

Portland, Oregon, Apr 11, 1880.

My Dear Friend:

Your kind and welcome letter reached me last evening. How like your own dear self. It brought back many memories of twenty years, and more ago. And yet it seems but yesterday since we were studying those, to me, hard lessons in the little school-house on the hill. How well I remember my humiliation, the day I entered the school, when I had to go down into the primary class in arithmetic. And then I met, and learned to love you and Helen, and I am free to say that affection has never diminished. But it was hard work to keep envy out of my heart, when I saw how bright you were, and how easy it was for you to learn. Spelling seemed to be second nature to you, while to me everything came so hard! And so it is, still. Every step forward, with me, is a battle. But as I go on, my victories are more easily won, and each adds strength to determination.

After we came home last fall from our "bridal tour," I spent several days looking over, and culling over old letters, saved out of the great mass of communications I have received during the last twenty years. Among these, I found packages from your mother and yourself, and Helen. Letters dating back to my Bruceport, and Oysterville school teaching; our trip to San Francisco, Lafayette, and so on. It was almost like a new revelation; for, with all my other defects, I am especially deficient in recalling past events.

I am very sorry to hear of your poor health, but hope as you grow older, you may grow stronger. You have great tenacity of life, and I have faith that you will be spared many, many years yet. My health is as usual, extremely good, and now that I have a husband whom I love, and who is devoted to me, my life is, indeed, a happy one. With my past life of hardship and constant struggle, it is indeed a great blessing to find one to whom you can at all times turn for consolation and advice. Such an one has God, in His great goodness, blessed me with in this late day of my life.

But now to business. I am indeed glad to hear of the advancement of Astoria, my old and first home, forty-two years ago, and shall look forward to much pleasure in meeting my friends there, in the near future, especially our ladies of the union. My heart is in the work, and with me you know what that means. I hope I shall not disappoint you, and your friends, when I do come. I shall hold myself in readiness to come at your call. I can come on the 26th of April, or the 3d of May; or, if you think that May tenth would suit better, I may make some change here in my present arrangements.

As to taking up a collection, I leave that with you. I charge nothing but my bare expenses, and, in this case, we have been expecting for some time to visit our folks, and so can combine business with pleasure. The subject of my lecture is:

"The necessity of educating our children, through our public schools, as to the effects of alcohol and narcotics on the human system."

Please let me know, at your earliest convenience, as to the day selected, that I may arrange the time of other engagements so as not to conflict. Sincerely yours,

B. A. OWENS-ADAIR.

Below is the lecture above referred to.

THE NECESSITY OF EDUCATING OUR CHILDREN SCIENTIFICALLY

THROUGH OUR PUBLIC SCHOOLS,

AS TO THE EFFECTS OF ALCOHOL AND NARCOTICS

UPON THE HUMAN SYSTEM

We know we are treading upon comparatively new ground, and subjecting ourselves to severe criticism when we suggest that our public schools should be required to assist in this great cause of temperance.

All, I think, will agree with me that it is through our public schools that we can most effectually reach the majority of the thinking minds of our country. Our public schools are fast wiping out superstition and prejudice, and training our boys and girls to think, to choose, and to act for themselves. This can but tend to broaden their minds, and deepen their intellectual perceptions, and give strength and firmness to their independence, which we know is, in our citizens, the view foundation of our republic.

As a nation we are looking to our public schools as the great source from which our youth are to receive correct ideas of self-government.

Our temperance movement is yet young; but we have reason to hope that within a short time it will absorb the whole people; therefore, we would begin now to educate our children as to the uses and abuses of alcohol. By instructing the children of today, we are educating the men and women of the near future, and I think that a child may be made a Catholic, a Protestant, or a "free-thinker" by the particular instruction given it in early life.

Let us, therefore, be very careful that the children of today shall not only be generally well-informed men and women, but that they shall grow up with intelligent and well-defined ideas as to the widespread, and far-reaching evil results attending the use of alcohol in any form, as a beverage.

Having suggested some of the many reasons for teaching the "evils of alcohol" in our schools, let us now see what objections may be reasonably raised against this movement. Certainly we need fear none in the name of religion, for alcohol is no respecter of persons or faith, but attacks Protestant and Catholic with equal force, and brings discord and dishonor upon the families of Christians, as well as "freethinkers."

Would those engaged in the liquor traffic stand alone as objectors? We believe they would; and further, we believe that a very respectable number of our liquor dealers would prefer that their children should begin life with a clear understanding of the baneful effects of this most insidious poison.

Physicians know that malignant diseases require radical treatment, and that in all cases, in order to cure disease, the cause must be removed.

This disease of intemperance, or alcoholism, to give its scientific name, has attacked our nation, and is fastening on, and gnawing at its very vitals! Its poison is infused through our whole system, and is coursing in the veins of all classes of our people! It may almost be called a contagious disease, and when once contracted, it can be transmitted from generation to generation, appearing in a thousand types, and forms.

No family in all our broad land is free from its baneful curse. We see it in the pinched and contracted features of the innocent babe. We hear it in the moans and cries of its disturbed slumbers. We find it exhibited in the ill-humors and vicious acts of the young and old. It comes to us in the form of chorea and paralysis. We meet it daily in the various forms of hysteria and other nervous diseases.

Visit our insane asylums, and trace the histories of those poor unfortunates therein, and you will find that at least three-fourths of them can be referred directly or indirectly to alcohol.

Then go to the poor-houses and penitentiaries and you will find a still greater percentage of their inmates who attribute their downfall to the same cause. And I ask: "Is there anything strange in all this, when we know, beyond a doubt, that alcohol has a special affinity for brain and nerve tissues? There are many physical and practical demonstrations which plainly prove the truth of this.

We know that the brain substance of heavy drinkers becomes hardened and contracted; and we have it asserted, on good authority, that the brains of long-continued drunkards who have died from the effects of alcohol, were so saturated with the spirits that it ignited when touched with a lighted match.

A very beautiful demonstration of the effects of alcohol on the circulation may be shown by placing the web of a frog's leg under a microscope; then drop one drop of dilute alcohol on it, and you will see the blood-vessels slowly dilate, or expand, and channels heretofore unseen will open before your eyes; and you will see the blood-corpuscles darting onward, at a far more rapid pace. Now touch the membrane with a drop of pure spirits, and you will see the blood-vessels quickly contract. The cells will slacken their speed, and finally cease to move. The flesh shrivels up, and dies for want of nourishment; the tissues no longer receiving their food-supply from the blood.

Alcohol is a poison. A quart drank at one time would be death to any person, but when diluted, as in wine, whisky and other drinks, it is a powerful stimulant. The experienced physician instantly detects the peculiar thrill conveyed to the pulse by the heart alcoholically stimulated. Like strychnia, and many other poisonous narcotics, alcohol (when in the hands of a skillful physician) is a safe, valuable, and harmless remedy. As a stimulant when delay means death, nothing has been found to excel it; and from age to age, it has proved itself one of the physician's strongest aids: but, like opium, only by the physician should it be prescribed, or used. Careful experiments show that two ounces of alcohol (an amount contained in the potations of a very moderate drinker) increase the heart-beats 6000 in 24 hours.

It is hard work to fight alcohol; harder than rowing, walking, wrestling, coal-heaving, or the tread-mill itself.

All this is only the first effect of alcohol on the heart. Its long-continued use will cause degeneration of its muscular fiber, so that the heart loses its power to drive the blood, and in time, it will fail to respond to even the spur of the stimulant that has driven it to destruction. When alcohol is taken into the stomach, it passes directly into the circulation, and in a few minutes, sweeps through the entire system. If taken in considerable quantities, its great affinity for water will induce it to absorb water from the red corpuscles, causing them to shrink, and change their form, thereby rendering them unfit to carry oxygen. They may adhere together in masses, which prevents their passage through the small capillaries, thus obstructing the flow of the vital current through the heart, lungs, liver, and other organs, and so laying the foundations of disease.

Should such obstructions occur in the brain, paralysis, or apoplexy may follow. Persons have died on the spot, from drinking large quantities of liquor, on a wager, and, upon examination, it has been found that the whole of the blood in the heart had formed into a clot, thus causing instant death.

The red corpuscles are the air-cells of the blood, and carry oxygen, which they receive from the lungs, to every part of the body, and give it up to the hungry tissues, after which they return to the lungs, upon their faithful and double mission, laden with carbonic acid gas, known as the debris of the tissues, which must be burned up in order to preserve health and life.

Now we have seen that from the effects of alcohol these little life-preservers are rendered unfit to perform their normal function of feeding and relieving the tissues, and further, from their abnormal condition they have become elements of constant danger. We know that alcohol alters, and impairs tissue, rendering it liable to disease; especially is this fact noticed in surgery. The blood being thinned, and depreciated, severe hemorrhage is always expected, and much dreaded; and the most skillful surgeon oft-times, in such eases, finds himself appalled, and powerless to check the flow of blood.

A Mr. Huber, who saw 2160 persons perish with cholera in twenty days in a Russian town, says:

"It is a most remarkable circumstance that persons given to drink have been swept away like flies. In Tiflis, with twenty thousand people, every drunkard has fallen. Not one remains!"

Alcohol is not a food, as many suppose; but, in case of weakly persons with poor digestive organs, its *judicious* use *may* prove beneficial, by stimulating the glands which supply the digestive fluids, thereby aiding digestion.

If you take bread or meat into the stomach, nature welcomes it, and the juices of the system at once take hold of, and prepare it for the nourishment of the body. A million tiny fingers, known as lactcals, reach out and grasp it. They pour upon it their digestive fluids, dissolving and working it over, and over again, thus preparing it for the circulation, which takes hold, and carries it onward to wherever it is needed to mend, build, or re-build "this house we live in." It is now no longer bread and meat, but has become a part of yourself. It is your flesh and blood. Its chemical energy has been imparted to you as strength.

But if you take *alcohol* into your stomach, nature does not receive it so kindly, but treats it as a poison, and seeks to rid herself of its presence as soon as possible. The glands join in giving up their protective juices, and try, through dilution, to weaken its power, and satisfy its greed for water thereby preventing its shriveling up the delicate membranes, with which it must come in contact.

The veins take it up, and carry it throughout the body; all the organs of alimentation (scavengers of the body) are vigorously at work in the effort to rid the system of this foe. Thus it rushes through the system, and passes off unchanged, as alcohol, nature seeming to make no effort to appropriate it to her use.

Dr. A. B. Hall, of Boston, states that he once bled a man who was dead drunk, catching the blood in a bowl, and upon touching a match to it, the liquor blazed up at once, proving that alcohol was there in an unchanged state.

Liquor (though many believe it) is not a protection against cold. Dr. Hayes, the Arctic explorer, says:

"While fat is absolutely essential to the inhabitants and travelers in Arctic countries, alcohol is not only completely useless, but positively injurious. I have known able-bodied men become utterly incapable of resisting the cold, in consequence of the long-continued use of alcoholic drinks." And it is also true in all cases where strength and endurance are required. Prize-fighters, racers, and the like, have given testimony to the truth of this assertion. The trainers of such persons absolutely refuse to allow alcoholic stimulants to be taken in any form, during the training process, so well do they know its deleterious effect upon the physical powers.

But, after all, the worst evil which alcohol brings upon humanity is the curse which the inebriate parent entails upon his innocent offspring. This law of heredity demands our most earnest consideration. The world is beginning to perceive that the life of each individual is, in some real sense, a continuation of the lives of his ancestors. "Each one of us is the footing up of a double column of figures that goes back to the first pair." As Emerson profoundly says:

"A man is the whole encyclopedia of facts. The creation of a thousand forests is in one acorn; and Egypt, Greece, Rome, Gaul, Britain and America, he folded already in the first man."

"We are omnibuses," remarked Holmes, "in which all our ancestors ride."

We inherit from our parents our features, our physical and mental vigor, and even much of our moral character, and often when one generation is skipped, these qualities will re-appear in the one following, or even later.

The vices of our forefathers, as well as their virtues, have subtracted from, or added to the strength of our brain and muscle. The evil tendencies of our nature constitute a part of our heirlooms from the past.

Our descendants, in turn, will have reason to bless us, *only* in the degree that we hand down to them a pure, healthy physical, mental and moral being.

There is a marked tendency in nature to transmit all diseased conditions,—the actual disease not always being transmitted, but a pre-disposition, or tendency toward the actual disease. Alcohol is the most potent of all agents in establishing hereditary traits which prove destructive to both mind and body.

The keen, morbid desire for liquor which demands gratification at any cost, is known as "alcoholism," and is transmitted from the parent to the child, and thus thousands of persons are cursed with the drink craze, and such of these as do not fall by the wayside, are compelled to make it the great struggle of their lives to resist the cravings of this unappeasable monster.

There are at least five distinct varieties of mental derangement which own alcohol as their direct cause.

Could men, with one accord, consent to give up all excesses, and live temperately.—which means a life of healthfulness and holiness,—what a glorious change would be wrought. What a diminution of disease, crime, and in-sanity. Though the reduction of misery and evil in *this* generation would be so great, that of the next would be vastly more.

But unfortunately, we know too well that men will not abandon their excesses; indeed, the experience of ages has taught us the futility of wasting much time and energy in the effort to change the fixed views and habits of adults, and the wisdom and necessity of concentrating our educator}' force upon the children, while their young, plastic minds are ready to receive indelible impressions, so as to forestall the baleful influences of evil, and implant the good in its stead.

FROM THE ASTORIAN OF MAY **12, 1885.**

"The exercises at the Congregational Church last Sunday evening were well deserving the large audience they attracted. Mrs. J. B. Wyatt, Mrs. C. H. Page, Mrs. T. W. Eaton, and Mrs. C. W. Fulton, together with Mr. D. A. McIntosh, Mr. H. G. Smith, and the church choir, gave some splendid vocal selections, after which a thoughtful and instructive address was delivered by Airs. Dr. Owens-Adair, the lecture being a subject of warm eulogy on the part of all who heard it."

PROHIBITION MEETING AT LIBERTY HALL, ASTORIA.

Dr. A. C. Kinney introduced the speaker of the evening, Airs. Dr. Owens-Adair, at the meeting last evening, who immediately began a thoughtful and instructive address, prefaced by a brief statement regarding the intents and purposes of the Prohibition party, and the work requisite for the Woman's Christian Temperance Union to do. She stated the subject of her discourse to be, "Habit in Forming Character." Habit is a prime factor in temperance reform. It may be defined in general as an internal principle that leads us to do anything naturally and without conscious volition. It may be inherited, or acquired. Rightly directed, it should begin with the pre-natal life of the child, and should he carefully nurtured in early years. We cannot stand still; we must go up or down. Motion is the universal law of nature, and misdirected energy will lead to bad, as proper efforts will lead to good results, and good habits. The common remark, "We are a bundle of habits," is a correct one, and one worthy of consideration by all who have their own welfare, and the good of their fellow-beings at heart.

The speaker then entered upon what may be styled practical physiology, and in well-chosen language, gave some excellent suggestions regarding the functions of different organs of the body; their normal and abnormal conditions, the important influence of our immediate surroundings; the mutual relations of mind and body; the laws of heredity, and the evils of opium, tobacco, and alcohol, which, though useful in medicine, are, if used habitually, destructive to life and usefulness.

The speaker was both pleasing and instructive. Her theme was well handled, her voice perfectly audible in all parts of the hall, her enunciation clear and distinct and impressive, and her logic and arguments convincing. Not the least part of her discourse was that relating rather more to the psychological than the physiological nature of man, and on points such as the discussion of our instincts, which were defined as but the transmitted habits of our ancestors.

The speaker shed new light on what has, at all times, been a favorite study of biologists.

She concluded with a fitting allusion to the priceless value of good habits, and gracefully illustrated the beauty of her text by quoting Longfellow's Psalm of Life," where our representative American poet says:

> "Lives of great men all remind us
> We can make our lives sublime;
> And, departing, leave behind us
> Footprints on the sands of Time.
> Let us, then, be up and doing;
> With a heart for any fate.
> Still achieving, still pursuing,
> Learn to labor, and to wait."

WOMEN TO THE FRONT

Under this inviting salutation, the *San Francisco Chronicle* of a recent date speaks very highly, and deservedly, too, of Mrs. L. M. F. Wauzer, a female student, who has been matriculated in the Medical Department of California, and who "will soon be sitting on the front seat of the lecture amphitheater, and cutting poor humanity to pieces in the dissecting room," and adds:

"She is the first woman on this coast who has ever been admitted to similar honor and companionship."

Here we take issue with the *Chronicle*. If our California editors would but see that Oregon is on this coast, with all her glorious history, they would find examples and precedents here for those important matters and things which are sure to follow in their own state, and of which, on the first occasion of notice of them, they boast so much.

Oregon has a daughter who has already received the highest honors in the medical profession, and is now reaping the fruits of a lucrative practice in this state. We allude to Mrs. B. A. Owens, M. D., of Portland. Mrs. Owens came to Oregon with her parents in 1843, being then a mere child. She early evinced a strong desire to learn; to acquire a scientific education. Having no means to enable her to pursue her studies, except what pioneers shared in common—just what their hands could procure—she struggled on, through great privation, in this new country, until she became, though young, the accomplished mistress of her own personal fortune. At that early day, and for years thereafter, the opportunities for learning were very few and far between. With the subject of this sketch it was an individual work.

She first prepared herself for a teacher, and followed the occupation until she removed to a more thickly settled portion of the state, among relatives and friends, and engaged in a more lucrative business, pursuing her medical studies at the same time. After a few years, being fully prepared, and having, by her industry, secured a competency, she entered the Medical University of Pennsylvania, at Philadelphia, where, in due time, she graduated with the honors of her class.

Mrs. Owens, therefore, is not only the first woman on this coast who has ever been admitted to such honor, but she is the first woman of the Pacific states who had the moral courage to enter a class of students in a medical college where men and women studied and practiced medicine together.

MRS. B. A. OWENS.

"This lady arrived on the last steamer from Europe, the Portland papers inform us. Mrs. Owens formerly practiced in Portland, where she had a large business in her profession. Three years since, she went east, and reviewed her studies in one of the first medical colleges in the United States. In this institution she graduated, receiving the highest degree in surgery, *materia medica*, and all the accomplishments of the profession of her choice. There is no lady, we venture to say, practicing medicine who has had the benefit of such thorough teaching as Mrs. Owens, and who comes to the practice with greater skill and ability. In her collegiate course she received the highest honors that could be bestowed upon one of the profession. For several months she has been visiting Europe, from which she returns to engage in her calling at Portland. A lucrative practice awaits her."—(July, 1881.)

PROHIBITION

Editor Gazette:

During our last State Woman's Christian Temperance Union convention, our state superintendent of state work asked me to reply to "Ekoms," in the *Gold Beach Gazette* of May 30th, which I had not, at that time, seen.

Whom this learned opponent is, I know not; but from the tone of his article, I should judge that his occupation is that of dispensing alcoholic drinks across a bar, to that very class of men whose rights and liberties he seems so anxious to champion. It is my belief that with even the average thinker, and reader, just such effusions as this from the pen of Ekoms must do our cause much good. The flimsy arguments which he sets forth, and seems to think conclusive, are old, and threadbare. They consist principally in assertions, sarcasms, ridicule, and slangy expressions. He says: "Physiology is a good thing to study, and so is hygiene, if we can get a proper conception of what it means." Also, that children in district schools will not reach these studies unless they skip geography, grammar, and arithmetic.

This shows that he has not a right conception of these subjects.

If he will but consult Dunglicon's Medical Dictionary, he will, I think, be able to learn that children not only six, but even three years of age, may begin the study of hygiene by learning what to eat, drink, and wear; and what not to eat, drink, and wear, that they may keep well and not get sick. They can also, even at this tender age, be taught the difference between the state of being sick or well, and how to avoid the one, and retain the other. All of which is the study of hygiene, physiology, and pathology, three big words, I admit; hut, like all other great problems, become comprehensive when simplified by knowledge, and clothed in simple words.

He also says: "And yet we find perfect health prevailing on an Indian ranch so filthy that the stench of it would turn your stomach wrong side out a mile and a half against the wind." (I presume he has reference to the distance from the ranch, and not the length of

378

your stomach.) "And a nice, Christian family, temperate and refined, prostrate with sickness, in the same climate, and atmosphere." Here I would gently remind our worthy opponent that we are not Indians; neither are we Chinamen. That which is life and health for one animal, is destruction and death to another. Who would think of placing a horse and a hog in the same pen, and expecting them to thrive on the same diet and exercise?

Just what Ekoms means by "a good, old-fashioned education," I do not understand. Neither do I believe that old-fashioned educations, or by-gone modes of instruction can equal those of today. I am only surprised that any person, at this age of science, who presumes to write for newspapers, could make the assertion that the effects of alcohol on the human system are not known. The effects of this drug (for it should only be known as such) have been for more than twenty years studied experimentally by many of the greatest scientists of the age. And today we know its effects upon every tissue of the body. We know, too that only as a medicine has it ever benefited a human being: for it must, of necessity, encroach upon that law that holds good throughout the universe: "Over-stimulation brings about a corresponding sedation."

It has been determined that two ounces of alcohol, taken as wines or liquors, will increase the heart-beats 6000 in 21 hours, which is equivalent to lifting seven tons one foot high. Or, reduced still further, corresponds to work done equal to lifting seven ounces 1493 times each hour. If we had no other proof than this one of its deleterious effects, this alone would be amply sufficient to prove to all reasonable thinking minds that alcohol does "shorten life," does "produce insanity and ill-health."

But, fortunately, we have thousands of proofs. If space permitted, I could fill pages with statistics, and opinions of scientific men and women to verify these assertions. If this is not so, why do insurance companies refuse to insure the lives of drunkards? Why is the question always asked by them: "Do you use alcoholic liquors? If so, to what ex tent?" Ignorance as to the effect of alcohol on the human system is, we consider, the cause of much drunkenness. Few persons understand or realize that they are being injured by this most insidious poison until the habit is formed. That habit now becomes the controlling and consuming element of their lives, which few persons have the moral or physical power to overcome. "We are a bundle of habits." We begin forming these habits even in the cradle; many of which go with us to the grave. Should not our little ones be taught by their foster-mother, the public school, how to avoid the evil, and select the good? What is the worth of education without morality? Give us this, and if needs be, less science. We deny that "nineteen out of twenty" want or need alcohol, in any form. And we contend that this nation has as much right to legislate and regulate the manufacture and sale of this poison, as it has that of opium, or any other deadly drug. Opium has never cost the nation one-thousandth part, either in wealth, disgrace, wretchedness, insanity or disease, as has alcohol. To say that men have the right, or should be allowed it, to use that which will not only ruin and bring disgrace upon themselves, but upon their families, as well, is, to my mind, equivalent to saying that a man has a right to take his own life, and that of his family. Were the drunkards the only sufferers through this indulgence, even then humane temperance people would be justified in interfering, and demanding that the strong arm of the law shall protect and shield those that cannot protect themselves. That this class should be permitted to not only disgrace our nation, and their own families, but that they should be allowed to poison the blood of their innocent offspring, and bring into our midst poverty, disease, idiocy, and insanity, is more than we are willing to allow. We deny that prohibition is a failure, and with pride we point to Iowa and Maine for ample proof. This temperance party has grown into a power that is felt throughout the land. For information, read "Prohibition in Portland, Maine," on the fifth page of the Union Signal, of July second. "In April, 1884, there were 115 arrests for drunkenness alone. In April, 1855, only 51 arrests. At the time of this writing, there has been no police court held for three mornings, there having been no arrests."

Ekoms, like many other such writers, closes his argument by placing this burden of purification on the shoulders of mothers. But he has taken the great precaution to instruct them in how they must work. Thanks, friend Ekoms for your gratuitous advice. But the last ten years have taught the W. C. T. U. that for their work, it is best to use their own brains. No, no, friend Ekoms, this laying on of your profane hand has not caused our holy sanctuary to "crumble and disappear, like frost in the morning sun." It is still secure, and we fear not the winds and storms of profanity; for our sanctuary is not built upon the sand. Yes, you are right, we are, indeed, "intrenched behind a breastwork"; a breastwork in which we have faith, for it is "For God and Home, and Native Land."

November 14, 1885.

Friend Ekoms:

It is with renewed interest, not to say pleasure, that I come forward to reply to your second article; especially now that I know you to be a friend, and more than suspect your identity. I shall strive not to "misunderstand" you in the future, and shall, therefore, have hopes of your ultimate conversion.

I should be glad to attempt the answering of all your questions, but to do so would require more space than any newspaper would allow in one or two issues. I shall, therefore, have to confine myself to reasonable space.

It was with thankfulness that my soul breathed a prayer, "Thank God," when my eyes fell on the sentence, "At present, I neither drink nor deal in liquor."

You "do not think that selling liquor has tarnished your honor, or that drinking it has impaired your intellectual ability." The first we will not discuss. But tell me, my friend, do you look back to your occupation of selling liquor with the same pride that you do to the time when your occupation was that of editing a newspaper in the interest of a young and growing community? The correctness of your second assertion depends much upon the quantity drank, and the conditions under which it was taken. If you drank liquor for years, or even months, as a beverage, then the weight of scientific authority is against you. But here comes a demand for statistics, and you seem to ignore statistics, especially those of recent date. If you have more faith in older statistics than those of modern times, I will refer you to Dr. Rush's essay, written one hundred years ago, the centennial birthday of which we temperance people celebrated last month throughout the United States.

For further proof, please study that eminent prize essay, written one hundred and thirty-six years ago, on the use and abuse of alcoholic liquors, by William B. Carpenter, examiner in physiology in the University of London, professor of medical jurisprudence in University College, and author of "The Principles of Physiology," etc.

You say you once heard me play a different tune,—that of woman suffrage.

T take pleasure in informing you that I have not forgotten that tune, neither have I ceased to play and sing it. It is just as near and dear to my heart today as it was \h years ago, when to advocate it was considered by the better (?) classes a disgrace, causing its advocates to be derisively called "blue-stockings." But, my friend, do you not know that away back in those days of my earnest enthusiasm I was as loyal a supporter of prohibition as I am now? In proof of this allow me to quote from my address printed in the *Roseburg Pantagraph,* in 1871. It was delivered before the Roseburg lodge of Good Templars, on my installation as worthy chief.

"I did not join this organization for honor or fame, but to labor in every honorable way for the abolition of king alcohol. This evil is deeply rooted in our system of government, and, like his satanic majesty, has set himself up as chief ruler in our governmental affairs."

Again I quote from my reply to Thomas Smith, of North Umpqua, whose article was headed "Anti-Prohibition." Near the close of my reply, I find this paragraph:

"Then I would say, let us work as one great family; let the women encourage the men to form political temperance organizations, where each man will pledge himself to throw party principles aside, and vote for the men who will pledge themselves to work for prohibition."

Yes, I do acknowledge that alcohol, like opium, is a valuable drug, and the great physician, Boerhaave, said: "Opium is the finger of

382

God," and those who, under its soothing power, have felt the cessation of unendurable pain, can respond to his sentiment. When rightly used, as a medicine, alcohol and opium are blessings. When perverted to sensual gratification, they inflict untold misery, and enslave their victims in chains that can be severed only by death. The strongest will is easily and insidiously overcome by the use of these drugs, and their victim believes that he is dying, will die, and that only opium (or alcohol, as the case may be)' can save him. Under such circumstances, the most conscientious will deceive, lie and steal to obtain the drug.

The use of all stimulants and narcotics, when taken in health, have the same destructive tendency, but the great difference in effect depends upon the special power of the drug itself. Opium stands at the head, both for good and evil. An eminent physician once said:

"If all drugs but one should be banished from use, may God grant that one to be opium."

Alcohol is the greatest curse to our nation, because it is more universally used. Tobacco ranks next in order, and yet, until the last few years, it was only objected to by "cranky" women, and the worst that was thought and said about it was that it was "a filthy habit." Today its deleterious effects upon the human system are scientifically studied and demonstrated. So great is the interest taken in this subject, not only for the present generation, but for the welfare of those unborn, that the law-makers of 16 states have passed laws requiring that the effects of alcoholic stimulants and narcotics on the human system shall be taught to all children educated by the public money.

Again you say that if I could be induced to study both sides of the question, I would still remain an honest laborer in the cause of temperance. I think few persons have had a better opportunity to study both sides of the question than myself. My early life was crushed by this common curse of humanity, alcohol. It robbed my home and childhood of every vestige of beauty and sunshine. It permitted me to grow up in ignorance of the contents of even the primary school books; and not until I had reached womanhood, and had earned money by the hardest manual labor, did I have the opportunity of learning to read and write.

For the last twelve years my profession has given me every opportunity to study the "other side"—the human side, which is, after all, the scientific side of this all-important question. God's laws do not excuse violations. No, nor even mistakes; and we, not only as individuals, but as a nation, should and must learn by our own and our neighbors' mistakes and failures.

More than eighteen hundred years ago we were told that "The sins of the fathers are visited upon the children, aye, even to the third and fourth generation."

Had we but heeded that warning, and studied the solution of the problem, we should not today require the use of jails, penitentiaries, and insane asylums. But for centuries, this warning has been allowed to go unheeded, and men and women in their ignorance and willfulness go blindly on propagating disease, insanity and wretchedness into this world. Today we have thousands of scientific men and women in the field devoting their earnest and faithful lives to the great work of elevating and purifying the race.

The W. C. T. U. is a grand educational organization which now numbers over 200,000 strong. For more than eleven, years we have been quietly educating, not only our women and children, but our men as well.

We have studied these questions thoroughly, and understand the elements with which we have to deal; and having trained and proficient workers in the field, we now feel prepared for the great conflict; ready to join hands with all temperance people; and willing to work for any measure that looks toward the restriction or abolition of alcohol, and all other sources of crime. And looking to this end, we shall stand by the third party. As to the assertions that prohibition is an enemy to temperance, and that it can never succeed, they will be decided in the near future. The gain of 20,000 votes in one year in Ohio is not very discouraging to us.

You and I remember well when it was said that slavery was a divine institution and could never be dethroned, yet we have lived to see that accursed institution which was so intimately interwoven into the very fiber and life of our government, literally torn up, root and branch, and consumed by public opinion. I doubt if there can be found in the south today a man who does not rejoice that the stain of slavery has been removed from the honor of our country.

Twenty-seven years ago the great Republican party that has governed our nation for nearly a quarter of a century, was, in point of numbers vastly inferior to the temperance party of today, and its object was not more humane. It received its life from various sources, which were of slow growth. Its primary germ was the old abolition party, which was near half a century in maturing, and proved to be its strongest root.

We temperance people have been working under various organizations, i e., Sons of Temperance, Woman Suffrage, State Temperance Alliance, Young Men's Christian Association, National League, Woman's Christian Temperance Union, etc.

The one great object of all these organizations is the advancement and elevation of humanity, and as alcohol is considered the curse of our country, it is the common enemy of all these societies, and, at no distant day, it will prove to be the issue which will firmly unite them all into one grand organization, in name, as they now are one in feeling. We are aware that this cannot be done without dissension. There are some men and women in our ranks opposing prohibition, because they have more interest in the Republican or the Democratic parties than in the principles of the organization to which they belong.

For years we have asked, prayed, and begged at the feet of these two great parties, only to be repulsed, or put off with faltering promises never meant to be fulfilled, until we have not only become discouraged, but disgusted. And now we are prepared to meet them in a way that will at least demand respectful consideration. No party realizes this more thoroughly than do the whisky leaders, themselves.

They are now calling lustily for "high license," while they are fighting prohibition, and woman suffrage. Only a few years ago they demanded equal privileges, recognition, and protection before the law. Today their only hope for protection is in high license. The time has also passed that they can smile at woman's power. They now consider her of sufficient consequence to require the adoption of a set of special resolutions, declaring that they will, at all times and places, work to defeat woman suffrage, for well they know that with woman's ballot, comes the fall of the liquor traffic.

Verily, verily the world moves forward.

MRS. OWENS-ADAIR, M. D.

WOMEN WORKERS

Portland, Oregon, April 27, 1886.

Editor Star:

Yesterday the subject of the advisability of women working at the polls was brought up at a regular meeting of our Portland \V. C. T. U.

The matter was deferred for one week, to give time for thought, consultation and plans. It was decided to meet at the First Presbyterian Church, this 10 a m., to make it a special subject of prayer, and consultation. At the close of this meeting', a committee of six ladies was appointed to call upon the Prohibition Central Committee, and ask for individual pledges from each candidate.

Today our beloved State President, Mrs. H. K. Plines, will request our corresponding secretary, Mrs. Robb, to send a special letter to each and every state officer of the W. C. T. U. of Oregon, asking her to authorize her name to be placed to a call which will soon be issued, if the consent of a* majority of all the state officers is secured.

This call will ask the earnest support of the W. C. T. U., and all other women who favor temperance, and the constitutional amendment. And further, it will invite all such to come and work at the polls for all good temperance candidates, irrespective of party, who will pledge themselves to work for a constitutional amendment.

We believe we know the mettle of which these grand women are possessed, who have charge of the W. C. T. U. of Oregon, and we expect to see within a few days, every name of every state officer attached to this important call. Our brave, noble women of the east have set us this good example. They have repeatedly worked side by side at the polls with their temperance brothers with success.

The Atlantic and Pacific must join hands in this great work. Oh, my sisters, this is a vital question, one of life and death! Do not, oh, do not shrink from this work. Let us think of our homes and dear ones in danger, and forget, as it were, all else but our duty to God and them.

Let us see to it that on the first Monday in next June we "make our record clean." And let us prove to the country that we can and will assist in protecting and defending our homes and loved ones.

MRS. OWENS-ADAIR, M. D.

WOMEN URGED TO ATTEND THE POLLS

Portland, Ore., April 27.

To the Editor of the Oregonian:

Allow me to thank Judge Bronaugh for his sensible and practical letter in this morning's Oregonian. Especially am I pleased with that portion wherein he appeals to women all over this stale to form themselves into committees, and wait upon every candidate for the legislature, and ask him to pledge himself, if elected, to work and vole for the proposed amendment to the Keady bill. I honor and thank Judge Bronaugh for his brave and earnest call for woman's aid in this great work. And let me say that I believe that his timely call will receive a hearty response. For myself, I not only endorse all that Judge Bronaugh said, in his letter, but I will go even farther than he has gone. I will advocate the advisability of women attacking this monster evil in its stronghold, the polls. I favor woman carrying her purifying influence to those places where her representatives are elected, and there laboring earnestly for those men only who will pledge their support, if elected, for the constitutional amendment. This will be no new departure for women. They have worked at the polls in the various states and territories where local option and prohibition now exist. Coffee, sandwiches, lemonade and ice water have been supplied in many places. In some localities, the children, our "Bands of Hope" were regaled, and with appropriate banners, and mottoes, were marched and counter-marched around and about the polling places.

And pure, refined women were there, earnestly laboring for the good of their country. Do not tell me that this is no place for women and children, and that this cannot have a beneficial influence. Purity and goodness are recognized, yes, and appreciated by the lowest, and most degraded. Nothing so easily touches and softens the heart of the hardest criminal as to look upon the innocent faces of childhood, and the thin, gray locks of motherhood. For a time he lives over again his own innocent childhood, and looks into the loving face of his long forgotten mother. A strange power seems to take possession of him, and he again resolves to atone for past wrongs, and' to be an honest man. For a time temptation loses its hold on him, and many men, under such influences, have been redeemed. The attempt, at least, should be made. I am aware that many of our good women shrink from the work. And yet the brave mothers of our beloved \Y. C. T. U. began this crusade, fourteen years ago, in the low, vile saloons of our land. And I am sure it was never claimed, even by the worst opponent, that these women were defiled through this unpleasant work, but to the contrary. The ministers all over our land held protracted meetings earnestly praying for their success, and urging out new recruits.

Now why should the women to-day not be strengthened and encouraged in performing this less objectionable work. One of our state officers, who is noted for her quiet manners, and good, sound judgment, said to me yesterday: "I not only think it is proper for a woman to work at the polls, but I look upon it as a duty, especially now, when we have an opportunity of accomplishing so much." Let us hear from some of our brothers and sisters on this subject.

MRS. OWENS-ADAIR.

A PLEA FOR WOMEN TO WORK AT THE POLLS

By Dr. Adair.

Portland, Or., May 6, 1886.

Ed. Plaindealer:

Will you allow me space to call the attention of the ladies of Douglas and surrounding counties to the fact that the ladies of the W. C. T. U. of Multnomah county have decided to work at the polls. Now, ladies, one and all, who are in favor of temperance, and the protection of your homes from the rum traffic, will you not join us, and lend your aid in every way that you think best, to further this good work? Let it be said that this election was presided over by women. Yes good, pure women, in whose presence men dare not sink below the level of the brute creation.

Rest assured, my good sisters, that wherever good women go, there good behavior will he found, and decency will prevail. This is no new departure,—women have worked at the polls in all the various states where prohibition or local option now exists, and at all limes they have done good. Many of our ministers have sanctioned the move. Yesterday one of the oldest, and clearest-headed ministers of Oregon not only sanctioned, hut encouraged us to go forward with this work.

All we need to do, my sisters, is to go forward and stand firm, and we will soon find an immense army of the moral element at our backs.

I hope, within a few days, to see an official state call to the W. C. T. U. [Women's Christian Temperance Movement] to take up this work. Put we want the aid of all good women outside of this organization to assist us in this work for "God, and home and native land."

NO TRUE WOMANS DUTY

Ed. Review:

In last, week's issue of the Review I see a letter, or a called plea, from Mrs. Owens-Adair, M. D., of Portland, in which she endeavors to induce ladies of Douglas and neighboring counties to an active interest in temperance and local option. Endeavors to persuade them to go boldly forward and mingle with the disreputable, hardened, careless and indifferent men, of which there are so many to be found at all voting places, or, in other words, desires that ladies "work at the polls" in the coming election.

Advising all ladies in favor of temperance and the protection of their homes to take part in this work with might and main in keeping the men from "falling below the brute creation."

This is all humbug. True, our ladies are all it is to be hoped, in favor of temperance, and will do all in their power to aid this great, grand, and good work; but, ladies, is this your duty? Is this the power of true ladies to do as advised by Mrs. Owens-Adair? To go among the men at the polls, to be jeered, insulted, scorned, and scoffed at, perhaps cursed. Is this your duty? No! What we want is to get the liquor out of the country, of course, but we can never do so by going to the polls, unless we can place our vote there, and thus eradicate the gloom cast over our country by whisky.

Ladies, your good, kind husbands would not care to see you at the polls, amid a crowd of shouting, noisy men, mingling among besotted wretches, drunkards staggering, swearing, in such conditions as you would not care to see. Your daughter would not desire to see her mother do thus, but would endeavor, to the best of her ability, to prevent any such contact on your part.

Your son would not have you see the wretched sights so common in such places, and horrifying to ladies. Oh, no, he would prefer to see his mother at home among her circle of friends, away from the vile, poisonous atmosphere of such places. With that sweet smile, that beaming countenance, those tender, kind, loving words that make home what it is. He would wish to protect you from such things, as a dutiful son should do. In God's name, ladies, I entreat you do not this; do what you can in other ways; exert your influence on those round about you. If you must work for the annihilation of the liquor traffic there are plenty of opportunities and methods offered to you which is much more ladylike, and will tend to greater good than that of the "worker at the polls."

I sincerely hope that these words will find their way to the minds of any lady readers, and after due consideration I am positive you will agree with me. Some time, perhaps, the victory will be ours, if we but do as we should. Sometime we will have the opportunity of walking, with brother or husband, son or friend, and cast your vote for right. Let us have no official state call for this work; we do not want it. Do this, ladies, "for God, and home, and native land." ORSINI.

The letter above is reproduced for several reasons, the first of which is to show public opinion as it was in those days as regards woman's position in society.

Second. To preserve the record of the past, by which to* judge the present, and estimate the future.

At that time the country was flooded with similar productions, usually written by men, though often under the guise of women.

Twenty-five years hence this letter will be looked upon as a real curiosity, and as such, and to show the progress we have made, should be preserved.

We have already passed far beyond that age, and thus, step by step, we have forged ahead, until now we are face to face with the "Smart Set,"—that great phalanx of wealth, fashion, and beauty.

This is a foe worthy our steel-, for we know that pots, and kettles, and other dirty things at least will not be used against us in this battle for humanity.

And, furthermore, we are encouraged in that we know that from the beginning of time it has always been the wheel horse that moved the cart.

Portland, Or., April 4, 1886.

Mrs. Davenport—My Dear Friend:

Yours just received and contents noted. First. We, the committee, do not wish to dictate to the ladies of any part of the state how they should or must work. We merely suggest. We believe they are as capable as we are, and are better judges of the people with whom they have to work.

As to working at the polls, I conscientiously believe that the end will justify the means. We are not working merely for the God-given right to vote, but for the great good we hope to accomplish through that power, privilege, or right, to vote. Now, if every man who will vote on this question knew and understood what he was voting for then I should object to working at the polls. But there will be hundreds yes, thousands, who will vote on this all-important question who will not have even a conception of what the amendment means. And as this element will be utilized I believe it is our duty to utilize it, as far as we honorably can, to further a good and just cause. Why should we stand idly by, and allow our enemies to win in this battle? No, no, my friend, God will answer our prayers when we prove our trust in Him by putting our shoulders to the wheel with a will, and a determination to defeat this, our enemy. Cromwell said to his soldiers: "Trust in God, and keep your powder dry." I believe we are justified in fighting this battle to win, and I am in favor of staying in the field until it is either won or lost. I am not willing to leave this question to ignorant voters, nor designing enemies. I confess that I have more faith in the solid, practical work of embodied spirits than I have in any good results that might be made upon ignorant voters through the agency of our "good guardian angels."

I have learned through long experience that if I do not attend to my own business, no one will attend to it for me. If we win, we will be honored; if we lose, we shall at least be respected. Did not the temperance women in the East, a few months ago, work at the polls? And have they not received praise and honor throughout the land?

No, I can see no wrong in our working at the polls. And I have been told by men that we could swell our vote by so doing, at least 1,000 in Portland alone.

I am sorry that I do not know of some speaker, but I do not. We must work with such material as we have.

Yours very respectfully,

WOMEN AT THE POLLS

Portland, Or., May *20.* 1886.

To the editor of the Oregonian:

I am pleased to see our able "Superintendent of Press Work" come to the front this morning with explanations and wise logic concerning that much-talked-of subject, "Women at the Polls."

Now, it is not strange that people of equal intelligence will see things from different standpoints, for such has been the case from the beginning of time. Therefore we are not surprised that this, one of the purest motives of the W. C. T. U., should be picked to pieces and shown up to say the least in aspects most objectionable.

We are admonished by one not to go to the polls as suppliants, as that would be degrading to our dignity and self-respect.

My friends, no person ever stultified his manhood, or injured his reputation by doing even the most disagreeable work for the good of humanity. Is it pleasant, and is it foolish for our officers of the Social Purity Department to go down into the dens of iniquity and vice, and there plead with depravity in its vilest forms? Was it pleasant, and was it foolish for the crusaders to begin this grand work where they did, in the lowest and vilest saloons in the land? That great organization, the W. C. T. U., which to-day numbers 300,000 earnest and devoted women, is the firstborn of that crusade of fourteen years ago.

The Prohibition party of to-day, which is shedding light upon our nation, is the grandchild of this same crusade movement.

We are accused of advocating this move in the hope of influencing voters by petty little feminine wiles, and also that we expect to buy votes with lemonade and buttonhole bouquets. Now, nothing could be more foreign to our intention than this. We all know" that it is not only right, but the duty of good men to go to the polls and work. Then why should not women be encouraged to do likewise? Where it is respectable for men to go, it should be respectable for women to go. It has been the custom for centuries, in great and small undertakings, especially when the social element entered into the

393

work, to provide some form of refreshment, or beverage by which the parties would pledge themselves to the work under consideration. It has been, and still is, the custom of our native Americans to have ready the pipe of peace, that it may be passed around as a sacred pledge of friendship. Alcoholic drinks have been used for generations as a pledge of fidelity and friendship in social gatherings. This custom has become so fixed upon us, as a nation, that few persons, even church members, are brave enough to give a dinner or marriage supper without champagne and other wines. "I do not believe in it myself, but then, you know, custom demands it."

Now, the W. C. T. U. does not object to pledges. Indeed, we advocate pledges, but we are particular as to the contents of the glass in which the pledge is taken and sealed. We would prefer that the pledge be taken with the beverage which God Himself provided for all mankind, "pure sparkling water." We do not, however, object to the addition of a spoonful of sugar and a few drops of lemon juice, for they are healthful and harmless. And, furthermore, wo do have faith in men, to believe that if they pledge themselves to vote for a temperance man or for our ticket, they will not forget their promise before they reach the ballot box.

Last year, during the long, hot summer, the W. C. T. U. kept a barrel of ice water in front of the rooms of the Y. M. C. A. to prevent men being forced to frequent beer halls to quench their thirst. One gentleman said he was sure that this was a loss of at least $50 a day to the saloonkeeper opposite. Said he:

"I was in the habit of spending 30 or 40 cents a day for beer, not that I cared for beer, just to keep cooled off."

Again, the temperance people all over the slate are taking lip subscriptions for temperance literature, and sending it wherever we think we can influence votes. And is this not legitimate? No, my friends, we are not proposing to buy votes, not even with flowers and lemonade. And should they be provided, too, I can see no objection, for they are innocent, and can do no harm. I am sure they cannot be accused of robbing any man of his senses, of sending him home reeling drunk from the polls.

Another very important reason why we should go to the polls next June is that we have a lady candidate on the ticket, whom we are very anxious to see elected. Should any woman in Portland he ashamed to go to the polls and ask any man to vote for Mrs. Alice Clauson Gove for School Superintendent?

I hope to see hundreds of her lady friends at the polls asking votes for her. Any lady has the right and privilege to go to the polls. I have no fears but that the ladies can, and will conduct themselves with as much propriety as they do in the streets of this city.

DR. OWENS-ADAIR.

WOMEN AT THE POLLING PLACES.

For the first time in the history of this city women have appeared at the polling places offering tickets and soliciting votes. The plan, as carried out, is simple and unostentatious. The women are stationed about half a block from each polling place, by a stand, covered with temperance literature, prohibition tickets, and flowers, and deal out to such as will take them their tracts and tickets, and to such as will listen, their arguments in favor of prohibition. The women engaged in the work are all past middle life, quiet and ladylike, and report having met kindness and consideration from the voters whom they addressed. Both their zeal in the cause of temperance and their bravery in its advocacy are unquestioned, and it is impossible to witness what must be, to an independent spirit, the humiliating position of these earnest workers without respecting their zeal, even if it is considered mistaken.

ANSWER TO CRITICISM

April 21, 1885.

To the Editor:

I beg space to reply to S. D. (Saloon Defender) in yours of the 20th, who would make sport of our worthy nominee, E. C. Bronaugh, who comes boldly forward and declares that he is an enemy of whisky, which is the acknowledged curse of the country.

I admit that the whisky traffic has been required to assist in the building of our penitentiaries, jails, and insane asylums; but I assert that it has furnished nine-tenths of all the occupants of these lamentable institutions. This is no wild assertion. Every lawyer and every doctor of eminence and ability knows that it is true.

A bright young attorney said to me the other day while discussing this subject:

"Well I know that nine-tenths of all the divorce cases and trouble in families are caused by liquor, and I would like to see it go."

In conversation with our estimable Governor Thayer last week on prohibition be said:

"I think perhaps nine-tenths of all the inmates of the penitentiary in this state may owe their incarceration to liquor, but I do not think you can claim that percentage of our insane."

My answer was that the cause is certainly one and the same, but the trouble is that while the cause is apparent and easily traced in the case of the convicted criminal, it is, in the majority of cases, obscure and hard to trace in the insane.

Hear what the eminent Dr. A. B. Palmer has to say on this vital subject—he who has been a professor of theory and practice for more than thirty years, who has been honored and quoted as authority by the great scientists, both of Europe and our own country. He says:

"Every permanent condition of the organism; every habit of body or mind in the parent, has an influence, greater or lesser, upon the qualities and tendencies of the offspring. We can make ourselves what we will, only within certain limitations, and our innate propensities, at least, however they may be controlled, are received from our ancestors, and are apt to govern us.

"Morbid qualities of a mild character in the parents may be exaggerated in the offspring. Thus, inebriety with its ordinary perversions in the parent may become idiocy or insanity in the child, and moderate drinking in the father, creating an appetite which in him is controlled, may produce drunkenness in the ,son, or dipsomania in the son or grandson, which may be beyond all control."

Add to this the testimony of the distinguished surgeon of London, Henry Thompson, who says:

"Few are aware of the great mischief done by the moderate use of fermented liquors."

I ask, should parents in their ignorance be allowed to poison the blood of their innocent and helpless offspring? Should men and women be allowed to contract disease, and vicious habits, and with them propagate, and bring forth mental and physical monstrosities with which to curse our land? Should our government have no will in these important matters? Must we forever be forced to build institutions with iron bars and grated doors to protect society? No, sir! We believe the time has come when our people shall be made to realize and understand the importance of these great questions which involve the life and well-being of our nation.

"OUR WANDERING BOY," AGAIN

Portland, Or., March 22, 1887. To the Editor of the Oregonian:

I have carefully read your article against prohibition in last Sunday's Oregonian headed, "Where Is My Wandering Boy To-Night?" Through your kindness I would like to reply briefly in the interest of "the wandering boy."

First, I say to that great array of talent and purity you cite to show that "prohibition is a delusion and vicious means to the end of the reduction of intemperance' we prohibitionists have brought forth equally as good proof in favor of the successful working of prohibition. And this, too, in the face of the fact that prohibition is still in its infancy. One of our latest proofs is found in today's Oregonian, and reads as follows:

"Leavenworth, Kas., March 18, 1887.

"J. W. Webb, Oregon:

"Your telegram received. There is not a saloon in Leavenworth.

397

(Signed)"F. S. NEALY."

Mr. Nealy is the Mayor of Leavenworth, and doubtless knows as much about his city as Mr. John Gates knows about Portland.

This is the kind of work, I am proud to say, that this "band of sentimental reformers" are engaged in. And this little band of "fools" and "cranks" I verily believe are fast reaching out into the millions, and will, in the near future, include a majority of all the thinking minds of our splendid country. "Father, dear father, why don't you come home?" will not be asked, by thousands of anxious wives and children in our own fair Portland two years hence, if the constitutional amendment is carried, and our Mayor and other city officials do their duty. Then if the dear father and "wandering boy" do not come home at the proper time their absence will not create so much fear and trembling.

We do not expect that prohibition is going to work miracles or make men good all at once, but we do expect it to make them better, by helping them to overcome their vicious tastes and habits. Who can expect to train up a child properly while allowing it to associate with low and degraded companions? What effect will your advice to your son against using tobacco have, if he sees you daily smoking? Or against liquor, if he is accustomed to see it at home upon your table, and sees his father and other respectable men going into saloons daily? Judge Cooley, the great jurist of Michigan, said to me: "What a blessing it would be if we could only get our children to profit by our experiences. But it seems to be a law of nature that each one must learn by his own experience, especially when surrounded by temptation."

The saloonkeeper pays the government for the privilege of carrying on his business, and thereby acquires a right to the respect and protection of the government. Our children are taught at home and at school that our government is a great and glorious institution—the best and greatest on earth. This great and good government authorizes the sale of rum so freely that her most respectable citizens offer it to their customers. Even our grocerymen pay a license for the privilege of supplying their customers with ale and beer. A few evenings since I happened into one of the best and oldest grocery stores in the city, and upon seeing several boxes filled with bottles I asked what was in them. The proprietor, whom I know to be an honorable man, answered: "Beer and ale." I said: "Is it possible you sell beer and ale?" He replied: "Yes, I do; but not because I want to sell it, for I don't use it myself, but my business requires me to keep it in stock." He added: "I pay for my license, and that is more than a good many do." To my amazement I then learned that every grocery store in Portland, with perhaps three exceptions, keep wine and beer for sale, and my friend further said that he intended voting for the amendment, and hoped to see the day when liquor licenses would he unobtainable. Yes, we do believe that a "change of law" prohibiting the sale of liquor would bring about a "change of heart." How often do we hear it said: "He is a good man, when not under the influence of liquor. Or, "He was a grand man, until liquor got the upper hand of him." You say that the law answers the mother that it does not know where her "wandering boy" is; it is none of its business.. Well, then, we think that the saloonkeeper who is cared for and protected by the law would have less difficulty in answering this mother's question, for it is part of her business to know where the dear father and wandering boy arc. We believe that the law should reach out its protecting arms, especially to the weak and helpless. It does say: "You shall not keep an opium joint, or gambling house," and to the druggist: "You shall not sell poison, except for medicinal purpose." But to the saloonkeeper it virtually says: "Go on selling liquor, which brings more distress and destruction to human life than all the other evils combined; sell away, and as long as you pay your license I will protect you against all damage suits."

The poet Whittier was, by nature, a moral man. He did not find it necessary to battle with vicious tendencies and appetites. Such persons as a rule are not so competent to judge of the proper treatment or punishment to be meted out to those more unfortunate. We usually judge others by ourselves, and if we are blessed with strong will power, and can easily surmount difficulties, and overcome bad habits, we frequently proceed to lay down rules for others to follow. Rules that would be just to us might be unjust to those who are differently constituted.

The lives of a few individuals cannot be taken to prove general laws. If they could, the lives of Daniel Webster. Edgar A. Poe, General Grant and a host of others would weigh heavily for prohibition.

MRS. OWENS-ADAIR, M. D.

"ANTI-SALOON MOVEMENT"

Portland, Or., August 1.

To the Editor of the Oregonian:

I cannot resist the temptation to make a few comments on the article "Anti-Saloon Movement" in to-day's Oregonian. Especially am I prompted to do this from the fact that, on my way home from the Congregational Church, where I had listened to a beautiful and impressive sermon on "Manhood and Manliness" by Rev. Dr. Clapp, I passed by two saloons on the same block, one with the side and the other with the front "door standing wide open, with streams of men pouring in and out. And this, too, in the face of a well-known Sunday law.

It fills my soul with great joy that the great Republican party has at last been forced to call an anti-saloon conference. However this may terminate; whatever course or plan they may decide upon, one thing is certain, the movement will add strength and power to prohibition. That in time it must come to this great issue, all deep thinkers and far-seers know, and that at no distant day this nation will be divided upon this the most momentous question our people have ever been called upon to decide. For soon the temperance people will drive this balance of power (the whisky element) from the center of the "teeter-board" into one or the other of the great political parties. Then we will meet them on the open field of battle; and will teach them what morality and "personal liberty" mean. We will teach them that the thousands of wretched wives and helpless children whom they have robbed have "personal rights," as well as distillers, brewers, and saloonkeepers. They will also learn that this nation can exist without a "little wine for the stomach's sake."

We are told in this article, as we are told even day, that a prohibition law has existed in several states, and in one for thirty years, and still prohibition is not a success. If this statement is true, why does the saloon power light it so desperately? That it spares no time, trouble or money to defeat a prohibition law, proves that it does practically prohibit, and they know it.

But supposing it to be true, J ask how could we expect to be a success in all those localities where there is either a Republican or a Democratic party holding the reins of state? Are not both controlled by the saloon power? One party rides into the White I louse on a barrel of whisky, while the other reaches that distinguished place of honor astride a keg of beer. Is it strange England should have called us a nation of drunkards? And this accursed beverage continues to flow unceasingly throughout each administration, unless the occupant of the presidential chair is blessed with a wife who possesses sufficient firmness of character and Christian fortitude to say:

"Wine shall not disgrace the table of the White House while I preside as its mistress."

Thank God that our Executive Mansion has been blessed by such a one. The honored name of Lucy Webb Hayes will continue to shine beside that of the immortal Frances Willard throughout the annals of history as a bright and luminous star to bless and encourage all womankind.

A prohibition party is what we want to secure; a national constitutional amendment. The breaking up of the Republican party in the North, and the prohibition element in the South, will furnish us a powerful leverage in this direction.

A prominent Republican politician said to me, in our present campaign: "Why are you prohibitionists working against your own interests? We have given you everything you asked for, and now you are repaying us by trying to elect your worst enemy, the whisky party."

I replied: "Oh, yes, we know how kind you have been, to give us just such laws as we want, but we also know that you never have enforced, and never intend to enforce the laws which you enacted. You will find that we are in earnest, and that we are not at all particular which of the whisky parties we work against. We are not fighting party, but whisky."

Never has the sky looked so cloudless to this young, but vigorous human party as today. Two years hence the prohibition party of Oregon will again come to the front with renewed courage and increased members, and show the doubting ones that she has not forgotten that her vote last June showed the greatest increase for prohibition for one and a half years, of any state in the Union.

MRS. OWENS-ADAIR, M. D.

DR. ADAIR'S REPORT

OF INTERVIEWS OF A COMMITTEE WITH BUSINESS MEN

A few weeks ago the W. C. T. U. of Portland, believing that the time had come when men aspiring to the position of law-makers should be asked to express themselves on the most important issue before the American people today, drew up a pledge, and published it in the leading newspapers, notifying the candidates of the three respective parties, that they would be waited upon by the ladies, and given an opportunity to make their record clean by appending their signatures to this pledge, that did not require them to vote for prohibition, or the third party, but simply to work and vote for the amendment to the Ready bill, which would make it effectual as a local option law. These gentlemen have been interviewed, with the exception of two or three, whose residences are remote, or who were out in the canvass, so that the committee was unable to find them. All the candidates for legislative honors on the third party ticket signed the petition, but the Republican and Democratic candidates declined. Now, voters of Oregon, and especially of Multnomah county, read, pause, and reflect before you cast your vote on Monday morning next. For the benefit of the curious, we give sketch of some of the interviews, which, after all, proved not to be so very unpleasant. To begin with: We are pleased to say we were in every ease most graciously received by all the candidates. This might be considered sufficient for us to report; still, there were some pleasing and interesting incidents connected with our work. One fine-looking legal gentleman informed the committee that he would take the matter under advisement until alter the 7th of June next. Another thought it was pretty hard to ask him to sign a pledge, when we had a ticket of our own in the field.

Another would not pledge himself to a party that would not pledge itself to support him.

Still another did not believe at all in pledges.

One good brother thought it was a trick to defeat the "Grand Old Party."

Others, notably a member of the educational board, com mended our work in the schools, and Bands of Hope, as affecting the habits of the rising generation for good. One informed us we should appeal to the party managers, instead of the candidates. This answer was, indeed, significant, and tells the whole story.

All were in favor of temperance, but did not wish to commit themselves by signing our pledge.

In behalf of the committee.

DR. OWENS-ADAIR WOMAN'S INFLUENCE

FOR EVIL,

HOW A CLERGYMAN WAS RUINED BY A HOSTESS' CRIMINAL THOUGHTLESSNESS

A recent sermon by Rev. Herbert Johnson, at the Warren avenue Baptist Church in Boston, was entitled, "The True Story of a Clergyman and a Glass of Wine." Its moral was that total abstinence is the only safe policy. Mr. Johnson's principal reason for declaring that wine is an enemy of human kind was that in taking a single glass, a man may awaken a hereditary and dormant taste for drink which can never afterward be assuaged, and that may eventually grow to proportions where it will be beyond his control. He then told the story of the clergyman and his glass of wine, the subject of the story having been a barkeeper and drunkard, who had reformed, and become a pulpit orator scarcely less powerful than Henry Ward Beecher.

This minister was one evening a guest at a reception given by a young, and very rich woman, a teacher in his Sunday-school, and a member of his church. Several of the guests urged the pastor to take wine, but he steadily refused. Finally the young hostess, who was very beautiful, begged him to join her in a glass, and though he several times declined, remembering his former weakness, her charms at last prevailed, and he fell.

That night after the reception, he disappeared, and was not found till four days later, while the church bells were calling the Godly to their morning devotions, the board of deacons found their pastor on an improvised bed in the rear of a bar-room, afflicted with the worst kind of an attack of delirium tremens.

He lost his pastorate, and became a wanderer on the face of the earth. The last heard of him, he was occupied in going on frequent sprees, and practicing law in his sober intervals.

Mr. Johnson drew two lessons from this incident: "Never take a drop of intoxicating liquor yourself, and never offer it to another."

(Many people of Oregon will remember the preacher above referred to as at one time one of Portland's most talented speakers; also the woman who tempted him. The last part of the program is quite familiar to the people of Marshfield.)

Salem, Oregon, January 15, 1885.

Mrs. Dr. Owens-Adair,

Dear Madame:

Yours received. We will be glad to see you. The Senate has its committees, but the House has not appointed its committees, up to this writing, though I learn that it will, during the day. Your hill is a good one, and ought to go through without much delay. Tt is a matter of education. There will be no committees called together this week.

Let me suggest how this business is done. Get a good man to introduce the bill, and have it referred to the Committee on Education. Then have it understood when the committee will meet, so the friends of the bill can he heard. The State Board of Education consists of the Governor, Secretary of State and the Superintendent of Public Instruction, and meets four times a year. This board has nothing to do with making laws. The Committee on Education in both Houses will control the matter, and they are to be consulted whenever they appoint a meeting. Their meetings will not be joint meetings.

S. F. CHADWICK.

CHAIRMAN EXECUTIVE COMMITTEE

Dear Sir:

Your card received. I was not aware that the Rev. Mr. Webb's mantle was to fall upon my shoulders, but if it has been placed there, I shall not refuse to wear it.

I shall, therefore, proceed immediately toward organizing a Multnomah county alliance.

I am willing to serve this cause in any capacity in which I am competent to work, and I shall not shirk from any duty required of me. Mrs. Riggs and I drove twelve miles into the country on last Sabbath, where a large congregation met us. I spoke at 11 a m and 2 p m., after which Mrs. Riggs organized a W. C. T. U.. with twenty-six members.

Next Sabbath we go to Beaverton, seven miles out of Portland, where I have an appointment at 2 p m., after which Mrs. Riggs will address the W. C. T. U., and instruct them in the importance of the work. In the evening we go to East Portland, where I speak in the Congregational church. In all places where I speak, I shall try to do something toward organizing our alliance.

You ask me for some items for our Bulletin. Well, one of the most important itcm of which I kuow, is the recent organization of the Y. W. C. T. U., of this place.

I am free to say that I am more interested in the Young Women's Union than I am in the old. It is just what our young women need to develop them, and bring out all their best powers for good. The power for good which they can and will wield is beyond all calculation. They can do for the young and the old men of our nation what married women and old women cannot do. The sweet, winning smile on the face of a pure, bright girl carries more power with it for the redemption of man, than tons of solid logic and scientific reasoning.

I have seen hundreds of young men, and many old ones also, march up to the table and sign the pledge, and stand up to have the blue ribbon tied on by the delicate white hands of our girls, who stood ready and willing to aid in this blessed work.

Where our girls go, there also will our boys be found; and they will make any sacrifice to obtain the good will of the young ladies.

' What a devoted mother fails to do with her wayward boy, his sweetheart can accomplish with ease.

All that is necessary for us to do is to teach our girls the importance and beauty of this grand work, and we can then safely trust it in their hands, and know that it will be well done.

May God bless our girls, for they will save and bless our boys. Our Portland Y. W. C. T. U. are going to work in earnest, and we expect much from them.

REPORT TO NATIONAL SUPERINTENDENT OF HEREDITY AND HYGIENE

Dear Doctor:

After begging' pardon for my delay in sending off my report (due to absence from the city and overwork;, I will say that my labors during the last year have been largely confined to writing and lecturing. I have delivered over twenty lectures in various part of the state. I had the honor of addressing the State Temperance Alliance, of from three to five thousand people. I delivered the essay on "Woman's Work" at the centennial celebration. Also addressed the

Band of Hope on that occasion. I delivered the address of welcome before the Grand Lodge of Good Templars.

Most of my lectures have been delivered in churches, to large audiences. I feel, however, that my best work has been done through the press. I have written very many essays and communications (far too many for me to enumerate here), which have been published in the Oregonian and our Prohibition Star, and from them copied throughout the state. This is my plan of work, and I feel that I can accomplish far more in this way than in any other. I instruct my local superintendents regularly through our State Bulletin.

When a communication goes into the Oregonian, it is read, perhaps, by 10,000 to 30,000 persons. When published in the Star, it reaches from three to five thousand sympathizing and interested individuals.

I have little time for practical work in the Unions. Aside from my professional duties, almost all my time is devoted to our temperance work in the way of communications through the press: and the calls upon me in this direction.

I assure you, are many. I will send you a late number of the Star, from which you can judge somewhat of my work.

Sincerely yours in the work,

DR. B. A. OWENS-ADAIR.

Portland, Oregon, December 26, 1886.

Mr. G. W. Dimick, Director Oregon Prohibition Publishing Society.

Dear Sir:

I had an interview with Mr. H. S. Lyman yesterday, and he, after talking with Professor James, agreed to take the editorial management of the Star on January 1, 1887, and continue during the year of 1887, in charge thereof, for four hundred dollars in money and three hundred dollars in paid up stock of the paper. This, with Mr. James' proposition to run the paper for one year (we, the stockholders, furnishing an editor), believe to be a good offer to accept.

Professor James is a practical printer, and a reliable man, is the Grand Worthy Secretary of the I. O. G. T. of Oregon, while Mr. Lyman is a well-known and able writer in our cause. He was a candidate at the last June election for joint Senator from Clatsop and Tillamook counties, and is, just now, filling the place of his brother, Professor W. D. Lyman, in the Forest Grove University. I think that we should at once place our paper in the hands of these gentlemen, and so does Mr. Z. T. Wright, and other friends here.

In order to avoid delay, I would like you to authorize me in writing to place them in charge, by proper agreement, and I would like you to come down yourself; but, unless you can come, please send me, or some other person (say Z. T. Wright), your proxy as director, as I think no time should be lost in accepting Mr. James' offer. He desires to take charge before January 1st, and I decidedly wish him to do so. Now, as to stock for Mr. Lyman. Mr. Chenoweth has already offered to donate $100 in paid up stock toward paying an editor's salary, and also to canvass personally to obtain further donations, believing he could secure the full $300 of stock, if Mr. Lyman could be induced to take charge of the paper as editor. Mr. Z. T. Wright agrees to pay $50 toward the cash part of Mr. Lyman's salary. Loth Professors James and Lyman feel confident of their ability to conduct the paper in such a way as to make our stock worth nearly, if not quite, at par at the end of 1887. Now, taking the present condition of our paper into consideration, and the outlook for placing it on a permanent and substantial basis, both Z. T. Wright and I have felt justified in promising Messrs. James and Lyman that their offers would be accepted, and they would be placed in charge of the paper just as soon as the formal action of the Hoard of Directors could be had to properly and legally complete the business. Please give this matter your immediate consideration, and give me an answer. I have written to Messrs. Roork and Young in regard to this matter.

Yours truly,

MRS. OWENS-ADAIR.

P. S.—Unless I am authorized to proceed, I shall feel obliged to call a meeting of our board -at an early date, in Portland.

LETTER FROM SEYMOUR CONDON

Salem, Oregon, January 31, 1889.

Mrs. Owens-Adair, M. D., Portland, Oregon.

Dear Madam—In reply to your letter, please find enclosed H. B. changing the age of consent, introduced by me.

How the bill will be received, remains a matter of conjecture. An amendment will probably be offered, making proof of previous chaste character necessary, when the female is over 14 and under 16 years.

Yours truly,

LETTERS ADDRESSED BY DR. ADAIR

TO MEMBERS OF THEOREGON LEGISLATURE

CONCERNING BILL FOR TEMPERANCE INSTRUCTION

IN THE PUBLICSCHOOLS OF OREGON **(1889)**

Honorable ,

Dear Sir—Through your letter, received today, I am pleased to learn that we can count you among our positive friends.

It is the intention of Mrs. Hoxter and myself to visit Salem at an early date, perhaps on next Saturday, if my professional engagements will permit.

One principal object of my visit will be to get a promise of a hearing before the Legislature at an early date, and any assistance you can give us in obtaining this hearing, say before a joint session for one hour, will be gratefully remembered.

Yours faithfully,

MRS. B. A. OWENS-ADAIR, M. D.

ADDRESS TO THE LEGISLATURE OF OREGON ON "THE AGE OFCONSENT" **(1889)**

Gentlemen—In the interests of humanity, it is right that a girl should be protected in her childhood from the possible loss of that which is of priceless value to her, and yet that which she has not yet sufficient knowledge or discretion to estimate at its true worth.

A girl child is liable to, and often does meet unprincipled and lecherous men, who look upon and lust after her very youth. We need not quote any special authority to support this declaration, for since the horrible disclosures and exposures recently made by the "Pall Mall Gazette," as to the wholesale debauchery of little girls carried on in London, England, it has come to be generally known and believed by the reading public, that the horrifying crime of debauching little girls, and enticing them to lives of shame, is carried on to an alarming extent in our own country, as well as in England.

Now we know that men may sin carnally many times, and still be received into society, and pass as one of wayward nature, "just a little too wild, you know, but then it is better that he sow his wild oats early."

Such expressions are made, not only as excuses, but as justifying immorality among men, any one of which would consign a poor girl to a life of ostracism from all that are, or pass for, good and pure. Women are most frequently accused of being violent and partisan in condemning one of their own unfortunate sex. This was more generally true twenty years ago in America, than it is today; for, without doubt much has been done in recent years by our women to make the downfall of girls and women more difficult, as well as to provide such means as are possible for the rescue of the fallen. We maintain that the protection, by law, of girls, is a powerful preventative against women becoming outcasts for life. In proof of this, I will offer the following dispatch, clipped from a late issue of the Daily Astorian: "London, February 5, 1889. The name of Sir Charles Dilke was presented to the rate-payers as a candidate for city counsellor. A protest signed by fifteen hundred women of the Social Purity League, was also presented, and his name was dropped."

This shows that the women of England are alive to the wrongs of their sex, as well as the women of America. And, gentlemen, when I tell you that the social purity question is one of the special departments in our great organization known as the Woman's Christian Temperance Union, which today numbers over 300,000 earnest and determined Christian women, I but tell you that which perhaps you already know. I come to you today as a representative of the W. C. T. U. of Oregon, in behalf of our girls.

It seems to me that it only needs to have the request made to our Legislature to pass the bill introduced by Mr. Condon, raising the "age of consent" to 16 years, in order to insure its passage by a unanimous vote. The objectors to such a law are not to represent the people of Oregon, as lawmakers, and, therefore, I do not feel like occupying more of your time than to represent that the W. C. T. U. of our state earnestly and emphatically urges you to pass the bill referred to above. And now I wish to say further, gentlemen, that the thinking and praying women of this nation are coming to the front, with outstretched arms to shield and protect the girlhood of this nation. I assure you that we will never let go of this work until we have induced the lawmakers of this nation to enact laws that will protect our young and innocent girls. And while we are working for our girls, remember we are greatly interested in the welfare of our boys, and in having laws enacted for their protection and benefit.

ADDRESS BEFORE THE WOMANS CONGRESS

AT PORTLAND, OREGON, JUNE 18 1896.

The following paper was prepared for and read before the Woman's Congress in Portland, Oregon, June 18, 1896, and by request, was read before the Pioneer Association the same year:

Ladies of the Woman Suffrage Association and Congress of Oregon:

It gives me great pleasure to meet you here today in this splendid city of our great Northwest. I see many faces that have been familiar to me nearly all my life; and knowing how faithfully, how honestly, and how persistently you have all worked in our great cause, I feel that this is the time for mutual and hearty congratulations upon the wonderful success which has crowned the efforts of the woman's cause in America.

And now, Madame President, I wish to say that my few brief and somewhat disjointed remarks are brought out by your letter, which reads as follows: "Your paper must be upon some phase of woman's work or ambitions." My mind took in the circuit of our great universe at one glance; then I asked myself: Is there any difference between woman's work and men's work? Is there anything under the sun that muscle or mind can do that the new woman cannot accomplish? We have no fear that the "new woman" will not find a place in the poet's theme, as well as in his heart. She will not cease to be the "ministering angel," the very inspiration of life. Like the fine gold that comes from the furnace, she will come forth, clothed in all the beauty and strength of a pure womanhood, for she will have been cleansed of the dross of dependence, helplessness and prejudice of past ages. Indeed, up to the present time, what has man done that woman could not do, or has not done?

Her muscles and mind are just as susceptible of being strengthened and cultivated as are those of man. We have but to reflect, to realize that this is undoubtedly true. I believe the champion marksman of the world is a young lady. The newspapers of recent date tell us that the champion swimmer and diver is a young woman. She jumps from a swinging trapeze seventy feet, down, down, into the water below. The papers also tell us that the champion lifter is a woman thirty-one years of age, and but five feet four inches in height. She weighs 197 pounds.

Yet even now we hear that old familiar question, "Can a woman fight?"

For an answer, you have but to turn your eyes toward Cuba, and read the startling accounts of the courage and daring exhibited on the battlefield by 1,500 brave women, who enlisted as soldiers to defend their homes and country.

If you go to the circus you will see feats of strength and daring performed by women, equal in all respects to those performed by men. I once saw a woman play with a cannon ball, tossing it up and catching it in her hands, and upon her bare shoulders, as a child would play with his toy ball. It required the united strength of two strong men to lift that cannon ball.

Yet she was not a giantess, but a strong, muscular woman, well developed during years of systematic training.

This brings to my mind a very remarkable young woman, a Miss Ann Hobson, a sister of the late John Hobson, and aunt of Senator Fulton's wife, a pioneer of '43. She deserves a chapter and life-size portrait in our pioneer history. She could row or sail a boat equal to a Columbia river fisherman. She could manage a canoe with all the skill of a Chinook Indian. She could ride a horse and swing a lasso equal to the most expert cowboy. In those days we bad only Spanish cattle, and to subdue them required great courage, skill and tact. They were possessed of frightfully long, sharp horns—dehorning was never heard of in those days. Miss Hobson was fully equal to the task. I have seen her often, riding at full speed, swinging the lasso around her head, in hot pursuit of a wild cow, that would not be driven into the corral. When near enough, she threw the lasso, and the cow's head was certain to be caught in the loop. If, by any chance, the lariat escaped from her grasp, she would continue the chase till it was within reach, when she would catch it from the ground (from the horse) and the next moment it was wound round

413

the high pommel of her saddle, and the cow was brought to a standstill. And she could catch a cow's foot with the lasso, with as much ease and grace as she could her head. There was not then in Clatsop county a man who could equal Miss Hibson in riding and lassoing. I, a little girl in those days, was Miss Hobson's especial pet, perhaps because I admired and loved her so much. Many a time did she pick me up from the ground, and placing me behind, or in front of her, put spurs to her horse, and away we would go, like mad, across the prairie. Her examples of courage and daring have been a blessing to me all through my life, and I gladly pay this tribute to her strong, vigorous and fearless girlhood. We have many examples of courage, endurance and marked ability among the early pioneer women.

Many of these have gone on to the better land, but some remain to tell the story of good accomplished, and to furnish grand examples for the bright, young generation that must take up their work, and carry it worthily forward. There is your president. I knew her before she made her first suffrage speech. I assisted her in starting the first suffrage paper in Oregon, and was a constant subscriber throughout its natural life. I was converted to woman suffrage by carefully reading "The Revolution," the pioneer equal suffrage paper, edited and published by our honored, and best beloved mother. Miss Susan B. Anthony, who now sits on this platform. I owe much of the success of my life to the brave words and deeds of this foster mother, and I take great pleasure now in doing her homage. Away back in those days when I was struggling, not only for an education, but for bread for myself and child, it was not pleasant, nor was it profitable to be called a "blue-stocking." It required more than common courage, as all pioneer suffragists can testify, to withstand the opposition, and endure the sarcastic smiles and distrust of the better classes, and the sneers and jeers, and even "rotten eggs" of the rabble. This was about the time an "honorable" Senator distinguished himself in the halls of Congress, while opposing an equal suffrage bill, by giving utterance to that most remarkable speech:

'We don't want our wives and daughters to be mathematicians, philosophers, or scientists. We don't love and honor them for what they know of such things, but rather for what they don't know. These things are not necessary for women. They are better off without such knowledge. Woman's place is the home, and it is her duty to love and care for her husband, and his children."

This is" on a par with what a fashionable lady, anxious to bring me back into the fold of respectability, once said to me: "What do you want to believe in that horrid woman's rights business for? I can't bear to see you mixed up in it." "Why, what is there wrong in it?" I queried. She answered: "I don't know anything about it, and I don't want to know anything about it, but I am opposed to it on general principles."

When I began the study of medicine, twenty-five years ago, I concealed it from my relatives and friends, fearing I might not have the courage to withstand the storm that would (and did) come, when I had matured my plans, and was ready to leave home for a medical college. Only two persons, of all my friends, ever gave me a word of encouragement. One of these was my highly honored friend, the late Governor S. Chadwick; the other the Hon. Jesse Applegate, who was ever a true friend and father to me.

He gave me many valued words of encouragement, and much fatherly advice, especially admonishing me not to say one word on equal suffrage during my medical course. Had I strictly followed his advice I might have -saved myself many tears and heartaches. On the day I left home two friends called to say good-bye. One of them said: "Well, I hardly know what to say to you, for I am thoroughly disgusted. I always gave you credit for having good sense. I really think you must have lost your head, to leave a good business and run off on such a wild goose chase."

I laughingly said: "Never mind: I will come home, after a few years, and be your doctor." Her reply came quickly: "No, indeed! You can make hats and bonnets all right, but you can never be a doctor. No woman doctor can ever doctor me!"

That good woman lived to change her mind, and laugh heartily at her former narrow-mindedness. Twenty-five years ago, when I was living in the beautiful little town of Roseburg, I was somewhat startled one bright morning to receive a characteristic telegram, which read as follows:

"Secure me a place to speak Saturday evening.

(Signed) "SUSAN B. ANTHONY."

Now what was to be done? There was the Court House, not a desirable place: a commodious hall under a saloon, and one nice large church. I decided to try and secure the church, so I made haste to call upon the minister. I said to him: "I have a telegram from Miss Anthony, who is to speak here tomorrow evening. I think she ought to have a church to speak in, don't you?" I looked him full in the face, and saw him wince, but he assented. I then said: "Your church is the largest and best. Cannot we have your church?" After he had consented, I called on the trustees, and succeeded in getting the key. I then repaired to the printing office, ordered several hundred posters printed, and secured a boy to post them in all the public places. The news spread in great haste, and the little town was stirred as though the coming of a circus had been announced. Men stood on the street corners, discussing the situation. Women stopped to read the posters, and make sure that the lecture was really to be in the church. That was the surprising point, which threw about it a halo of respectability! Late in the evening the proprietor of one of Roseburg's largest saloons called at my store, and jokingly said: "Well, you have played your cards very nicely; but we will checkmate you, for we are getting up a free supper and a free dance at the hotel, and I'll bet you don't have a baker's dozen at the church."

That was sad news to me, for I knew if there was anything that would draw in that town it was a free dance. Saloon-keepers, in those days, were most respectable citizens, and their wives and daughters were much sought after as desirable members of church societies and ladies' guilds. It was customary then for candidates to leave money with proprietors of saloons for electioneering purposes, for the distribution of free drinks. Election days were days of

416

drunkenness and riot, and it was hardly considered respectable or safe for a lady to be seen on the street on election day. On such days you could locate every saloon by the surging masses of half-drunken men around its doors, should you cast your eye up and down the street. Indeed, there were few men who could withstand the pressure on election day with breath uncontaminated by at least one drink. I will briefly relate what I saw on one election day, more than twenty-five years ago. That was before the memorable crusade which gave birth to the W. C. T. l., to which every nation today pays respect. My little store stood on the principal street. Three doors above me stood a large saloon. A few doors above, on the opposite side, was another. These were the largest saloons in town, and were the rendezvous of gentlemen in those days. About three blocks away stood the court house, the principal polling-place, in full view of my house, owing to a vacant lot in front. I invited in several of my lady friends, among whom was the wife of my nearest saloon neighbor. She was in favor of progress, and afterward attended Miss Anthony's lecture, while her husband assisted in the opposition dance. We locked the door, and removed everything from the show window. This enabled us from behind the lace curtains, to see all that went on at the polls, and in the street, without ourselves being seen. Long before 12 o'clock there were plenty of drunken men. Then, as the common expression went, "the circus began." Some of the men laughed; some sang; others quarreled, and some swore, with much loud, and some confidential talking. Thus they kept up a continuous stream, by twos and threes and fours, going to and from the polls and saloons. Several times we saw men start with a drunken fellow, who stopped half way, declaring he would go no farther to the polls without another drink. We saw men going to and from the polls with bottles of whisky in their hands and pockets, and saw them drink from bottles on their way. We also saw two men of prominence, one a judge and the other a lawyer, take, by actual count, eight men to the polls, some of them so beastly intoxicated that it took their united efforts to get them to and from the voting place, and before the voting closed these gentlemen were in about as helpless a condition themselves. Without looking backward we can hardly realize the changes for the better that have taken place in the last quarter of a century. The young people now growing up can scarcely believe such a state of society could have once existed. But such were the conditions in the little town of Roseburg, so beautifully situated on the banks of the Umpqua river. Nearby also flowed picturesque Deer creek, known in former days as "the hunter's paradise," where roamed great herds of deer, who drank of its crystal, cool waters, or grazed on the flower-bedecked hills, and basked in the shade of the giant oaks which abounded in that locality. Yes, that was the state of society in that little village of 500 souls, and sixteen saloons!

When Miss Anthony, then in the prime of her womanhood, alighted from the south-bound stage, in-front of the McClellen hotel, I was there to greet her; and so, also, was a , large and curious crowd, anxious to get a sight of her. In the evening, when, on our way to church, we passed the hotel, we heard the violins sending out strains of music, to which many merry feet were keeping time. This was truly an anti-Anthony dance. We found the church well filled, and the lecture was all it should have been. I-was gratified beyond all expression without success. It gave me new courage and determination to adhere to my convictions. We had then only fifty-five miles of railroad in Oregon. Nor were an}' of the great transcontinental railroads in existence at that time. The old-time stagecoach traveled from Salem by way of the beautiful Willamette valley, and across the now famous "Shasta route" to Sacramento. Woman, in all these advanced movements, has forged ahead, and taken her rightful place beside man. To what place of honorable business can you go today and not find pure women using their hands and brains in the uplifting of the human race? Every business of importance must have a woman bookkeeper and typewriter and the stores fairly swarm with woman clerks. Woman has proved her ability to use the ballot, and to perform any official duties with as much discretion and wisdom as does man, and the time is not far distant when the ballot will be awarded her in every state in the Union.

WHAT HEREDITY DOES FOR HORSES AND MEN

North Yakima, Wash., April 1, 1903.

To the Editor: I have just read B. S. Botsford's comments on Mrs. Dumiway's communication in Sunday's Oregonian. I regret I did not see the sketch referred to, and I also regret that I am unable to determine whether Botsford is a man or a woman. I believe with Botsford in precept and example, and I also believe in strict discipline, from infancy to maturity, but I do not believe that parents should be held responsible in all cases for their children's misdeeds.

I am a true believer in heredity and hereditary influences. I received an object lesson in my early life which thoroughly convinced me of this great power which may work for good or evil. My father was a Kentuckian, and, like most Kentuckians, he was a great lover and a good judge of fine horses, and from the early fifties to his death he always kept a fine stallion—the best the state afforded.

When I was about nine years old my father bought me a pretty little spotted cayuse pony. Unlike most of her breed, she was gentle, faithful and trusty. I loved my little Dolly. In time she was bred to Royal Prince, and she brought me a beautiful bay, who was the picture of her sire, and I named her Princess. In time Princess was bred to another of royal blood, and she excelled herself in a beautiful dappled bay, with soft brown eyes. I began riding her before she was six months old. She was so gentle and affectionate, so beautiful tall and graceful that I called her Queen. When she matured my father owned a celebrated horse, known far and near in Oregon. He was a beautiful sorrel. His coat shone like satin, and he was kind, intelligent and obedient. My father said: "Now you shall have a thoroughbred, for Queen is perfect." My hopes were high in anticipation.

One bright morning father came in, convulsed with laughter, saying: "Queen has a colt. You had better go out and see it." I rushed to the barn-yard, and there stood my beautiful Queen, with her broad, intelligent brow and soft brown eyes, and around her was playing a little ugly, spotted, blaze-faced cayuse colt. I was amazed. Lady Queen came up and rubbed her nose against my cheek, and I almost fancied I could hear her say: "I could not help it. Don't blame me."

She afterward had other colts, and they were beautiful. This was the only cayuse; and he was a typical cayuse. His mean, treacherous nature dated back beyond his great-grandmother, for she was true and good. No amount of training could ever make him anything but a cayuse, and a very mean one at that.

We have but to use our eyes to see this object lesson verified all about us, both in the human and animal kingdom. How often we see this illustrated in the same family, some of which will be good, honest and faithful, while the others will be dishonest and vicious. They have all received the same mental, moral and physical training, yet are unlike in principle and practice. How can we account for these differences, except through the law of heredity? Yes, "blood will tell," but it is like a double-edged sword; it may cut one way or the other, and sometimes it cuts both ways in the same family.

We often find different complexions, dispositions and traits of character in the same family springing from the same parents:

And this-holds good in the lower animal kingdom as well. This is a great subject, and one little understood. Probably not much better now than it was 1,000 years ago, when attempts were made to prevent the propagation of diseases and deformities.

The writer of the letter I referred to seems to think that if the ballots were placed in the hands of women they would proceed to destroy this nation. Observe his or her prophecy. "God shield us from the evil days that will come upon this nation when women are given the ballot, for no chain is stronger than the weakest link. So no nation can be stronger than its weakest people, who are Indians, Chinamen, idiots, and women."

Now I find myself repeating to myself over and over: "Can this be a woman who is publicly declaring herself one of the weaklings, and that, too, when she has been reading us a lecture on reaping and sowing and the training of the young. I am wondering, too, if this writer is aware of the fact that there are several states in this Union where women have enjoyed equal suffrage with men, "lo, these many years.' Now, I object to being classed with Indians, Chinamen, and idiots! I have been voting for these twenty-five years at school meetings, and I hope to live to see the day that I can vote for the President of our United States.

I do not believe there are as many bad women as there are bad men. Just visit the penitentiaries and jails, and compare notes. A few weeks ago we had a school election in this city. A good, worthy man was elected for director by a large majority. The mothers of families and school teachers were out in force: They wanted a good director, and they elected him. They were not interested in the political deal.

Consistency, consistency, thou art indeed a jewel of great price! Would that we all might possess you.

THE "RACE SUICIDE" QUESTION

Since President [Theodore] Roosevelt's speech on "race suicide" there has been much discussion of the question by the press and public. Mrs. Owens-Adair of this city contributed an interesting article on the subject in the Portland Oregonian of May 3, which the Herald reproduces:

"I have been watching the discussion of the race problem with great interest, and I was highly pleased this morning with grandmother's discussion of the family question.'

"This is a many-sided subject, and as a physician I have had the opportunity of viewing it from various standpoints. As grandmother says, the question is no longer sacred, but through newspaper discussion has become very common. President Roosevelt is a great man, and we all rejoice that the White House is the home of five happy children—not a large family, as compared with Oregon and Washington pioneer families. Many pioneer mothers have given thrice that number to their state. But, judging from the signs of the times,' such mothers will soon become obsolete, and remembered only in history.

"As President Roosevelt said of his convalescing son, 'He is coming out of the woods with leaps and bounds so it is with our nation; we are going ahead 'with leaps and bounds.' We have no time for old-fashioned ways, or old-fashioned living. They are cast behind us, like worn-out garments. Nothing but high pressure and rapid transit will satisfy us. Education is our nation's watchword. Our daily papers are volumes within themselves. We read them principally through their headlines, editorials and telegraphic dispatches. There is no place set aside nowadays in which to file away our papers. We are deluged with periodicals filled with good reading, which we would like to read if we only had time. Sixty years ago we were glad to get one mail in twelve months. We were delighted when we received two mails a year. Now we are not satisfied with two free deliveries a day.

"No one thinks of doing business without a telephone. The doctor calls the family or nurse up, inquires about his patient; then calls the

422

druggist, dictates a prescription and orders the medicine sent. And so with other business. The housewife, the neighbors, all give orders and gossip over the 'phone. Even the little tots know how to climb up to the 'phone, ring up central and make their little wants known.

"Is there any wonder that, when we are living so fast, and rushing ahead with such speed, that the wife finds neither time nor desire for maternity? Child-bearing is hard, and the rearing of children requires constant care; and as society is today, our girls are not reared and drilled, as their grandmothers were, in the care of children and the home. From the ages of seven to twenty they are kept in school. From the high school they go to the university. Then they are ushered into matrimony and are expected to rear a large family. When such a mother, without wealth at her disposal, attempts to bring a child into the world every two, or even three, years, as a rule she breaks down, and becomes a physical wreck. It matters not how much sentiment or glamour is thrown about motherhood, all the stern reality falls to her lot, and society has augmented her sufferings and responsibilities ten-fold. No children nowadays 'grow' up, like Tops'. No more girls marry, with parents' consent, at the age of fourteen, to begin raising a large family. No more boys and girls at the ages of fourteen and fifteen can be found on the farm, or in the home, doing men's and women's work. Certainly not in Oregon, where we have a humane law to protect children under sixteen from doing work after stated hours.

"Sixty or seventy, or even thirty years ago the labor question was not under discussion. Girls could be obtained at from one to two dollars a week. They could wash, iron, clean, cook, take care of the children and the house. A week meant seven full days. But those days are gone. The new girl, as well as the 'new woman,' has come to stay. Education has lifted her out and beyond those 'old-fashioned' ways. Now we can talk with the nations of the world by wires under the seas, and without wires over the seas. We open our eyes in the morning, and press the button. The morning papers are sent up, and we read what the heads of nations will tell us tomorrow. All this interferes with baby-raising. For 'babies must cry to be healthy,' and society has excluded them from churches, theaters, banquets, receptions, and, indeed, almost every public place (even the most desirable flats and cottages are forbidden to the possessors of children). Papa must go, and mamma wants to go; but who will stay with baby, The hired girl? O no, not she! And now comes the time of the young mother's trials. She is left alone with her baby, or babies. Day and night she must be at her post. Now she finds time for reflection, and she usually does so about in this wise:

"'What was I educated for? I am shut out from everything. I have no time for society, and must, of necessity, be dropped out. I am already a nurse, and am fast becoming a household drudge. And yet my husband expects me to meet him with a smile, and look as fresh as I did before we were married.'

"This brings to mind an instance that occurred at my home a few years ago. A young widow had a handsome young lad of three years, who required a great deal of will power to manage. After a tussle with him one day which completely exhausted her, she dropped into a chair, and with a most distressed expression of countenance exclaimed: 'Oh, my God! What shall I do?' Turning to me she said in the most pitiful tones: 'Tell me, Doctor, is this the only way the world must be populated?' My heart went out to her in sympathy, but I could not refrain a smile. I said: 'Never mind, my dear friend, it will all come out right. Children are very much alike, and one is not so bad as a dozen!'

"'A dozen!' she echoed. I would be in the insane asylum if I had more than one, and I will tell you now that I will never again get married, to have this repeated.' Thus far she has kept her word.

"As I have said, this is a many-sided question; but it is in the hands of the public, and I have faith that it will be examined, analyzed and disposed of for the good of our nation. Since the landing of the pilgrims our women have not been lacking in their duty and she will be found in the future, as in the past, faithful and loyal to her country.

"The best article I have seen on this subject was an editorial published some weeks ago in the Oregonian—'Eliot on Population.' I believe a reprint of this article at this time would be very beneficial."

OREGONIANS EDITORIAL ON "RACE SUICIDE"

The article referred to is as follows:

"President Eliot's strictures on excess in athletics, and his opinion that post-graduate studies conduce to celibacy may be unreservedly endorsed, but when he deplores the small families or no families, of the highly cultivated as a thing to be reprimanded, if not, indeed, extirpated, he gives himself bootless concern about something for which there is no help, and something which is probably, on the whole, the best arrangement possible. Agitation is undesirable in a Harvard man, anyway, and the course of nature is something it is rarely profitable to seek to interfere with. The fertility of the human race is in inverse ratio to culture, possibly to intelligence. This is a universal law. It applies to modern London or Boston as much as to the ancient world—to Germany as well as to France. It forms a part of the general system by which nature prevents overcrowding of the race. Every stage of human development has its peculiar checks on population. What starvation and massacre achieve in savagery, the love of ease and the pride of luxury afford to the cultivated. It is unnecessary to expatiate upon the reasons why devotees of literature, art and fashion content themselves with small families, or with no children at all, or even without marriage. They are familiar to all, and are not amenable to reason. These matters are no more referable to public policy, or religious mandates, than love is to the locksmith. Accept them, therefore, without protest or alarm.

"There is no great loss. The highly cultivated are not necessarily more fitted for the perpetuation of the race than are the children of the soil. We require many things for offense and defense of organized society in advance of poise and intonation. The highly cultivated are not the best soldiers, builders, or traders. They are not the most desirable parents, either, in many ways. Their children are likely to be without the struggle which in early life, or not at all, gives strength for the supreme battles. Inheritance can give the child strong body, and to some extent a moral intensity, but it is one of the plainest and most pathetic facts of human experience that intellectual power cannot be transmitted. The greatest of earth left no descendants. The family of Shakespeare has perished from among the living, and Napoleon's only child died a weakling at twenty-one. So of Milton, so of Cromwell, so of Washington. The children of the great, as a rule, belong to hopeless mediocrity. Many of them are imbecile, many are vicious and depraved, many of them are crushed by the weight of their name and expectations, or seduced by the indulgence which power puts within their reach.

"And it is better so. If the superior circumstances in life perpetuated themselves, as prosperously as the poor, the result would be an aristocracy of brains and accomplishments, which would do away with the healthy ferment of society, and prevent the present accession to power of the sons of the soil. The ruling classes would be impregnable, and Markham's 'man with the hoe' would be a reality, instead of a libel. How long would this continent resist the encroachments of Europe if it were peopled with Charles Eliot Nortons and Edward Atkinsons? How long would the world have looked in vain for escape if it had looked for the devotees of philosophy and fashion to clear the way?"

FINDS MAN ON THE ROAD

LOOKS LIKE CASE OF DRUNKENNESS, BUT REALLY WAS RHEUMATISM.

North Yakima, Wash., December 15, 1003.

To the Editor: I have noticed the editorial and other notices of the case of the man who was taken to jail, supposed to be drunk, but after two or three days—too late to save his life—was found to be suffering from concussion of the brain. Today's paper reports a similar case in Chicago. Now society demands that a competent physician be called in such cases by the police.

I had an experience last Saturday, December 13, which is along this line and worth relating. It was a cold, foggy day, the foggiest day I have seen in North Yakima. At 3 PM. I ordered my rig and started to see a patient three miles out. The ground had been frozen for some time, the roads were quite smooth and the driving good. When a mile or more out I saw something in the middle of the road loom up in the fog. I thought it might be a mattress or roll of bedding lost off a wagon, but to my surprise I saw an active movement for a moment, then all was still. As we neared it Pride, my horse, swerved, and tried to run, but he knows my voice and always obeys it. I reined in close to the object, and, to my surprise, I saw it was a large man in a long overcoat. I am sure he was over six feet and would weigh nearly 300 pounds. His knees were drawn up and his overcoat covered him completely. His face was toward me, and it was swollen and bloated, and he was looking straight at me. I thought he was drunk, as he looked like a man who had been on a debauch for a week or two. I have seen many drunken men in my day, and believed I could diagnose drunkenness. I am not afraid of drunken men. I looked at him and said: "What is the matter with you?" He replied: "I fell down, and can't get up." I said: "Do you think you can get up if I help you?" He answered: "Yes." I stopped and took hold of his big bloated hand, expecting to be greeted by the fumes of whisky, but to my astonishment there were neither fumes of whisky or tobacco. Saying, "Now, do your best, and only try to get on your knees first," I pulled and pulled and he puffed, and with his big

427

hand, long arm and hard work he got on his knees. "Now rest," I said, "and you will make it next time." A few more pulls and he was on his feet and I was holding to him to keep him from falling. He looked down on me and asked: "What is your name?" I said: "My name is Dr. Adair. I am a physician; where are you going?"

He responded: "Right there, to the next house. I have been in the hospital for two months with rheumatism. I am an expert pork packer and have come out here to oversee the packing of pork. I fell down and could not get up, though I tried four times, but I can get to the house now." He reeled and staggered, and his voice was thick and husky like a drunken man's, but he was not drunk, neither had he been drinking, for there was no smell of drinking about him. My family all have the sense of smell highly developed, and my power of smell is not impaired. I have always boasted that I could detect whisky or tobacco on a man twenty feet off, and I am sure I was not mistaken in this man. I looked back and saw him slowly making his way to the house. Had he been two hours later he might have been run over and killed, for the night was very dark, and in that case his death would very likely have been reported as "due to drunkenness."

WILL ALWAYS LOVE 'EM

MEN WILL BE TRUE TO WOMEN, EVEN ATHLETIC WOMEN

North Yakima, Wash., December 28, 1902.

To the Editor: I see that President Eliot of Harvard is again finding fault with the American women of the present age. A short time ago he was taking women in the higher walks of life to task for not raising large families. Now he is criticising her for developing her muscular system, and increasing her physical strength. He objects to her ability to row, to hunt, to jump the bar, to kick the ball, to punch the bag, to put the shot. He declares women were not originally intended for such vigorous and violent exercise, which belongs to man. Furthermore, he says: "There may be some women who are made in such a strange, unnatural way that it would not be injurious to them to put the shot, etc., but to the great majority of women it would hurt them for life."

Now to a physician, who has made woman a study for years, this sounds like the merest twaddle. I admit that the glamor of sentiment interspersed through the writings of eminent people adds much to their attractiveness, as spices tickle the palate and give flavor to delicate and delicious dishes; but facts are facts, although expressed in a homely manner. Physically the frailest and most delicate woman is made identically the same as the Amazon or the renowned fish-woman of Europe, or even man, in that she has the same number of bones, muscles, vesicles, nerves, internal viscera, fingers, toes, hands and feet, etc. Every child has its beginning, development and growth by and through the same natural lanes. God created man and He then created woman. And to the end of time, if there is to be any end, man will go on loving woman because she is a woman, and woman will love man because he is a man. No amount of precept or training will change this, and yet they are unlike in a marked degree. No amount of education or training will change this law. God is superior and He has put us here to work out the problems of this life. If physical exercise is good for man, and we all admit that it is, then it is equally beneficial to woman. It adds to her strength, her beauty, her usefulness and her longevity. Violent exercise is no more hurtful to woman than to man. President Eliot ought to know that the strength and power of the muscular system depends upon its constant and systematic use, as the mental faculties are improved by the mental educational drill. Any amount of mental or physical wealth acquired by woman will not prevent man from loving and cherishing her. For he is a true cavalier, and will love her more for every added charm. Though he may not be called upon to defend her, or lead her in the chase, he will think none the less of her should she pass him in the race, or be the first to accomplish that wonderful feat of swimming across the English channel. No, it is man's nature to love woman. He was made for her; and she for him. As time goes on, and the nations become more educated, refined and cultivated, love will become more purified and intensified.

MRS. OWENS-ADAIR, M. D.

GO TO BED WITH THE CHICKENS

AND THEN THE CHILDRENWILL BE UP WITH THE LARK

North Yakima, Wash., July 15, 1903.

To the Editor: I always read or look through your editorial page, and I beg to differ with parts of the following:

"Will not the State Commission on Child Labor divest parents in the country of their tyrannical power to drag their children out of bed at an early hour and force them to milk the cows, hoe the garden and do the drudgery generally that children in the country so greatly detest? Shall we not have complete emancipation of the American child? Shop and factory labor is nothing to farm drudgery. It is horrible that a child should be compelled to work. Moreover, if not

4UI taught to work when a child he never will work when a man; so this law, if rightly administered, would make life for every individual one long holiday."

First. I do not believe farm work should be termed drudgery any more than factory and shop labor. In my opinion farm labor is far more healthy and to be desired. Boys and girls who are reared on a farm and are taught to do all kinds of farm work are, as a rule, much stronger and more vigorous than city-reared children. This stands to reason. Their work is out of doors, where they can breathe God's pure, health-giving air, which purifies their blood, and gives food and strength to their young and growing tissues. The country, in my estimation, is the place to raise children. There is plenty of pure milk, fresh eggs, butter and vegetables, which are the best food for children. Then they get wholesome exercise to develop and strengthen their muscles. These are the essentials to be sought in giving us a foundation for healthy men and women. Milking cows, feeding pigs and chickens, breaking calves and colts, riding horses and cultivating the garden should and can be made pleasant and wholesome employment, and not "drudgery." If children were required to go to bed when the birds go to roost, they would be ready to rise with the birds, and, like them, with a song in their mouths. They would be ready to greet the faithful cow, and have an appetite for her warm, sweet, rich milk.

I do not like that expression, "tyrannical." Country parents have as much love for their children as have city people, and my observation is that country children do not "detest" work anymore than city children.

As a rule children do not like work and do love play, and as too much work "makes Jack a dull boy," and too much play makes him a bad boy, to make him both good and bright he must have both work and play.

Who can have the welfare of the child at heart so much as the natural father and mother? I do not think it is "horrible" for children to work. I believe that all children should be required to work intelligently and systematically with their hands and that they should be taught that mental and physical activity are essential to health, happiness and long life. Just now, when many of the old pioneers are passing away, may we not learn a lesson from their lives? Where and how were they raised? Most of them have lived out their three-score and ten years. Many have reached fourscore and some are near the century mark. How did these sturdy men and women begin their valuable and useful lives? Inquire and you will find that most of them were raised on a farm and were taught that wholesome lesson, "Early to bed and early to rise makes a man healthy, wealthy and wise." Do not let us, in these times of fast living, lose sight of all that was good in the past. Let us stop, consider and compare notes, and let us remember that old ways have been tried, while news ones have yet to stand the test.

MRS. OWENS-ADAIR, M. D.

LADIES SHOULD RIDE ASTRIDE

North Yakima, Wash., April 14, 1904.

I was handed a copy of the Daily Seattle Times and requested to reply to "What a Man Thinks of a Woman Who Rides Astride." The request came from three young ladies, farmers' daughters, who have ridden horseback all their lives and are all good horsewomen. But during the last three or four years they have discarded the side-saddle, and now use the cross-saddle. One of them came near losing her life about four years ago by being thrown from a horse. Her father said in my presence: "Had you been riding in the sensible way this would not have happened."

I judge, from Dr. Montague Tallack's name and style of writing, that he must be a foreigner, and, as I am a woman and a physician of thirty years' standing, I feel that I can speak for American women from a woman's standpoint. The writer starts out by criticising a physician's opinion. To my mind, if there is any person who should be entitled to a logical opinion on this subject it is a physician, who is supposed to have a knowledge of the anatomy and physiology of the human body and its capabilities. Mr. Tallack has but to visit a first-class circus and watch those beautiful muscular women riding and performing on the bars to have his little "60 and 70-angle degree" theory exploded. Oh, no, Mr. Tallack, God gave women legs for their use, and for the same use for which He gave them to men. The writer discusses the length and mold of the legs of men and women to give strength to his argument. He says men's legs are long and flat and women's are short and round. Well, in my time I have seen a good many women with long legs and a good many men with short ones. It was often said of Senator Douglas that he was taller sitting down than he was standing up. You could not say that of President Lincoln. President Grant had short legs. And so has Lord Roberts. I was astonished to hear that a Mr. Smith of England uses the side-saddle for breaking his high jumpers. I wonder if President Roosevelt and General Wood knew of that. They might have filled out their Rough Riders with side-saddles and made a great hit. Mr. Tallack tells us that if women make a practice of riding astride they will become fat and gross. I take issue with him on that point. It is a fact, however, that women, as a rule, do grow corpulent after middle age but so often do men as well.

Nothing will preserve woman's grace and her symmetrical form so much as vigorous and systematic exercise, and horseback riding stands at the head of the list, providing she has a foot in each stirrup, instead of having the right limb twisted around a horn, and the left foot in a stirrup twelve or fifteen inches above where it ought to be. If she sits astride her saddle she will relieve herself of those imaginary injurious "jolts" and "jars" received from a rough trotter. This she could not do sitting sidewise. I have been a horseback rider all my life. I was raised on a farm and learned to ride before I can remember. As I grew to womanhood society demanded a side-saddle, and I had to adopt it. Some ten years ago, when cross-riding was beginning to be advocated, I adopted the new style. Now, when a pale, delicate, nervous patient is brought to me, especially if from the country, I say: "Now, in addition to your medicine I want you to take a horseback ride every day, but mind you must ride the new style. I forbid the side-saddle, and in addition, if you have a flower garden or a vegetable garden, give them special attention, and you will soon be strong and have roses in your cheeks."

The testimony of the Baroness who taught the Russian Empress and most of the Queens of Europe is rather ancient and not to the point, as all women rode sideways in those days. We are now discussing cross-riding for women. This is an age of progress and rapid transit. It seems that we have no time or patience for the slow old styles and ways, and women are keeping pace with the age. Indian women have ridden astride for centuries. To them motherhood has no terrors.

I would advise Mr. Tallack to come up to our state fair next October, and he will have the pleasure of seeing many pretty and graceful women riding crosswise, and he will have an opportunity of witnessing the squaw races, a great attraction.. He would see eight or ten Indian maidens, decked in gay colors, ride out on the track and take their positions in front of the grandstand and wait for the belltap. They bestride their horses with grace and ease, for they are riders. I have witnessed these races for four years, and every time these Indian maidens come on I have heard both men and women all around me saying: "Now, that is the way women should ride. That's the sensible way.",

No, no, Mr. Tallack, you are quite behind the times. The side-saddle will soon be a thing of the past, and will soon be found only in museums, where it will be kept and viewed as a relic of barbarism, not only to woman, but to that noblest of animals, the horse.

MRS. OWENS-ADAIR, M. D.

AN OLD FRIEND

North Yakima, Wash., April 24, 1904.

My Dear Old Friend, Dr. Mattie Hughes: You will doubtless be surprised to hear from me, but today I was reading Mr. Cannon's testimony in the "Smoot" case, and I see by his testimony that he is 70 years old, and that he married you in 1884, that you were his fourth wife, and that in 1886 he married two other women, and that his six wives were all living in Salt Lake City or county. If I remember rightly, you were about 22 or 24 when we were at Ann Arbor. Reading this testimony has brought back many memories of you during our stay at the old widow's. (I have forgotten her name.)

You will remember that I was reducing my body weight under Dr. Vaughn. I shall never forget the pangs of hunger that I suffered in getting rid of thirty-five pounds. And how the good old landlady would go waddling around under her two hundred pounds getting my scanty meals and showing her disgust for my scanty fare. She gave expression to her views one day by saying: "Well, I don't think I would die in debt to my belly." I told her that many people died before their time by being too good to their stomachs. I have thought of you many times and wondered what you were doing. Some years ago Colonel Adair opened a periodical and said: "Here is a woman doctor who is in the state legislature." I said: "I will bet that is Dr. Mattie Hughes." He replied: "Yes, that is her name." It was a published interview by some woman. It was the first time I had heard of you since we parted at A. A. I thought then that I would write to you, but "Procrastination is the thief of time." The article said that you had two small children, so I supposed then that you had only been married a short time, but from the testimony you were married the same year that I was. Colonel Adair is only seven months older than I am. The reporter said you were very gray. Well, twenty-four years have brought many changes, but I am not very gray yet, and though past, I am seldom taken to be more than 45 or 50. My health is good, and I drive and come and go just as I did twenty-five years ago.

And how are you? How many children have you, and how old are they? Is not this Mr. Cannon the same man that stopped over Sunday at Ann Arbor to visit you? And do you remember the conversation we had the next morning in my room? You were much pleased with his visit, and told me that he was a high official in the church and had two or three wives. I said: "Mattie, you will go back to Salt Lake and marry some man that has more than one wife, for you will marry for influence and power, and you may be sure that all the influential men of your church will enjoy the luxury of fresh wives." You said: "Polygamy belongs to our church, and I would not mind it if I could be the favorite wife." I replied: "You will be for a time, but you may depend upon it, the man who has the privilege of taking another wife will soon tire of the last and will find a new one. And the older and more influential he becomes the more wives he will have." From his testimony he confesses he married two women in 1886, which must have been after he served six months in prison, which he says was nineteen years ago. I am wondering if your marriage brought you any real pleasure. I gave birth to a baby girl at 47. About your age now. You are still young, and ought to have a husband near your own age. Are you devoting your time to medicine or politics? I should be glad to hear from you. If the spirit moves you write to me. As ever, your friend and classmate,

R. A. OWENS-ADAIR.

SOCIAL LIFE AND PROFESSIONAL WORK

1904.

Social claims and pleasures are largely crowded out of a busy professional life, and to one of a warm social nature, like Dr. Adair, this is a real privation. She often regrets her inability to return her many social calls, or to accept her frequent society invitations. When she does attempt to attend some particularly attractive social function she is almost sure to receive an imperative professional call at the same time. One example of this will serve as an illustration. Having received a special invitation to a Shakespearean reading, given by an exclusive ladies' club, whose members are the *elute* of the city, she prepared to attend, expecting to enjoy a social and intellectual treat. After arraying herself with careful elegance and placing herself in the hands of the hairdresser and "beauty doctor," she was on her way to the club rooms chatting with her lady friends, who thronged the adjacent street, entrance and stairway, when she was overtaken by Mrs., her office assistant, who breathlessly announced:

"Doctor, you are wanted in a confinement case."

"Where is it?" asked the doctor.

"Two miles out of town," was the answer. "I have ordered your horse, and the man is waiting."

In the meantime they were hurrying back to the office, where the doctor hastily changed her festal garments for those more suited to the case in hand, seized her medicine case and other necessary appliances and drove rapidly away at the very hour when she should have been exchanging pleasant greetings with her friends and acquaintances.

She found the patient, a German woman, in a neglected, cheerless, disorderly house, with three young children, and with no aid but that of the husband; but she proceeded promptly to assist the suffering woman, bring order out of chaos, and make the best of things as they Were. Here she spent seven weary hours, doing the work of a nurse, as well as that of a physician, and finally left the woman comfortable and grateful, with a new baby boy beside her. This was the fifth child, one having previously died, and the mother declared that she had never before gotten through so well in every respect as at this time. The husband also was greatly pleased and assured the doctor that he would pay her bill cheerfully and promptly, and he kept his word. This was some compensation for all she had missed, but, as she said at the time and often repeats: "It is useless for me to attempt to keep up with my social duties. Society life and professional life are well-night incompatible. The one must inevitably yield to the other."

A week later the father, a rosy-cheeked, jolly German, called at Dr. Adair's office, and, drawing several gold twenties from his pocket, asked what her bill amounted to.

"Twenty dollars," said the doctor, and he handed her the money with alacrity, and jokingly asked: ' "How much would you charge to bring him a mate?"

"Just twenty dollars," she laughingly responded.

"You shall have it when you bring him," emphatically declared the jovial farmer as he took his departure.

LOST IN THE FOG

(1904.)

An amusing as well as exasperating episode occurred one night when the doctor was called by telephone to attend a case of confinement in what is called "Old Town," four miles south of North Yakima.

She was perfectly familiar with the road, having driven over it hundreds of times day and night, but on this occasion it was so foggy that she could not see three feet ahead. As she left the stable her carriage lights showed not more that two feet of the road before her, but she had no thought of missing the way. After traveling, as she supposed, about half way to her destination, the lights of North Yakima loomed up in the mist just ahead! Dismayed, but undaunted, she determined to try it again, but the horse was of an opposite mind, and she got him turned about with difficulty, and the next minute found herself run up against a familiar rockpile. This gave her her bearings again and she pulled her horse into the road and urged him onward. But, after some time, by closely watching the roadside, she know she was lost again. Convinced now that she could not guide the horse correctly, she gave him the rein and a command to "go."

It was impossible for her to tell where they were, and she soon found herself in an alley so narrow she could see both sides of it in dim outline, by the aid of her carriage lights.

It seemed as if they would never reach the street at the end of the alley, but in time she drove over a sidewalk, and in trying to turn up the street had driven into the middle of it. She could see the city lights only dimly half a block away. Continuing on, she soon drove up to the stable from which she had originally started just as the town clock struck two.

Then she knew it was just an hour since she left. She called to the stablemen:

"How many of you are there here?"

"Two," was the response.

"Then one of you must go with me. Can *you* find the way to Old Town?" to a grizzled old fellow who appeared.

"Yes, madam, I can drive anywhere in this valley, but the first thing you should do is to put out those lights."

This done they set out, and this time succeeded in reaching Old Town, but not without getting off the right road several times, which took some of the conceit out of the old stage driver.

What was still more gratifying to the doctor, they arrived, after all, in time for her to attend the case to a successful issue.

NIGHT WORK

(1904.)

Untiring energy and unfailing strength are surely needed by the faithful physician who responds to the call of distress at all hours of the night, as well as the day—in summer and winter—in storm and shine. The impatient patient and family who querulously complain that "the doctor is so slow," and later, perhaps, at the bill, little realize the sacrifice often made for them or pause to think that, after having been hard at work all day, the doctor is often called from a greatly needed rest, out of a warm bed, to dress in haste, and drive five or ten miles into the country, with the temperature very near zero—sometimes below that—and, on returning home, must attend to business the following day, instead of taking rest and sleep; very likely to be called out the next night also. People *should* think of these things, and remember that the least they can do is to pay the doctor's bill cheerfully and as promptly as possible. Money often cannot pay for the services a faithful, efficient physician renders. A few appreciate this, but far too many do not.

The following true experience will give some idea of what a physician not infrequently undergoes in a rigorous climate. In any climate it would be trying enough. not many men could have gone through it unharmed, but Dr. Adair was equal to the occasion.

The doctor was called very early one morning in February, 1903, ten miles out into the country to attend a young lady said to be sick with a serious sore throat. On arriving she found that it was diphtheria of the worst type and that the child of the young lady's brother (at whose house she was visiting when taken ill) was then lying dead in the ' house. Another physician had been called the night before, and had pronounced the child's disease diphtheria. It had died an hour after he left. Dr. Adair immediately telephoned the health officer in town the situation, and he, replying, directed her to allow no one to leave the house until he arrived. He came that afternoon, disinfected the elder father, an aunt and an elder sister of the patient, that they might return to the paternal home, and removed and buried the body of the child. Dr. Adair, meantime, had done all that could be done for the young lady, though she told the parents frankly that it would be nothing short of a miracle, if she recovered. She then returned home and attended to her office business and usual professional calls. At seven o'clock that evening she received a message by telephone that the young lady's heart was failing, and she must come to her with all speed. Ordering her horse the doctor soon started alone on that long ten-mile drive, in a heavy snowstorm, which continued all the way out.

On arriving at the bedside of the sinking patient she administered strychnia hypodermically, and stimulant and nourishment by enema, which brought relief, and quiet sleep to the sufferer. Leaving the patient comfortable, the doctor set out on her return home. The snow had ceased, and the temperature was falling. It should be stated that she was her own driver and made her professional calls night and day into the country alone. She felt no fear, and knew that few men could excel her in handling a horse. She reached home, on this occasion, between 12 and I A M., and retired directly to bed. Between I and 2, only an hour later, she was -called up to attend a case in town, but some distance away. She again ordered her horse and started out. The temperature had fallen so low that it was now the coldest night of the season, but weather of any sort never kept the doctor from her professional duty.

After attending to this case she returned home at 4 A M., two hours later, and sought her bed a second time. Soon after o she was up and had a light breakfast, after which she ordered a horse and sleigh and was off within the hour on the ten-mile drive to visit the diphtheria patient. She found her apparently much better from the restful sleep of the night before—the best night, they said, that she had had in all her three weeks' illness. The doctor then returned home, attended to her office patients, and answered a call into the country. Returning from this call, at 5 r M., she found the father of the diphtheria patient waiting with a double team to take her back to his home, eleven miles in another direction, as his youngest daughter was also taken with a sore throat, and they feared it was diphtheria. He added: "After you have prescribed for her, there will be another team ready to take yon the ten miles farther to my son's, where you *must* stay all night, doctor. Money is no consideration now!"

She found the youngest daughter was, indeed, coming down with the same dread disease, and after doing all that could be done for this new patient she was driven rapidly on to see her sister. At the gate they were met by the son. "How is Maggie?" were the doctor's first words;

"She seems to be having a bad spell," was the reply, and the doctor hurried on.

At the door the unmistakable sounds of dissolution met her ear and exclaiming, "My God, she is dying!" she hurried to the bedside to render what aid she could, well knowing that all would soon be over for that beautiful and beloved young girl.

When the son's wife realized that her favorite sister-in-law was indeed dying she was seized with the pains of premature labor. The mother of the dying girl became frantic with grief. All three demanded immediate attention, and as there was no other woman on whom she could call for aid, upon the doctor fell the duties of both nurse and physician for them all. Will any one have the effrontery to assert that a woman physician was not a thousand-fold better than a male doctor in such a time as this? Dr. Adair, as always, was equal to the emergency. Knowing that they had been watching five days and nights without sleep, and were completely exhausted, she first administered a powerful opiate to the young expectant mother, and directed her husband to take her upstairs and put her to bed at once. This he did. Then giving the elder mother a soothing potion, and leaving her somewhat calmer, she again turned her attention to the dying girl, who soon breathed her last. The doctor then telephoned to the health officer in town to come out and remove the corpse immediately. He replied that it was impossible, as he was engaged in a special Elks' celebration, and could not then leave, but would come out in the morning. Dr. Adair insisted on his coming at once, and appealed to him in these words: "Doctor, you are a father yourself. You know that in all probability, if a child is ushered into this infected house, both mother and child will never go out of it alive. Now take it home to yourself. I beg of you to come and take the corpse out of the house as soon as possible."

The health officer, unable to resist this moving appeal, yielded, and said:

"I will come now if the undertaker will come. I will see him, and if I can get him I will come."

Dr. Adair then called up the undertaker and appealed to him in similar language. He replied that if the health officer would come, he would accompany him. The doctor told him what he had just said to her. "Very well," said the undertaker; "measure the corpse, and give me the measurements, and I will make all necessary preparations, and we will come as soon as we can possibly get there."

This she did, and phoned to the health officer what the undertaker had said, requesting him to let her know when they were ready to start, which he did, and added:

"Shall I order a carriage to bring you home?"

"No," answered the doctor, "Do you think I would leave this house tonight? I cannot desert this afflicted family in their trouble."

"Well, but you will be quarantined," he urged.

"I am not worrying about the quarantine," she responded. "I want you to get out here and disinfect this house in the shortest possible time."

On his arrival he repeated:

"Well, you are in quarantine, Doctor."

"I will not remain in it, though," she retorted. "I have as much right to go, with proper precautions, as you have. Give me the formaldehyde, and I will disinfect myself when I am ready to go."

So he left her a good supply, and they parted good friends, as usual, at 4 a m.

Dr. Adair then proceeded to disinfect and carry out into the snow all the infected clothing, and set the house in order, as she then felt no desire for sleep. This occupied her until (a m., when she heard the father at the gate, asking after Maggie, and thus, in addition to all she had gone through, on her fell that hardest of all tasks, the telling him that his precious daughter was dead, and buried.

He then said: "We must still care for the living. You must return home with me to see her sister." ,

So they started for another eleven-mile drive. The doctor found this, also, a well-defined case of diphtheria. From this case the elder (and third) sister, the aunt, and the only remaining grandchild, all contracted the terrible malady, but through the administration of antitoxin, and the most faithful attention and careful nursing, they all finally recovered.

Thus, during sixty consecutive hours, Dr. Adair, then in her' sixty-fifth year, accomplished an almost incredible amount of labor, under great mental strain (as the parties were her warm personal friends, as well as patients), having traveled in that time over one hundred miles, with but two hours' sleep, out of the whole sixty hours; yet she continued her regular practice with no cessation, and without extreme exhaustion—a record very few male physicians, if any, could equal, and surely none excel. This was after her sixty-fourth year.

LEGAL COMMENDATION

1905.

Dr. Adair never takes any serious step unreflectingly, but, always thinks out her subject clearly before acting, consequently her statements in any important matter are concise, yet comprehensive.

In cases where she has been called upon to give expert medical testimony in court she is always commended by legal gentlemen as an unusually good witness.

Judge Rudkin, Superior Judge of the Yakima District,—now one of the Supreme Judges of the State of Washington,—after hearing her testimony in a case of infanticide tried before him, said:

"If I were practicing law, I would give Dr. Adair pointers, and have her for an expert witness in all my cases."

The prosecuting attorney of the district thanked her warmly for her evidence on the same occasion, saying: "Your testimony was just what I wanted."

Dr. Adair has received similar commendations and compliments on her expert testimony in similar cases in Portland, Oregon, which shows how much her strong common sense can and does add to her extensive medical and surgical knowledge. For common sense (the rarest sense in the world) is, after all, the foundation of all law and equity, and without it the most astute display of legal phraseology only confuses and befogs the mind of the average juror.

ADDRESS OF WELCOME

TO THE STATE W. C. T. U. OF WASHINGTON
BY DR. OWENS-ADAIR.

Madam President, Mr. Mayor and Honored Guests:

We are here to greet you, as you come from your various homes and fields of labor, to report your progress, and to enquire as to ours;—to receive, as well as to give encouragement;—and it is my pleasant privilege, in the name of the Medical Profession of the State of Washington, and the City of North Yakima in particular, to extend to you a cordial welcome. We offer you our hospitality, and our hearty sympathy in your commendable work; and we shall be glad, in our turn, of the uplift we expect to receive from your presence among us. For, though we believe the advantages and attractions of our thriving little city are equal to those of any other place of its size, we have to admit that there is great room for improvement. The enemy you seek to vanquish has a foothold here, as elsewhere, and he is not easily dislodged.

We need more of that spirit tersely described by President Roosevelt as "an aggressive spirit, which not only deplores evil and corruption, but wars against it, and tramples it under foot."

No victory of value is lightly won, and the fight against the saloon is waged against invisible foes, without and within, as well as with their material manifestations,—a combination against which only our most determined efforts, reinforced by divine aid, can prevail. But, my sisters, we shall eventual win.

"To doubt would be disloyalty.

To falter would be sin."

I speak feelingly, from a pungent personal experience, having borne my part in the fore-front of the battle in our sister state of Oregon, thirty-five years ago; and having suffered in person the unspeakable abuse which is, in itself, a sure indication that our work is telling.

448

Popular opinion was by no means with us then, as now. The first temperance petition ever sent to an Oregon Legislature was contemptuously voted to be "thrown under the table!"

Liquor sellers and their families were then received in polite society, and social drinking was almost universal. Declining wine at dinners and banquets was considered not only as an indication of personal fanaticism, but as an insult to the host and other guests. In those days a majority of the working men drank hard or "moderately," and employers expected their men to "go on a spree," and lose one or two days in a month, if not in every week. This was made an excuse, sometimes, for hiring Chinamen, who never drank, or lost a day.

I well remember the scenes of the never-to-be-forgotten "Woman's Crusade," as they occurred in Portland, Oregon, about 1874.

Some of you may recall how that devoted band of Christian women, comprising members of the most refined and influential families in the city, marched solemnly through the streets, kneeling on the foul pavements in front of the worst saloons, amid the curious and ribald throng, praying, singing hymns, and making personal appeals to the liquor sellers, and their customers. Sometimes, on going inside to plead with them, they were met with insult, and told to "Go home, and mind their own business."

At one place, while the white-haired mothers appealed to the bar-keeper, with drinking and gambling going on all around them, one impious man raised his glass of brandy, saying, *"This* is *my* Christ," and drank it down! In one instance, lighted matches were thrown among the kneeling women, setting fire to the skirt of one lady. Finally the climax came, when they were all arrested, and taken to the police station, at the instigation of a prominent liquor man.

And then there was hurrying to and fro among fathers, husbands and sons for the speedy release of those most honored and dear to them.

Many sad and heart-rending scenes were enacted during those exciting times; and some had their amusing side. In some of the smaller towns, the dear old pioneer mothers banded together, and

449

went in relays, with their knitting and sewing, and spent the day in the saloons,—one set going in the forenoon, another relieving them at noon, and remaining till night, then a third band took their places till closing up time, much to the disgust of the proprietors and their customers. Some of these dealers poured out their whiskey, shut up their places, and joined the crusade. Others were defiant, and not to be "intimidated by women and their devices."

The mother heart was aroused, as never before, and multitudes of delicate and timid women threw themselves into the excitement of the hour, determined to rid the country of this giant evil. But they soon realized that the victory was not to be won in a day, and settled down to a steadier, but no less determined effort. Out of that tempestuous crusade was evolved the beneficent, white-winged army known as "The Woman's Christian Temperance Union," which has for years waged the most powerful and effective war on intemperance, and kindred evils. Years ago our own beloved Francis Willard clasped hands with Lady Somerset, across the broad Atlantic Ocean, and now the tiny white ribbon flutters on the bosoms of hundreds of thousands of earnest women, devoted to our holy cause.

Say you that all this has been in vain? No, no! A thousand times *no!*

You have but to compare the conditions of thirty to forty years ago with those of today to realize the great good accomplished.

, How is it today? The Salvation Army, and other out-of-door evangelistic organizations, are now accepted with thankful appreciation, whereas, in those days, they were abused, and even stoned.

It is a matter of common knowledge that no railroad company in the United States will now employ a man who drinks intoxicants, or even frequents a saloon; and all the large railroads are establishing Young Men's Christian Associations and reading rooms for their men, at their own expense. Other responsible business establishments are falling into line, and refusing to employ drunkards and gamblers. *Their* prohibition *prohibits;* and no complaint is heard from their employees of any interference with their "personal liberty."

Social drinking has largely ceased A lost fraternal societies exclude saloon-keepers and their families from membership; and drinking places are being forbidden the most desirable streets, as on our own beautiful Yakima avenue; and, in time, our progressive and aggressive public sentiment will demand that the sale of intoxicants, as a beverage, must cease.

Mothers of sons and daughters, the love and loyalty to truth and purity that has burned so brightly in your breasts all these years, *has* borne grand fruit in this new generation of the twentieth century, richer in that same Heaven-born love of Freedom and Righteousness, than any gone before it! Witness, in additional proof of this, the place woman now takes, unrebuked,—nay, welcomed, beside her brother. In all the walks of life, she is his equal partner, in business, as well as in pleasure; and in some sections of our country, in the administration of the law, through the exercise of the ballot. Nor have the breaking of family ties, or the destruction of womanly modesty, or manly chivalry, in any instance resulted therefrom especially on behalf of the Medical Fraternity, whom I have the honor, on this occasion, to represent, I give you God-speed. Your work and ours should go hand in hand. "A sound mind in a sound body," is the ideal of the highest mortal perfection. Our province is the physical and mental, as yours is the spiritual. To aid in restoring, and maintaining, by the best known methods, the highest health of all three, is your mission, and ours.

We physicians, particularly, welcome all efforts to increase the general intelligence, and educate the general conscience, since the lack of these, in the nurse, so often defeats our best endeavors.

The progress and prosperity of the commonwealth is identical with that of our profession, and no person will rejoice more heartily at all indications of improvement than the physician.

I trust your sojourn among us will be as profitable to you as it has been profitable to us.

Again *we* thank you for your good work, at home and abroad, and for the compliment of your presence among us.

ADDRESS OF PRESENTATION

1904.

Worthy Past Matron:

In the name of Syringa Chapter No. 38, I have the honor of presenting you with this jewel, as a slight token of our appreciation of the faithful and impartial services you have rendered us as first officer of our Chapter during the last year.

Take it, my beloved sister, and wear it upon your bosom nearest your heart, for our sakes. It will there shine and sparkle, for your honor, and for ours, where, through its brilliant scintillations, it will remind our great sisterhood of the noble deeds of our ancient heroines, Adah, Ruth, Esther, Martha, and Electa.

RESPONSE TO THE TOAST: "THE EASTERN STAR IS THE TRUE HOME OF THE MASONS"

The key of this sentiment is "Home." The home is of Divine origin. The very name sends a thrill to every loyal heart. The ideal home is found only in the family circle; around the hearthstone, where the love and loyalty of husband, wife and children reign supreme, and give us a glimpse of the home beyond.

Such a home can only come of the union of the sexes. From this union, comes the nation, and the rise and fall of the nation depend upon the foundation stone of the home.

It has been said that "The hand that rocks the cradle, is the hand that moves the world." Woman, therefore, is an essential element in both the home and the nation.

To appreciate the true worth of home, in its broadest sense, you should travel, for a time, in a foreign country, where you see only strange faces, and hear strange voices and tongues. At last you come to a harbor, where the ships of all nations are anchored; and there, floating in the breeze, you behold the emblem of your own country. The sight of the Star Spangled Banner quickens your heart-throbs, and you give vent to your pent-up patriotism in exclamations of, "My Country, oh, my Country!" "Sweet Land of Liberty, thy name I love." And you will find yourself repeating over and over, "Home, home, sweet, sweet home."

The Masonic order, great and grand as it is, had first only a bachelor's home, which is but half a home, until the Eastern Star opened her doors, and invited her brothers to come and abide with her.

The Eastern Star possesses all the essential elements of an ideal home. Here you find the father, mother, husband, wife, sister and brother, all united in one grand, fraternal fellowship, and ill striving for one great purpose,—that of the uplifting of humanity, through the home and the nation.

And now, my brothers, one and all, in the name of Syringa Chapter, I bid you welcome to our home. The latch-string you will find at the outer door, and a welcome within.

ADDRESS REFORE THE "EASTERN STAR"

Brothers and Sisters:

I have been requested to say something for the good of the order, and as I cannot express myself extemporaneously, I have just jotted down a few thoughts.

The first thing, to put it logically, is to *have* an order; and the next, and far more important thing, is to support it.

We have an order, and I think I know whereof I speak, as I have an opportunity of judging, when I say that the Eastern Star is the Queen Bee of all the other orders, social and otherwise.

And now, what *is* our duty? And what can we do for the good of our chapter?

Our worthy sister from Portland,, at our banquet said: "You must stand by your officers." And I ask you, "What can the officers do without the support of the members?" I answer, "Nothing."

What could our immortal Washington have done without the support of the determined band of men and women who, in their poverty, never once thought of deserting him, but through long months and years of anxiety and struggle, never once showed the "white feather"? And from those first faithful thirteen stars and stripes has come the greatest nation on this broad earth. What could our martyred Lincoln have done in holding together our glorious union, without the aid of his loyal Cabinet and Congress? What could our Dewey have done without his men behind the guns? What can any general do without his trained lieutenants, and his faithful and obedient soldiers at his back? And what can our worthy matron do without her assistants, and the still more important loyal support of the members of this chapter?

We have placed her in the East, and have pledged her our support. She has the advantages of youth, education, and charming manners. She is worthy in every way of the high position we have given her. Therefore, our duty is plain. One word will cover it all, and that word is "loyalty."

And what shall I say of our worthy patron? He needs no encomiums from me. He has served us before, and he will serve us again with honor. I now turn my eyes toward the west, and there I see a bright and brilliant star in the ascendency. Our records are in the hands of an honorable and tried expert. Our cash is as safe as if it were in the bank of the United States.

The five points of our star are yet in bud, but ere long they will open out in full bloom. Then their combination of beautiful colors will attract and charm all beholders.

Our conductress and marshal, upon whom so much depends, I am confident, will not be found wanting in their duty.

Our doors are securely protected by competent and trusty guards. You have chosen a worthy set of officers (not including the speaker), who, I have faith, will successfully navigate this ship through pleasant channels (avoiding Russia and Japan), and will bring her into a harbor of unity, beauty, and prosperity.

PHYSICIAN RECOMMENDS OPERATION FOR DEFECTIVES.

MEANS CHANCE OF RECOVERY FOR UNFORTUNATES
THEMSELVES.

PREVENTS THE PROCREATION OF UNFIT CHILDREN

Eugenics—the belief and practice which aims at improving the genetic quality of the human population. As a social movement, eugenics reached its height in the early decades of the 20th century. At this point, eugenics was practiced around the world and was promoted by governments and influential individuals and institutions. Its greatest abuses came during the Nazi era in Germany prior to WWII.—Ed.

North Yakima, Wash., March 11th, 1905.—(To the Editor.)

I have been much interested always in the problem of race improvement, and especially of late in the discussion in your invaluable paper, on the humanity, or inhumanity of sparing, or cutting off at birth, the lives of physical and mental defectives.

However strongly I might believe that the death, at birth, of all such would be the best for them and humanity, I could never accept the solemn responsibility of taking a human life, and I am persuaded that it is a power not to be safely or properly entrusted to any private human judgment.

And yet the human race should, and could be largely protected from monstrosities and deadly diseases without resort to the taking of life. Certainly parents should think and live rightly. This course, in time, through generations of parents, would doubtless produce a race very near to physical and mental perfection; but at present, unfavorable ancestral influences are too strong for one right-living pair to more than partially overcome them; therefore, it is not wholly within the control of parents to produce just the kind of children they desire. If it were, we should soon have a whole race of Roosevelts, Willards, and Shakespeares,—a condition delightful to contemplate, but, I fear, still far in the future.

Here is a case in point, which occurred recently in my own practice, of a handsome young Scotchman, full of life and health, with a beautiful young American wife—ages 27 and 24—(the most vigorous time of life, according to Dr. Osier). This happy young couple of eighteen months' wedded life were looking forward, with joyful anticipation, to the stork's visit to their home. In time he came, and brought a poor, frail, six-pound babe, with an unnaturally long neck, and an abnormal growth of the size of a hen's egg on each side of its throat. Can you attach any blame to these healthy, right-living, offspring-desiring parents? No, for it would be palpable injustice. Should I have killed that child? No, a thousand times no.

Besides, who can tell at the child's birth whether, though seriously handicapped physically, it' may not become a power in, and a blessing to the world? For instance, Alexander Pope, Lord Byron, the present Emperor of Germany, and, to come near home, our own able historian, and man of letters, Professor H. S. Lyman, all physically imperfect at birth, might have come under the proposed plan of extermination.,

That we have not complete control of the situation, however, is no reason why we should not use our best efforts by right thinking and living, to have our children, so far as our power and responsibility go, well-born.

This is a deep and serious subject, and one too great to cope with in its entirety, yet, I repeat, much can and should be done. Some of the worst ills to which humanity is heir, such as insanity, epilepsy and cancer, are almost certainly transmitted by the immediate progenitors.

The greatest curse of the race conies through our vicious and criminal classes, and to my mind this is the element that should be dealt with—not by chloroform or strangulation, but by the science of surgery, for if their power to reproduce themselves were rendered null, a tremendous important step in advance would have been taken, not only without injury to life, but often with positive benefit to the victims themselves.

Over twenty years ago I visited our State Insane Asylum at Salem. My friend, Dr. R., then in charge, received me graciously, and conducted me through the various wards. On our way from the wards back to luncheon I said:

"Doctor, this is a horrible phase of life; and when is it to end?"

"I do not know. It is hard to tell," he replied.

"If I had the power," I continued, "I would curtail it; for I would see to it that not one of this class should ever be permitted to curse the world with offspring."

He stared at me, and finally said: "Would you advocate that method?"

"I certainly should, if I were not a woman, and a woman M. D., to whom, at this day and age, I know too well it would simply mean ostracism," I answered.

"Well. Doctor," he rejoined, "I beg you not to mention this subject to my wife, for she would be shocked and horrified."

"I shall not mention it to your wife," I assured him. "but I want to tell you right here that if I were in control of this institution, as you are, I would at least give many of these pitiable unfortunates the one chance of recovery through a surgical operation, which might restore their reason. You know, Doctor, as well as I do, that hysteria and insanity are often due to diseased reproductive organs. Think of these loathsome victims of an unnamable vice under your charge. It would be nothing less than common humanity to relieve them of the source of their curse and destruction by a simple surgical operation that might give them a chance to recover their reason."

Eight or ten years since, in a conversation with an eminent attorney concerning a mutual friend and near neighbor, whose wife had recently called upon this attorney at dead of night to protect her and her children from her husband, who had for the second time become suddenly insane, he said to me: "This is terrible; but who would have thought of that level-headed business man going insane?"

457

I responded: "Remember we know it is in his blood by family inheritance. And now I am going to say what will shock you, which is that every person admitted into an insane asylum should be so dealt with as to preclude reproduction."

Instantly and warmly he exclaimed: "I sanction that, and I will go farther, by including every criminal that goes through the penitentiary doors."

Thereupon we shook hands on it, then and there, feeling sure that the time would come when the commonwealth, forced to grapple with this vital subject, would be able to adopt these measures with the full assent of a majority of its citizens.

MRS. OWENS-ADAIR.

LETTER TO SUSAN B. ANTHONY

North Yakima, Wash., March 28, 1905.

My Dear Beloved Miss Anthony: I see by today's Oregonian that you may come to our great Lewis and Clark Centennial, and my heart responded with a strong throb of pleasure at the thought of again seeing you.

Can you recall me, my friend, among your many thousand special friends? Yes, I think you will, when I remind you that I am that little Roseburg milliner to whom you wrote November 15, 1871, by the advice of Mrs. Duniway, to secure you a lecture room and audience; how I engaged the largest of the three churches then in town, and, through posting bills, and house-to-house work, got out a good audience.

And do you recall how, as we passed the McClellan Hotel, we heard the sound of the "fiddle" at a free dance, gotten up purposely to detract from your lecture?

Ah, how well I remember your visit with me in every detail. I can see you now, in the strength of your vigorous womanhood, as you've finished your toilet before a bright wood fire in my little sitting-room, while I prepared the breakfast, with the door open between us. How we did talk! For, as you said, "The stage will start in two hours, and we have so little time, and so much to say."

Those were days that tried women's souls. I was then taking your little paper, the Revolution, and after f had read it I would send it to a lady in the country, who was a leader in her community.

The next time I saw you was at the Woman's Congress in Portland, Oregon. I called on you at Mrs. Duniway's, and you asked me: "Who is this?" I said: "Think a moment."

You looked keenly at me and exclaimed: "Yes, you are the Roseburg milliner, but not a milliner now, but an M. D.'"

I replied: "Yes, and there will be no more rotten eggs; no vile epithets; no opposition dance for us now. Crowds will Hock to hear the honored Miss Anthony."

A few evenings later at one of your receptions I saw a beautiful young girl gazing at you intently and said to her: "Kiss Miss Anthony, my dear, for she is one of the greatest women the world has ever produced."

"*May* I kiss her?" she eagerly asked.

"Surely you may," and I led her forward. "Miss Anthony, may I kiss you?" she timidly asked. You reached out your hand to her, and as she stooped and kissed you I saw tears sparkling in your eyes. If death has not claimed that sweet young girl she has long since blossomed into womanhood and has taught her children to honor and bless your well-beloved name

Now, my dear and honored friend, *do* come to see and delight us with your presence. Oregon needs you. Our whole broad state is your home. Friends and physicians of your own making will stand proudly by your side and ascribe to you praise.

The old stagecoaches and lumbering wagons that plowed through the mud and rattled and jolted us over rocks, roots, ruts and logs in the past, bringing us health, strength and vigor at the same time and preparing us for the hard work before us, have given place to the palace car, which can bring you to us with comfort and pleasure, and I believe the trip will "give you a new lease of life" in renewed health and strength.

My beloved mother is now in her eighty-eighth year, and last fall she took a sea voyage of three hundred miles, stood the trip well and was benefited by the trip and the change. She intends to return to Portland in June to visit our great fair. Last summer she walked five miles in one day several times.

I am now in my sixty-sixth year, am still in active practice, and am strong and well. I often drive fifteen or twenty miles into the country. I handle my horse today as well as I did twenty-five years ago. Not long ago I drove in from the country, fifteen miles, alone, reaching home at 2 A ar.

You and I have had the advantage of *not* having been reared "in the lap of luxury." The hard battles we have fought give us strength and increased longevity.

I enclose a clipping from the Portland Oregonian, which I believe you will indorse. I have received many congratulatory commendations for my "heroic" letter. One old M. D. wrote that he "had for many years rested in the belief that God's reserved force to reform the world is woman," and that he is "glad to have read the public enunciation of such views from a woman." And I must tell you, my dear friend, that I have waited twenty-five years to give public expression to my views on this subject, and now seemed the first fitting time for it.

And now, my dear friend, I bid you adieu, with the earnest hope that I may have the extreme pleasure of taking you by the hand at our great convention this summer.

Sincerely and fraternally yours,

DR. B. A. OWENS-ADAIR.

MARRIAGE AND DIVORCE

EVILS OF LEGAL SEPARATION SHOULD BE RESTRICTED BY LAW

North Yakima, Wash., May 5, 1895.

To the Editor:

I have watched with special interest the controversy on the divorce question, which has been going on for more than a year, first taken up by the Episcopal Church and now generally participated in by other churches. That the frequency of divorce has brought disrepute and scandal on our nation is acknowledged and deplored by all. Tut how to prevent it is the question. To say that God sanctions all marriages that record their vows before the pulpit and receive the blessing of the minister is simply absurd, as hundreds of thousands of unhappy marriages will affirm, while many happy marriages, and affectionate and honorable families have had their origin from vows given before a Justice of the Peace, whose breath, at the time, may have savored of bad whisky and tobacco. (I do not wish here to be understood as placing the civil ceremony on a level with the religious marriage service, which I approve, and personally prefer.)

To my mind the success of the marriage relation depends upon the disposition, education and sterling principles of the contracting parties—not upon one, but upon all, i. e. where those conditions may be made to blend, through the power of the affections—love. Then we can say: "What God hath joined let no man put asunder." We have this illustrated day in and clay out, especially in these times of fast living, when the electric spark seems to move the world. How long can we continue along these lines? Every day brings to light some great discovery, or the accomplishment of some startling feat, each, in turn, to live, to thrive, to blossom for a time; then to be crowded back, to prove its worth or be lost in oblivion. But not so with marriage and divorce. Like the poor, they are "always with us."

As a nation we should be, and are, striving to improve the marriage relation, realizing, as we do, that the home is the foundation of our Government. The essentials of a home are love,

462

honesty, loyalty. With the American people to decide is to act, and to act is to accomplish; and I have faith to believe that we shall find a way out of this national affliction, which seems to have become a veritable contagion, attacking rich and poor, high and low alike, and which should be met with stringent measures and remedies. A divorce no longer carries with it the stigma of disgrace that it did thirty or forty years ago, which required a lifelong struggle to overcome. The most disgraceful feature of these modern divorces is that, in the majority of the cases, it can be proved that one, and sometimes both of the parties, contract new engagements of marriage before having even made application for separation from the old relation. Sunday's Oregonian tells us of a courtship of three days, a marriage of three days, and a suit for divorce filed on the sixth day! The newspapers are flooded with similar cases, until they cease to shock us, proving the truth of what the poet says: "We first endure, then pity, then embrace."

A halt must be called. The people will find a way to check this great evil. The churches are laboring with the question, while the courts are grinding out divorces by the thousands, and the ministers and all others having authority are equally busy in joining people together in "holy matrimony." (?) The press—the great educator of the world—is performing its part by giving publicity to all sides.

As a free and independent nation our laws must be sanctioned and upheld by public opinion, and with divorce, as with other evils, we should have stringent regulating laws; but to enforce these laws the people must be educated up to a recognition of their value.

In my opinion we should have laws forbidding the remarriage of any divorced person under five or ten years after their divorce was obtained, this would effectually cut off outside love-making, and future matrimonial engagements during married life. Five or ten years' probation would act as an ice bath in cooling off a good deal of lovesick, sentimental passion, and would bring many of its victims to a wholesome sense of their manhood and womanhood, and would enable them to live more upright and clean lives. I believe in divorce for proper cause. I do not believe that people should be forced to bear and rear children in an unholy union. Proof of the wisdom of this can be found in the Oregonian, telling of the shooting of his brutal father by the 18-year-old son, Tom Brown, in Chehalis, Wash. Such occurrences speak more powerfully than words.

BARE HEADS ON THE STREETS

North Yakima, Wash., September 28, 1905.

To the Editor:

I read the "She-Pope of Milliners," Madame Hunt's tirade on "Bare Heads on the Streets" (in the Oregonian of recent date), which she chooses to call indecent. Who, forsooth, is this president of the national milliners' convention, who declares war on a great army of women who choose to appear on the streets, to walk or ride, with uncovered heads? I admit that any person has the right to improve and protect his business, but he has no right to wage war on the community by so doing. The madame may "sigh" and "shudder" and be "horrified" and perhaps suffer an attack of hysteria from coming in contact with a bare-headed woman on the street or in the store, but "war, and no compromise" is a declaration that will be resented by the average American woman, who is fast becoming mistress of her own ideas. The woman that charms the world today is the woman of courage, of original and independent character; not a bundle of dry goods and millinery. She can select a hat to her taste, and she can, and will, go bareheaded, if she choose to do so. If she wishes her hair to have a sun bath, or to have the soft breezes fan her scalp or play with her silken tresses, why should she be denied that pleasure? Poets have raved over the wealth and beauty of woman's hair.

Every woman should retain her good looks as long as possible, the loss of the hair is a grief to any person. Baldness, which is so prevalent among men, is due, principally, ' to their headgear. Proof of this can be found among the natives and all people who do not wear head coverings. All theater-goers are expected to leave their hats at home or remove them before the play begins.

We have a bright and up-to-date minister in this city who requested the ladies of his congregation to remove their hats during service, and I understand this is the common custom in the largest churches of Portland. It is a sensible request, for who wants to sit behind one of those hats that spreads half across the pew, while a long feather or spray of flowers keeps nodding in your face, completely shutting out the speaker from view?

Madame says: "If it is the intention of the followers of the uncovered-head fad to give their hair a bath in the sunlight, let them find a nook in their home, where they can sit and enjoy the rays of the sun in seclusion." Pretty advice this, but where is the nook and where is the time i Again, everybody does not enjoy seclusion. It is a real pleasure to feel that you can call upon a neighbor or run down town to the store and not be compelled to stop five, ten or fifteen minutes to arrange your hair to suit your hat, and to be sure every pin is placed so that it will not be lop-sided. Public opinion would not have permitted this a few years ago. The busy mother and housewife was compelled to don her hat under all conditions. And how many scenes like this have occurred. In great haste the precious hat is snatched from the bandbox and pinned on, while several tots are pulling at her dress, promising to be good and rock the baby if she will bring them candy. She rushes to the store, finds it full, must wait. Home again, finds the baby crying, and beans dry and burning. She runs to the bureau to remove her hat amid the clamor for candy, and, to her horror and disgust, finds she has been down in town with her hat on wrong side before. This accounts for that broad smile Airs gave her. Whom had she seen? Everybody, yes, everybody. Oh, dear, dear, everything goes wrong. Dinner late: husband will be here any minute: hair all mussed, and such confusion! She feels that she is threatened with, nervous prostration. This is not an overdrawn picture.

Let me tell you my experience of twenty-four years ago. I had a hysterical patient in South Portland, who gave me a good deal of worry. One bright morning my reception room was well filled with ladies, and I was rushing to get through. I heard the office girl say:

"The doctor will be out in a few minutes' But a man's voice replied: "I must see her at once."

I stepped to the door. The husband of the aforesaid patient said: "I fear my wife is dying; you must come at once." I replied: "Oh, no, she is not dying." He exclaimed: "You must come at once, or I will get another doctor." "Well," I said, "go and bring my rig." He was back all too soon.

"Now, how many of you ladies can wait till I get back? I'll not be long," I said; and to the man: "Get in the buggy, and be all ready, so I will not be detained."

I finished with the last hurry patient, and, seizing my case, I rushed downstairs and sprang in, and taking the reins I said "Go" to my good horse, Frank, who was always ready to obey that order.

Just beyond First street bridge I saw two of my sisters coming. When they saw me, they rushed to the curb, and as I saw they were in great distress I stopped, saying: "What is the matter?"

One of them said: "Where is your hat?" I said "Go" to my horse, and turning to the man at my side I asked: "Why didn't you tell me I was bareheaded?"

The distressed expression on his face as he was holding on to prevent being thrown out by my reckless driving brought the ludicrous side of the picture to view, and I laughed till we reached our destination. I found my patient not dead, gave her a good "dope" and left her medicine to be taken every ten minutes till relieved, borrowed an old hat to save my reputation, and rushed back to my office. I expected to receive a free advertisement the next day, but fortunately for me, cartoonists were not numerous in those days. Our own Homer Davenport was not known to the world of fame. He was occupied about that time with big lumps of chalk and a can of whitewash decorating board fences, barns and outhouses.

I should not have taken the time to reply to madame's war notes had I not been urged to do so by several indignant ladies of this place.

DR. OWENS-ADAIR.

As a matter of record I feel it incumbent on me to give the public dates of some of my earliest surgical operations.

My first plastic work was for Mrs. A. F. Brown, of Oakland, Oregon, in August, 1881. Dr. Carpenter, professor of surgery in Willamette University, administered chloroform, Dr. Cardwell assisting. For that operation I received one hundred dollars in gold twenty-dollar pieces. I believe that was the first personal perineal operation performed in Oregon by a woman, and I distinctly recall Dr. Cardwell's remark at the time.

"Well, Doctor, we men must look to our laurels when we see a woman do such skillful work as this."

That case brought me wide notoriety, not, however, in the same sense as did the autopsy case of seven years before, for this patient was well and favorably known, and public opinion has marvelously changed toward "she doctors."

My next case was a Mrs. Kent, of Portland. Oregon,. soon after. Dr. C. C. Strong administered the anaesthetic. She, too, was a grateful patient, often saying: "I don't pretend to be a very good Christian, but I do think the most Christian act I can perform is to hunt up other poor, miserable women and get them to go to Dr. Owens and let her perform an operation that will give them some comfort in this world," and she was as good as her word, and brought me many patients.

Surgery in those days was not so common as now, and a woman surgeon was rare indeed. My esteemed friend, Dr. G. M. Wells, has assisted me in many operations. In December, 1886, I was called by Dr. August C. Kinney to Astoria to operate on Mrs. Ward for complete procidentia.

After moving to North Yakima, Wash., I did a great deal of surgical work. For Mrs. S. B. Smith, of Clatsop, who came to be at North Yakima for medical assistance, I removed the entire mammary gland, including three cancerous growths (one as large as a hen's egg) from the axilla. Dr. Fletcher administered the anaesthetic, Dr.

T. B. Gunn assisting. On our way home Dr. Gunn said: "Doctor, do you know you have performed a major operation?"

Later Dr. J. A. Fulton, of Astoria-(to whom I had sent Mrs. Smith for any needed advice), laughingly said: "The idea of your doing that operation!"

"Why? Don't you think it ought to have been done?"

"Yes, of course, but I never thought you would have tackled such a job as that."

From surgery has come a large part of my income from my professional work, and it is the branch which I best love. Had I not taken upon myself matrimony and motherhood I would have continued to drink at Europe's and American's freshest fountains of surgical knowledge until I should have gained the confidence to stand beside any surgeon in the land. This is no idle boast, for the two principal requisites of a first-class surgeon are, first, knowledge, and, second, confidence in his ability to put it into practice.

This recalls what Professor McLean of the University of Michigan once said in the lecture room:

"Medicine and surgery may, as a whole, be compared to a house of many rooms. Surgery is the parlor, wherein you will find the most valuable and sacred contents of the house."

If the Death Angel defers his call on me for a few years more I shall endeavor to compile a small book from the gleanings of my thirty odd years of practice, which may be of some value to Oregon in contrasting the work of the early pioneer doctor with that of the physician of modern times, especially showing ' the immense forward strides taken by surgery.

DR. OWENS-ADAIR AGAIN AT SUNNYMEAD FARM

NEAR WARRENTON—ABSENT SEVEN YEARS

The local world of Astoria will find pleasure in the announcement that Mrs. Dr. Owens-Adair, with her husband, Col. John Adair, is again comfortably installed at the family home on Sunnymead farm, after an absence of seven years in North Yakima, Wash., where she practiced her profession with constant success and made worlds of friends. Dr. Adair will remain at Sunnymead for some little time, until weather conditions become more propitious, when she will leave for Southern California, where she will remain until 'she has finished the chosen task of her later years, that of writing a book, biographical and historical in character, and as wide as the state in scope, and including much of her life in this city and county, all closely interwoven with the lives of other prominent pioneer families of this section. The following excerpts from the Yakima press will best serve to tell those who know and admire this sturdy and accomplished lady of her experiences there, and of all she accomplished professionally and socially.

The Yakima Herald, in a recent issue, says:

"After over thirty years spent in the practice of medicine, Dr. Owens-Adair announces her intention of retiring and taking a well-earned rest. Dr. Adair is the only woman physician in this city, and she has built up a large practice during the six or seven years she has resided in North Yakima. She will spend the remainder of her years on her Sunnymead, farm of several hundred acres near the mouth of the Columbia river, where every boat that enters the river and every pound of freight that goes to the ocean must pass her doors. Mrs. Adair believes she has earned a rest from the activities of her professional life, and she knows of no more attractive place than the old farm to recuperate. The doctor still holds considerable Yakima realty, which she believes gilt-edged as an investment. The best wishes of a host of warm friend here will go with her."

And the Daily Republic speaks no less kindly when it says:

"Dr. Owens-Adair has informed the Republic that she will close her office and retire from business here October 10. Dr. Adair has been in active practice for over thirty years, having been the first woman graduate in medicine in both Oregon and Washington. She has practiced in both states since the early '70s.

"It is the doctor's intention to devote the remainder of her life to literary work, and she hopes to have her first book for the press by early next spring, when she will return to her home in Clatsop County, Oregon. The doctor will remain with her son, Dr. Hill, till the morning of the 14th. After a visit of a month with Col. Adair and their son John at their ranch she will go to San Diego, Cal.

"On the eve of her departure from North Yakima Dr. Adair was the guest of honor at a splendid banquet given by the order of the Eastern Star, as represented at that place, and was made the recipient of a superb gold pen from the lodge as a testimonial of the high estimate in which she was held in that city.

"Mrs. Adair may well use this suggestive gift in the new volume she is about to write, thus giving a host of others some share in the beauty and utility of the gift."

RECOGNITION OF WOMEN PHYSICIANS

BY THE AMERICAN MEDICAL ASSOCIATION

A unique feature in the series of entertainments to be given during the visit of the A. M. A. to Portland will be the banquet to the women physicians in attendance under the auspices of the Portland Medical Club. This banquet will take place at the Hotel Portland on the evening of July 12 (1905.)

This is the first time in the history of the sessions of the A. M. A. that the women have had a distinct recognition. It certainly marks a step in the progress of the association. It is worthy of note that it occurs at the Portland meeting, and at the suggestion of the women physicians of this city. It is another instance of the West setting the pace and establishing precedents for the rest of the country to follow. We may expect, hereafter, to see such recognition a regular thing at the A. M. A. meetings wherever held.

I take great pleasure in giving space to the above from the Oregon Medical Sentinel of July 12th, 1905. It speaks volumes in contrasting the standing of the professional woman of today with the standing, or the lack of it, of a generation ago.

I had the honor of attending the banquet referred to by the Sentinel, which far excelled anything of the kind in my previous experience. A most remarkable feature of this banquet was the absence of wines and cigars. Pure, cold water and tiny cups of coffee were the beverages which slaked the thirst, and calmed the nerve-centers of the lady M. D.'s, and enabled them to suitably respond to toasts presented by our own Dr. Mae Cardwell, whose name, so well-known at home and abroad, assures success in whatever she undertakes.

The banquet was a triumph of the twentieth century art, taste and genius. Words are inadequate to do it justice. The tables were literally banked with smilax and fragrant and gorgeous flowers, which also formed a canopy overhead, and among which thickly sparkled countless tiny electric lights, whose soft, heaven-lighted rays twinkled and scintillated like radiant star-jewels. The tables were presided over by men in swallow-tailed coats, and kid gloves,— the only members of their sex privileged to be present.

The California Poppy, the Oregon Grape, and the Washington Rhododendron, were commingled in artistic decoration, representing the united interests of the three great commonwealths, and eloquently voicing in sweet flower language, a cordial welcome from each to all.

Most of the ladies present were in full dress, white, so beautiful and becoming to young and old, and so much worn at the present time, prevailing in the exquisite costumes. Mine was of white, with a corsage bouquet of white sweet peas, my favorite flowers. One of my colleagues said, "Why, Doctor, you look like a bride!"

"I feel like one," I responded. "For this day, in which I behold the full fruition of all our labors, is the happiest of my life. I thank God that I have been spared to see this day, when women are acknowledged before the world as the equal of men in medicine and surgery; and, above all, that my own Oregon is in the forefront of this grand forward movement."

By special invitation, the professions of the Pulpit, Press, Law and Medicine, were each represented by a woman prominent in her chosen life-work.

After our physical needs were satisfied by the delicious viands so profusely provided, our glasses were re-filled with the sparkling dew of Heaven, and then began "The feast of reason, and the flow of soul."

Our accomplished toast-mistress then stepped within the charmed circle, and sprung a surprise upon ns, for, as no one had been requested beforehand to prepare to respond to a toast, no one was prepared to be called on, for that purpose. After the address of welcome, the toast of "Oregon" was announced, and I was called on for the response! To use a slang phrase, I was "floored," and had to receive a second call before I could "pull myself together," and get on my feet. Naturally deficient in extemporaneous speaking, especially in the presence of such an august body, with assembly-room, doors, and passageways a sea of faces, I was for a moment speechless; but, inspired by the intelligence and beauty around me, and the products of our evergreen states in such lavish profusion, my thoughts began to take form, and I said, in substance:

"We are here to do honor to Lewis and Clark, and to celebrate their inestimable services in exploring this great Northwest Coast, and all honor is certainly their due: and yet,—that pregnant 'yet,'— had it not been for a woman—the Princess Sacajawea—who knows if ever they could have succeeded in their momentous quest? Sacajawea, who, bearing her babe on her shoulders, with unfaltering strength, courage, and fidelity, guided those intrepid men steadily and unerringly all the long journey, protecting them by her presence and explanations, from the savage tribes on the way, even to the very verge of the Pacific, which was as strange to her as to them, remaining, and acting as a safeguard on their return trip also! Truly, we can say that woman had a vital part in the very beginning, as well as in the later destiny of this great Northwest Empire!"

Many, very many, were the beautiful and graceful sentiments evoked by the toasts proposed at that memorable banquet, none of which were better than those of Rev. Anna

Shaw, the first woman ordained minister in the United States, and perhaps in the world. She said, in part:

"I have been traveling on the trail all my life. It was the blazing of the first trails that has been the hardest work, and the travelers in them were few for many difficult and lonely years, but the road has widened, and straightened, and the travelers in it have increased, until now it has become a broad, smooth highway, in which the untrammeled women of our own country, and ultimately of all nations, may freely and gladly walk."

THE PROGRESS OF WOMEN

(By Lydia Kingsmill Commander, "Scrap Book.")

"Nothing is more wonderful in this age of wonders than the progress of women in all the civilized countries of the world. Never before were the doors of opportunity so widely opened; never before were the barriers of sex so low.

"The last census shows that in the United States women are following every trade and profession except the Army and Navy, and even the Navy has a woman physician, Dr. Anna McGee, who wears a uniform. In Europe the uniformed woman is by no means a rarity. Almost every royal woman wears military honors. It will be remembered that Queen Victoria was carried to her grave on a gun-carriage, like an officer, because, as Queen of England and Empress of India, she was the head of the British army, and of the greatest navy in the world.

"To have an occupation is almost as natural to the American girl of today as to her brother. For a woman to go into business used to be like climbing a mountain; now it is almost like going down a toboggan-slide. When she leaves school, she expects to work. Sometimes she finishes her education in the public school, and goes into a shop, factory, or mill. She may become one of the 75,000 milliners, the 100,000 saleswomen, the 120,000 cotton workers, the 275,000 laundresses, or the 340,000 dressmakers.

"If she stay longer in school, she may become one of the 320,000 school teachers. Or she may go to a college which sternly closed its doors in the face of her grandmother, and carry off the prizes and honors from the men. She can enter a university, come out a B. A., M. A., or Ph. D., and join the thousand women who are already college professors.

"If she fancies law, medicine, or the church, her way is clear. All three professions number their women members by the thousand, though a generation ago the pioneers in each line were struggling against ridicule and bitter opposition.

"Even the more unusual occupations are well represented. There are 261 wholesale merchants, 1,271 officials in banks, 1,932 stock-raisers, 378 butchers, and 193 blacksmiths, all women.

"The traveling public depends for its safety (and its accidents) principally upon men; but women already claim 2 motormen, 13 conductors, 4 station agents, 2 pilots, I lighthouse keeper, 127 engineers, and 153 boatmen among their number.

"Almost every paper one picks up tells of women's successes in some line of work. The product of her brain and pen have long blessed the world. A dozen women in Chicago, and probably three times as many in New York, are making $10,000 a year or more, either as salaries, or profits from business. It is said that Hetty Green, the shrewdest business woman in the world, can stand in City Hall Square, New York, and see five millions of dollars' worth of her own property; and everyone knows she owes her millions to her own cleverness, and not to either father, husband, son or brother.

THE END.

BIG BYTE BOOKS is your source for great lost history!

Made in the USA
Coppell, TX
11 April 2021